Insurance
Information
Systems

Insurance Information Systems

H. THOMAS KRAUSE, CPCU
Assistant Vice President
State Farm Mutual Automobile Insurance Company

DOUGLAS R. BEAN, CISA, CSP
Computer Audit Assistance Group Partner
Coopers & Lybrand

ROBERT L. CAWTHON
Assistant Vice President and Assistant Controller
The Hartford

ROBERT A. OAKLEY, PhD.
Vice President—Corporate Controller
Nationwide Insurance

First Edition • 1985

INSURANCE INSTITUTE OF AMERICA
720 Providence Road, Malvern, Pennsylvania 19355-0770

First Printing • December 1985

Library of Congress Catalog Number 85-81541
International Standard Book Number 0-89462-023-1

Printed in the United States of America

Foreword

Over the years, the American Institute for Property and Liability Underwriters and the Insurance Institute of America have responded to the educational needs of the property-liability insurance industry by developing programs specifically for insurance personnel. These companion nonprofit educational organizations receive the support of the entire property-liability industry in fulfilling this task.

The American Institute maintains and administers the program leading to the Chartered Property Casualty Underwriter (CPCU) professional designation.

The Insurance Institute of America offers programs leading to the Certificate in General Insurance, the Associate in Claims (AIC) designation, the Associate in Management (AIM) designation, the Associate in Risk Management (ARM) designation, the Associate in Underwriting (AU) designation, the Associate in Loss Control Management (ALCM) designation, the Accredited Adviser in Insurance (AAI) designation, the Associate in Premium Auditing (APA) designation, the Associate in Research and Planning (ARP) designation, the Associate in Insurance Accounting and Finance (AIAF) designation, the Introduction to Property and Liability Insurance (INTRO) certificate, and the Supervisory Management (SM) certificate.

This text was written specifically for the AIAF program. The development of the program involved the identification of educational objectives, the drafting of course outlines, the coordination of authors' responsibilities, and finally the writing and the revision through several stages of this text. Dr. Robert J. Gibbons, CPCU, CLU, Vice President of the Institutes, executed these responsibilities as an integral part of his professional duties as an Institute staff member. In this capacity he had the assistance of the many contributors to this volume. All of these individuals generously gave their time out of dedication to continuing

v

professional education. No one will receive any royalties from the sales of this text. We have proceeded in this way to avoid any possibility of conflicts of interests.

As with all Institute publications, this text has been extensively reviewed by industry personnel. Thus it is not limited to one company's practices, but strives to represent a consensus view as far as possible in such a pioneering work. The text which has emerged with the benefit of this review process should have substantial value for everyone working with insurance information systems.

Edwin S. Overman, Ph.D., CPCU
President

Preface

Given the importance of information systems for the insurance business, the paucity of corresponding educational materials is surprising. In order to be effective in their jobs, many insurance people need to understand the workings of their company's information systems, including the capabilities and the limitations. Moreover, the need transcends the ranks of company personnel, since auditors and financial examiners require a grasp of the system as well.

Of course, information systems differ from company to company. This book attempts to sketch the fundamental needs, tasks, and controls for insurance information systems generally. This approach emphasizes the underlying logic rather than the specific characteristics of a system. Since most users need the logic more than the detailed characteristics, this approach should prove beneficial.

Appropriately for the subject, this book resulted from the efforts of a diverse project team. The four principal authors—Tom Krause, Doug Bean, Bob Cauthon, and Bob Oakley—conceived the framework for the book, took responsibility for writing multiple chapters each, and reviewed and rewrote other portions of the text to assure a consistent approach throughout. The contributing authors wrote significant sections that were incorporated into the final text. Several others also helped with the development of material for the text. The Continental Insurance Company contributed material for Chapters 1, 2, and 7. In addition to those listed as contributing authors, Barbara Bush, William Earl, James Heffron, and Joseph Lash—all of the Continental Data Center—assisted in developing this material. Several employees of the Hartford Insurance group, Donald LaValley, P.A. DeFrancesco, Augusto Gautier, Christine Zweigle, and Janet Cook, drafted material for Chapters 3 and 4. Chapters 5 and 6 incorporated the efforts of several Nationwide Insurance Company employees: W.E. Anderson, Michael L.

Bates, Richard C. Brough, Michael A. Flack, Diana L. Grapes, William H. Hoch, Michael W. O'Laughlin, George C. White, and Stuart A. Whittaker.

Chapters 8, 9 and 10 are based on information found in diverse written materials and publications from Coopers & Lybrand's United States, United Kingdom, and International Firms. This source material is used by the Firm constantly, both in training and in the field, to develop EDP auditors and apply auditing techniques. A complete presentation of the range of EDP auditing skills and technology is found in the C&L-authored book, *Handbook of EDP Auditing*, published by Warren, Gorham & Lamont. This material was rewritten, edited, and customized for the insurance industry by Doug Bean and by John W. Cassella, Partner, Coopers & Lybrand; John E. Malley, Gary C. McWilliams, Xenia Ley Parker and Pamela R. Pfau, Managers, Coopers & Lybrand; with the assistance of Seto Jew, Myra D. Cleary, and Florence Mazzella.

Credit for much of this effort also goes to three individuals whose exceptional interest and encouragement greatly facilitated the project. They are Kenneth J. Burk, CPCU, Senior Vice President, Continental Corporation; Lon A. Smith, Vice President and Group Comptroller, The Hartford Insurance Group; and Stanley D. Halper, Partner, Coopers & Lybrand.

The Advisory Committee for the Associate in Insurance Accounting and Finance Program reviewed the entire text and offered innumerable suggestions for improvement. In addition to Tom Krause, the members of this Advisory Committee are A.M. Cunningham, Director of Finance, Texas Farm Bureau Insurance Companies; Arthur J. Laberge, CLU, Assistant Vice President and Director of Group Sales and Service, Reliance Standard Life Insurance Company; John R. Lanz, CPCU, Treasurer, Utica Mutual Insurance Company; Gerald I. Lenrow, J.D., Partner, Coopers & Lybrand; Katherine S. Perry, Assistant Vice President, Planning and Control Unit, CIGNA Corporation; and Robert W. Strain, D.B.A., CPCU, CLU, President, Robert W. Strain Seminars, Inc.

Additional reviewers who offered insightful suggestions included Patricia Henry, Planning and Control Consultant, Continental Data Center and Gary Knoble, Assistant Vice President, The Hartford Insurance Group.

Ultimate responsibility for the project rests with the Curriculum Department of the Insurance Institute of America, which welcomes comments and suggestions for further improvements in this text.

Robert J. Gibbons

Contributing Authors

The Insurance Institute of America and the authors acknowledge, with deep appreciation, the help of the following contributing authors who drafted initial manuscripts for significant sections of this book:

John M. Fcasni
President
J M F Associates

Robert Kehoe
Senior Project Manager
Continental Insurance

Joseph A. Mahaney
Director—Line Operations Controls
Nationwide Insurance Company

John McRee
Project Manager
Continental Insurance

Eugene Sogliuzzo
Systems Consultant
Continental Insurance

Thomas D. Steele, CPCU
Statistical Manager
Wausau Insurance Companies

P. K. Vichare
Assistant Vice President
Continental Insurance

Bernard L. Webb, CPCU, FCAS
Professor of Actuarial Science and Insurance
Georgia State University

Table of Contents

Chapter 5—Budgeting and Planning............................ 189

Introduction ~ *Coordinate Actions of Diverse Organizational Units; Communication; Motivate Performance; Evaluate Performance; Support Delegation of Authority; Link Strategic and "Tactical" Planning*

Essentials of Budgeting and Reporting System Design ~ *Fundamental Issues; Budgeting Systems; Reporting Essentials*

Budgeting ~ *Budgeting Principles; Budgeting Procedures*

Strategic Planning ~ *The Need for Strategic Planning; The Strategic Planning Process; Progress in Strategic Planning*

Capital Planning

Summary

Chapter 6—Management Reporting 225

Introduction

Regular Management Reports ~ *Sales Activity; Underwriting Activity; Claims Activity; Loss Control Services; Administrative and Human Resources; Investment Performance; Profitability*

Responsibility Accounting ~ *Organizational Structure; Goal Planning Responsibility Centers*

Decision Support

Summary

Chapter 7—Statistical Reporting 257

Introduction

Statistics and Ratemaking ~ *Ratemaking Concepts; Rate Regulation and Statistical Requirements*

CHAPTER 1

An Overview of Insurance Information Systems

INTRODUCTION

As one authority observed over a decade ago, "The insurance business is unique among businesses in the quantity of statistical data that are compiled and in the degree to which such data are utilized in everyday practice."[1] Meeting information needs for insurance operations demands an understanding of the needs of a variety of users. First, there is the insurance provider, including its owners, management, investors, and creditors. Next come the customer who is buying protection and the agent selling this protection. Tax authorities also require detailed information on insurance operations. Due to the social nature of insurance, many private and regulatory bodies are interested in insurance operations. These include the state insurance commissioners whose unique interests and concerns have led to statutory accounting principles. Special credit rating and statistical organizations require information to be used in research, rate making, and dissemination of information about the insurance organization. Publicly held companies are also subject to Securities and Exchange Commission (SEC) regulation and to specific legislation including requirements for adequate records and systems of internal controls mandated by the Foreign Corrupt Practices Act of 1977. Financial reports for the SEC are based on generally accepted accounting principles. These extensive and complex requirements influence the development of all insurance information systems.

Information systems are as complex and unique as the particular company using the system. The information system of an organization

1

performs the service function of transforming financial data into useful information that aids management and others in making decisions. The accounting information system accumulates, classifies, processes, analyzes, and communicates relevant financial information. Since non-financial information also influences decisions, a management information system may perform these functions for all types of information affecting a company's operation.

An information system is an organizational component that provides a service to management. System definition to provide this service requires development of the general specifications of the system objectives, design of the input and output formats, and development of processing logic to convert inputs into outputs. These specifications are realized in *system life cycles* which are a sequence of events that involve initiation, analysis and evaluation, design and selection, implementation, and maintenance of a particular system.

Nature of Insurance Operations

Due to the social nature of the protection offered by most insurance coverages, many private and regulatory segments of the economy are interested in insurance operations. The social responsibilities of the insurance business, along with normal regulatory requirements, require that insurance information systems recognize the demand for additional information capabilities.

Customers of most business organizations have no direct financial interest in the company beyond the price paid for the product purchased. When the product fails to perform as anticipated, the customer can demand a refund of the purchase price, a replacement or repair of the product, or perhaps some negotiated or litigated damages. However, insurance buyers have a direct financial interest in the insurance provider that goes beyond that of the customers of most businesses. Insurance buyers are purchasing protection against a potential economic loss, such as hospitalization or incapacity after an accident or sickness, an unforeseen loss of or damage to property, or responsibility for damages or injuries to other individuals. The loss that is insured against is almost always greater than the price (premium) paid at the time the product (policy) is acquired.

Insurance providers, unlike most other businesses, have another user of financial information in addition to the usual owner, management, investor, creditor, analyst, or regulator. Due to the public nature of insurance, each state's insurance commissioner charged with the regulatory responsibility of insurance companies requires meaningful financial, statistical, marketing, and operating information about insurance companies. The commissioner's interest and concerns vary from those of others, and in recognition of these concerns and responsibilities, statutory accounting principles have been established by statute, regulation, and practice.

Internal Accounting Controls

The information system of any business must maintain accurate records and adequate internal controls. Accurate records are the essential foundation for accumulating and reporting financial information.

A number of business practices and laws have created an interest in internal accounting controls. These developments include the following:

- The Foreign Corrupt Practices Act of 1977.
- The SEC's concern about corporate compliance with the Foreign Corrupt Practices Act.
- Disclosure of questionable business transactions which led to bankruptcy.
- General information concerning cases of computer fraud.
- Concerns expressed by corporate audit committees.

The Foreign Corrupt Practices Act, which amended the Security Exchange Act of 1934, contains provisions that apply to U.S. corporations whether they are involved in international operations or not. These provisions require companies registered with the United States Securities and Exchange Commission to (1) make and keep books, records, and accounts that accurately and fairly reflect, in reasonable detail, the transactions of the registrant and the disposition of its assets, and (2) devise and maintain a system of internal accounting controls sufficient to provide reasonable assurances that certain specified control objectives are met. Property-liability insurers and insurance holding companies with assets exceeding $1 million and 500 or more shareholders are subject to both the 1934 and the 1977 acts.

Historically, the authoritative directives of state insurance departments and the opinions of independent public accountants have well established the responsibility of insurance company management for establishing and maintaining adequate internal controls. The SEC reinforced this responsibility in the following pronouncement:

> The establishment and maintenance of a system of internal controls is an important management obligation. A fundamental aspect of management's stewardship responsibility is to provide shareholders with reasonable assurance that the business is adequately controlled. Additionally, management has a responsibility to furnish shareholders and potential investors with reliable financial information on a

timely basis. An adequate system of internal accounting control is necessary to management's discharge of these obligations.[2]

Additionally, independent auditors must review internal controls as part of any audit engagement. Generally accepted auditing standards require that, "There is to be a proper study and evaluation of the existing internal control as a basis for reliance thereon and for the determination of the resultant extent of the tests to which auditing procedures are to be restricted."[3]

Because both of the foregoing professional statements apply to virtually all accounting systems, the management of an insurance operation should be certain that its internal controls adhere to these guidelines.

In its Statement of Auditing Standards (SAS) No. 1, the American Institute of Certified Public Accountants distinguished two types of internal controls, administrative and accounting. The definitions of these two types of internal controls are as follows:

Administrative control includes, but is not limited to, the plan of organization and the procedures and records that are concerned with the decision processes leading to management's authorization of transactions. Such authorization is a management function directly associated with the responsibility for achieving the objectives of the organization and is the starting point for establishing accounting control of transactions.[4]

Accounting control comprises the plan of organization and the procedures and records that are concerned with the safeguarding of assets and the reliability of financial records and consequently are designed to provide reasonable assurance that:

— Transactions are executed in accordance with management's general or specific authorization.
— Transactions are recorded as necessary (1) to permit preparation of financial statements in conformity with generally accepted accounting principles or any other criteria applicable to such statements and (2) to maintain accountability for assets.
— Access to assets is permitted only in accordance with management's authorization.
— The recorded accountability for assets is compared with the existing assets at reasonable intervals and appropriate action is taken with respect to any differences.[5]

Thus an insurer's accounting system should be designed to satisfy these standards for both types of internal control.

MANAGEMENT INFORMATION NEEDS

All too frequently, the data provided to managers are inadequate. Have you ever been surrounded by (or had access to) volumes of statistical reports yet no clear-cut answer to the question at hand could be found? If so, you know the difference between information and data. Information tells you something; data alone does not.

Information in a business sense can be defined as the carefully constructed compilation of data, qualitative and quantitative, in a clear form that contributes to decision-making. The value of information lies in the improved quality of decision-making that results.

Organizations require feedback to regulate business activity and to evaluate business goals. Information provides a substantial portion of the operational feedback required by an organization.

Feedback information has been classified into three types: scorekeeping, attention directing, and decision making. Each of these types of information is useful in evaluating the operation of an organization. *Scorekeeping information* describes what has occurred in the past. Financial statements such as income statements and balance sheets are prime examples of scorekeeping information. *Attention directing information* refers to business facts that arouse the interest of the information user. Budget reports which provide a comparison of planned to actual experience are an example of attention directing information. *Decision making information* relates to the future and generally provides information which is pro-forma or forecasts the outcome of a series of decisions. Annual plans and strategic plans which are composites of various financial planning forecasts are examples of decision making information.

Information is essential for planning and budgeting, pricing, performance reviews, and operational assessments. The objective of a management information system is to provide the appropriate information in such a way that it results in timely input and support to all levels of management in carrying out assigned duties and responsibilities.

It might be thought that information, once provided, can remain in static form; once it becomes information, it will forever remain information. Nothing could be further from the truth. Today's business environment, particularly in the insurance industry, is as volatile as it has ever been. The issues and decisions facing all levels of management are many and varied. Management's need for information cannot help but be dynamic in nature—that is, forever changing. Information developed for use in the "days of old" becomes historical, antiquated data if it has not been updated and upgraded to reflect current business conditions or corporate strategic and operational plans and activities.

Forms and Types of Management Information

Management information is most often thought of as organized data in a statistical form. Every insurance organization must prepare financial statements. Insurance companies are always concerned with market share percentages, incurred loss ratios, number and types of agents, number of employees, economic conditions, and so on.

But management information can be composed of qualitative data as well. Information such as changes in state insurance regulations, releases of new standard industry policy forms, and revised underwriting rules all qualify as a form of management information.

In addition to the forms management information can take, it can also be categorized by a variety of types. Management information can be obtained externally as well as generated internally by a company. External management information can be general or specific in nature. Examples of the former might include statements and statistics on national or state economic conditions and associated political environments. Specific external industry information might include that provided by rate-making organizations such as the Insurance Services Office and the National Council on Compensation Insurance. It might also take the form of statistics provided by such data gathering bodies as Best's or Argus.

As these examples show, information also varies in the level of aggregation. Statistics reported to the Insurance Services Office are summaries of exposures, premiums, and losses by classification and by territory for each line of business. Reports to the National Council on Compensation Insurance, however, are on a unit transaction basis. That is, the National Council receives a detailed report of exposures, premiums, and losses for *each* workers' compensation policy.

The most evident type of management information is that which a company creates itself about itself. This internally generated management information can be about an organization's past, present, or future situations. Historical results often provide a basis for judging current operating results and assisting in the projection of future trends and directions. Current operating results are generally measured against current period expectations and plans. Projected results are used to ascertain the appropriateness of various strategic decisions and long-term directions.

The manner in which management information is reported can also vary. It can be periodic; that is, monthly, quarterly, semi-annual, annual, or some other calendar schedule form. It can also be "on-request" or on an exception basis. Management information that is provided "on-request" is delivered to a user only if that person requests it. The data is readily available in a pre-planned information form but is not distributed according to any pre-arranged schedule. "Exception reporting" occurs only when predetermined conditions exist. For example, a line of business result exceeds an established target such as an incurred loss ratio of 75.0. When this happens, a detailed information document about that line, including supporting detail, is produced and distributed to the appropriate person. However, nothing goes to this person unless the measured variable, in this case a line of business, has an incurred loss ratio result for the current reporting period in excess of 75.0.

Key Management Information Questions

Data abounds in most business organizations, and insurance companies are no exception. Information, however, does not. In order to overcome this condition, information development efforts must be organized and managed in a systematic way. There are four real or implied series of questions that a compiler of information must ask in preparing data for transformation into information. This same individual must re-visit these same questions for information already in existence if this "old" information is to remain current, or if it is to remain at all. These questions are:

1. *How is the desired information to be used?* Information must be presented in a communicative form in order for it to be effective. This requires a thorough understanding of the reason for the information request by both the end-user and the data compiler. Failure to accomplish this requirement can only result in an information effort that misses its mark.

2. *How much information is required and how often must it be produced?* This is a very important "two-pronged" question. There is a tendency on the part of end-users initially to request repeated volumes of information in support of a primary information requirement. Once this detail is provided, because of the volume (often caused by frequency), the end-user becomes frustrated, losing sight of the primary objective— comprehensible knowledge—and gaining an office filled with detailed reports and no time to read or comprehend them. The end-user and the data compiler can be accused of having turned information back into data, a common condition known as "information overload."

3. *Does the data necessary to support the information request exist within the organization and, if so, is it readily accessible?* These questions result in cost estimates useful in determining whether or not an organization can afford to produce the information requested. If the desired data exist somewhere on an existing report or within an existing system, it should not prove to be too difficult nor too costly to obtain. However, if this is not the case, then the cost to compile the

requested information will more than likely be substantial and time consuming, which are important considerations.

4. *What is the cost or loss to an organization to go without the requested information?* This can be a very difficult question to answer as information, particularly management information, very seldom produces short-term "hard dollar" benefits that can be attributed to it directly. For example, how do we directly quantify additional premium production resulting from information that permitted a company to better understand and manage its agency plant more productively? In fact, we can't; at least not directly, as other conditions such as increased competitive pricing or revised underwriting rules also may have contributed to the improved premium production condition. Despite this difficulty, an insurance organization must attempt to place some value on its information development efforts if it is going to be able to justify their development and production costs.

Management Information Tools

What tools exist to compile information? There are manual efforts that can be applied, and then there is the computer. The computer is a very powerful tool. It can store large volumes of data, manipulate all of it, and employ a variety of statistical techniques such as linear programming and regression and correlation analysis.

Decision support systems are becoming very popular information tools as they permit management to review alternative future scenarios as a result of changes in a variety of management decisions.

If management has a goal of making informed decisions, then it must be supplied with the appropriate management information on a timely basis. If management is to make "active" decisions, they must be based upon the most up-to-date, comprehensive information possible. Active decision-making involves a conscious decision being made; the decision does not happen by default or inaction. These requirements hold true regardless if the decision at hand is strategic or operational.

In order to support active, informed decision-making, an organization's systems must be dynamic, flexible, timely, accurate, accessible, and secure. Failure to meet any one of these criteria causes management to make less than fully informed decisions, or worse, totally inactive decisions due to a lack of management information.

Many individuals believe that computers can make decisions. This can be true only if the computer's logic has been programmed by a person to review alternatives and then select "a best one" based upon some humanly predetermined decision selection criteria.

The same can be said about people's perceptions of information and decision-making. Even the most obvious of decisions requires human intervention. Information, by itself, does not make the decision; it only "points out" the appropriate decision, and then only if the responsible person interpreting the information decides that way. Therefore information is only the input into the decision-making process. It is not the decision itself. However, the importance of information cannot be overstated. Failure to provide accurate timely information can only take away from an organization's well-managed decision processes.

USES OF INFORMATION

There are a number of users of insurance information. Each has a particular reason for wanting the information. These users include both those with an economic interest in the insurance organization and those with an interest that is mandated by law. Some of the typical users are management, actuaries, statistical organizations, policyholders and agents, regulators, tax authorities, and reinsurers. Because they rely on the output of the information system, these users may also insist on an adequate audit trail or description of how information flows through the system. The following section examines each of these users in regard to who they are, what kind of information they use, and how they use the information.

Managing

Insurance company management is, or at least should be, the primary user of information provided by the insurance information system. By definition, it is responsible for planning, organizing, directing, and controlling the destiny of the insurance organization. Consequently, the management has a duty to uphold the economic and statutory interests of all concerned.

As a result of these responsibilities, insurance company management uses many kinds of information both internal and external to the organization. It may be financial, statistical, economic, demographic, or social in nature, and it may represent either historical experience or future projections. Each phase of the management process may require some or all of the various types of information. Although the insurance information system does not provide all the information that management uses, it should satisfy most management needs. In addition, it must be flexible, responsive, and accurate.

Planning The planning cycle involves the establishment of goals for the insurance organization. Generally, the management states those goals in quantifiable terms so that success of achievement can be measured. Financial terms are most often used to express the desired results. The goal may be a dollar amount of underwriting or operating profit or profit expressed as a percentage of premium volume. A growth objective might be established in terms of a dollar amount, or percentage increase in premium volume, or a share of the insurance market as expressed by a percentage of industry premium volume. Growth goals may also be expressed in units such as insurance applications submitted or policies issued. They may also be subdivided into separate goals for each organizational unit, geographic area, product line, or customer group.

Planning is often characterized as "short" term or "long" term. The short term is one-to-eighteen months while the long term may be one-to-five years. The information needs for the short term are very specific and detailed. Extending into the longer term, they become somewhat less specific. In any case, planning relies on information developed from past experience, as well as forecasts of future economic, industry, and company specific variables. Therefore, information systems for insurance organizations must be designed to facilitate planning. The information needs for planning are no different than for other functions, but the information must represent continuous time series data to allow extrapolation into the future.

The computer has had a very large impact on planning. Insurance organizations can now plan for the future on the basis of large amounts of historical data. Prior to the advent of large computer systems, it was impractical to perform the complex compilations and manipulations of data now generated readily by computer models. These models mimic the structural relationships among important variables derived either from logic or from the historical record. For planning purposes, data reflecting possible changes under consideration can be put into the model. The model then determines results that can be expected.

A typical insurance organization may use the following variables for planning purposes:

- Number of employees for expense purposes
- Number of policies written
- Number of policies-in-force
- Written premium
- Earned premium
- Catastrophe losses
- Noncatastrophe losses
- Expenses
- Profit and losses

The results of several models describing environmental, organizational, and desired change variables are used by management to set objectives to be used in budgeting, controlling, and performance evaluation.

Budgeting Budgeting is a critical component in an insurer's information system. The health of any organization requires proper expense control.

The National Association of Insurance Commissioners (NAIC) has developed a set of operating expense classifications. The company management must determine whether it wants to use the NAIC expense classifications and groupings, or if the expense information system should be structured according to its own requirements. Some systems or parts of systems are necessary for tax and regulatory purposes. But the diversity of insurance organizations requires many additional systems for proper expense control.

Budgeting information needs stem from these expense controls. The NAIC specified operating expense classifications for property and liability insurers are:

1. Claim Adjustment Services
   Direct
   Reinsurance Assumed
   Reinsurance Ceded
2. Commission and Brokerage
   Direct
   Reinsurance Assumed
   Reinsurance Ceded
   Contingent—Net
   Policy and Membership Fees
3. Allowances to Managers and Agents
4. Advertising
5. Boards, Bureaus, and Associations
6. Surveys and Underwriting Reports
7. Audit of Assured's Records
8. Salaries
9. Employee Relations and Welfare
10. Insurance
11. Directors' Fees
12. Travel and Travel Items
13. Rent and Rent Items
14. Equipment
15. Printing and Stationary
16. Postage, Telephone and Telegraph, Exchange and Expenses
17. Legal and Auditing

18. Taxes, Licenses, and Fees
    State and Local Insurance Taxes
    Insurance Department Licenses and Fees
    Payroll Taxes
    All Other (excluding Federal Income and Real Estate)
19. Real Estate Expenses
20. Real Estate Taxes
21. Miscellaneous[6]

Regardless of how an insurance organization chooses to develop, manage, control, and implement its budgeting processes, management information provides the key to a successful budgeting activity.

Management information which includes historical expenditure results, current results to date, future economic expectations, and management's direction and assumptions is necessary to establish the organization's budgets. Then actual expenditures must be tracked against these plans in order to ensure the budget's appropriateness and the degree to which the organization is on or off target. Significant budget variances, particularly overages, can have significant impacts on a company's financial position and pricing and product structures and strategies.

Management information has to be provided in support of all three budgeting categories: operational budgets for both line and staff functions, long-range planning budgets for activities such as the penetration of new geographic markets, and capital budgets for acquisitions such as computer hardware and new office buildings.

Controlling The organizing and directing phases of the management process bring together all the resources needed, in the right amounts and the proper structure, to achieve the goals established in the planning phase. The control phase is the guidance system of the management process. In this phase management monitors how well its decisions in the organizing and directing phases propel the insurance organization toward the goals established in the planning phase. It is here that the insurance information system plays a vital role for management. It is the heart of management's monitoring system.

Management must monitor the activities and results of the insurance organization. In this way, they can control or attempt to control the functioning of the company. The computer has enhanced the control function by enabling organizations to provide many reports presenting information for control purposes.

The essential information needs in this area involve those that verify the actual operation of the organization in comparison to the planned operation.

As with planning, the number of employees, number of policies, premium (both written and earned), losses, and expenses are important control informational items.

Evaluating The evaluation of the control reports are then the final process, prior to needed action, which require information considerations. Management requires the ability to track actual results and compare them to its plan.

The information needs are the same as for planning, budgeting, and controlling, but the information must also be organized in a fashion which facilitates analysis. The comparison of current period data to historical data allows management to see patterns.

The types of performance reviews an organization's management might make include actual results versus current plan, historical performance against current performance, and current trends measured against future desired directions.

The monitoring of performance may provide management with a "current status"; or "after the fact" assessments; or early warnings of future problems or opportunities. In any event, management information provided in support of performance reviews should indicate that current directions are:

- on-target and should not be changed, or
- on-target but should be changed, or
- off-target and should be brought back on-target, or
- off-target and appropriately so, or
- some combination of the above.

These indications may even suggest that management's decision processes themselves need to be reviewed, a key performance decision itself.

During the early 1980s business graphics have been developed to enhance this process greatly. The use of the computer has allowed the graphic display of information for evaluation purposes to be developed quickly and efficiently. These visual displays have made the evaluation process much more orderly and disciplined.

Information should be summarized in a manner corresponding to the scope of responsibility of each level of management. At the detail level the accounting records must be developed, and maintained, in the smallest detail possible. This level must also recognize that the quality of information provided at higher levels, as management responsibilities expand, depends on accuracy at this detail level.

The supervisory level focuses on results, performance measurement, and the responsiveness of the information system. This level has taken on even more significance in recent years because of the complexity of computer systems. In order that these complex systems be maintained properly, information must be timely and accurate.

Finally, middle and top managers need information showing overall performance and financial results. They make their decisions on the basis of information received so that sound management decisions result. To accomplish this, management needs not only actual results which will become public records but also detail on what was planned or expected. This permits an assessment of performance, analysis of variance from plans, and development of any corrective action needed.

Pricing

One of the most difficult decisions for insurers is to determine the best price for their products. Unlike other business firms, insurers do not know the actual cost of their product at the time of sale. The cost depends on the future occurrence of events covered by the insurance. Thus the insurer must estimate the cost of such future losses on the basis of past experience. The need for precision in making these estimates is crucial. If the insurer underestimates the cost of future losses or expenses, its obligation to pay those costs could drain its surplus and impair its financial condition. On the other hand, if the insurer overprices the product in an effort to be conservative, the business will go to competitors instead and the insurer may not have sufficient volume to justify its expenses.

Pricing of insurance products is the function of actuaries. Historically, insurers have pooled their statistics and depended on the actuarial expertise of rating organizations. Since the rating laws of many states now encourage greater competition, however, insurers have a greater need for their own actuarial analysis. Some states, for example, permit rating organizations solely to calculate and file pure premium data. Individual insurers must calculate their own expense data and file gross rates independently.

The rate-making data needed by actuaries include data on premiums, losses, and expenses. It might have to be grouped by line of business, by state, by territory, by classification, or by other rating variables. For actuarial projections, it is important that premium, loss, and expense data represent the same group of policies. Thus the most accurate method is to tabulate all the data on a policy-year basis. That method also has disadvantages, however, and the calendar-year method or the calendar-accident-year method might be preferred for some purposes.

Premium data include not only the amount but also the exposures and the number of policies. Loss statistics must include the number of claims as well as the amounts, properly coded according to the relevant statistical plan. Expense data, including loss adjustment expenses, commissions, other acquisition expenses, general expenses, and taxes, must also be incorporated into the rate-making process. In some cases, budgeted expenses may be more appropriate than past experience, if such information can be provided to the actuaries.

In addition to rate making for current products, actuaries also perform special studies and analyses. These special studies may suggest new classification plans, new underwriting standards, or other improvements in the existing operations. They may also analyze the potential profitability of new products or new markets. For these special studies, they may need information relating to certain variables or grouped in certain ways previously not foreseen.

Statistical Reporting

All insurance organizations are required to report information for the states in which they do business to those states. To fulfill this requirement, data must be collected and organized so that the resulting information will satisfy the state statutes. This type of statistical data is essentially scorekeeping information.

Independent statistical agencies collect the data from insurers and then report that data to the states. This service assists insurers in that rather than reporting to each state separately, they can report the data for all states to the agency (for a fee). The statistical agency then reports the appropriate data to each state. In this system, the states receive summaries of all industry information by state so that little more manipulation of data is necessary.

The statistical organizations engaged in rate making and reporting to insurance departments, such as the Insurance Services Office and the National Association of Independent Insurers, require a great deal of detailed information for each line of business. Premium and loss statistics are needed for each geographic location of the risk such as state, territory, county, zip code, or public protection code for insurance coverage on the risk such as policy type, deductible, and amount of insurance; and for conditions peculiar to each insured, such as building construction type, vehicle identification numbers, age and sex of the driver, payroll dollars and numbers of employees, and type and value of insured merchandise. Such detail is required so that insurance rates can be properly developed or analyzed by the insurance departments to determine if they are reasonable, adequate, and not unfairly discriminatory. In addition, regulators require information measuring the volume of each line of insurance written in their states.

For these purposes, premiums and losses are collected by a variety of identifications. Typical identifications needed for premium information include:

- State
- Territory
- City
- County
- Construction
- Public Protection
- Deductible—Type and Amount
- Insurance Amount
- Construction Year

In addition to those required for premiums, typical identifications needed for loss information include:

- Catastrophe Code
- Loss Cause

For each of these identifications the following is reported:

- Written exposures
- Written premium
- Paid losses
- Unpaid losses
- Number of paid losses
- Number of unpaid losses

The computer environment dictates that a minimum amount of redundancy resides in a company's information systems. Therefore, the same data used to develop financial and management information is used for statistical reporting.

Statistical agencies notify insurers of the information requirements for each line of business. This notification comes through statistical "calls" which specify the time frame within which the information must be reported, whether monthly, quarterly, or annually. In addition to the time frame, options are specified with respect to the medium to be used. Nearly all reporting can be done on computer tape rather than hard copy, or punch cards, which were common in the past.

Early in the 1980s insurance regulators established requirements that determine the quality of an insurer's information. The state of New York (NY Regulation 103) requires that all insurance organizations writing private passenger automobile business follow a specified Statistical Data Monitoring System. This requires that, in addition to the information needs described above, insurance organizations must determine if that information accurately represents the insured entity.

A comparison of the information used for statistical reporting must be made to the insurance organizations' financial information.

The principal insurance statistical organizations are those organized for rate-making purposes and those that act as statistical agents to fulfill reporting requirements mandated by state insurance departments. Other insurance statistical organizations are established for purposes of loss prevention, research, and dissemination of information about the insurance industry.

The other types of statistical organizations generally do not require as much detail as the rating and reporting organizations. Examples of other types of statistical organizations include the National Auto Theft Bureau, the Insurance Crime Prevention Institute, the Bodily Injury Index Bureau, the Property Insurance Register, the Insurance Institute for Highway Safety, and the A. M. Best Company.

Financial Reporting

Insurers must provide additional scorekeeping information to parties concerned with their financial condition. Foremost in this regard is the concern of insurance regulators to protect the public interest by assuring the solvency of insurance companies. In addition, investors, creditors, agents, policyholders, and tax authorities all have an interest in an insurer's financial condition. Two specific sets of accounting standards have evolved to facilitate accurate comparisons of insurers' financial reports. State insurance commissioners require financial information reported according to principles prescribed by the National Association of Insurance Commissioners. These so-called Statutory Accounting Principles (SAP) emphasize the presentation of financial information relating to solvency. Since potential investors, however, may be more interested in an insurer's earnings potential in comparison to firms in other industries, many insurers also report financial results according to generally accepted accounting principles (GAAP).

The insurance organizations information needs must support these various requirements for financial accounting. Information needed for the balance sheet and statement of income and retained earnings includes:

- Fixed maturities
- Equity securities
- Cash and short-term securities
- Investment income accrued
- Premium balances receivable
- Deferred acquisition costs
- Company occupied real estate

- Furniture and equipment
- Loss reserves
- Loss adjustment expense reserves
- Unearned premium reserves
- Excess of statutory reserves over statement
- Federal income taxes:
  - Current
  - Deferred
- Common stock
- Additional paid-in capital
- Unrealized capital gains
- Retained earnings
- Shareholder equity, SAP
- Permanent impairment of bonds for GAAP in excess of the SAP write-downs to market mandated by the NAIC
- Restoration of premium balances receivable deemed to be collectible under GAAP, but required to be written off under SAP
- Capitalization of certain policy acquisition costs
- Certain furniture and equipment counted as GAAP assets, not admitted under SAP
- Formula loss reserves required by SAP restored to retained earnings under GAAP
- Shareholder equity, GAAP
- Premiums written
- Increase in unearned premium reserves
- Premiums earned
- Investment income
- Losses
- Amortization of deferred acquisition costs
- Investment expenses
- General and administrative expenses
- Dividends to policyholders
- Realized investment losses, net of taxes
- Retained earnings, beginning of year
- Required addition to loss reserves
- Dividends to shareholders

Statutory Basis   Statutory accounting principles are prescribed by the insurance department of the state in which the organization is domiciled. These principles have developed over the years to assist insurance regulatory authorities in the discharge of one of their primary obligations, which is to keep insurance companies solvent and in sufficiently liquid financial position to discharge all of their obligations to policyholders. For this reason, statutory accounting differs from generally accepted accounting principles in the following ways:

- Business acquisition costs under statutory accounting are charged against income as they are incurred.
- Statutory accounting treats certain assets as nonadmitted, i.e., their values are removed from the balance sheet.
- Federal income taxes are reflected on the "liability methods" (tax actually payable) under statutory accounting.
- Statutory accounting does not recognize salvage and subrogation until collected.
- Redeemable preferred stocks whose terms and conditions meet certain requirements are carried at cost in statutory accounting.
- Under statutory accounting a number of states prohibit the accrual of debit adjustments (additional premiums) on policies with retrospective premium provisions.
- Statutory accounting does not require accrual for a probable loss from premium inadequacy affecting an entire line of business.

GAAP Basis Generally accepted accounting principles have been developed to prepare financial statements that provide investors with information about insurance companies on a going-concern basis. GAAP statements present a snapshot of a company's financial condition at a point in time. From GAAP statements, trends of growth in premium, investment income, claims, and other operating expenses can be analyzed.

For this reason, GAAP procedures capitalize acquisition costs that are primarily related to and vary with the volume of premium income by periodic charges to earnings over the policy terms. Also according to GAAP procedures, equipment and furniture, leasehold improvements, balances due from agents, and amounts recoverable from salvage and subrogation are shown on the balance sheet subject to the tests of recoverability or realization. Similarly, dividends to policyholders are accrued at balance sheet date using the best available estimates.

Deferred federal income taxes are required to be provided on all timing differences between pre-tax GAAP earnings and taxable income on the federal income tax return. Under GAAP the deferred tax on the unrealized appreciation on any equity investments must be provided. These practices lead to a more realistic presentation of an insurer's earnings performance in a particular period.

Stockholders in an insurance company are no different from stockholders in any other type of company. Annual reports of the financial condition and operating results of the company and other investment publications are their main sources of information. Their primary concerns are safeguarding their investment and making a fair return on their money. Therefore, the Securities and Exchange Commission requires financial reports on a GAAP basis for all companies whose stock is traded publicly.

Not all insurance companies are owned by stockholders. Mutual companies, reciprocals, and Lloyds represent other forms of insurance organizations. The size and form of the organization influence the information needs of its owners. Some need no more information than the average policyholder while others need as much information as the organization's management. In many cases they may prefer financial reports stated according to generally accepted accounting principles even when a GAAP basis is not required by law.

Customer Service

As users of information, policyholders and agents can be considered together, because information used by the policyholder becomes an information need of the agent. The policyholder looks to the agent as the primary source of insurance information. To acquire and retain the policyholder as a customer, the agent must provide the needed information either personally or through the insurance organization.

Policyholders' information needs are relatively simple and are much the same as purchasers of other products. They want to know what products and services are available that will meet their insurance needs, who has them, and how much they cost. The agent can provide the information from printed or electronically displayed rating manuals developed by the actuarial function from data in the insurance information system.

In addition to satisfying the policyholders' needs, the agent uses additional information in operating the business. This information includes personal data about customers and prospective customers; policy and coverage identification data, including type, limits, and deductibles; premium charges and premium collection data; and data relating to the productivity and profitability of the agency operation.

The information needs of an insurance organization for customer service emanate from the following requirements:

- Policy service
- Claims handling
- Annual report to policyholders
- Agency communication

Policy Service The information needed for customer service in the policy area is derived from the policyholder (customer), by the agent, when the application is taken. Additionally, the premium (rate) information developed by the insurance organization must be available for the customer.

The agent as a representative of the company collects the information in discussions with the customer and sends that information to the organization. The organization writes and issues the policy, which contains the pertinent rate information, including a description of the risk. The customer can use the description provided by the organization to verify the accuracy of what is insured and the amount of insurance provided. At each policy renewal time this information should be available for the customer. Typically this information is:

- Automobile
  - Make and model of auto
  - Deductible applicable
  - Estimate of mileage driver
  - Principal garaging location
  - Coverage applicable
- Homeowners
  - Amount of insurance
  - Deductible applicable
  - Insured location-address
  - Coverages applicable

This information must also be available to respond to customer questions. Today, most organizations have access to electronic data files that store all the information available for a policy.

Claim Handling and Processing Upon notification of a loss, the insurance organization creates a data record to represent that claim for reimbursement. Typically, the customer will inform the agent of a loss on property insured by the organization. The agent will then notify the organization. A claim handler will then be assigned to adjust, i.e., investigate and settle (pay) the claim if coverage is applicable.

To enable the adjuster to do this, the information with respect to the customer and insured property must be available. The adjuster confirms coverage does exist by comparing the claim information to the coverage information.

At the time of claim payment, the information on the policy and on the claim must be available for proper customer service. Information for claims handling in addition to the policy information is:

- Automobile
  - Location of the loss
  - Time and date of the loss
  - Type or kind of loss

- Amount of damage
- Homeowners
    - Type of kind of loss
    - Amount of damage
    - Time and date of loss
    - Location of loss (if off the insured premises)

As with policy information, access to the claim information must be readily available in order to respond to customer questions.

Annual Report to Policyholder In today's consumer oriented environment, it is important that the organization inform customers of the operating results and health of that organization. Insurance organizations make the financial information available to customers through an annual report. Typically, the information provided is:

- Premiums
- Losses
- Expenses for adjusting losses
- Administrative expenses
- Profit or loss
- Investment income
- Dividends
- Income taxes

Generally, the operating results are explained, as well as notification of the annual meeting time, date, and place. Primarily the information needed is a summarized form of the financial information reported to state regulators.

Agency Communication The information needs for agency communication primarily require compilation of data on each aspect of an agency's book of business. Computer systems have been developed to facilitate the requirements.

Each insurance organization develops a series of agency reports to reflect the information for that agency. In addition to the typical annual report to the agency, some insurers develop semi-annual, quarterly, or monthly reports.

The information is organized into its various components to facilitate reporting. For automobile insurance, these reports segregate voluntary business and nonvoluntary business, that is, insurance written due to a regulatory requirement. For homeowners business, distinctions may be made between policies covering owner-occupied and nonowner-occupied dwellings.

Several categories of information may be provided. A policy

activity section may display the number of policies at the beginning and ending of the period. The policy gain or loss can then be derived.

A productivity section may show items such as company cancellations, policyholder cancellations, new policies writings, and number of policies not renewed. This information provides both the insurer and the agency with a view of that agency's production.

To indicate an agency's loss experience, a loss activity section may be included. Typically the frequency of losses—how many losses per policy have resulted over the report time period, and severity—the average paid cost of each loss, will be shown.

A profitability section may be included to show the profit or loss of the agency. Written premium, earned premium, paid loss amounts, outstanding loss amounts, incurred loss amounts, incurred expenses, and dividends are included.

A number of factors affect the rate, such as amount charged for a policy period. These factors can be displayed in an "analysis section." For automobile business, these factors may include number of private passenger autos insured, number of recreational vehicles insured, number of vehicles based on the deductibles, and model year of the vehicles. For homeowners, these may be year of construction, public protection class, and so on.

These various sections are designed to communicate specific pieces of information to the agency.

During the early 1980s, substantial effort has been made to establish a computer link between insurance organizations and insurance agencies. The computer link will allow for enhanced communication for both the organization and the agent. The efforts expended in this regard do not materially change the information needs, but as in any use of the computer, the new system will:

1. require greater attention to accuracy to assure quality information,
2. substantially speed up the communication process, enabling faster response to problems, and
3. require greater security of the information used.

Regulation

Like most businesses "affected with public interest," insurance is subject to extensive government regulation. In the United States, the individual states are primarily responsible for the regulation of the insurance industry. In 1945 the United States Congress reaffirmed this responsibility in Public Law 15. This law exempts insurance from federal anti-trust regulation as long as there is adequate regulation by the states.

Each state has established a commissioner, superintendent, or director of insurance whose staff constitutes the state insurance department. These state insurance departments regulate insurance within their state boundaries to determine the financial stability of the insurance organizations doing business there. This regulation helps to assure the availability of insurance for the state's consumers.

Market Conduct A major responsibility of state insurance departments is to evaluate compliance with statutes and regulations relating to market conduct practices of insurers and their dealings with policyholders and claimants in the state. According to the NAIC Model Market Conduct Examination Handbook:

> The four key market conduct areas are: (1) sales and advertising, (2) underwriting, (3) rating, and (4) claims.... The department is also concerned with ensuring that a climate of competition continues to exist within the marketplace of insurance. State Unfair Trade Practice Acts prohibit practices in restraint of trade or tending to foster monopoly such as unfairly discriminatory underwriting practices, much as the federal antitrust law applies to other industries....[7]

In examining a company's market practices, regulators rely primarily on financial examiners and on information developed by the staff members who process complaints, who review and approve rates and policy forms, and who regulate agents and brokers. Complaint analysis, information from other states, and other indicators play a role. In addition, regulators may conduct examinations of sale and advertising, underwriting, rating, and claims to determine factually the business practices of a company.

Solvency To provide some consistency and uniformity in regulation among the various states, the state insurance commissioners formed the National Association of Insurance Commissioners. This association, with the assistance of members of the insurance industry, developed the annual statement blank that must be filed in each state. This statement is the primary source of information for monitoring the solvency of the insurers doing business in each of the states.

The statement consists of a balance sheet and income statement supported by a number of exhibits and schedules that show the financial data by line of business, by type of transaction, or its development over time. At least two exhibits in the fire and casualty annual statements require a breakdown of premium and loss information by state and territory.

In 1971, the NAIC established a property and liability "early warning system," later named the Insurance Regulatory Information System (IRIS), which consists of a series of eleven ratio analyses using the data submitted on the annual statements. Three of the analyses deal with the overall financial results, three with profitability, two with liquidity, and three with the adequacy of loss reserves. The purpose of these analyses is to quickly assess the financial condition of insurers and identify those that need to be scutinized in more detail.

In addition to the annual statement, some state insurance departments require their own special financial exhibits and on a more frequent basis. They also periodically conduct Financial Condition Examinations of individual insurers in which they review the source documents and processes to verify the accuracy of the amounts stated in the annual statement and that internal controls are consistent with standard regulatory practices.

The Securities and Exchange Commission is also interested in similar financial information for stock insurance companies. The SEC is concerned with the protection of the stockholders' interests and has its own financial reporting requirements.

Rate Adequacy   State insurance regulators are also interested in the rates charged for the various types of insurance coverages sold in the state. They want to ensure that the rates are "reasonable, adequate, and not unfairly discriminatory." Rating laws vary by state and line of business. In a few states, rates are mandated by the insurance department. Other states have prior approval, file-and-use, or open competition laws. Regardless of the type of rating law, insurers must support their rates with historical and projected data derived from their own or a pooled insurance information system. The data is filed directly by the insurer or through an approved rating organization to the state insurance department or its designated agency.

Taxes, Fees, and Assessments

Insurance companies deal with a myriad of taxing bodies, especially those companies that do business on a national or international scale. Each of the taxing bodies needs not only the money due, but also the supporting data and documentation that were used to calculate the amount due. The insurance information system must be geared to provide the supporting information for the various taxing authorities. Generally, however, that requirement poses little difficulty, since in many cases the data used to support the development of the annual statements can be used.

Like all businesses, insurers must pay federal income and payroll related taxes. They must also pay a number of state and local taxes, fees, and assessments similar to other business such as state income taxes, state unemployment taxes, license fees, filing fees, real estate and personal property taxes, sale and use taxes, and franchise taxes. In addition, there are a number of taxes, fees, and assessments peculiar to the insurance business. Most state and local taxing bodies base these taxes, fees, and assessments by location, by line of business, or both. All fifty-three state or territorial taxing jurisdictions impose a gross premium tax. It is computed on gross premiums received by the insurer, less deductions for such items as returned premiums, cancellations, and dividends. Some states require the inclusion of other premium related items, such as finance or service charges and membership fees. On the other hand, some states allow reductions for certain lines of business that are taxed separately or allow tax credits and tax allowances for such things as investment incentives and other types of taxes paid.

Other taxes, fees, and assessments peculiar to insurance companies include fire marshall, fire department and fire pension fund taxes; workers compensation taxes; secondary injury and special workers compensation funds; guaranty funds; automobile insurance funds; special boards and bureau assessments; county and municipal taxes, licenses, and fees; and retaliatory and reciprocal taxes.

Reinsurance Relationships

Reinsurance is "the transaction whereby an insurance company (known as the reinsurer) for consideration, agrees to idemnify another insurance company known as the ceding company (the reinsurer or the primary insurer) against all or part of a loss which the reinsured may sustain under a policy or policies it has issued."[8] It is the transfer of insurance from one insurer to another insurer, the insuring of insurance. Such agreements may be advantageous to an insurance company for several reasons: (1) to help the company increase its capacity to write more insurance, either more or larger risks than it normally could cover; (2) to provide protection against catastrophic losses; (3) to provide stable underwriting results for the insured; (4) to improve financial strength through surplus relief; and (5) in some cases, to provide the reinsured with expert help and advice.

The various forms of reinsurance agreements dictate the type and amount of information that the reinsurer needs to reflect properly the reinsurance transactions on its own information system. Essentially, however, the reinsurer needs much the same information as the primary insurer.

Two problems often arise in the flow of information from the primary insurer and the reinsurer. One is the timeliness of the data received, the other is the amount of detail. Information is often slow in reaching the insurer and in not enough detail to classify the data properly. The increasing sophistication of insurance information systems, and greater use of computers in particular, is important in managing these reinsurance problems as well as meeting information requirements of all other users.

SYSTEMS DEVELOPMENT

People use the word "system" in many ways. One frequently hears: "He beat the system," or "The system isn't working." A system may be considered a method of doing something or getting something accomplished. Some systems are very simple; some are very complicated. Almost everything one does on a daily basis can be characterized as a system. Getting dressed to go to work, feeding a family, buying a house or a car, and numerous other activities a person does routinely can be called a system. In each case there is some sort of input, some processing steps or procedures are followed, and there is a final outcome or objective achieved.

A system usually consists of a formalized set of procedures for accomplishing an objective. For business purposes, we might define a system as an operating combination of human and machine functions which interact in a controlled fashion to satisfy business objectives and user requirements. Management establishes objectives or reasons for existence in the specific goals for a system and its relationship to all other systems within a corporation. There are system operating costs for people and machines, and there is interaction between people and machines and among individuals in various departments. Systems use data which are processed through equipment to produce the desired information. The processing is usually done during established time constraints, that is, at certain times of the day and of the month and for a certain period of hours. The entire system operates in a controlled environment to insure accuracy and security.

The system environment is divided into two parts—hardware environment and software environment. The hardware environment contains all the equipment used in the system, while the software environment contains all the instructions and logic that control everything the hardware does. Years ago, hardware was the dominant factor because it was so expensive and limited. Gradually, the cost of hardware has decreased because of technological advances and increasing competition among manufacturers. During this same time, the cost of software has increased so much that software is now the dominant consideration in developing systems. Because it requires large amounts of costly programming time, software is very expensive. In fact, it is recommended that the software be designed without considering the hardware. Then, after deciding what you want done and how you are going to do it, the hardware can be chosen from the large selection of equipment that is available.

Project Development Life Cycle

It is difficult to overstate the need for carefully planning systems development and involving the necessary people in the process. The lead time required to develop an effective system is nearly always far longer than the casual observer might guess.

One reason is that today's computerized systems tend to be large and complex. Another reason is that there is a considerable ripple effect associated with systems development. What might seem a small, painless change in one isolated area can have very painful consequences in another part of the system. So, the system impact of any new initiative has to be carefully considered by users and systems people.

Developing systems that work effectively and efficiently is a big responsibility and there are frequently big dollars involved. To achieve the desired result, systems development should proceed through a series of logical steps. Users have to get involved in systems development at the planning stage and assume a significant portion of the responsibility for the outcome.

The increasing complexity of system development projects necessitates a standard methodology. Following a standard methodology for system development will:

- Increase the efficient use of resources
- Provide a standard set of activities for project development
- Provide the project team members with models of phase-end reports
- Provide management with information for interpreting alternate courses of action, assessing progress, budgeting, and planning
- Enable project team members to see clearly how their activity fits into the total project
- Identify and explain the logical phases of project development

The project development life cycle standardizes the processes involved in systems development and modification, promotes communication among concerned groups, and insures that the end product meets the original objectives of the project. To achieve these goals, a handbook or manual should be available to provide guidance concerning the organization, objectives, activities, and responsibilities of the project team which is composed of representatives of the application systems departments, the end-user, and other groups. The project development methodology helps everyone involved in a project increase the efficient use of resources, improve productivity of personnel, and control project time and costs.

The creation of a system is an evolutionary process, which may be divided into discrete phases. Each phase has specific objectives, contributing to the progressive completion of the project. The phases of a project must be completed in sequence because each subsequent phase depends on products of preceding phases.

Each phase consists of numerous activities necessary for achieving the objectives of that phase. An activity is defined as the basic unit of work within a phase. Each activity has a defined purpose and may require a number of steps to accomplish the purpose. The outcome of each of these activities is generally documentation.

The creation of a specific report signifies the completion of each phase. These reports are easily assembled from the documentation produced as a result of each activity. Phase-end reports are reviewed and evaluated by data processing management and approved by user management. This procedure insures that the project continues to meet the objectives of the business entity as well as the defined requirements of the proposed system.

If, at the end of any phase in the life cycle, approval to continue development is not received, reasons for declining approval should be stated. Consequently, it may be necessary to adjust requirements (with user agreement), alter the approach, or terminate the project if it is decided that acceptable modifications cannot be made.

The number of phases in a project development life cycle may vary from four to twelve, depending on how the activities are grouped. This discussion presents the life cycle in seven phases: (1) initiation, (2) feasibility, (3) definition, (4) design, (5) development, (6) implementation, and (7) post-implementation.

Depending on the estimated cost of a project, this life cycle can be abbreviated. For projects estimated to cost between $50,000 and $250,000, the feasibility phase may be eliminated. For projects estimated to cost between $10,000 and $50,000, the feasibility, definition, and post-implementation phases may be eliminated. Regardless of a project's estimated cost, it may be a good idea to review the requirements of each phase to make sure that nothing important is overlooked. In fact, it is advisable to review the project development life cycle manual even when the estimated cost of a project is less than $10,000.

Initiation Phase The initiation phase provides the foundation for all succeeding phases of the project development life cycle. During the initiation phase, the *project request document* is analyzed and evaluated from the client or user's viewpoint. The user's requirement must be initially identified in this phase. Since all succeeding phases build upon and refine project requirements, the user should actively participate in identifying requirements. A user representative should be assigned to the project team to provide assistance and guidance as the project development proceeds.

The initiation phase is critical to the success of any systems development project. Systems development disasters often occur because not enough time was spent analyzing systems needs and planning a realistic schedule for the execution of the project. When the right questions are addressed initially, the remainder of the project flows smoothly. The early involvement of both systems analysts and users facilitates planning, but early involvement is not enough. The key is precise communication concerning system needs and possibilities. Ideas bounce back and forth from users to analysts until they reach a clear common understanding of the system to be developed.

Feasibility Phase The feasibility phase expands the ideas and broad problem statements generated in the project request document into the objectives and performance specifications to be met by the system. In addition to stating what the system must do, specific information, schedules, and alternatives are developed, and a cost/benefit analysis is prepared.

Definition Phase The definition phase emphasizes the user's view of the system and defines the problem the system is expected to solve. Since different requirements stem from different needs, it is essential to clarify the precise need for the system. The definition phase leads to specification of the input, output, and processing requirements. User requirements and specifications are in effect an outline of the project in clear, nontechnical language that communicates to users and technicians what the project should accomplish.

The most useful technique for specifying user requirements is to model the current logical system. Used carefully, flowcharts can depict the logical processes of a system. However, they do not incorporate user preferences when there are tradeoffs involved in the system design, such as between immediate access to data and absolute accuracy. Moreover, flowcharts commit the systems designers to certain choices unnecessarily. For these reasons, it has been said that flowcharts do more harm than good.[9] Even so, there is nothing wrong with using them as a tool to help systems analysts and users achieve a common understanding of the system requirements.

Systems needs of insurance companies may be divided into five general categories. Although the possible variations are endless and the specific requirements unique, the classification of systems needs may help to identify particular needs. The following description presents some of the issues involved in planning each general type of system.

Manual Systems. All companies have some system or systems for manually processing work. The terms workflow or methods and procedures are sometimes used to describe these systems. Planning a manual system requires consideration of the following issues:

- What will be the manual work flows?
- What areas will handle the required processing?
- What are the forms requirements including design, development, and lead times for printing? This consideration is frequently overlooked until the only option is to delay implementation of a project because the forms are not ready.
- What training, follow-up, and documentation will be required?
- Based on volume projections and complexity of the work to be done, what will be the staffing requirements?

Automated Systems. Automated computer systems perform high volume, highly structured tasks in most companies. They support the manual systems and tie into manual systems to some point. Thus questions to address in planning an automated system include:

- What will the manual to computer interface look like?
- Will it be electronic?
- Physical pieces of paper keyed into the computer?
- What are the cost trade-offs to consider?

Interfacing of automated systems is a key question. The processing system for a new line of business has to "talk" to the accounting and billing systems or there will be big trouble.

If a new processing system is required, there is another group of questions to consider.

- Should you custom develop or purchase and modify an existing package?
- Is the cost for either option justified based on volume and market share projections?
- What about interfaces (again)?
- How much time will it take?
- How does that time requirement fit with the overall plan?

Premium Processing. Front-end systems, which may be either manual or computerized, are designed to process policies. This processing can include underwriting, rating, coding, and policy insurance. Relevant considerations in planning such a system include:

- How will the specifics of getting policies quoted, underwritten, rated, and issued be handled?
- What about handling endorsements and audits, if required?
- Is a new line of business code needed for booking the premium?
- Are there new state reporting requirements involved?
- How will cancellation processing be handled? Does this project require anything special?
- Can an existing system be used for premium billing? If yes, are all the interfaces covered?
- Might reinsurance be involved?

Claims Processing. Like the front-end systems, claims processing systems are sometimes manual and sometimes computerized. They are designed for the physical processing of claim data and for monitoring claims through the adjustment process.

Important considerations include reserving practices (particularly when a project involves a new line of business), incurred but not reported losses, and reinsurance.

Work flow for claim processing is particularly important because it usually involves both staff adjusters and independent adjusters. Keeping procedures relatively consistent is therefore a special concern.

Support Processing and Reporting. Support systems perform the accounting, reporting, and analysis necessary to run the business. Financial statements, annual statements to insurance departments, statistical reports to rating bureaus, and internal management reports all depend on such systems. Key questions in planning such systems are:

- What kind of reports and information do we want?
- How frequently are the reports going to be processed?
- Are all the support systems interfaced properly so the books will balance?
- What about premium billing? Does the premium system handle that or is a separate system dedicated to billing only?[10]

Design Phase The design phase deals with refining "what" the system will do and "how" it will be done. From the system description presented in the previous phase, the project team develops complete system specifications. Issues like file structure, field definition, and record layouts are addressed in this stage. The discussion and documentation are time-consuming and often tedious. However, only precise technical requirements and specifications can communicate effectively to the programmers what the systems should do. These specifications include enough detail to allow the programming, testing, and implementation of the system to proceed.

Development Phase All parts of the system are built and tested during the development phase. Systems programs and modules are coded and tested. Clerical procedures are formalized. Systems, operations, and user documention are compiled and reviewed. Plans for user training are developed. All of these activities are performed in accordance with the plans and specifications developed in the previous phases.

Implementation Phase The implementation phase encompasses conversion to the new system and all the associated training and documentation. During this phase the system is installed in the user's organization, acceptance testing is performed, and the old methods and procedures are phased out. The completed system and the data to be processed are placed in operational readiness. During acceptance testing, all parts of the system are tested in combination with each other to insure that they meet all of the established system requirements. Testing may include *parallel testing*, that is, running both the new and old systems until the user is satisfied that the new system is satisfactory. Documentation, run guides, and training should have been completed prior to turning the new system over to production. System acceptance is obtained from the data processing and user managers.

Post-implementation Phase The post-implementation phase is a period of assessment during which the operational system is evaluated to determine whether it has met the previously defined objectives and performance criteria. It is a good idea to do some form of checking with the user to insure that the new system is doing what it is supposed to be doing.

Structured Techniques

Although building systems can be a time-consuming activity, tools to help perform the complex tasks involved have only recently emerged. These "structured techniques" have also been called productivity tools or programmer aids.

They include structured analysis, top-down design, structured programming, chief programmer teams, and structured walkthroughs.

Structured Analysis What happens in the beginning phases of a project has a big impact on what takes place in subsequent phases. The "front end" activities uncover the user needs, desires, and wishes. If these needs, desires, and wishes are not defined correctly, inaccurate estimates of time and cost result, and delivering the system really needed becomes impossible. In such situations there are inevitably conflicts between the user community and the data processing community.

User unrest with the standard project life cycle methodology has encouraged the increasing use of structured analysis. Communication difficulties between users and analysts, ignorance of data processing staff development efforts, and uncertainty regarding the eventual delivery time and cost figure all contribute to user unrest. Analysts, however, might say that the users really did not know what they wanted. In most cases they have user sign-off on a three-inch stack of paper that describes user needs. Unfortunately, these "functional specifications" are very tedious and boring to verify. Even if read very carefully, they can be difficult to understand because of the prevalence of data processing jargon.

The outputs of the standard analysis phase commonly involve several problems:

- Functional specifications are like a book—in order to get anything out of them, you have to read from beginning to end.
- The same type of information is repeated over and over again.
- They are inflexible—too often they are very difficult to change. A simple change to the user's requirements requires changes to several parts of the functional specifications.
- They describe how things will be done instead of what needs to be done. For example, they describe the hardware and file structures needed to implement the system. These details confuse the users and interfere with their conception of what has to be done.

Structured analysis tries to solve these difficulties with a specification that is graphic, easy to read, and easy to understand. The tools of structured analysis are data flow diagrams, data dictionaries, and structured English.

Data flow diagrams provide an easy, graphic means of modeling the flow of information through a system. Exhibit 1-1 shows a sample data flow diagram for a policy issuance system.

The second tool is the *data dictionary*. A data dictionary is a collection of definitions of all of the data elements that are shown in the data flow diagram. For a typical system, there may be several thousand definitions. For example, the data element *Customer-File* in Exhibit 1-1 would be defined as follows:

> Customer-File = Application and Loss Control
> Report and Financial Reports

The third tool of structured analysis is *structured English*. It is a

Exhibit 1-1
Data Flow Diagram

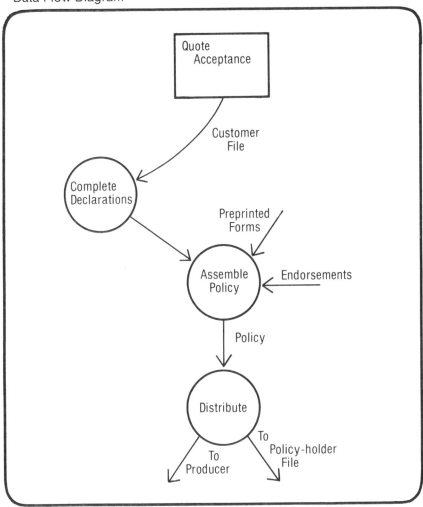

limited set of verbs and nouns organized in a way that is a fairly good compromise between readability and rigor.

As an example, the process called *Assemble-Policy* might have the following structured English associated with it.

> Take completed declarations combine
> with necessary forms and endorsements.

Top-Down and Structured Design Another structured technique is structured design. Sometimes it is referred to as top-down design, but structured design concerns inter-relationships between programs and other systems while top-down design primarily deals with a method of designing a system.

Structured design can be defined as the process which determines the best way to solve some well-defined problem through the proper connection of programs. The key issue is efficiency. If you were to put any number of computer analysts in a room together, give them a problem and ask for solutions, you would receive a limitless supply. Structured design attempts to eliminate all of the designs that are not good. If it works, the remaining designs provide a greater opportunity for success.

Two tools used to assist in structured design are HIPO (hierarchical input process output) diagrams and structure charts. The purpose of these tools is to concentrate on what has to be done as opposed to how it needs to be done. HIPO permits dividing the system into its component parts for ease of understanding and design. Each of the modules indicates the name of a particular process. Each module can be broken down into finer levels of detail until you reach the lowest level of input, processing, and output.

The primary advantage of HIPO is that it encourages analysts and programmers to examine the system from the top down (from the more abstract general ideas to more specific, concrete). The result is a more structured design. Many say, however, that the amount of paper generated when constructing HIPO diagrams does not correspond to the probable success of the system.

When using the tools of structured design, it becomes easier to identify bad design. As the designer/analysts become more familiar with the tools, they quickly recognize:

- The interrelationships between the modules
- The restrictivity/generality between modules
- The error reporting capabilities
- The correspondence of system structure to data flow structure

Structured Programming   Structured programming is the oldest of the structured techniques. To many in the programming field, structured programming is a generic term and covers everything that is not done by structured analysis. This loose definition, however, is misleading, since structured programming is essentially coding technique.

The underlying theory of structured programming is that any program's logic can be put together from combinations of any of the three constructs shown in Exhibit 1-2.

The implication of this theory is that all high-level programming languages can build programs that are built from combinations of:

Exhibit 1-2
Logical Constructs

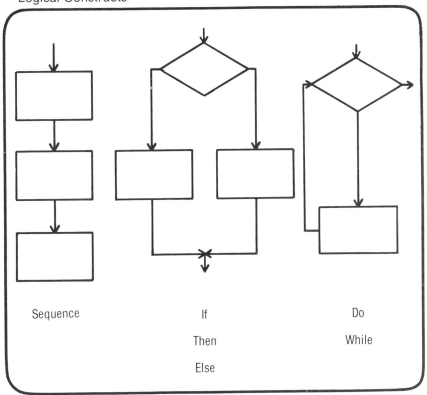

Sequence   If   Do

Then   While

Else

- Simple statements of reading files, writing records, and determining values
- If-Then-Else statements for decision making points
- Do-While and Do-Until statements to complete repetitive processes

These three constructs can form all program logic. It becomes unnecessary to use an uncontrolled branching statement—the GO TO—in structured programs.

Structured programming may not be a cure-all, however. There are problems that structured programming may not resolve. The skill level of the programming staff is an important factor. Do they understand the tools and techniques? Do they have sufficient experience with the programming language? How much time does the programming staff spend on actual programming tasks and maintenance tasks? The primary language used in the development process. Some languages, such as PL/1, ALGOL, and Pascal, are more appropriate for writing structured code than others. There are some clumsy features of structured programming as well.

Chief Programmer Teams A critical factor in systems development is the organization of project teams to accomplish the programming tasks. IBM carried out an experimental project several years ago in the organization of a programming team. The result was the concept of the chief programmer team. As the name implies, the team is built around a chief superprogrammer. The ideal superprogrammer is an individual with at least a dozen years of experience who can develop software much more rapidly than the average programmer, is capable of doing both the front end analysis and final implementation, and can supervise the group. There are few such people around, but if every data processing organization had one, miracles could be accomplished.

That person would not be the only individual needed. You would have to supplement their skills with others. Assuming the chief programmer is the leader, other members of the team should be: a copilot, a paperwork administrator, application expert, a toolsmith, and a librarian. Their functions are described below:

Copilot:
: The second in command. A minichief programmer. Ready to take over if the chief programmer had to leave the project for some reason.

Paperwork Administrator:
: As the name implies, this person would handle all of the paperwork, contractual agreements, scheduling of computer time, and other administrative duties that might keep the Chief Programmer from getting any work done.

Application Experts:
: The project team ought to have one or two people who are expert in the system being developed. This is the person who could answer the question, "What happens in this circumstance?"

Toolsmith:
: This person excels in building "software tools" or "utility programs" for use by the chief programmer and other members of the team. In the best sense, this person's expertise is in showing other people how to do things.

Librarian: The person who files, updates, and organizes all material associated with the development effort.

Many companies have not been able to develop chief programmer teams because superprogrammers are difficult to find. Most organizations that have implemented chief programmer teams have done so only on one or two projects and not on a wholesale basis.

Structured Walkthroughs   A structured walkthrough is an organized procedure for a group of peers (systems analysts or programmers) to review a technical product for correctness and goodness.

Walkthroughs can and should take place at several places during the development process: analysis, functional specifications, design, code, and testing. The emphasis, however, has been on conducting code walkthroughs.

Although there is much confusion between a walkthrough and a review, the difference between them is fairly simple. A walkthrough is conducted by members of a team who work together on a day-to-day basis; reviews involve the presentation of a piece of work to an audience that usually includes management people. A walkthrough permits fast, effective reviews of the technical correctness and accuracy of the specification, the design, and the code for the system. A formal review provides an official stamp of approval.

Project Management

Systems development usually requires committing extensive equipment and personnel resources to the project on a temporary basis. Because of its temporary nature, managing the project requires special techniques for project control and project organization.

Project Control   Perhaps the most difficult task undertaken in a data processing project, outside of design, is that of control. Data processing remains an art, not having developed the rigorous constraints and rules that mark the true sciences such as engineering, chemistry, or biology. The application of project control (scheduling, resource estimation and allocation, and actual project monitoring) varies greatly from project to project. The ability (or inability) of the project manager to estimate correctly the human and machine resources needed, to schedule those resources efficiently, and finally to monitor their performance spells the difference between a successful project—one delivered on time and within budget—or a disaster marked by high cost overruns and massive delays. Typically, project managers take years to amass the required experience and management ability to successfully perform these three critical tasks.

Resource Identification and Allocation. When a data processing project begins, there exist only ideas and concepts that must grow into a completed system. The resources needed to accomplish this growth at each successive phase of the project are what must be identified at the beginning of each phase. At the start of a typical project, senior management (both user and data processing) agree that a computer solution to a known problem is appropriate. With only this agreement, the project manager begins. Estimates of the number of users needed to identify and document the system requirements must be generated. Identification of the experience level of users needed for each separate area and the duration of the assignment are required. Next comes an estimate of the level and number of system persons needed to assist the users and ensure that the specifications produced are usable for the design phase, along with the identification of clerical support required. For design, the number and experience level of analysts required must be estimated.

Later, for development, the number of programmers needed must be estimated. Various levels of programming skill will be needed to perform the many tasks associated with coding and testing.

After the human resources required have been estimated, the machine time and storage space requirements must be developed. While there are a number of software products that will assist the project manager in identifying and qualifying all these resource requirements in the final run, the project manager must generate a custom resource estimate since each and every project is unique.

Scheduling. After the resources for the current phase of the project have been estimated, these individual pieces must be calibrated and made to function properly to produce the desired product. Certain activities cannot begin until other tasks have been accomplished. Even within an activity, there will be many smaller tasks to be accomplished. Which tasks should be undertaken first and which resources will be needed at which time? During a single phase of a project, hundreds of activities must be completed. Large projects can consist of thousands of individual tasks which must be scheduled correctly.

Fortunately, a number of techniques have been developed to assist with these efforts. Two very widely known ones are CPM and PERT.

The critical path method (CPM) emphasizes the identification of the critical path—the longest chain of events that must occur before the project can be completed. It permits all other nondependent events to be scheduled around the critical path.

PERT, which stands for program evaluation and review techniques, was developed in the late 1950s. It is a scheduling technique that employs the concept of an "event" or the reaching of a certain stage of completion coupled with the expected time required to complete activities leading up to that event.

A PERT network usually consists of two symbols: a circle or rectangle which represents an event or milestone in a project, and a line which represents the time an activity takes. Events are placed in the network depending on whether they are done at the same time or one before another. The critical path is the sequence of events which will take the longest to complete and therefore determine the total duration of a project. If the events in the critical path fall behind schedule, the final event will be late. This technique highlights key steps, shows progress and allows flexibility. PERT is a tool, and it can be altered to meet changing needs while a project is in progress.

Monitoring. We have identified what resources we will need as well as when and how they will be used. This is fine for today, but what about tomorrow? Some people become ill, and other people quit. Tasks are delayed. Some tasks are dropped since they may no longer be needed as when a statutory requirement is eliminated. Others are added. How is the constant precession of change going to be handled? Even if no change were to occur, how is progress on the various tasks going to be watched? The project manager could easily spend all day just checking with each member of the project team to ensure that they stay on schedule. On a few key tasks this daily personal interfacing may well be needed. But what about all the other tasks?

A *project management system* may be utilized in the monitoring phase. All the resources that have been identified can be entered into this type of system. All the schedules generated along with all the interdependencies can also be entered. By the introduction of daily or weekly data from each project member, an automated tracking of the project schedule can be accomplished. Tasks that fall behind schedule are highlighted so that corrective action can be taken, while tasks that are completed early can have resources reassigned to other activities.

There are many project management systems currently on the market. They typically run on a computer (anything from a PC to a mainframe is available). A good project management system will support the resource estimation function and the scheduling function.

One main area of concern regarding the need for monitoring that cannot be over-emphasized is the need for change control. Rarely is a system developed without changes being requested. As the user learns more about the means of satisfying business requirements, many new ideas are generated. These ideas often entail changes. Change may take any of a number of forms including cosmetic, logic, data, or strategic.

Changes are generally easiest to make during the earliest phase of the life cycle. During those times, changes can be made to the functional requirements without further repercussions. Changes made in any phase after completion of the planning phase are expensive and time-consuming. Not only must the change itself be made, but all documentation must be examined and updated. In addition, activities may have to be redone to reflect the change. Therefore, careful consideration should be given before requesting changes after the planning phase.

Change procedures must be established early in the life of a project. These procedures must be mutually agreed upon by both the users and the systems people. In establishing these procedures, the following must be considered:

1. Who may request a change?
2. How may a change be requested?
3. Who has approval authority for changes?
4. Documentation of all requests for change; assignment of a control number.
5. Criteria for acceptance, alteration, or deferral of change (based on impacts on costs and implementation).

The project manager must recognize a change that will have significant impact on project cost. In such a case, an update to the cost/benefit analysis should be initiated immediately rather than at the completion of the phase. If the total cost of the system has been altered in excess of the allowable overrun, the appropriate approval authorities must re-approve the project before it continues.

Project Organization   The basic principles of maintaining direct and clear lines of communication, responsibility, and authority are vital for systems development. The proposed system may encompass a number of organizations, departments, or groups. Ideally, a project organization should be established which has the authority and jurisdiction to develop the total system regardless of traditional organizational structure. Functional departmental lines must not be allowed to cause problems of control, communication, and responsibility.

A team effort is necessary to develop a sound and complete system. Many people with diverse skills and specialties from different functional areas must collaborate on related and independent activities. Formal reorganization of these people is not required to enable them to function as effective project team members as long as their efforts are subject to coordination by the project manager.

The responsibilities of project team members depend on the nature and complexity of the project. It is important that all responsibilities be identified and assigned.

While the project manager is the person responsible for the project's overall success or failure, many people fulfill many different project roles. Normally, there are three managers beneath whom the entire project staff operates. All three typically exist on medium and large scale projects; however, on smaller projects one person may perform all three roles. These three are known as the project manager, the user manager, and the system manager.

Major responsibility for the planning phase rests with the user, who must organize a project team to define in detail what the system should do. This involves what data should enter the system, where it will come from, what should be produced, its destination, and control and performance requirements. The system area has major responsibility for defining an operating environment and a detailed automation approach, as well as determining whether to "buy or build" the system. After estimating costs and benefits, the user area must publish a phase-end report.

The design phase is primarily the responsibility of the systems group. The actual design of the system, including record and file design, data base considerations, hardware selection, and other technical aspects, is performed by systems personnel. The user personnel are responsible for manual procedures and quality assurance criteria. The design report, which includes a revision of the cost and benefits estimates, must be published at phase end.

During the development phase, systems personnel continue to perform their traditional activities, mainly writing and testing programs. The user is responsible for various levels of acceptance and pilot testing, training, and documentation, as well as producing the phase-end report.

During the implementation phase, the systems staff is essentially responsible for the installation of hardware and getting the system up and running. User personnel provide training and implementation to the end-users of the system.

Project Manager. The project manager has overall responsibility for the project and performs all the functions associated with the role including planning and control.

The project manager may reside at any level of the organization. The level of the project manager should be commensurate with the objectives and scope of the project. The project manager is usually a member of the system's staff since the majority of project life cycle activities are performed by this staff. The project manager must maintain cooperation and communication among project team members in order to successfully complete the project.

In addition, it is the project manager's responsibility to:

1. Coordinate the numerous project activities of the diverse project effort.
2. Consolidate estimates of system development costs and schedules which are prepared by project participants.
3. Monitor the status of project progress and cost.
4. Report the status of project progress and cost to management having approval authority over such functions and expenses.

User Manager. The users that are assigned to a project represent that part of the corporation that will use the system for the duration of its existence. They come from various functional areas and bring their own ideas and needs to the project. They have many responsibilities during the development of a new data processing system. They must define the requirements of the process they seek to automate so that the data processing people can design and build the system. As each phase of a project is completed, the users are normally charged with the production of the phase-end report. This report documents the activities of the just completed phase and lays out the plans for the next phase. Since they are the ones that the system is being built for they will perform the cost benefit analysis that justifies the expenditure of monies for the project. Typically, at each subsequent phase-end this analysis is updated to reflect the actual expenditures made to date and to refine planned future expenditures. The user team is also responsible for generating all the documentation that will be required to use the system and to train the user staff in the use of the system. The actual design, execution, and evaluation of the acceptance tests to verify that the new system can be placed into production are also the responsibilities of the user team.

The user manager is charged with the planning, coordinating, and controlling of all the members of the user team and for assigning their work. This person must balance the needs of all users on the project team, especially when projects cross existing functional lines. The user manager is responsible for the production of a set of requirements that addresses the needs of the company and controls the "wish list" that has ruined many projects. The user manager must control requested changes (to the stated requirements) once design has begun and must ensure that the user team performs its many project tasks, some of which will be new and strange to many users.

The user team will typically contain a number of junior to middle-level user managers who are assigned to the project and who most likely will return to their respective areas along with the completed system to oversee the day-to-day functioning of the system.

The user manager coordinates all user activity, and ensures that the various users assigned to the projects complete their assignments as required.

System Manager. The system manager is responsible for providing the appropriate system expertise and support; that is, ensuring that all systems personnel perform as required.

The system manager provides the technical knowledge and experience in the systems design, programming, and testing procedures areas and is responsible for:

1. System design
2. Program development, related processing, training practices, and system documentation
3. System testing
4. System implementation

The system manager must ensure that the functional specifications that are produced by the user manager and the users are sufficient and complete so proper design can be accomplished. The system manager must have sufficient experience to permit the identification of a reasonable number of alternate design approaches, analyze each and select the most suitable one. Any application has an infinite number of possible design solutions. Of the few that are practical, the one most suitable must be identified. Next the system manager must oversee the efforts of turning the system design into a series of programs. Program specifications must be written, coded, and tested. The tested modules are then assembled and tested as a sub-system and finally the sub-systems are assembled and tested as a system. The system manager must be familiar with proper programming techniques and the programming language. The generation of proper test plans at each stage of testing is overseen by the system manager along with the actual execution of these plans. Many projects have fallen by the wayside because testing was cut short or not done at all. The system manager must ensure that proper testing is done. Perhaps the greatest challenge to the system manager is the actual management of the systems staff.

SUMMARY

Information systems play an important role in the successful operation of today's businesses. Due to the fiduciary nature of the services provided, insurance information systems must supply information not required in other businesses, while also meeting the requirements of federal and state regulatory statutes. At the same time, it is possible for an insurance organization to be buried in data unless the information system is designed to respond to the needs of the organization.

There are a number of users of insurance information, each with a particular reason for wanting the information. Users have an economic or statutory interest in insurance information; both groups are interested in data that is timely and accurate. Each of the user groups has a specific interest in the data that will assist in accomplishing an assigned task. Users include statistical organizations, management, policyholders and agents, regulators, tax authorities, and reinsurers.

Organizations have different information needs at each level of management and the people at the various levels have needs based on the scope of their responsibility. The statutory basis of accounting practices are those prescribed by the organization's domiciled insurance department. On the other hand, generally accepted accounting principles (GAAP) have been developed to prepare financial statements which will provide investors with information about insurance companies on a going concern basis. In addition, all insurance organizations are required to report information for the states in which they do business to those states. Independent statistical agencies have come into being to collect the statistical data from the companies and then report that data to the states. Information systems must be designed to facilitate planning within insurance organizations. Planning must be done by using information developed from past experience. The information needs for agency communication primarily require compilation of data on each aspect of an agency's book of business. Each insurance organization may develop a series of agency reports to reflect the information for a specific agency. In today's consumer-oriented environment, it is important that the organization inform customers of the operating results and financial health of that organization. Insurance organizations make financial information available to customers through an annual report. Finally, tax filing requires documentation of taxes owed to federal, state, and local governments.

The development or modification of an information system can be an elaborate and complex project. It requires the involvement of both the analysts who design the system and the departments that will use the system. To coordinate these perspectives, systems development projects usually follow a project life cycle including an initiation phase, a feasibility phase, a definition phase, a design phase, a development phase, an implementation phase, and a post-implementation phase. In addition, structured techniques such as structured analysis, top-down design, structured programming, chief programmer teams, and structured walkthroughs facilitate the communication between analysts and users and thus help to assure that the system developed actually meets the needs of the users. The management of a system development project may also require sophisticated techniques of project control and project organization.

As this overview has demonstrated, effective management of an insurance company depends on effective information systems, and making those systems effective requires the coordination of multiple requirements, reflecting varied concerns and perspectives. The next chapter traces the flow of data through an insurance information system and explores ways of storing data to meet those varied requirements.

Chapter Notes

1. Norton E. Masterson, "Statistics for Management," *Multiple-Line Insurers: Their Nature and Operation*, edited by G. F. Michelbacher and Nestor R. Roos (New York: McGraw-Hill, 1970), p. 224.
2. Securities and Exchange Commission, Securities Release 34-13185 (January 19, 1977).
3. Committee on Auditing Procedure, *Statement on Auditing Standards* No. 1 (New York: American Institute of Certified Public Accountants, 1973), 320.01.
4. *Statement on Auditing Standards* No. 1, 320.27.
5. *Statement on Auditing Standards* No. 1, 320.28.
6. National Association of Insurance Commissioners, "Uniform Accounting," *Financial Condition Examiners Handbook* (1976), p. 225.
7. National Association of Insurance Commissioners, *NAIC Model Market Conduct Examination Handbook* (1984), p. 5.
8. Robert W. Strain, et al., *Insurance Words and Their Meanings* (Indianapolis, IN: Rough Notes Co., Inc., 1981), p. 102.
9. Chris Gane and Trish Sarson, *Structured Systems Analysis: Tools and Techniques* (Englewood Cliffs, NJ: Prentice-Hall, 1979), pp. 6–9.
10. This section is adapted from Ben L. Griffin, Jr., "Systems Development," in Robert J. Gibbons, ed. *Dimensions of Corporate Strategy: Selected Readings* (Malvern, PA: Insurance Institute of America, 1983), pp. 534–538.

CHAPTER 2

Data Flows and Data Storage

INTRODUCTION

The information systems of an insurance company can be exceedingly complex. Most insurance companies process an enormous volume of transactions. As the volume of transactions increases, the need for state of the art electronic computers, point of origin input devices, and communication networks also increases. Systems must be designed and installed not only to produce ledger balances from which the required financial statements are prepared, but also to report management and operating information for timely decision making.

For every insurance policy written, claim incurred, and expense paid, an insurer's information system must collect detailed information. This detailed information must be validated, corrected if necessary, accumulated in a variety of ways, and recorded for permanent reference. As the needs of the industry for statistical information grow, more and more people, time, and machinery are employed in capturing, processing, analyzing, and reporting this data.

Information systems depend on the flow of data through various processing subsystems. The system should assure that the data flow is managed, controlled, and expedited. The three essential characteristics of valid data are accuracy, completeness, and timeliness. These characteristics should be the guidelines toward which an information system should strive. The more successful an information system is in achieving these goals, the more effective the system.

Regardless of the complexity of an insurance company's systems, independent public accountants, internal company auditors, and others find it necessary to study how the systems work and what controls exist. Information systems include both the logical flow of data through computer programs and the physical flow of documents through various departments of the organization. Document flowcharts can be combined with computer system flowcharts to indicate data flows. Document flowcharts assist accountants when documenting an accounting information system, auditors when examining an audit trail, and system designers when performing a system study. This chapter examines the normal flow of data in insurance companies and the possibilities for storing it in an efficient manner.

DATA FLOWS

The information system of any business must be built upon accurate records and adequate internal control. Economic events affecting the firm should be recognized in consistent procedures for accumulating and reporting financial information. In order to trace the flow of data through the system, the resulting network of transactions, systems, processing procedures, and data bases can be logically divided into a limited number of cycles. Each cycle recognizes economic events that are converted into entries and processed through the company's systems to the financial statements, statistical reports, and management reports.

Every organization uses accounting as a method of communications, and society regards the practice of accounting as a business norm. Traditionally, accounting has been regarded as the process of recording, classifying, summarizing, and reporting business transactions. With the introduction of quantitative tools such as the computer, accounting has expanded to support managerial control and decision making. As the American Accounting Association asserted in 1966, it is now generally accepted that "Accounting is essentially an information system."[1]

To apply the principles of accounting, organizations follow a standard set of systems and procedures. Those systems create a set of records completed in a specific series of steps. Records are the foundation of all accounting systems, regardless of whether they are manual or computerized, and include ledgers, journals, and registers. All of the financial activity in an organization is recorded in these formats so that there is a physical place where the information is available for reference, the actual numbers can be reconciled, and the material is available for use the creation of reports and financial statements.

To enter this data, or "keep the books," both computer and manual record-keeping systems generally follow standard procedures for:

- Creating and processing business transactions documents, such as policy applications or claims forms, and ensuring the accuracy of those documents and transactions.
- Keeping records of all transactions in the appropriate place, such as premiums written in the premium statistical file or loss data in the loss register.
- Processing all transactions from original entries through ledger accounts to ultimate financial statements such as the balance sheet, income statement, statement of cash flow, statement of changes in financial position (source and allocation of funds), and any other statements that may be required to depict an organization's position or operating results.
- Creating reports and projections for management, based on existing financial data.

Management must also safeguard the accuracy of the system response and data on which important decisions are based. Data may be inaccurate because of flaws in the system's ability to catch erroneous transactions or because of a lack of security over the data. Those who can access data may also be able to change the data unless controls exist.

Systems should demonstrate that they restrict access to data to authorized users of the data. Individual data elements may be used by many applications and the users and providers of the data may be different. For example, certain users may only retrieve data elements, while others may have the authority to add, delete, or modify the data elements. Finally, certain users may have no reason, or permission, to access the data element at all, simply because it has no relationship to their tasks. For example, the premium entry clerk has no need to see the employee pay rates.

Accounting is the act of accumulating and reporting information concerning an *economic event*. All insurance companies participate in economic events that affect their financial statements and information bases. An economic event is an actual occurrence.

Many economic events directly involve an insurance company in exchanges with outsiders. Some examples are:

- Issuance of an insurance policy
- Acceptance of premium payments for policies
- Cancellation of coverage on the remaining policy term
- Receipt of a notice of loss
- Claim payments
- Receipts of life insurance policy loan repayments

Other economic events involve external forces, but do not involve exchanges, such as changes in economic conditions or changes in laws and regulations. The passage of time is also an external economic event which results in the accrual of interest and the expiration of policies. Some economic events, such as operating decisions or correction of errors, are internal occurrences.

The economic events affecting the organization first must be identified. Once recognized, they should be approved or authorized by appropriate levels of management. They may require additional processing steps such as calculating, classifying, and recording. These steps are usually followed by summarization from which journal entries are prepared for posting in the general ledger. Finally, general ledger balances are reflected in the financial statements. This entire process may be totally manual, totally automated, or a combination of manual and automated systems.

All economic events involving an insurance company in any monetary exchange should be reflected in the financial statements. In addition, generally accepted accounting principles and statutory accounting procedures require the recognition in insurance industry financial statements of certain external and internal economic events not related to an exchange. GAAP accounting principles involve such events as the handling of deferred acquisition costs while statutory accounting requires the recognition of excess of statutory reserves over statement loss reserves.

An economic event has only the potential of having an effect upon an insurance company's financial statement. A *transaction* is an economic event that has been recognized as having a monetary impact on a financial statement. In addition, a transaction must be rendered in a form that can be processed and accepted for processing by the company's accounting system.

An accounting "business transaction" results from any monetary event that causes a change in an asset, liability, owners' equity, revenue, or expense account. Separate accounts are maintained for every monetary item so that information is available regarding individual accounts. Transactions can occur from business activities between a company and either some external party or an internal party. For a business transaction to enter an organization's accounting system, it must be quantitative and measurable in monetary terms. Business transactions result in the creation of *source documents*. Source documents represent visual evidence regarding the occurrence of business transactions.

The initial task of an accounting system is the timely recognition of an economic event that should be processed by the system. Transactions should be authorized for entry prior to input for initial processing. Many transactions may also be authorized for entry as a result of the structure of the processing system, such as renewal premium billing. A single economic event may result in several transactions, such as the sale of a policy and the recognition of income, asset, and commission transactions.

One of the main characteristics of accounting information is that it is financial in nature. Accounting systems process business transactions that are measured in monetary units and produce reports which provide financial information. Financial reports such as income statements, balance sheets, budgets, and planning forecasts are presented in financial terms. In addition, financial information excludes the processing and storage of nonquantifiable and nonfinancial information. It is important to recognize this limitation of accounting systems because management relies on both financial and nonfinancial information in controlling the current activities of an organization and in planning for the future.

The Accounting Cycle

An accounting system is a series of fundamental tasks by which transactions are processed. This series of tasks should be viewed as a complete cycle of activities. The accounting cycle generally includes the recognition of an economic event as a transaction, followed by approval, computation, journalizing, posting, summarization in trial balances, accumulation on worksheets, and reporting in financial statements.

Internal accounting controls are methods employed to prevent and detect errors in processing, to safeguard assets, and to protect the reliability of financial records. Various internal control techniques should be included in a system so that the controls appear to be part of the system's normal processing routine. If the purpose of a routine is to control the processing of transactions, it should be viewed as part of the internal controls.

It is important to recognize that an insurance company may function with weak internal accounting controls, but that it will cease to operate if the accounting processing systems fail.

The inputs to financial accounting systems are transactions measured in monetary terms. An audit trail of accounting transactions should be maintained within the system to permit the analysis of the flow of data through the system. The processing of transactions involves the recording of journal entries from source documents, posting these entries to general and subsidiary ledger accounts and preparing a trial balance from the general ledger account balances. Financial statements prepared from general ledger accounts provide

Exhibit 2-1
Accounting Cycle

A - 1. Analyze transactions.

A - 2. Record busines transaction in a journal.

A - 3. Post business transactions from journal to general ledger and determine account balances.

A - 4. *Prepare a trial balance.*

A - 5. Record adjusting entries in a journal, post adjusting journal entries to the general ledger, update accounts balance and *prepare adjusted trial balance.*

A - 6. Complete financial statements from adjusted trial balance.

A - 7. Record closing entries in a journal, post to general ledger, update balance of accounts affected by closing entries and *prepare post-closing trial balance.*

useful information to investors, creditors, and management through the following statements:

- Income statement provides information regarding the periodic (monthly, quarterly, annually) profit or loss operating success of a company.
- Balance sheet states the financial condition of a company as of a specific date.
- Statement of change in financial position discloses the periodic sources and uses of working capital.

In order to obtain monetary amounts for these financial statements, organizations maintain a daily record-keeping system. Such a system transforms data that is generated by a company's daily business transactions into meaningful information for presentation to management and external parties. The routine for this data transformation process is called the accounting cycle. (See Exhibit 2-1)

Analyzing Transactions An accounting transaction results from a monetary event that causes a change in an asset, liability, owner's equity, revenue, or expense account. Separate accounts are maintained in a general ledger for every monetary item so that information is available regarding the dollar balance of individual financial items. Ledger accounts are identified through a chart of accounts, a table of numerical codes with each code representing a

Exhibit 2-2
Chart of Accounts

Account Code	Title
Assets	
212–	Bank Account
216–	Petty Cash
287–	Accounts Receivable
Liabilities/Owners' Equity	
339–	Accounts Payable
352–	Reserve for Uncashed Checks
Revenue	
010–	Premium
020–	Return Premium
Expenses	
101–	Losses
140–	Salaries
148–	Travel

Note: Assets, liabilities, owners equity are balance sheet accounts. Revenue and expenses are income statement accounts.

general ledger account (an abbreviated example is shown in Exhibit 2-2).

Transactions occur from business activities between a company and either some external concern or internal employee. In order for a business transaction to be entered into an organization's accounting information system, it must be quantitative and measurable in monetary terms. Business transactions result in the creation of various types of source documents or original records.

Source documents are visual evidence that a business transaction has occurred. In most companies, a financial transaction is not prepared for entry into the accounting information system until proper source documents are received and approved. The types of source documents used by businesses will vary in accord with each firm's operating characteristics. Some of the more common source documents used by business organizations are employee time cards, sales invoices, purchase invoices, receiving reports, bills of lading, and voucher checks.

The accounting systems insurance organizations commonly recognize transactions in the following ways:

- Online or remote entries on a terminal keyport such as an online claim reporting system
- Entries on magnetic tape or disc file such as a computer-generated loss expense calculation
- Manually prepared documents such as subrogation, registers, insurance applications, or capital expenditure requests
- General ledger entries
- Cash disbursement system entries

In order to maintain internal control, most companies designate a level of management to approve source documents for processing. After approval, the source documents are analyzed for assignment of the proper chart of account code. By utilizing source documents, a company prepares its transaction data for subsequent entry into the accounting information system. In addition, the source documents represent the starting point of a company's audit trail through an information system's accounting cycle.

Journalizing Business Transactions   Once accounting items are substantiated with source documents, the data is recorded in a company's journal. A journal is maintained as an integral part of an accounting information system in order to provide an organization with a chronological record of the monetary events that occur as a result of operations.

When someone needs information regarding monetary activities that occur on a specific date, one can refer to the pages of the company's journal used on that date. In those instances in which a company processes accounting data with a computer, the journal information may be maintained on a storage medium such as magnetic tape. When this occurs, a computer printout of the specific day's journal entries would have to be prepared.

In many organizations, innumerable monetary transactions occur during an accounting period, but normally a majority of these transactions can be classified into a few broad categories. Policy premium entries, for example, may be considered a single category, since they are all processed in the same way. The classification of transactions by categories makes it possible to design an accounting information system that efficiently processes the large volume of economic events affecting insurance companies. In many cases, the growing volume of transactions compels organizations to replace manual accounting systems with computerized accounting information systems.

Some of the more common types of transactions that must be handled by all organizations are: (1) the purchase of assets, (2) an incurring of operation expenses, (3) the sale of products and services, and (4) the receipt and payment of cash. An important category of business transaction commonly processed in insurance companies relates to investments. Owing to the special significance of investment activity and cash management, an insurance company may establish a separate accounting information system that is designed to deal solely with the special features of securities investment.

Posting from the Journals to the General Ledger   Within an accounting system, a general ledger is the control containing summary monetary information concerning an organization's various assets, liabilities, owner's equity, revenues, and expenses. The ledger is organized with a separate account (sometimes called a "T" account) for each type of monetary classification in a firm's chart of accounts.

Without information about the dollar balances or a firm's specific accounts, business performances would be difficult to evaluate because effective business decisions by external and internal parties are often based on account balances, relationships, or ratios.

In the discussion of journalizing business transactions, it was noted that the journal provides a chronological record of all monetary events occurring in a company which indicates the accounts and amounts of the offsetting debits and credits for each business transaction. However, the journal does not provide information regarding the individual dollar balances of the various monetary transactions in an account. For example, if an organization's management needs to know the monetary balance of the company's accounts receivable assets, this information would be found in the special "T" account maintained for accounts receivable in the general ledger. The journal would not provide information regarding the balance of the accounts receivable but rather only the individual debit and credits that were recorded to the accounts receivable during a specific time period.

In order to provide management with information concerning the accounts receivable dollar balance, the specific debits and credits recorded in the journal for accounts receivable must be transferred to the "T" account in the general ledger through a process called posting. After the posting process is completed, the dollar balance of each general ledger account is determined.

Most accounting systems include a series of journals and a general ledger. This arrangement supports both a good accounting system and an effective information system. The major benefit of a series of journals is that it provides a complete chronological listing of an organization's monetary transactions. The journal provides a history of each specific business transaction, because the debit and credit sides of the transaction are shown along with identification of the event either through the use of a specific journal or a short narrative in the general journal. However, with a general ledger, it might be difficult to determine the monetary balances of the individual accounts. The general ledger contains a summary of the journal activity by providing information regarding the balances of an organization's accounts. On the other hand, the general ledger does not disclose in a single account the complete picture of a monetary transaction. For example, the debit part of a transaction may be recorded in an asset account in the general ledger, while the credit half of the same transaction might be recorded in a liability account. Functioning together in a company's accounting system, the journal and the general ledger each serve a particular need and provide relevant information about the monetary transactions that have occurred. As an integral part of the posting process, an audit trail is established as a cross-referencing code is used between the two.

Trial Balance Preparation   All financial statements represent either a company's financial position at a particular date (balance sheet) or operating results for a period of time at a particular date (income statement). Individual company policy determines the period for which companies prepare financial statements. They may present monthly, quarterly, semi-annually, or yearly results. Due to the fact that both federal and state income tax statements usually need to be filed annually, a firm must prepare financial statements at least once a year as the basis for computing tax liability.

When a company needs to prepare an income statement or a balance sheet, all of the posting routine must be completed so that the dollar balances of the various general ledger accounts, used to prepare the financial statements, can be determined.

After these account balances are computed, a financial worksheet called a trial balance is prepared. A trial balance lists all the general ledger account numbers together with the respective end-of-period account balances. The trial balance makes it possible to determine if the total debit and total credit account balances are equal and facilitates the preparation of the company's financial statements. The trial balance is a preliminary statement to determine that the debit and credit balances in the company's ledger accounts balance before formally preparing the organization's financial statements.

Adjusting Entries   The complete routine involving adjusting entries includes recording adjusting entries in a journal, posting adjusting entries to the general ledger, updating accounts balance, and preparing an adjusted trial balance. After preparing the trial balance, a company's general ledger accounts will have dollar balances which represent the account balances at the end of the specified time period (as of a month, a year). Prior to preparing the company's financial statements, certain adjusting journal entries may be necessary to the general ledger accounts. The need for adjusting entries may be necessary to the general ledger accounts. The need for adjusting entries within an accounting information system is based on two primary accounting principles: the periodicity principle and the matching principle.

The *periodicity principle* is derived from the word periodic, which means "occurring at regular intervals." In accounting, it is held that after a specific time period, a company can accurately determine the dollar balances of its general ledger accounts and then prepare financial statements. This process is usually called adjusting and closing the books. The books are an organization's specific journals, general journal, and the general ledger. At the end of a month, for example, when an organization wants to prepare the income statement and balance sheet, the periodicity principle holds that the firm is at a specific cutoff point in its operating activities and can therefore provide relevant financial information to interested parties such as potential investors, creditors, and management. These parties do not want to wait until the end of a firm's existence to acquire financial information but rather want it at specific times throughout the organization's existence. The periodicity principle enables a company to provide financial statements at specific time intervals. In addition, at the end of its fiscal year, an organization should attempt to present to its financial users the most accurate income statement and balance sheet possible. The interim financial statements will provide an overall indication of the organization's operation, while the fiscal year report will provide exact information for financial decision making regarding the organization.

The objective of the *matching principle* is to compute precisely a company's net income (or net loss), as well as to determine accurately the dollar amounts of balance sheet accounts each time the organization's financial statements are prepared. In keeping with the matching principle, revenues should be recognized when earned, either by selling products or providing services to customers even though cash has not yet been received. Expenses should be recognized when a product or service is used even though cash is not paid at the time.

The matching principle attempts to relate accurately an organization's revenues earned to the expenses incurred in earning those revenues, prior to the preparation of the financial statements. This effort is necessary in order to smooth the distortion in the flow of monetary transactions caused by the receipt of money for products and services sold when matched to the disbursement of funds for goods and services purchased in a given accounting period. Management is interested in the comparative success of various business periods and this is attainable only by the uniform comparison made possible by matching.

There are four major types of adjusting entries to be considered at the end of a company's accounting period. These adjustments are as follows:

1. Adjusting entries for accrued liabilities (commonly defined as unrecorded expenses). Such as:

Salary Expense	Debit
Accrued Salary Payable	Credit

2. Adjusting entries for accrued assets (commonly defined as unrecorded revenues). Such as:

Accrued Rent Receivable	Debit
Rent Revenue	Credit

   (The most common entry in an insurance company would be for accrued interest receivable. However, this classification is a nonledger asset, and entries are not made for nonledger assets.)

3. Adjusting entries for prepaid assets (commonly defined as deferred or prepaid expenses). Such as:

Insurance Expense	Debit
Prepaid Insurance	Credit

4. Adjusting entries for advanced payments by customers (commonly defined as deferred revenue). Such as:

Advance Payment for Services	Debit
Service Revenue	Credit

These four examples of adjusting entries do not represent all the types of adjustments an organization may need at the end of an accounting period, but they do illustrate the adjusting entry concept. At the end of an accounting period, when a company wants to prepare financial statements, it should strive for accuracy in financial data. In order to achieve this accuracy, all the monetary activities for the accounting period should be examined to determine if any transactions have occurred that are not properly recognized in the accounting records. If unrecorded monetary events exist, adjusting entries are required. After all adjusting entries are recorded an organization's financial data has been updated. The financial statements prepared from this adjusted data reflect a more accurate picture of the organization's business activities for the accounting period and provide better information for decision-making.

After a firm's adjusting entries are recorded in the journal, the debits and credits of these entries are posted to the correct general ledger accounts in the same manner as the regular business transactions recorded during the accounting period. Upon completion of the posting routine, the updated balances of those accounts affected by the adjusting journal entries are determined. After this is accomplished, a company's financial data is current for the preparation of the financial statements. Preceding the completion of the income statement and balance sheet, it is necessary to prepare an adjusted trial balance. Initially, a trial balance was prepared after all business transactions occurring during an accounting period are rounded, posted, and the balance of each general ledger account determined. In addition, the equality of total debits and total credits between the accounts was resolved before the adjusting journal entries were recorded and posted. Preparing a second trial balance, called the adjusted trial balance, determines that the equality of the debit and credit account balances still exists after the adjusting entry process.

Completion of Financial Statements from the Adjusted Trial Balance When the adjusted trial balance routine is finished and reflects all updated financial data, the balance sheet, income statement, and other financial statements can be completed. The adjusted trial balance should contain all the information needed for the preparation of the financial statements.

Because the financial statements are prepared on a regular basis, probably monthly, standardized statement worksheets and controls can be used in completing the statement. These worksheets and controls may be prepared manually to insure detail review and analysis of the statements prior to publication. When the statements are prepared directly from the accounting information system, an analysis and review of the financial statements must be provided.

Closing Entries The complete routine involving closing entries includes recording closing entries in a journal, posting closing entries to the general ledger, updating account balances, and preparing a post-closing trial balance. An organization's revenue and expense accounts are subdivisions of the owners' equity accounts. The main reason for using separate revenue and expense accounts is to provide complete accounting information about operating activities to the firm's management and other interested concerns. At the end of each accounting period, a company records and posts closing entries to eliminate the individual revenue and expense account balances and transfer the net income or loss into the owner's equity account, because the business firm's net income or loss belongs to its owners.

Because revenue and expense accounts are subdivisions of the owners' equity accounts, whose balances are closed at the end of an accounting period, revenue and expense accounts are often called temporary or nominal accounts. On the other hand, asset, liability, and owners' equity accounts are not closed at period-end. Thus they are referred to as permanent or real accounts. In other words, the revenue and expense accounts reflect activity of only the current accounting period, while asset, liability, and owners' equity accounts reflect the continuing history of the business.

It is important for a company to prepare financial statements as soon as possible after the close of its accounting period so that information contained in the financial statement is available for analysis by groups such as management, investors and creditors. As indicated previously, the owners' equity accounts on the company's balance sheet will reflect the net income (or net loss) for the particular period. Needless to state, before the recording and posting of the closing journal entries, the owners' equity general ledger accounts do not include the net income or loss for the accounting period. Net income occurs when the total of the revenue accounts exceed the total of the expense accounts; net loss occurs when expense exceeds revenue.

Once a company's closing entries are journalized and posted, all the revenue and expense accounts zero dollar balance and the new balances of the owners' equity capital accounts include the effect of the current period's net income or loss. A post-closing trial balance is then prepared to determine that the accounts with debit balances equal those with credit balances. The preparation of the post-closing trial balance is the final step in the accounting cycle. The post-closing trial balance offset of debit and credit account balances provides a company some indication that no errors were made in its accounting records during the period. After closing, a company is then ready to repeat the accounting cycle for the next period.

Since the major objective of the accounting cycle is to enable a business to prepare its financial statements as well as update the dollar balances of its general ledger accounts, the length of the cycle is determined by how often managements want these statements prepared. If monthly financial statements are needed the accounting cycle is repeated every month. However, there can be exceptions to this rule which some firms incorporate into the accounting information systems. For instance, some organizations may prepare monthly financial statements without going through the formal process of recording and posting their closing journal entries each month, rather waiting until year-end to journalize and post the closing entries.

The Data Processing Cycle

Processing is the actual execution of the tasks in a system.

Processing methods within a system may be performed manually while other tasks may be done with a computer. Some systems may be designed to process a continuous flow of similar types of transactions, while others may process only occasional transactions.

The data processing cycle consists of four separate steps: (1) data collection, (2) data classification, (3) data maintenance and summarization, and (4) report generation. Data collecting includes gathering and recording raw data in a logical manner, using pre-designed source documents such as invoices, purchase orders, and time records. Data classification organizes data by verifying and sorting in order to reduce data errors and to prepare the data for further processing. Data maintenance involves the operations of calculating, comparing, summarizing, and storing data for future reference. Report generation transfers information from files to reports that are usable as business documents.

As Exhibit 2-3 reveals, the accounting cycle and the data processing cycle are comparable in nature. The making of journal entries in the accounting cycle is equivalent to data collection and classification in the data processing cycle. Posting to ledgers and completing a trial balance in the accounting cycle are similar to data maintenance and summarization in the data processing cycle. Preparing financial statements in the accounting cycle is the same as report generation in the data processing cycle.

Recent changes from batch to interactive systems in the data processing area have greatly affected both the data collection and data classification steps.

Data Collection The design of information systems usually begins by considering the outputs from the system. The bulk of accounting data collected by an organization ultimately appears in some type of internal or external report. No degree of sophistication in information reporting can compensate for deficiencies in data collection. If the required data is not captured, meaningful reports cannot be generated. Thus the requirements of these reports serve as a prerequisite in establishing an organization's data collection processes.

From the standpoint of the information system, the primary concerns in the data collection process are accuracy, timeliness, and cost-effectiveness. An activity or process is considered cost-effective if the anticipated benefits are expected to exceed the anticipated costs.

Source documents serve to substantiate transactions and help manage the flow of accounting data. First, source documents prescribe the kind of data to be collected and help ensure legibility, consistency, and accuracy in the recording of data. Secondly, source documents encourage the completeness of accounting data because the informa-

Exhibit 2-3
The Parallel of the Accounting Cycle to the Data Processing Cycle

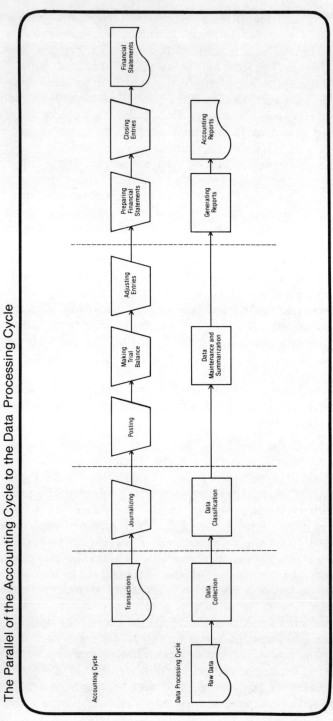

tion required is clearly enumerated on the various forms. Third, source documents serve as distributors of information because multiple copies of the same form can be sent to those individuals or departments that need the information. Finally, source documents aid in establishing the authenticity of the accounting data which is useful for such purposes as establishing an audit trail, determining authorization of payment or inventory disbursements or serving as back-up for computer files.

The source document can be completed by one or many participants in the process. For instance, the agent servicing the account may code some data. Subsequently the document may be processed by the underwriter who in turn adds additional data. In many cases, each completed source document translates into one or more transactions in the system. Once the document is completed, it is given to a person who enters the information into the system. This process of entering the information into the system is called data entry. The data entry process may use a terminal, a keypunch machine, or some other device that translates the information into a form that can be read by the computer.

In a system, a transaction becomes a request to perform some action. There are two major categories of processing transactions: update and inquiry. Some typical update transactions include a new policy, an endorsement, or a loss report. Inquiry transactions retrieve information which is on the file, either by producing a printed report or by displaying the information requested on a terminal screen. Systems may perform many different types of update or inquiry transactions. The system recognizes each type of transaction by a code, often called a transaction code. Each transaction code identifies a particular task and therefore the data which should be present on the record. Each type of transaction usually requires some additional data to perform the designated task. This additional data is contained within the data fields of the transaction. A field is one unit of data on the transaction. Some examples of fields on a transaction are:

- Transaction Code
- Policy Number
- Insured Name
- Expiration Date
- Coverage Code

Sometimes only minimal information is needed to complete a transaction, as, for example, with inquiry transactions. In this case, the operator may enter the complete transaction on a terminal without using a source document for reference. In all other cases, however, the source document provides a reference for the data entry person to enter all fields of the transaction into the system.

In a batch system, operators enter transactions on keypunch machines capable of producing machine readable output such as cards. The system subsequently processes transactions at pre-determined intervals, usually once a day. The output from each transaction returns to the location or person who requested the transaction. The interval between the request for action (keying the transaction) and the results of the processing is called turnaround time. The turnaround time in a batch system is usually twenty-four hours.

In an online system, data entry operators key the required entries on a terminal. The system which collects the transactions may validate the keying for accuracy and verify that the correct entries are made. All collected transactions are accumulated for processing at a later time. Usually this processing occurs in a batch environment and the results return the same way as in batch processing. Terminal data entry allows front end editing. This process edits a transaction for possible errors while the transaction is being entered and reports the errors to the terminal operator immediately for correction. Front end editing precludes many transactions which contain errors from entering the system. Once the operator has corrected all indicated errors, the error free transaction is added to the transaction file. The process of performing front end edits reduces the number of transactions rejected by the system.

In a real time system, operators enter transactions at a terminal, the transaction is processed, and the output is made available on the terminal. This type of system resembles a conversation between the operator and the system. The operator must wait for the output of one transaction before entering a second transaction. The interval between entering the transaction and receiving the output is called *response time*. The response time in a real time system is usually measured in seconds. The output from transaction processing in this case may be a confirmation message, error message, or a report. Real time processing differs from online processing primarily in that real time processing updates the applicable files immediately. However, further processing may occur at a later time to produce other required outputs.

Often a system is a combination of these types. A system might include online inquiry and data entry with batch updating. This combination is usually referred to as online data entry/inquiry. In such a system, inquiry transactions are processed via online system. The operator's screen displays the reports requested. These reports are usually short and limited in information due to the restrictions of screen display. More detailed reports are usually available through the batch component of the system. Update transactions may be entered on the terminal and front end editing performed. However, the update transactions are not processed immediately, but collected in a transaction file to be processed by the batch system later. Some inquiry transactions may also be routed to the transaction file. For example, a request for a larger report may be processed in the nightly run of the batch system. The functions performed by the online system as opposed to the batch system are defined at the time of system design according to the needs and requirements of the users of the system.

Data Classification Data classification organizes the data according to the requirements of the system. This step normally involves two fundamental tasks, editing and coding.

Editing. Editing a transaction is normally the first step taken after the system reads the transaction and before actual processing takes place. This step ensures the accuracy of data entered for all transactions to be processed. The editing process includes three essential types of edits.

Transaction Validation. This type of editing checks the transaction code to ensure that it is one the system recognizes. If the system cannot recognize the transaction, there is no need to process it further.

Transaction Fields. Within a given transaction, certain fields must be coded. The system can edit for these fields as well as check their validity. Four types of checks may be formed on the fields within a transaction.

1. Numeric Edit: Certain fields must contain numeric information. An example of such a field might be premium amount.
2. Length Edit: The data within a field must have a minimum, maximum, or exact length. An example of such a field might be a social security number.
3. Range Edit: Some fields must have values within a certain range. For example, commission ranges may extend from five percent to twenty percent. Any entry below or above this range would be considered invalid.
4. List Edit: Some fields must contain values which appear in a list of values. These lists of values are available to the system, and fields can be checked against this list.

Cross Field Checks. These edits check one field in a transaction against another field in the same transaction or against the applicable master file record in order to validate the value coded in the field checked. For example, if the data entry operator indicated that the addition of a new driver to a personal auto policy is driver number three, the system would check for the presence of driver one and driver two on the master record. If present, that transaction field would be valid and further editing would be performed. Edits of this type are common in many systems.

The more errors that can be detected at the time of data entry, the fewer the error reports that will occur at update time. In a real time system that performs updates immediately, all edits are performed at once and the operator receives immediate confirmation of the transaction processing. In an online data entry system, some of the edits discussed above may be performed. If the master file is available to the data entry system, as it usually is in an online data entry/inquiry system, all of the edits may be performed. In a pure batch system, all edits occur at the time that the system processes the transactions. No edits can be performed prior to the processing of the transactions file.

Coding. Data classification also involves coding the data according to predetermined categories.

Classification codes serve many purposes in an accounting information system. The primary purpose is to identify accounting data. Information systems may need to contain information to identify individual accounts or transactions. Bank account or payroll files may use social security numbers or internally assigned account numbers rather than individual names to identify data. Codes not only facilitate identification but also aid in information retrieval.

A second purpose of coding is to condense data. In general, written descriptions waste space, while coders are simple to use and do not require as much space. It is much easier to code the data than to write it out.

Codes are also used to classify transactions. Usually, it is important to classify accounts or to classify transactions by type, date, or location. For example, a one-digit code may identify the type of claim transaction being processed.

Finally, codes serve to communicate information. Sometimes it is necessary to convey information in such a way that it is meaningless except to the intended user. The credit rating, computer access password, or price may be useful only to the intended user.

The essential types of codes for an information system, are mnemonic codes, sequence codes, block codes, and group codes.

Mnemonic codes are codes that by their very nature help the user to remember what the code means. Usually mnemonic codes are alphabetic and acronyms, made up of the first letter or the first few letters of a term or phrase. An example of the use of mnemonic codes is the code for states used by the U.S. Post Office. The disadvantage of mnemonic codes is that a large number of codes can be similar, and it is simpler to sort items by number than alphabetically.

A *sequence code* is merely a sequential set of numbers that are used to identify specific items such as check numbers. Sequence codes are easy to understand and facilitate record retrieval because the code naturally orders the data in a meaningful manner. Sequence codes may also act as an important accounting control to identify missing items by gaps in pre-numbered series.

Block codes are actually sequential codes in which specific blocks of numbers are reserved for a particular use. Usually, the lead digits in the sequence code serve as the block designator, and the subsequent digits are identifiers. For example, in some policy numbering schemes, the first two digits represent state code and the following digits the individual policy.

A *group code* consists of two or more subcodes that have been combined. Each subcode is identified as a field of the group code, and each field describes separate data. Group codes are very flexible, since mnemonic, sequence, and block codes can be combined. With this flexibility, group codes can summarize a great deal of information in a limited space. On the other hand, group codes can easily become overly complex and not serve the purpose for which the code is intended.

In designing codes, it is important that the code serve some useful purpose. Whenever possible, codes should be consistent with others already in use. For an accounting system, the primary consideration is the established chart of accounts. In any case, codes should be standardized, organized for future expansion, and as efficient as possible.

Data Maintenance Data maintenance involves the processing operations of calculating, comparing, summarizing, and storing. These functions involve the actual processing or manipulation of data in a computer system using a combination of computer programs and computer hardware to execute predetermined tasks. Calculating implies mathematical operations on data, while comparing involves logical operations such as determining whether data is "greater than," "equal to," and "less than" other data. Summarization refers to the condensation of individual data into meaningful totals, while storing is the function of keeping the results of calculating, comparing, and summarizing in one location for future use.

The order of processing transactions differs with batch, online, and real time environments. In a real time system, transactions are processed as they are entered. All transactions are edited. If a transaction passes the editing step, it is then processed against the file. In the case of an update transaction, the master file is updated and the operator who entered the transaction receives a confirmation of the update. After processing, the updated record becomes available to all other operators using the system.

If online data entry is used, transactions are edited as they are entered on the terminal. Transaction validation and transaction field edits can be performed at the time of data entry. Cross field editing may or may not occur at data entry time. Cross field editing may not be possible if the files required are not available to the online system. In this case, the final editing occurs during the batch cycle which processes the transactions collected online. When a transaction passes all edits, it goes into a transaction file that serves as a repository of all transactions collected. At some later time the system takes the transaction file containing the day's work and begins to process the transactions. The processing of a transaction file by a batch update system can involve many different steps.

The master file for a system might contain all policies for the particular company. This file may be organized as a keyed file or a sequential file.

A keyed file provides a means of locating the policy needed by supplying the key information such as the policy number. If the key to the record requested is known, it is possible to read that record directly. It is also possible to access the records of a keyed file in a random order. Most new systems use a keyed file as the master file, but there are still many systems that use sequential files to hold policy information. Although a sequential file has a key, the key cannot be used directly to locate a record on the file. In order to find a record on a sequential file, one must read each record and compare the key on the transaction to the key on the file. If the records are arranged in order according to the key to the file, it is possible to determine whether the desired record is on the file, without having to read the entire file.

In many batch systems the transaction file is sorted using the value of the key to determine the sort order. The sorted transaction file is then processed against the master file. When a master file is a sequential file, this method enables the system to process the transaction file against the master file by only reading the master file once. By matching the keys on both files the system can process all transactions.

When a keyed file is used as a master file, the transaction file does not have to be sorted, but it may still be sorted to improve system performance.

The process of sorting files is usually repeated many times during the update function. In addition to the transaction file, other files may also require sorting. These include output reports and files to be processed by subsequent jobs or steps.

Report Generation and System Interfaces Updated files contain information which can be useful and relevant to information users. Report generation transfers information from files to a form suitable for utilization by company management and other interested parties. The forms most frequently used are business documents such as paychecks and billing statements or business reports such as income statements and balance sheets. In addition to printed reports, some systems display business information on CRTs or visual display terminals that are linked directly to a computer storage device. In order to have value for the user, reports should be timely and in a standard format. Output reports and output files are the end products of the information system and become the goal of the system.

Reports. System reports generally fall into one of three categories. These are error reports, processing reports, and transaction request reports.

Error Reports. These reports usually list all transactions which did not pass the editing criteria. The list also provides some information identifying the error and the field which was in error. These reports may be segregated into many smaller error reports by location or by operator to assist in the process of reconciling and correcting the errors.

Processing Reports. Application systems produce various processing reports.

Confirmation reports generally list all transactions processed. The confirmation reports may be reconciled with the error reports to determine that all input has been processed.

Balancing reports generally serve to indicate the dollar amount of change resulting from the activity represented in the processing. This activity might include changes in receivable amounts due to cash transactions processed or changes to premium amounts due to endorsements.

Output documents maybe printed on standard forms and distributed to the receiving department. They could include declaration pages, premium bills, policy renewals, annual statement pages, or any other documents. The number of different documents produced in insurance information systems is almost unlimited.

Transaction Request Reports. Inquiry transactions are commonly used to request special reports. Each inquiry transaction produces a report of some type. The type of report depends on the transaction code issued. An example of such a report might be to list all policies which will expire in the next sixty days. This request may have a transaction code assigned to it. When the batch system encounters this transaction code, the report will be generated.

In each system, the reports produced by the batch run are routed back to the person requesting the report. Usually in the past the data center printed all the reports and mailed them back to the appropriate people. It is more common today to produce the reports on a file and to transmit the files back to the location requesting the report on telephone lines.

Output Files. Systems frequently must communicate or interface with each other. An interface is a link at which a transaction exits from one system and enters another. Interfaces include the points at which:

- Premium payments received by lock boxes are forwarded to the premium accounting to update the policyholder's account.
- Premiums recorded or booked are used to update the unearned premium reserve.
- Daily general ledger entries such as premiums, losses, and investments are sent to the general ledger systems.

In a computerized system, the interface medium generally is a file shared by several programs or a file that contains output from one system that can be used as input into another system. In manual systems, the sending of a document from one department to another and the routing of various copies of a multipart form to several departments are interfaces.

Examples of output files in a computerized processing system include transaction error recycle files, backup files, and utility files.

Transaction Error Recycle File. This file contains all transactions which the update run did not process due to errors. The operator can then review the error report and determine the necessary corrections. The erroneous transactions can be located via a terminal and corrected without rekeying the entire transaction. This procedure prevents additional errors from occurring while rekeying the entire transaction. Some transactions, especially new policy transactions, contain many required fields, and a total rekeying effort can be substantial.

Backup Files. Backup files are created to copy a file in case some event occurs in the system which could destroy the original file. In an online data entry system, a backup may be taken from the transaction file. Real time update systems take the backup from the master file at the end of each day when the online system stops. In a batch update system, a backup copy of the master file would be created after the system has updated the master file.

Utility Files. Other files may be created to serve as input to another system. In an online data entry system, for example, certain tables of values may be generated for front end editing of the online system nightly. All files required are defined at the time of system design. New files may be added to the system because of new requirements.

DATA STORAGE

Insurance organizations store an enormous volume of data. The initial data are used for underwriting, rating, recording of certain statistical information, and production of the actual policy. The same data are used to develop such items as premium notices, agency commission entries, and claims statistical information when a loss occurs. The sample matrix in Exhibit 2-4 shows insurance activities or functions and some of the operating data involved.

In this sample matrix, types of information are shown on the horizontal lines, and the functions which are performed on the vertical lines. The *X's* indicate the functions for which the data are used. For example, the policyholder's name, the second item of information, is used in the issuance of the policy, billing of the premium, verification of the coverage when a claim is presented, and the drawing of the check or draft in payment or a claim.

Most policyholder data comes from the original application or coding sheets. Additionally, data are derived and created internally in order to provide information in a manner different from that on the application, such as by statistical codes. Further, as claims develop, another group of data will be put into the computer to reflect the claims activity. Internal to the computer, other data will be created as claims information is paired with policy information. There is a great volume of this type of internal generation of data, limited only by the defined needs of the company or the limitations of the computer system. A *data base* is a pool of stored information that results from processing transactions. While transactions are processed partially or completely within a given period of time, a data base crosses time periods and passes information about transactions from one period to another and from one system to another.

Data base elements are of two types: static and dynamic. *Static* or reference data provide input for processing transactions or producing reports. Examples of static data are name and address information, premium rates and terms in a policyholder master file, and salary rates in a payroll file. *Dynamic* data include current balances that are stored or summarized transaction activities that are updated during normal transaction processing. Examples of dynamic data are premium and loss payment transactions and account balances in a general ledger.

Data bases may exist on magnetic discs, drums, and tapes or in card files, tab files, or drawers. Regardless of the storage medium, however, it is essential to understand the organization of the stored data.

Exhibit 2-4
Insurance Information Matrix*

	New Policy Risk Analysis	Premium Calculation	Policy Issue	Endorsement Underwriting/Issue	Client Billing	Agency Reconciliation	Agency Recording	Verification of Coverage	Claim Recording	Claim Payment	Renewal Underwriting/Issue
Client Number	X		X	X	X	X	X	X		X	X
Name			X		X				X		X
Address	X	X	X	X	X			X		X	X
Policy Number	X		X	X	X	X	X	X		X	X
Line of Business	X	X		X	X	X	X		X		X
Coverage/Limits	X	X	X	X				X	X	X	X
Deductible	X	X	X	X				X	X	X	X
Risk/Exposure	X	X	X	X				X	X		X
Policy Dates	X	X	X	X	X	X	X	X	X	X	X
Rate Data	X	X		X							X
Premium Amounts	X	X	X	X	X	X	X				X
Claim Number									X	X	X
Claimant Number									X	X	X
Claimant N/A									X		X
Reserve Amount									X	X	X
Agent Number	X		X	X	X	X	X			X	X
Commission Percent	X			X	X	X	X				X
Due Dates					X	X					
Amount Due					X	X					
Loss Summaries	X			X							X

*Reprinted with permission from *Property/Liability Personal Lines Insurance: DB/DC Information Systems Design Concepts*, IBM Corporation, 2nd Ed., October 1974, p. 33.

Data Files

The conversion of manual office systems to automatic data processing systems carried over many common terms to a new context. This continuation of familiar terminology helped people in applying their current knowledge to the new automated systems. Reviewing the meaning of these terms in manual systems clarifies the new data processing language.

File Content   Thus, to illustrate the concept of files, consider a familiar example. Almost everyone maintains a file in the form of a personal checkbook. This is generally called a check register. The check register contains related sets of records. The data contained in this file include the date of the ckeck, the check number, the payee, the amount of payment, and sometimes the purpose of the check. Although the appearance of computer files differs greatly from personal check registers, they contain similar information. That is, a computer file also contains related sets of records.

Manual Data Files.   In a manual system, an organized system of alphabetic characters and numbers represents all kinds of facts. The organized system with its related characters and numbers constitutes the language of the system users.

When the characters and numbers are organized according to well defined rules, literate people can interpret the results. Characters and numbers displayed without following the rules become unreadable items. Misspelling would be one example of the misuse of the rules.

Automated Data Files.   In an automated system, the same set of characters and numbers can be used to display facts. There must also be a defined set of rules to govern usage. These rules are programmed for the computer. Most modern business computers must be supplied with data using individual characters. These characters include alphabetic letters (A to Z), numeric digits (0-9), and any set of predefined symbols ($, *, /, ?, :, ,,).

Traditionally, accounting information was recorded on visible accounting documents (such as agents' accounts current, direct bills, and claim checks) and in ledgers and journals. In a computerized system, data are recorded and held in machine-readable form, which may be referred to as an "invisible" record. Unlike manual files, computer files are readable only by the machine. Physically, computer files consist of decks of punched cards, magnetic tape reels, magnetic disk packs, magnetic drums, or data cells. Magnetic tape reels resemble those used on tape recorders, but they store bits of information rather than recorded music. One inch of magnetic tape can typically store up

Exhibit 2-5
Data Hierarchy

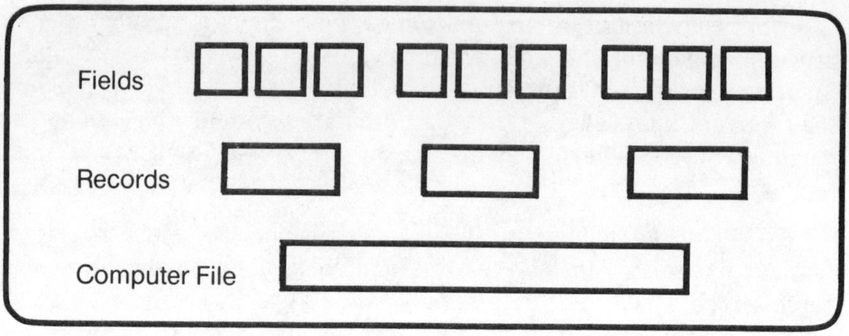

to 1,600 characters. A single large reel of tape can store up to 25 million characters.

Another major difference between computer files and manual files is that computer files can be changed and updated without physical human intervention. This ability improves the speed and accuracy of EDP systems, but introduces some limitations as well. These limitations stem from the fact that computer files must be more formal or rigid in their design than manual files. For instance, the record for each check must be of a specified length and be located in an exact area in the file. The computer does not have the capability of interpreting general instructions and must be given the exact location data. As an example, consider a situation where all the checks to a particular payee must be listed for a period of time. For a computer file, the name of the company must be spelled the same way on each check. Without the use of complicated programming, computers do not have the flexibility to match names which are similar but not exactly the same. For this reason, therefore, computer files generally list payees by account numbers. Still another difference between computer files and manual files is the coding required in computer files. For example, the computer must use distinctive record codes in order for the computer to know whether the transaction is to be treated as a credit or a debit.

When computer applications were first introduced to business, punched cards constituted the predominant medium for storage. The nature of the cards and the fact that they had to be processed by using mechanical equipment limited the variety of choices and file design. However, some of the terminology developed for use with punched cards is still in use today. The term "field" was used to denote the exact location for a data element within a record. Exhibit 2-5 shows the hierarchy in a computer file.

Exhibit 2-6
Hierarchical Groupings Compared

	Manual	Automatic
Characters	A to Z	A to Z
	0 to 9	0 to 9
	Special Symbols	Special Symbols
Groupings	Words	
	Phrases	Fields
	Sentences	Records
	Paragraphs	Files
	Pages	Databases
	Books	
Size	Variable for each word	Fixed and predefined for each field
Control	English and Math rules governing language	Preset instructions defined by program

Data into Fields. For computers to process data, individual characters are grouped into more meaningful relationships called fields. In the context of manual systems, similar groupings are called words or numbers. Exhibit 2-6 compares the hierarchical groupings of data used in manual systems to those used in automated systems. The field is the smallest unit that has some logical meaning. This collection of characters can be treated as one unit. In processing, the characters in the field are always addressed or used as one single unit.

Field examples on a mailing label could be: Last Name, First Name, Middle Initial, Address, City, State, and Zip Code.

Fields into Records. Fields are grouped into the next larger unit called a record. A record is a collection of fields that have some common factor or denominator. These collected fields may represent all the information needed to complete a mailing label.

Data	Fields	Record
Jones	Last Name	
John	First Name	
J	Middle Initial	Jones John J
115	Address	115 Cary
Cary		Lakewood Texas 07185
Lakewood	City	
Texas	State	
07185	Zip Code	

Each record contains the fields related to one person, one transaction, one policy, or any one complete unit.

Records into Files. All of the records that can be collected and assigned a common factor or denominator are grouped into a unit called a file. The mailing label records that are needed to mail a certain group of books would be collected into a file.

Files Become Data Bases. In today's environment, all files may be collected into one or more large corporate data bases. These data bases are joined together to make all corporate data available to a larger number of users.

Types of Files In an ongoing data processing system, there are three primary types of files. File types are generally assigned names that reflect the reason they exist or the items they contain. These file types are the master file, the transaction file, and sort file. An additional file type, the suspense or error file, may be used to hold those transactions that cannot be processed automatically because of some problem condition. Special files may also be created for unique purposes.

Master Files. Every ongoing system has some file of data which holds the permanent source of data for the application group. This master file is the major repository of the records that are used on a scheduled basis to supply needed information. The master file must be kept up-to-date to provide current accurate information. These files represent the subledgers or books of account, such as the premium statistical master with name and address for each policy, loss master with name and address of each claimant, or general ledger chart of accounts with account numbers and descriptions.

Master file data are data of a permanent or semipermanent nature, such as policy number, annual premium, policy type, payment mode, and policyholder's name and address. Frequently, master file data operate on transaction data for purposes of control, such as validation of claims, or accounting, as when original premium amounts are used to calculate earned and unearned premium values.

Transaction Files. The transaction file contains the transactions or records which represent the activity against the master file. These transactions generally are either:

- ADDS—Adding an entire new record to the master file.
- DELETES—Removing an entire record from the master file.
- CHANGES—Changing information or an existing record. The change may involve replacing information currently on the record or adding or deleting parts of the record.

Transaction data is specific to individual transactions. It may be held in its original form (such as by policy number, effective date, or premium amount) or in a summary form (such as current inforce).

Examples of transaction files are renewal premiums billed, open collections, and accounts receivable; the transactions are often sorted in sequence by policy number or date. In the master file, the same information would probably be stored in sequence by company. Normally, the renewed premiums billed file is stored in sequence by branch, line of business, and policy number.

Sort Files. In processing it is often necessary to arrange the record within a file in some special order. For example, placing the transaction file in the same order as the master file generally saves processing time. This arrangement is known as sorting. Sorting produces an additional file with the same contents as the original file in a special order. The sorted copy may or may not be retained after the process is completed.

Suspense Files. Suspense files, or error files, contain transactions held pending some further action. Not all records contain the proper information to allow processing. Erroneous transactions, such as claims with invalid policy numbers, must be held awaiting correction.

The cause may be data entry errors or processing transactions out of order. Data entry errors may be the result of typing mistakes or violation of any of the predetermined rules set for the file. An example of such a violation would be attempting to delete a policy that is not on the master file.

Any record lacking the proper information could be placed in a special file. It is necessary to investigate each error separately to correct the error condition and allow processing with the next batch of transactions.

Special Files. There are a number of other files that represent special conditions. These files generally have a name that reflects their special content.

The most common special files are grouped together as *backup files*. This group includes any files created to protect against loss. Backup files duplicate existing production files. They are stored at a separate location, sometimes even in another state. In case of major damage at the data center, these files would restore the destroyed data.

Another form of backup is a copy of all the files on a certain device such as a disk-drive. This file would be used to replace or relocate the data from a device that had a hardware failure.

A data base system maintains a special backup file called a *log file* to help recover the data base in case of failure. These log files are copies of all changes to the data bases.

Of special interest to insurance companies is a special file called a *rate table file*. This file is a set of tables containing the rate schedules for different coverages and conditions. If these rate files were maintained within a program, the program would have to be changed every time a rate was adjusted. Rate tables kept in a special file are more easily maintained and available to many different users.

Many insurance companies use another special file to serve a similar purpose in the statistical area. A table of statistical codes is kept on a file separate from any program. These statistical coding master files are maintained separately and can be used by many different users.

Organization of Files   Whatever information is maintained in a file, the files must be organized to allow for speedy retrieval of its content at the lowest possible cost. Major factors that determine cost are file size, frequency of use, frequency of change, and type of processing.

Size of Files and Records.   File size varies widely from small files that contain a small number of records to very large files that contain millions of records. Record size varies from a few bytes to thousands of bytes or characters.

Records on a file are generally fixed in length; that is, every record has the same number of characters. The fixed length record is most common in payroll and inventory files.

Of more interest to the insurance industry is the variable length record. In this case, the length of each individual record varies according to the information contained in the record. A record that represents one family's auto insurance policy includes a number of fixed length segments or parts. For example, the first part of the record contains control information such as the insured's name, address, and rating territory information. Another segment contains information about the producing agent and commission rate. Additional segments describe the payment plan if the policy is paid in installments. Following these segments are a number of segments, one for each auto, that identify the auto covered. Additional segments list special coverages on each driver such as life or medical insurance.

Many families have two or more cars with two or more drivers. Without the variable length record, each car would have to be reflected on a separate fixed length record, with each record repeating the common policy information.

A variable length record that combines all the features offered in an auto policy could easily represent thousands of bytes of information. The beginning of each variable record tells the computer in a field of two or more bytes, the length of the record on a read instruction. Using this record length indicator, each record can be read with no lost or idle space.

Many insurance companies are working on policies that will combine all lines of personal coverage using the variable length record. One very large record with many sections could contain the necessary data for one family's auto, homeowners, and life and health insurance.

The combination of lengthy records and many records in the file may result in a very large file that spans volumes of magnetic tape or requires a number of online devices.

Frequency of Use. The frequency of reference to the information on a file influences the best organization. If a file is used many times during a single day it will be necessary to have the file organized and available for this frequent reference.

Frequency of Change. If the file is used only as a source file, it is called a static file. A file that has many changes is called a volatile file. Whether files are volatile must also be considered in determining the best organization.

Type of Processing. Another consideration is the type of processing the file receives. Traditionally transactions were collected or grouped together in batches, to be processed against the master file at a convenient or appropriate time. With online processing, the file must have an organization and be housed on a device that allows for continuous reference. The file must always be available. Many business applications depend on such online variable information.

Types of File Organization There are two major types of file organization used at the present time—sequential and direct.

Sequential Processing. Most files are organized in a sequential order. The records in the files follow one after the other according to the sequence of some common element. This arrangement lends itself to the use of punch cards or magnetic tape. Although punch cards are largely obsolete, magnetic tape is still the common storage media for vast amounts of business data. Magnetic tape survives because of its relative low cost and the major cost of converting many existing systems to online systems.

To use sequential organization, the master file and any transaction files must first be arranged in a predetermined order. Establishing a unique field on the record as a key sort field generally facilitates sequential arrangement. The key sort field must be unique. Examples of unique fields are the social security number on a payroll record or the assigned policy number on a policy system. When a key field is selected, the file can be sorted or placed in an ascending or descending order.

Direct Processing. The development of a new range of storage devices made direct processing possible. A direct access storage device such as a magnetic disc or drum allows records to be located anywhere on the recording surface of the device. Any record may be located without reference to the other records on the file. No matter how large the master file, data can be retrieved and processed online. This feature of these new storage devices offers a significant advantage over magnetic tape, since searching for data on tape requires starting at the beginning and reading to the end of a file.

Address Systems The computer storage system can be compared to a vast room or rooms full of filing cabinets. Each and every location in the system must have a specific address.

If a file is in sequential order on a tape, the address system is very simple. The system needs only to know the *data set name* of the tape. The location of the record on the tape will be found by reading the tape from beginning to end.

If a file is on a direct access storage device, there must be a directory of the locations on the device as well as a directory of all the devices on the system. Because of the complexity of these directories and the high level of maintenance, it would not be possible for a programmer to keep track of where or how this data is stored. The directories must be established and maintained by the system. Each major manufacturer has developed an address system that performs this task for its equipment and devices.

Indexed File Organization. In most systems the directory is based on a key or control field. This key is maintained in an index area within the directory. Along with the key the directory stores pointers or indicators showing where the entire record or the larger data item is stored.

Index Sequential. In the index sequential access method, three separate areas are established on a storage device. These are the index, main storage area, and an overflow area.

The index area contains only the key fields and pointers. These key fields are placed in sequential order in much the same way as a sequential tape file. The index facilitates rapid location of the individual record.

The data records are stored in another area. This area may even be on another device in a large system. These records are not kept in sequential order. Their arrangement may depend on size, available space, or on when the record was added to the file. The order varies according to the system manufacturer and its written software.

The third area holds overflow when the major storage area is filled. When records or the index straddle the primary and overflow area, a slower processing time results. Systems that use an index and overflow storage area must be rearranged or reorganized as processing time slows.

Some manufacturers no longer support the index sequential storage method. These manufacturers have developed a new addressing system where the index and storage area are more dynamic.

Relative File Organization. Relative file organization avoids the use of an index of key values. Each record is stored in a uniquely identified area. These areas are located by a relative position from a point of origin. This original position becomes the key value and is used to retrieve the record. This system requires more control by the programmer.

Data Dictionaries

Organizations create data files in order to perform certain processing functions efficiently. As computer systems expand, more and more files are created to support new applications. Often different files contain the same data although in time contradictions inevitably appear. Moreover, executives may not obtain desired information because it combines data contained in different files. Separate departments may even use different names for the same data items. Data modeling can help to overcome these problems. The data modeling process should develop and maintain precise documentation regarding the requirements of the system, data items necessary, logical and physical structures, security requirements, and general system documentation. Most organizations today use a data dictionary to capture and store this documentation.

Data dictionaries serve three essential purposes for the whole organization: (1) they inform people of the existence of data, (2) they help to control the definition and representation of data, and (3) they indicate what programs are affected by changes in the structure or representation of data.

Using a data dictionary during the design of a data base helps to ensure that agreed upon definitions of data requirements are maintained throughout the design phase. The definition of a given data item may include information regarding length, format, narrative description, editing criteria, and alternative names commonly used for the data item. The dictionary also indicates in what records and segments the individual data items are contained and in what data bases the segments reside. This information is captured and maintained over the life of the development effort as well as after the data base is designed and implemented. A data dictionary model appears in Exhibit 2-7.

Most data dictionary products can produce reports on all of this documentation for the individuals on the development team, which is a significant benefit for a team defining a large data base. Insurance applications normally contain massive amounts of data and therefore require this type of product to control the effort. The reports generated can normally be produced either in a computer printout form or be returned to an online screen if the capability for online retrieval is part of the product. Exhibit 2-8 illustrates a data dictionary report.

In addition to the documentation used by the development team, most dictionaries allow for the generation of control blocks which can in turn be processed by the data base management product in use by the company. This ensures that a central repository is available for use in the implementation phase as well as in the future when modifications are required.

Once the data base design is implemented and more and more application systems begin accessing the data base, a dictionary can also be used to capture application access intact information. It is then possible to maintain an accurate description of the usage of the data base by the applications and ensure that security of the information is being maintained. During this period the dictionary also helps to determine if the requirements of a new application can be supported by a current data base design. This determination entails reviewing the needs of the new system regarding the data required and ascertaining if in fact the data exists and is in a format suitable for use by the application. Without tight control over the documentation for a data base, these questions cannot be readily answered. In addition, the lack of such documentation can lead to the development of new or modified data bases where a need may not exist. The benefits which can be derived from data sharing will not be realized when data is replicated in multiple files in an uncontrolled fashion. The implementation of a data base management system by itself will not produce the maximum benefit without adequate controls over the data base. One of the essential control tools is a data dictionary.

Successful data sharing requires both a strong management

Exhibit 2-7
Data Dictionary Model

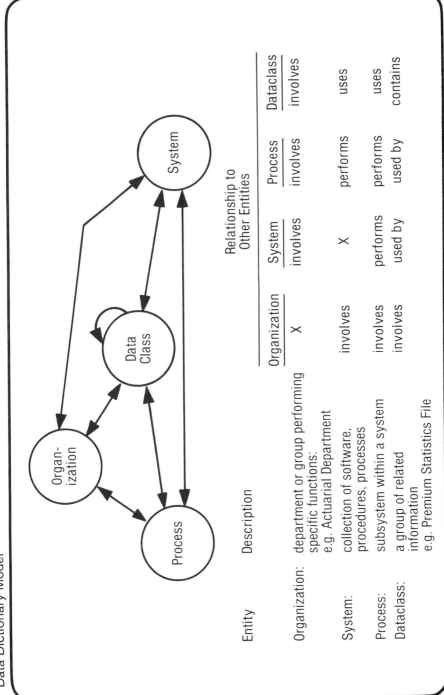

Relationship to
Other Entities

Entity	Description	Organization	System	Process	Dataclass
			involves	involves	involves
Organization:	department or group performing specific functions: e.g. Actuarial Department	X	involves	involves	involves
System:	collection of software, procedures, processes	involves	X	performs	uses
Process:	subsystem within a system	involves	performs	performs	uses
Dataclass:	a group of related information e.g. Premium Statistics File	involves	used by	used by	contains

Exhibit 2-8
Data Dictionary Report

```
****   DATA MANAGEMENT REPORT   ****   DATE 09/16/82   PAGE 2

CATEGORY: DATACLAS                    *  DICTIONARY / DIRECTORY  *

PRIMARY NAME: LOSS-STAT-FILE   LANG CODE:   OCC: 000 STATUS: B
RELATIONSHIPS:
    USED-BY         SYSTEM
    AGENCY-EXPERIENCE-SYSTEM
    CLAIM-MANAGEMENT-SYSTEM
    DATA-COMPILING-SYSTEM
    WORKSHEETS-SYSTEM
    PCOS-SYSTEM

+  +  +  +  +  +  +  +  +  +  +  +  +  +  +  +  +  +  +  +  +  +

    **  INVALID RSN CALL                     00046

INPUT RECORD   /EXEC PGM DDP6DICT PARM-'ORGANZTNB UNDERWRITING-
               DEPT!R-(*,SYSTEM)
INPUT RECORD   /D-(DESC,ATTR)!RD-YES!'  ;
```

commitment to incorporating a data dictionary into the organization
and the total cooperation of the application areas and end users in its
use. In addition, procedures for the use and maintenance of a dictionary
must be established and tuned to fit best into the daily operation of the
company. Without these commitments, the use of the data dictionary
tool will become cumbersome and eventually be circumvented.

Data Bases

As explained earlier, files are used to capture and store data for
further processing. The arrangement and organization methods give
the ability to store data captured from the ongoing data collection
effort. This data can then be processed by an application program and
saved on a master file for future updates.

As technology has improved, so has our desire to provide more
flexibility regarding the storage and retrieval of data. With the advent
of storage devices that had the capability of random retrieval versus a
tape device, which was primarily used for sequential processing, and

the increasing need to provide immediate access to the stored data, the data base approach has become more viable. The remainder of this section is devoted to a definition of the term data base as well as discussion of its benefits and features.

Advantages of Data Bases Most organizations purchase a package which can provide a data base management system (DBMS) suited to their specific needs. Various data base management systems are available, and each has its own strong points. The review and selection of an individual product should be based upon the processing requirements of each company. The important point is that the realization of any benefits from a data base will be through the use of either a purchased DBMS or the in-house development of a tailored system. The goal of both approaches should be to provide one common approach to the management of the data bases created. Without a standard methodology, some of the potential benefits of a data base approach will not be realized. A common approach is required because as each data base is created and implemented, the application program that accesses the data base calls upon the services of the DBMS to perform the functions of retrieval, updating, insertion, and deletion of data items on the data bases. It is the purpose of the DBMS to coordinate these activities and to provide a consistent approach. An analogy can be made with a standard office filing cabinet. If more than one approach to filing daily reports was used in a branch office, it would soon become impossible to locate a given file in this cabinet. It would not be possible to share one common file among various users. However, once a standard approach is implemented regarding inserts and deletions, sharing becomes possible and the benefits of one central file to be used by various areas can be realized. Although this is a rather simplistic example, the data base approach depends on the same concept. As shown in Exhibit 2-9, a data base management system controls access to a central claims data base and allows it to be used by four separate application programs.

Collection of Interrelated Data. One of the most important considerations in the design and implementation of data bases is the concept of *subject data bases*. This approach to data base design has been shown to be the most effective method of meeting current needs while still providing for the capability to support future business requirements. This method is based upon the assumption that data which has been arranged to fit the basic business relations will be much more capable of being used without re-arrangement for a much longer period of time. The alternative approach which many organizations fall prey to is the implementation of data bases based upon the requirements of a given application. An *application data base* leads to

Exhibit 2-9
DBMS Controlling Access to Data Bases

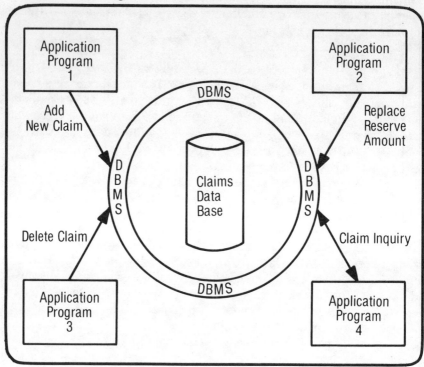

problems as companies reorganize and new functions have to be added to a system. By developing subject oriented data bases, such as claims information, policy information, and billing information, and trying to keep each class of data on its respective data base, many more applications can be developed to use this data.

One implication of subject data bases is that a given application may have to process multiple data bases concurrently. Multiple data bases being processed by one application, because of the segregation imposed by subject data bases, may at first appear to be an inconvenience to an application development team. However, most data base management systems allow the combination of more than one physical data base into a logical data base. This enables the application development group to view and process what appears to be one data base when in fact it would be multiple physical files. For example, a policywriting application may require loss information as well as policy information in order to rate a policy properly. In this case, information regarding losses could be contained on a claims data base and information specifically related to the policies could be contained on a

Exhibit 2-10
Logical View Versus Physical Data Base

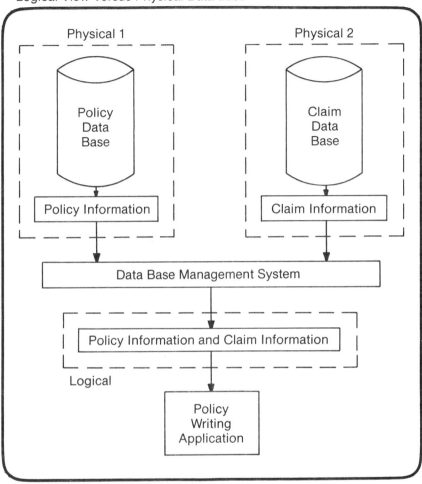

policy data base. The application programmers, however, could view these separate data bases as if they were one data base. Exhibit 2-10 contrasts the logical and physical views of such a data base.

As shown in Exhibit 2-11, in traditional systems, which were developed in the past with the use of files and not data bases, a similar application would result in data being passed from a claims processing application to the policywriting system and subsequently store the data in multiple files. This type of processing results not only in duplicate data but also, as time progresses, in inconsistent data. In this example, the transactions sent from the claims system to the policywriting system could be misapplied or rejected due to some type of editing error. This in turn will result in inconsistent results between the applications. Additionally, the extra processing, which includes the transaction creation from the claims application, the processing by the policywriting application, and the storage costs of the data, adds to the expense that an organization would incur.

In summary, the approach to be used for development of new systems should be the creation of subject oriented data bases which contain only interrelated data. Overall the organization will benefit substantially more from this approach than from the implementation of data bases to fit individual application systems that therefore do not provide the capability for sharing data.

Minimum Redundant Data. As we have seen from the previous discussion regarding subject data bases, duplication of data between multiple systems and files should be reduced as much as possible. The cost of not doing so can be significant if we consider the impact of inconsistent data being processed and subsequently reported throughout the organization.

It is important to remember that the data base approach strives for "minimum redundant data," not total elimination of redundant data. It has been a common misconception that with the implementation of a data base management system and the related data bases that all duplicate data will be eliminated. A much more accurate statement would be that duplicate data will be controlled. With today's technology it is not possible or practical to totally eliminate all redundant data. In order to process the data bases in the most effective fashion as well as be able to meet some of the restrictions imposed by the various data base management systems, some duplication is necessary. Therefore, most organizations attempt to implement the concept of *controlled redundancy.* This concept essentially means that if duplication of data is required, then it must be incorporated into a design in a controlled fashion. The reasons for taking this action must be agreed upon by the design team and documented. In addition to the reasons for this decision, every effort must be made to keep track of where this duplication exists. This is normally accomplished with the aid of a data dictionary product. Although redundant data will not be totally eliminated, a positive effort must be made to control and document this duplication.

Physical Storage Independence. With traditional systems, it was necessary that the programming area always be aware of the physical storage for data on a given file. This meant that the programming staff had to know such things as the length of the data on a file, the positions of the data fields on the records, and the format of these fields. All changes that affected this layout had to be programmed accordingly. If

Exhibit 2-11
Traditional Approach

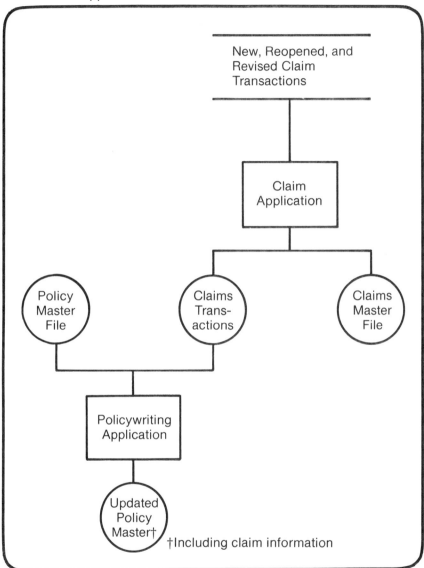

New, Reopened, and
Revised Claim
Transactions

Claim
Application

Policy
Master
File

Claims
Trans-
actions

Claims
Master
File

Policywriting
Application

Updated
Policy
Master†

†Including claim information

multiple areas were accessing a given file, the job of communicating and controlling changes to the layout of files became more and more difficult. If the information regarding these changes did not reach all concerned parties, the results could be disastrous. The impact of such changes can be significantly reduced with the proper implementation of a data base management system.

One of the significant features of a data base management system is the ability to allow changes to a data base and still provide the same view of the data even though changes had been made. Changes could have been required because of processing efficiencies such as the movement of data base from one device type to another or reorganizations of data base to provide improved processing. In addition to these types of changes, new or modified functions may be required. This could possibly result in more data being captured on the data base. The data base may be used by many applications and the new data may only be required for one of these applications. The applications which do not require the new data should be able to continue to process without impact.

As we have seen, multiple data bases can be combined into one view as though they are processing as a single data base. This same concept can be applied on a lower level regarding segments of a data base or individual fields. A very simplistic example of this can be seen in Exhibit 2-12. In this example, make the assumption that the data base contains information on policyholders, but does not contain information regarding dependent children. If a requirement comes along to provide for an automatic diary to indicate that a dependent child may have reached the appropriate driving age and should therefore be reviewed by the underwriting staff, then new data must be added to the data base. After reviewing the requirements of this new function, it is determined that a new segment of information will be added to the data base. The ability to implement this change without impact on the current applications is required. A data base system can provide this capability. Current applications that do not require the new data would not be affected. With traditional files, the applications currently using this file would have had to make the programming changes necessary to be able to process a record that contained the new data. This same concept can be applied to a situation that may have resulted in only new data fields being added to an existing segment of the data base.

As can be seen very quickly, this ability can dramatically reduce the amount of time and effort required to implement a change and also reduce the amount of time spent in handling normal maintenance activities. The amount of activity required either on a regulatory basis or just to improve a competitive position can sometimes be overwhelming. Any reduction in the impact of these changes can result in substantial savings.

Recoverability. One of the most important features of a data base management system is the capability to recover from an error situation

Exhibit 2-12
Hierarchy Old/New Physical Versus Logical View After Adding a
New Segment

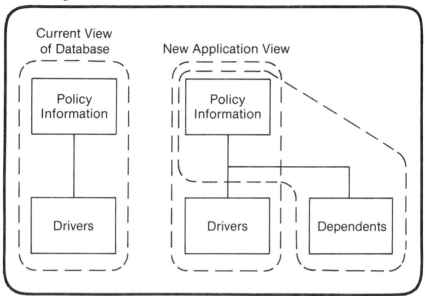

as quickly as possible. This is very important when we consider that many application systems could be using a given data base. If that data base becomes unusable for any reason, the impact will be much more dramatic than in a traditional environment where each application system usually had its own copy of data. In addition to this problem the data base may also be one which is being used in an online environment and the impact on many terminal users must be considered.

Methods of recovering from failures fall into two general categories. The first is a *forward recovery*. This type of recovery is generally required when the device that contains the data base becomes inoperable. There are many reasons why a physical device can fail; suffice to say that essentially the data base can no longer be read or updated. The first step taken when this occurs is to locate a copy or backup of the data base and load it to a new device. However, the backup copy could have been a day, a week, or even a month old. Since this backup copy was taken, there could have been many updates applied to the data base. Two methods are available for bringing the data base up to date. The first method is to rerun all jobs that have updated the data base since the backup copy was taken. Although this method will work, the amount of processing time required to perform this is sometimes not practical. The second method is keep track of all updates to a data base as the jobs that update the data base are running; this is referred to as *logging*. A data base log file contains images of all records updated on the data base as they looked after the transactions were processed by an application program. If this is done then the option exists to take these log files and process them with a generalized utility type of program and place them out on the data base which has been reloaded. This activity will result in the data base appearing exactly as it did prior to the device failure. The benefits of this method over rerunning all of the application programs is that the utility program will process the logged records very rapidly because it is only a matter of putting them back on the data base. The utility program does not perform any of the original logic that the application program initially did to process the transactions which resulted in these updates.

The second type of recovery is called a *backout*. This type of recovery is necessary because in a data base environment the application program is changing the data base in place as opposed to reading in a file and writing out an updated version. If during the update process the program fails and must be restarted, all changes up until the time of program failure must be removed from the data base before the program can be restarted. The methods of doing this basically fall into two categories. The first method is to take a copy of the data base before any updates take place. If the program fails, this backup copy can be loaded back and the program can be restarted. For large data bases this is not usually a practical method due to the amount of time it takes to copy the data base before starting the program. The alternative method is very similar to the method described above for forward recovery. Data base logging is implemented but, in addition to keeping the after images of all updated records, the before images are also captured. If it then becomes necessary to backout the effects of a failing program it is only necessary to process the log file with a backout utility program and locate the before image records and place them out on the data base.

Security. In a traditional file-oriented environment where each application had a copy of its own data and sharing of data was not very extensive, the need for security was less pressing than in a data base environment. When multiple groups begin sharing data it becomes mandatory to restrict access and update privileges solely to individuals with valid reasons for these functions. Most data base management systems provide the means of controlling the access capabilities to only a given set of records or segments and also down to a data field level.

Data Base Structures Prior to the introduction of data bases and the capabilities of data base management systems, data fields were arranged in records and records placed on files according to the requirements of each individual application system. This meant that data was replicated in these multiple files and therefore maintained by various groups. With the capabilities provided by the introduction of data base management systems, it became possible to arrange data into a logical organization. One of these arrangements is based upon the premise that there exists a natural hierarchy to the data that is processed. For example, it is readily apparent that for a personal auto policy, from one to many drivers may be associated with a given policy number; it is also apparent that for a given policy there can be from one to many accidents associated with these drivers. It can also be seen that it is not possible to have an accident without having previously captured the driver information. This data can therefore be arranged in a hierarchical fashion. Exhibit 2-13 shows this arrangement of data, which is also referred to as a parent-to-child relationship.

In this example the policy segment of information is considered to be the parent segment of the driver information. A child segment (driver segment) cannot exist without a parent. This concept also points out the relationship of one parent having many children. In our example, for one policy it is possible to have many drivers. This same concept can be expanded so that information regarding the vehicles associated with a policy and their respective coverages can be included along with claims and billing information. Exhibit 2-14 shows these segments of information added to the original hierarchy.

This structure then becomes the logical data base that will be processed. By creating a hierarchical structure of this type, multiple application systems can access the data and only view the information related to their specific needs. For example, a claims processing system may require only the policy segment and the claims segment; it may not need access to the other pieces of information. This means that if it becomes necessary to add a new segment of information for another system being developed, claims processing can continue without being impacted. It also means that the amount of redundant data has been eliminated. For example, if some of the data in the policy segment is the insured's name and address, then there exists only one copy of that data for all of the applications using this data base. If it is necessary to change the insured's address, it will be changed once for all applications. If this data base did not exist and multiple applications had the insured's name and address, it would be necessary that all of the applications be notified to update the address. This can result in unnecessary processing expense as well as inconsistent data if one of these systems fails to update the information in a timely fashion.

In order to develop and control the design and implementation of data bases, it is necessary to have a central area coordinating and

Exhibit 2-13
Hierarchical Arrangement of Policy Driver and Accident Data

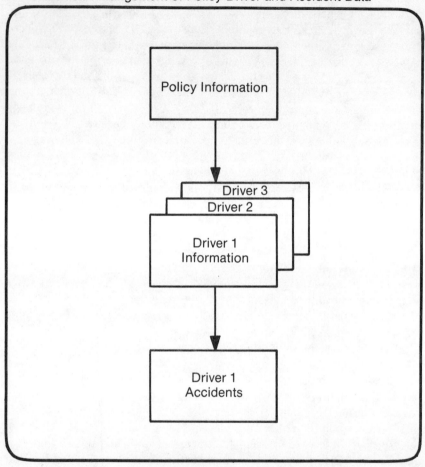

implementing the designs required. In the past this group was referred to as the *data base administration area*. Recently, however, organizations have begun modifying the responsibilities of the area to encompass all of the data being processed by an organization and have modified the name of this area to *data administration*. Normally the area will divide into groups—one responsible for the physical implementation and maintenance of the data bases and another responsible for logical design of data bases. The logical design group may also have responsibility for the implementation of methods and procedures to allow for the documentation and control of both data bases being developed and the conventional files maintained by an organization. This function not only serves to define these files so that the application

Exhibit 2-14
Hierarchical Arrangement of Policy Driver and Accident Data and
Including Vehicle, Coverage Claims and Billing

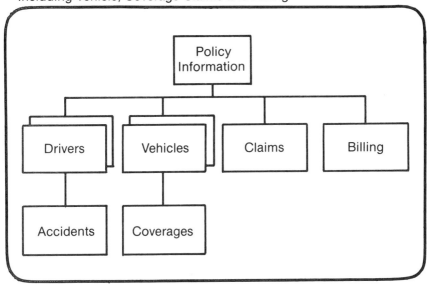

areas have supporting documentation, but also begins to establish a central inventory of all data resources in the organization. This can then be used to perform modeling functions for long-range planning and to perform impact analysis when questions are asked regarding potential changes to data items which may be required. These changes could be the result of requirements outside the organization's control, such as expansion of zip codes or internal requirements. The impact of changes required to data items can only be measured after collecting the total inventory of data determining and how often the changes are needed and where the data resides. This is one of the main reasons for establishment of a data administration area.

Regarding the logical design of the data bases, it is mandatory that the design be undertaken in a team approach with representatives from the application, data administration, and user areas. The goal of this team is to define all of the business requirements of the system and to convert these requirements into data structures capable of supporting the needs.

Once the logical structures have been defined and finalized, the logical design is turned over to the physical design unit. The data base designer now has the responsibility to turn this logical structure into a physical definition based upon the rules and constraints of the given data base management system used. It is during this process that consideration must be given to efficiency factors so that processing and online response times can be met. This normally requires developing several alternative approaches and either manually reviewing each design or processing the design through a prototype in order to predict the eventual processing effectiveness. The entire effort is composed of repetitive attempts to examine each alternative and make the necessary adjustments to the design. Once this stage has been completed, the final data base definition can be developed and supporting procedures can be defined and implemented so that the data base can be supported and maintained in the most effective manner.

Development Aids   With the ever-increasing cost of developing applications, it is becoming much more important that applications be developed with a minimum amount of time expended by the programming staff. It is also becoming much more common for users to develop small applications or one-time programs. These requirements make it necessary to locate products that can be used to reduce the amount of effort it requires to develop a new application or that can be used by someone without a programming background.

Various products are available that cover the area of simple queries up to application generators. Usually these products can be used online to interrogate a data base based on some selection criteria or they can be run in a batch type of environment to produce a report suited to the specific requirements. Most organizations today require multiple packages to support varying needs within the company. The primary reason is that the available products that are truly user-friendly and can be used by someone not trained as a programmer may not be suitable for more complex types of queries or procedures. In order to support these needs effectively, it becomes necessary to review and select multiple packages. Since the goal of a data base implementation is to provide the most flexibility in the area of data sharing, either internal features in the data base management system or purchased products become necessary. These features will allow an organization to gain the most benefits from the data bases they implement.

SUMMARY

Two major considerations in an insurance information system are the flow of data through the system and the manner of storing data within the system. Tracing data as it flows through the system from the original input to the final output reveals the tasks performed by the system. Examining the design of data files and data bases clarifies the capabilities and the limitations of the system.

Insurance information systems must be designed both to produce ledger balances from which financial statements are prepared and to produce management and operating informational reports in nonaccounting terms. An accounting system is a series of tasks by which transactions are processed. The fundamental tasks of an accounting system generally include the recognition of an economic event as a transaction, followed by approval, computation, journalizing, posting, summarization in trial balances, accumulation on worksheets, and reporting in financial statements. These tasks follow the seven steps of the accounting cycle, beginning with analyzing transactions and concluding with the preparation of the post-closing trial balance. This conventional definition of tasks in the accounting cycle originated in a manual environment. In a computerized environment, the same tasks are performed within the four steps of the data processing cycle. These four steps are data collection, data classification, data maintenance, and report generation.

Data may be stored on magnetic tapes, discs, or drums, just as it would be stored manually in paper files and filing cabinets. Regardless of the storage medium, the essential factor is the organization of the data. A hierarchical structure organizes data into separate files of related data, within each file into separate records, and within each record into separate fields.

Because different departments may rely on the same data items, data file structures can inhibit the most efficient utilization of data within the organization. One way to overcome this problem is the use of a data dictionary to identify the various uses of data and to promote uniform definitions of the same data items.

When organizations recognize the multiple uses of data, data sharing becomes a realistic and highly desirable possibility. A data base approach facilitates the collection of inter-related data into subject data bases, minimizes redundant data, allows physical storage independence, provides the capability for quick recovery from an error situation, and formalizes the necessary security precautions.

Chapter Note

1. AAA Committee to Prepare a Statement of Basic Accounting Theory, *A Statement of Basic Accounting Theory* (Evanston, IL: American Accounting Association, 1966), p. 64.

CHAPTER 3

Cycles of Insurance Activity: Premiums, Losses, Reserves, and Reinsurance

INTRODUCTION

One approach to analyzing the web of transactions, systems, processing procedures, interfaces, and data bases in an insurance information system is to separate them into a limited number of logical cycles. The definition of each cycle stems from the objectives accomplished within that cycle. This chapter and the one that follows describe the logical cycles of activities within an insurance company.[1] They are:

- premiums,
- claims service and loss and loss expense reporting,
- reserve reporting,
- reinsurance,
- treasury,
- investment,
- payroll expenses, and
- purchasing.

Another cycle, financial reporting, also exists in an insurance company. Unlike the others, this cycle usually does not process transactions but reports results of processing to the various levels of management, investors, and regulatory bodies.

In addition to processing transactions, the cycles usually exercise physical control over the insurance company's assets. For example, the treasury cycle is responsible for cash and cash items, while the investment cycle covers securities.

Each cycle includes one or more functions. A *function* is a major processing task or an element of an insurance information system that processes logically related transactions. Although each insurance company's functions are unique, every company must perform the functions identified within each cycle. With the exception of financial planning and control, which consists of management's supervision, control, and review of the cycles, every function involved in processing transactions or preparing financial statements can be identified within the eight cycles described here. This cycle concept focuses attention on the flow of data through the system rather than on the effect of transactions on particular static accounts. This focus emphasizes the interrelations of the various cycles and reveals the impact of a single event on many elements of an insurance information system.[2]

This description of insurance activity cycles is not intended to typify normal organizational arrangements. Companies frequently establish separate organizational units to perform functions integral to a particular cycle. However, the function performed, not the department performing it, determines the cycle to which it belongs.

PREMIUM CYCLE

Typical activities within the premium cycle include policy underwriting and issue, billing, cash receipts, maintenance of policy master file data and, depending on the company, commission accounting. This cycle also encompasses the agents' balance (premiums receivable) function. The premium cycle is a company's prime source of funds and includes the master file maintenance function, which is of particular importance to the accurate and efficient operation of an insurance company. Internal control objectives for an insurance company premium cycle are:

- producing accurate quotes and, when the coverage is written, capturing all the necessary information for proper rating;
- processing the policy and the reinsurance;
- establishing the proper premium entry in the appropriate receivable file; and
- collection.

Functions

Typical functions of the premium cycle are quoting and rating, policy processing, premium processing, cash receipts, master file maintenance, and journal preparation.

Quoting and Rating The rates charged by an insurance company provide for four basic components; (1) acquisition costs, (2) general overhead, (3) loss and loss adjusting costs, and (4) profit. The *rate* is the unit of measure on which the insurance price or *premium* is based. Just as commodity prices are quoted in terms of cost per pound, per dozen, or per quart, insurance prices or rates are quoted in terms of cost per unit, depending on the kind of coverage.

Ratemaking is a complex process. Costs need to be developed separately for the many different types of insurance coverages because a different policy form is used and a different rate charged for each type of insurance. Rates are further broken down to recognize characteristics of a state or rating territory where the exposure to losses could be materially different.

A company may determine rates based on its own statistical files of accumulated expenses, or it may pool its costs and experience with that of other companies to arrive at an average cost in each territory. Companies may belong to "rating bureaus" where statistics furnished by member companies are compiled and rates calculated based on averages. The bureaus monitor these rates, continuously adjusting them to reflect the most recent experience. Companies may also be bound by rates promulgated by state insurance departments.

Quoting is the act of conveying to the agent or customer the price at which an insurance company is willing to assume the liabilities under a certain insurance policy. That price is determined by *rating* the policy, which means applying the insurer's established rate for each exposure class to the amount of the exposure. The sum of these computations is the *policy premium.*

Policy Processing In the United States, property and liability insurance is often sold through agents or brokers. When the customer and the agent mutually agree on the desired insurance coverage, an application is usually completed specifying the type and the amount of coverage requested. Since rates vary by type of exposure, the application may require additional information to classify or identify the exposure. (For example, type of business would be required on a workers' compensation application and miles driven to and from work on an automobile application). Although agents may have available the rates needed to calculate the premium, usually they must transmit the completed application to the insurance company where rating and underwriting the policy take place.

Underwriting is the evaluation of hazards, selection of acceptable applications and determination of price and conditions coverage. This process assures that the application is complete, that proper rates are used to calculate the premium, and that the character of the application is such that the company wants to assume the risk. For routine exposures, basic underwriting can be done within a computer system using predetermined edit criteria. In the case of more hazardous exposures, a review by specialized personnel maybe necessary.

Once the company has accepted or approved the submission, the agent receives the premium quote. If the premium quote is acceptable to the customer, the agent requests the company to issue the policy. The increasing use of telecommunication links between the agent and the insurance companies often means that premium quotes can be accomplished almost instantaneously.

The policy is a written agreement between an insurance company and the insured describing the insurance protection provided. The policy between the insurer and the customer is called *primary insurance* and gives rise to the insurer's *direct* insurance premiums. In contrast, another insurer's assumption of a portion of the risk under the policies issued by a primary insurer is referred to as *reinsurance*. The consideration paid to the reinsurer represents reinsurance premiums.

Computer systems in insurance company home offices or processing centers issue most policies. Highly advanced policy issuance systems have internally generated rating, statistical coding, and policywriting capabilities. They support all transactions including new business, renewals, endorsements, cancellations, and reinstatement processing. Policies are printed overnight in the home office or processing center and mailed directly to the customer or to the agent for delivery to the customer. Policies may also be printed in agents' offices via an online terminal system linked to an insurance company's data processing system. A company may have one or more policy issuance systems, depending on the types and variety of business written. In a small company or when a nonstandard policy is required, policies may still be prepared manually.

Premium Processing Premium processing differs depending on whether the premiums are for primary insurance, for reinsurance, or for syndicates, pools, or associations. Within these broad groupings, further distinctions can be made depending on the practices chosen by a particular company.

Primary Insurance Premiums. When a company bills the premium charge directly to the insured, it is called *direct billing*. The customer is required to remit payment directly to the company by a specified date if coverage is to remain in force. If a commission allowance is due to an agent, the payments applicable to the agent's account or sales number are accumulated and accounted for in a periodic commission statement mailed to the agent, normally with a check attached. The direct billed approach is common on personal lines business such as automobile and homeowners where high volume makes computer-issued policies and bills cost effective.

In contrast, since commercial lines business requires more agency involvement in structuring of coverages and price negotiations, a large portion of this business is billed to the agent. When dealing directly with an agent, premiums are normally received in one of three ways. A broker may remit on an *item* basis. An agent may remit using his or her own *account current* submitted to the company or on the basis of a statement prepared by the company and mailed to the agent. In all three of these arrangements the agent or broker collects the appropriate premium from each insured, deducts commissions due for writing and servicing the business, and remits the net amount due to the company. The commission allowance retained by the agent is the result of a specific agreement with the insurance company and may vary on different types of insurance. The agent is expected to remit for all policies due within a specified credit period, normally thirty to sixty days, or to cancel the policies for nonpayment. If the agent or broker fails to collect the premium from the customer and does not cancel on a timely basis, he or she becomes responsible for that part of the premium which has been earned during the period the policy was in force.

It is important to note that the insurance company's liability begins the day the contract is effective, often before the policy is issued. If an agent does not collect the premium, and the policy has not been canceled, the company would be liable for a loss that occurred even though it had received none of the premium.

Premiums may be subject to financing via a finance arrangement with an outside third party or through a company installment or finance plan. Where a financing arrangement involves an outside third party, no special accounting entries are necessary, but in the event of cancellation, the return is owed to the finance company. When the insurer does the financing, the finance premium must be transferred from "premiums in process of collection" to "premiums billed but deferred" or to "premiums receivable taken for premiums." Under a company finance plan or installment arrangement, premiums normally are reported and paid based on the provisions of the financing arrangement.

Reinsurance Premiums. Reinsurance premiums represent the consideration due the reinsurer for accepting liability on either an individual risk (facultative) or under a treaty relationship covering a class or type of exposure. Premiums may be determined in several ways—a percentage of the subject base premium, a flat rate, or a preliminary rate subject to adjustment based on loss experience. A primary company normally would remit to the reinsurer on either an item or an account current basis. Agreed-to credit terms would govern the actual payment due dates.

Premiums from Syndicates, Pools, or Associations. An insurer may develop premium income from membership or participation in underwriting syndicates, pools, and mandated statutory associations. Commonly, statements showing a company's participation are received quarterly with the actual results often on a three- or six-months lag basis. Premiums, losses, and expenses are usually combined in a single statement which accompanies the quarterly accounting. If money is due the insurer, a check accompanies the statement.

Collection No matter where the first accounting entry in an insurance company is recorded, the entry is always the same, debit accounts receivable and credit income. The accounts receivable may be due from agents or from policyholders. The income credit goes to an account known as premiums written, the term used for the amount of dollars charged for the policies issued. The premiums written account really represents deferred income, since the premium is paid for services to be delivered in the future. The following is a typical accounting entry to record a premium transaction:

Dr. Premiums Receivable	$900	
Dr. Commission Expense	$100	
Cr. Premiums Written		$1,000

Adequate internal control systems are essential to monitor the premium and commission recording since this record is the basis for cash receipts.

The collection of premiums billed should be a process separated from the recording of premium transactions. Thus it is usually performed in a cashiers or premium accounting department. The entry to record cash is always a debit to cash for the amount received and a credit to the receivable account which it represents.

Controls over cash are established to prevent defalcations rather than to provide statistical accuracy. Common controls are as follows:

- Individuals responsible for opening mail and depositing cash should not be responsible for maintaining cash receipts records.
- Checks received should be restrictively endorsed early in the processing cycle.
- Cash receipts should be deposited intact, daily.

- Independent validation of deposit slips with cash receipts record.
- Bank statements should be promptly reconciled to company records by an independent control unit.

Companies use a variety of methods to make cash available quickly for investment or operations. As an alternative to centralized or decentralized collections within company offices, insureds or agents are sometimes directed to send payments to a post office box number controlled by a bank. The bank deposits the receipts to the insurer's account, providing the insurance company with payment information accompanying the receipt, or a copy of the check. The company uses this information to post the cash receipts entry in its ledgers or computer file.

When branch offices receive and deposit premium collections locally, usually the depository bank transmits daily all funds in excess of a minimum balance to a centrally located bank. A home office control unit receives notice of the transferred funds and monitors the disposition of the receipts.

A company should make every effort to ensure that remittances are made in accordance with the agreed-to credit terms. If there is earned premium due from an insured or overdue outstanding balances from an agent, every effort should be made to collect these funds. These funds should be aged. Those over ninety days are *not admitted* assets. Outside collection agencies and an attorney should be used if company efforts have failed to obtain results. When all efforts to collect a billed item have failed, the premium receivable should be written off by debiting "return premiums" and crediting the appropriate control and subsidiary "accounts receivable."

Master File Maintenance Selection criteria for premium forecasts, policyholder requirements, policy costs, legal restrictions, economic and underwriting decisions, insurance policy terms, and underwriting standards can all be contained in one or more of the master files interacting within the premium cycle. Data bases containing policyholder information, agency information, and reinsurance companies and standards are some of the more common master files used in this cycle.

Proper master file maintenance insures that the company is writing the type of business authorized by management utilizing the criteria established in the financial planning and control function. Some of the techniques employed to maintain the integrity of the various master files are as follows:

- Documented statements of criteria being utilized.

- Control procedures for adding to, changing, or deleting data from a master file. This would include authorization by supervisory personnel, review and approval of "before" and "after" change reports, and so on.
- Periodic balancing of random access files.
- Limiting access to data contained in on-line computerized data bases through use of passwords, physical control over terminals, or other applicable security measures.
- Validity of checks on critical data fields such as premiums rates.
- Pre-numbered standard forms to control output documents.

Any or all of the following problems can result from lack of proper master file maintenance and control:

- Insurance policies may be sold by unauthorized agents or reinsurance placed with unapproved companies.
- Premiums could be billed to the wrong customer or agent.
- Insurance coverage could be denied to an individual meeting the selection criteria.
- Premium rates may be too high or too low.
- Premium rates may not be in accordance with regulatory guidelines.

Journal Preparation In most insurance companies, journal entries prepared in the revenue cycle are submitted to the financial reporting cycle for review and posting. Written premium data is usually collected at an individual policy level, then summarized by product line and by branch or regional office, and journal entries are prepared from the summarized data. General ledger entries in the premium cycle include the recording of cash, premium adjustments, prepayments or accruals, suspense or unreconciled differences, and agents' balances.

Some of the basic accounting controls which should be in place to ensure the proper and timely recording of journal entries are as follows:

- A written chart of accounts should exist containing a description of each account.
- Changes in the chart of general ledger accounts should be done in a controlled environment utilizing written procedures.
- Written cutoff and closing schedules should exist.
- Supervisors who do not actively participate in the journal voucher preparation should review and approve each entry.
- Period-to-period comparisons of recurring entries should be made.
- A standard general ledger entry register to provide reasonable assurance of all required entries are prepared.

- Validity, checking, and verification of key data fields of each general ledger entry.
- Assignment of an individual to be responsible for each account.
- Budgeting and reporting using same accounts.
- Variance analysis between actual and planned account balances.

If an error is detected requiring an adjustment to premium revenues, related policy master file premium data and current distribution should be accurately and promptly classified, summarized, and reported. If required, adjustments should be made to the proper policyholders' accounts, including policy issued, billings, charges to policy master file data, and premiums collected.

A common adjustment to the premium account is the liquidation of uncollectible accounts. Other adjustments may include advertising allowances to agents, volume rates, or the application of a finance or surcharge for late payments.

Source Documents

Since the premium cycle is the primary revenue source of an insurance company, well designed source documents are essential since they become the basis for the company's interaction with customers, agents, and reinsurance companies, those entities which ultimately remit cash to the insurer. Critical source documents are:

- policy applications,
- actual insurance policies,
- premium notices, and
- reinsurance agreements.

Policy Applications The first step in the process of providing insurance coverage requires completion of a signed policy application. The application is designed to give the company the information it needs to determine the rate or rates to be used in calculating the premium and to decide whether the risk is desirable. This application is usually the company's only source of information about the customer and all required data must be available before a policy can be issued. This document also protects the company in the event of fraud or misstatement of facts by the policyholder.

Insurance Policies The contract between the insured and the company is an insurance policy. The information contained in the policy application may be entered into a computer system, where a series of interacting master files (such as rate tables or underwriting selection criteria) decide on the acceptability of the submission, calculate the premium charge, and ultimately produce a policy with one or more copies.

The policy contains specific contract terms such as the period covered, the name and address of the policyholder, information relating to the producing agent, the company name and address, the premium charged for each type of coverage, and the basic limits of liability. The original policy is sent to the policyholder, a copy to the agent, and one or more copies may be retained by the issuing company. In most larger companies, no policy copy is retained, since the information resides in a policy master file and can be printed out when needed by accounting, underwriting, or claim personnel. Policy issuance also generates various statistical files needed for bureau reporting, financial statement preparation, billings, and issuance of renewal notices and renewal policies.

Premium Notices On agency billed business, the premium notice prepared by the company takes the form of a monthly statement which supplements the policy copy that displays the premium and is forwarded to the agent when the policy is issued or renewed. As indicated previously, this billing information is a by-product of the policy issuance function where the agency information, policyholder name and address, and premium information is generated.

On direct billed business, the billing invoice is generated and mailed directly to the policyholder with a copy to the producing agent. On new business, the initial billing often accompanies the policy.

Regardless of the billing mode, the premium notice contains such information as policy number, producing agent, insured, premium amount, due date, and where the remittance is to be mailed. When the premium notice is in the form of a monthly statement to the producing agent, commission due the agent is displayed.

Reinsurance Agreements A reinsurance agreement is a contract transferring part or all of the risk of loss under policies issued from a primary carrier to another carrier. The company providing reinsurance protection is the reinsuring company or *reinsurer*. The company receiving reinsurance protection is the *ceding company*. A reinsurance agreement may cover a single policy contract or may cover a group of losses exceeding a certain limit specified in advance. The liability retained by the ceding company is known as its *retention*.

Data Bases

The data bases normally affected in the premium cycle include the policy master file, the agents file, the policy statistical file, the premium rate book, the commission rate book, and the application file.

Policy Master File The policy master file is the insurance company's record of who it has insured. This file is created from and updated by transactions flowing from a policy issuance or controlled manual input. It contains all of the key data appearing on the actual insurance policy and is the primary vehicle for recording, storing, and reporting a company's premium activity. Key reports from this master file are:

- in-force policies by producing agency,
- in-force policies by risk, state, branch office, and so on, and
- policy expiration lists.

This valuable file represents the company's inventory of customers complete with addresses and effective and expiration dates of coverages. Security measures should be in place to make certain this information does not become public.

Agents File Since a company has contractual agreements with its agents, it must maintain a file of those currently approved, complete with addresses, types of coverage to be written, and credit terms for payment of balances to the company. This file interacts with billing systems to produce account and commission statements. In addition to agency name, most companies assign a numerical code to each producer and use that identifier in most of their internal systems. This numerical code can then be matched against the master file to generate the actual name and address of the agent.

Policy Statistical Files Insurers are required to file statistical reports of premiums in jurisdictions in which they are licensed to conduct business. These reports are the output of statistical files containing standardized coding from the policy issuance process. Statistical filings may be made through authorized statistical agencies or directly to the state insurance department. The statistical agency or the individual insurer prepares the required reports in sufficient detail to permit relating corresponding premium and loss data.

The level of statistics compiled varies in detail, depending on the line of business and the number of policies for coverage categories within a line of business. Codes exist for the geographic location of insureds, the insurance coverage provided, conditions peculiar to a policy, and any other information required by the applicable statistical plan.

This statistical information on premiums along with related loss data also becomes the basis for line of business reporting in the statutory quarterly and annual statements filed with state insurance departments and the National Association of Insurance Commissioners.

Premium Rate Book Rating bureaus compile statistics furnished by member companies and establish rates based on averages. These rates are established separately for types of coverage. Rates also vary by classifications that recognize characteristics of insureds, including location, that cause the exposure to loss to be materially different. The bureaus provide member companies with premium rate books showing what rates should be used in calculating the policy premium. If the company uses its own experience to produce a statistical base and resulting rates, the company must produce its own premium rate book to be used in the premium calculation process. Most companies store their rates in a computer data base utilizing this information for the policy quoting and issuing process. Since rate changes occur frequently, the rate book must be updated constantly to ensure that the appropriate premium is charged.

Commission Rate Book Producing agents receive commissions for business they produce. Commission rates vary by type of business, new or renewal premiums, volume, and sometimes profitability. The commission arrangement is covered in an "agency agreement" or "contract" issued between the company and the agent. This commission information resides in a master file that identifies the agency, usually by a numerical code. This file is matched against new and renewal policies issued to assign the proper commission.

Application File The application master file contains all of the information furnished by the insured on the initial application submitted to the company and any updated information resulting from endorsements or renewal rating of the policy.

Outputs and Interfaces

The premium cycle produces essential documents and feeds several other activity cycles of an insurance company. Some major outputs of the premium cycle are the policies, endorsements, and bills processed in the cycle. The premium cycle also provides information regarding cash receipts to the treasury cycle. Policy data from the premium cycle also feeds the reserve reporting cycle. General ledger entries and statistical data come from the premium cycle. Finally, management information systems depend on premium information collected during the premium cycle.

Exhibit 3-1 illustrates the essential outputs and interfaces of the premium cycle.

Exhibit 3-1
The Premium Cycle

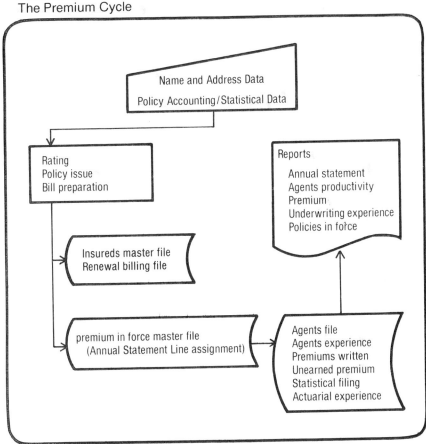

LOSS AND LOSS EXPENSE CYCLE

The major cost of doing business for a property and liability insurance company is loss and loss expense. Thus, management should develop standard procedures to service claims. It is important that these procedures be properly communicated to all claim adjusters and that all claims be processed, handled, and paid in a common manner. The accounting and statistical data that result from these transactions should be timely and accurately recorded so that the company's insurance information system properly reflects the company's activity.

In the underwriting operation of a property/liability insurance company, the revenue for any accounting period is the premiums earned for coverage provided during that accounting period. In order to follow the fundamental accounting principles of matching cost and revenue, claims incurred from that coverage are costs of that period. These costs include not only the dollars of all present and future loss payments on those claims, but also the dollars of expense that will be paid on the adjustment of those claims. The liabilities at the end of an accounting period provide for the cost of losses and loss adjustment expense on claims that have occurred prior to the end of that accounting period that have not been paid. The estimated liabilities for losses and loss adjustment expenses are probably the most important and critical items in the balance sheet because of their relative size and because of the degree of difficulty in achieving acceptable accuracy.

Functions

Typical functions of the loss and loss expense cycle include initial reporting of claims, processing of claims, payment of claims, cash receipts, and establishing loss and loss expense liabilities.

Initial Reporting of Claims The reporting of a claim starts a series of events, initiated when an insured or claimant suffers an economic loss that may be recoverable under a contract of insurance. Loss reporting practices will vary either because of company claim procedures or because of the line of business. Perhaps the most common is for the insured or claimant to contact the agent from whom the policy was purchased. Upon notification of the loss, the agent will complete a notice of loss. The company must have this document to set the claim processing mechanism in motion.

Processing of Claims The establishment of a claim begins when the company receives a notice of loss from the agent, insured, or claimant. Based on the initial information contained in a notice of loss, the claim supervisor determines if the claim can be paid immediately or if additional information is required and a case reserve needs to be established.

After the initial information has been obtained and a claim number assigned, the claim jacket file is established and the claim information entered into the company's claim processing system. Claims should be numbered consecutively so they can be uniquely identified in all of the company's systems. Claim information is entered into a company data base in order to record either the paid or outstanding case reserve accounting and statistical data on the books of the company.

At the same time, claims that require additional investigation, and for which outstanding case reserves have been established, are assigned to claim adjusters. The adjuster has the responsibility to contact the insured, and if applicable, the claimant and witnesses to obtain necessary statements.

Payment of Claims When a case reserve is established on a claim, the draft or check to settle this claim is not issued immediately. After a *property loss* is settled and the amount of the claim is determined, the company may not pay the claim until the home office is contacted and a release is secured from the claimant, subject to the amount of the claim. The obligation of the company is covered by a written contract, the insurance policy; therefore, to protect the company the claim adjuster may have the claimant sign a proof of loss release.

Releases are usually obtained at the time of negotiations with the checks or drafts issued at a later point in the process. Most companies use drafts because of the volume of claims and because claims are not always paid directly by the company. Field adjusters and agents often have authority to make payments on specified types of claims; therefore, payment of claims by checks issued at the home office is not always practical or desirable. In the claim payment process, promptness—the ability to issue a draft immediately—is very important. To expedite claim payments, field adjusters or agents may have drafts in their possession and, where authorized, issue them to the claimant. The company could not stop payment on a check but it incurs no legal liability in rejecting a draft. Since most payments made outside the home office are done by draft, the home office may issue drafts to settle claims, too, so that all claims are handled in a uniform manner.

Insurance companies usually make arrangements with the banks to give them time to review drafts before payment is made. The insurance company uses this review process to protect against forgery or against having an adjuster issue drafts that the company judges to be improper.

Third-party claims occur under liability, compensation, and other casualty coverages that insure the policyholders against liability to third parties. When an accident or other insured event occurs, the injured person becomes a claimant. The event makes the claimant a third party to the insurance contract along with the insurer and the insured.

The initial procedures followed in a third-party claim are essentially the same as for a policyholder's claim with the notice of loss report being completed and forwarded to the company where a claim file is created and an initial case reserve estimate established. Unlike a policyholder's claim the adjuster or claim investigator assesses damages to the third-party, obtains police reports, and tries to obtain the facts surrounding the injury or damages. At some point, the claimant or injured party will make contact with the insurance company demanding payment for damages sustained.

Certain provisions in the liability policy guarantee direct relationships between the third party and the insurance company, even though no prior connection existed. In these claims, the insurance company deals chiefly with the third party, except when it needs the policyholder's assistance in adjusting the claim, mainly as a witness to the accident. Under the policy contract, the insured must cooperate with the company and not jeopardize its rights by any action that might increase the amount of the judgment.

A policyholder's claim is more or less fixed while a third-party liability claim is always subject to discussion. In determining the cost of a third-party claim two questions need to be asked: (1) Is there any liability at all? and (2) What is the extent of the liability if liability does exist?

A claim in the process of adjustment may go to court to be litigated in an effort to determine the company's obligation. Many suits are filed, not always to try issues but to bargain. If the claimant wants an unreasonable amount of money, the company may let the case go to trial. Negotiations may take five minutes or drag on for years, with the final outcome being a paid claim or a "no cause" verdict.

Once the liability has been determined, the damages found, or a judgment rendered, payment is due. As in first-party claims, no payment is made until the adjuster obtains a "release" from every claimant involved in the third-party claim. After the release or releases have been secured, payment is made by draft (or check) and the draft accepted upon presentation just as for the policyholder's claim.

Loss payments may be made on a scheduled, partial, or additional basis prior to the final payment. In order to properly match loss statistics with premium statistics, loss payments require the same coding as premium entries. Loss indemnity payments are generally coded to a specific claim and related to a specific policy. The proper matching of premium and loss statistics is extremely important for ratemaking purposes, underwriting analysis, and the development and use of loss reserve statistics.

In recent years, it has become increasingly common to pay for bodily injury claims with annuities. Future payments are typically funded by purchasing an annuity from a life insurer with such annuity payments made either for the lifetime of the claimant or for a fixed period.

Loss Adjustment Expenses These expenses are those amounts incurred by an insurance company in the total process of settling its losses, as distinguished from loss payments to claimants:

Loss adjustment expenses shall comprise all expenses incurred wholly or partially in connection with the adjustment and recording of policy claims, including the totals of the operating expense classification, Claim Adjustment Services; the type of expenses included in Claim Adjustment Services, when the activities resulting in such types of expenses are performed by employees; and including related expenses incurred in the following activities; estimating amounts of claims, paying and receiving; entering and keeping general and detail records; general clerical, secretarial, office maintenance supervisory and executive duties; handling personnel, supplies, mail, etc.; and all other activities reasonably attributable to the adjustment and recording of policy claims in connection with claims reported, paid and outstanding, and reinsurance thereon.[3]

Circumstances involving each claim vary significantly according to the degree of difficulty in settling a claim, the amount of the claim, and the type of coverage. A property claim is usually adjusted quickly and easily, with a complex liability claim often taking years of litigation to settle. Litigation impacts both loss payment and loss adjustment expenses.

Allocated adjustment expenses are identified with a specific claim number. This expense is usually identified with statistical coding appearing on the related indemnity payment instrument. In most instances, allocated adjustment expenses result from either the billing by independent adjusters for numbered claims or from file costs associated with legal expenses.

Unallocated adjustment expenses are those expenses incurred in the claims handling processes that are not associated with a specific claim file. This includes expenses of both claim and nonclaim departments which directly or indirectly assist in processing claims. Claim department expenses should be identified as claim expense when coded. Nonclaim department expense can be allocated to claim expense on the basis of salaries or special studies.

Just as premium revenue represents the largest source of cash to an insurance company, claim payments represent the largest single outgo of cash. The claim processing and disbursement procedures in an insurance information system should be established and maintained to ensure the following:

- ● Only those claims covered by terms of the policy contract are approved for payment, over the proper deductible or retention.
- ● The existence or nonexistence of reinsurance coverage should be ascertained.
- ● Reinsurers should be properly and promptly charged for their share of loss and loss expenses paid.
- ● Disbursements for claims or claim adjustment expenses should be based on recognized and supported claims.

- Claim adjustment expenses should be accurately prepared and appropriately authorized.
- Claim payments should be accurately applied to the proper claims and promptly reported.
- Recorded balances of paid losses and related accounts should be periodically substantiated and evaluated.

Cash Receipts Certain transactions occur that offset the payment of losses. These offsets should contain the loss and policy statistical data associated with the original transactions so that the net result is properly reflected by state and line of business. These offsets include salvage, subrogation, claim refunds, and reinsurance.

Salvage occurs when the insurance company obtains title to and sells damaged property for its remaining value. Subrogation is common in automobile physical damage claims, where the insurer recovers the claim amount from the third party's insurance company. Claim refunds generally arise from the correction of scheduled payments or the overpayments of advances for such items as living expense. Reinsurance recoveries from reinsurers are contract recoveries, which permits the insurer to spread its risk and protect its surplus.

Loss and Loss Expense Liabilities Losses and loss adjustment expenses incurred are determined by subtracting reserves at the beginning of the accounting period from payments made during the period and adding the reserves at the end of the period. The payments during the period are easy to determine, but reserves (liabilities) are a different matter.

The goal of loss reserving is to establish as accurate a liability as possible. The purpose is to establish, as of a statement date, the liability amount in the form of reserves which are equal to all losses a company would owe if it ceased doing business as of the statement date. Companies develop or select a method of calculating their liability based on the type and level of data they record, their size, the type of business they write, and similar considerations. Some techniques utilized may be simple and some quite sophisticated. Overall, the method employed is not important as long as the result is credible; that is, it is a statistically acceptable measure of outstanding loss liabilities.

The losses paid in an accounting period are usually easy to identify because they are definite in amount and purpose. The real problem with losses is the establishment of proper reserves so that current period income and expenses are matched. Four types of reserves are used in dealing with this problem (see Exhibit 3-2). These reserves are case loss reserves, bulk reserves, in-suit reserves, and supplemental reserves.

Case Loss Reserves. Case reserves are reserves established by claim number through data obtained from the loss reports and the

Exhibit 3-2
Loss Transactions

Payment	Reserves	Off-Sets
Check	Case	Salvage
Draft	Bulk	Subrogation
	Incurred but not	Refunds
	Reported	Reinsurance
	Catastrophe	
	Quick Payments	
	In Suit	
	Supplemental	

policy file. Case reserving practices vary among companies, with the two major differences being claim philosophy and type of accounting/statistical system.

Bulk Reserves. Loss reserves that are not established on a claim number basis are identified as bulk reserves. In most property/liability insurance companies, a number of claim reserve situations may be handled with bulk reserves. Most bulk reserves are provided for in the incurred but not reported (IBNR) statistical base.

Unreported Losses. Losses not reported are those claims which have occurred prior to the company's balance sheet date but which are not yet recorded by the company. At the time of financial statement preparation, such unreported losses are considered incurred but not reported (IBNR), and are valued by estimates. Various statistical methods are used to estimate IBNR loss reserves.

Quick Payment Claims. Due to the expense of establishing case reserves and the problem of properly matching reserves and payment data, the use of bulk reserves is being expanded. Some companies are bulk reserving all claims of $25,000 or less that are likely to be settled within sixty days. These liability amounts are used to provide reserves for quick claim payments regardless of the type of coverage.

Catastrophe Situations. Some companies may also use a quick payment technique to pay catastrophe occurrence damage that results in large numbers of claims. The amount of each catastrophe involvement will be bulk reserved as a separate estimate by state and coverage. As payments are made, the reserve is adjusted to reflect the estimated amount of the catastrophe occurrence. A time limit is usually established for such handling of catastrophe reserves and after a specified number of days, the open claims are case reserved.

In-Suit Reserves. All claims inventories will contain certain claims that are "in suit" or litigation. An indicator may be provided in the outstanding claim record to indicate the in-suit status of a claim. Using this information, some companies will maintain a suit count and a single in-suit liability amount, while other companies maintain a reserve for each in-suit claim and do not average in-suit claim amounts because some claims are very large.

Supplemental Reserve. Supplemental reserves are used in relation to either case reserves or incurred but not reported reserves. These bulk reserves are used when statistical analysis indicates that the ultimate development of the original reserve will be deficient.

Loss Adjustment Expense. Allocated loss adjustment expense reserves should be established for outstanding case reserves, bulk, in-suit, and supplemental. These reserves are usually determined by applying factors developed from experience to the loss reserves, usually by annual statement lines of business.

A similar technique is used to provide a reserve for unallocated loss adjustment expenses. Factors developed from a historical statistical base are applied separately to the outstanding loss reserve and incurred but not reported losses.

Source Documents

Source documents are vital in the processing of loss and loss expense because of the legal aspects of claim handling and the need to substantiate the transactions in the cycle. (See Exhibit 3-3.)

Source documents associated with the insurance information system loss and loss expense cycle include loss notices, claim jacket files, claim coverage forms, proofs of loss, payment authorization forms, claim offset and correction memos, and reinsurance worksheets.

Notice of Loss The notice of loss is completed by the agent when the insured or claimant gives notification of the loss. It should contain the information needed to begin adjusting the claim. A typical notice of loss contains such information as (1) the name of the policyholder and policy number so that coverage can be verified; (2) a description of the property or place of loss; and (3) the nature of the loss, including an estimate of the extent of the loss and the circumstances surrounding the loss.

Claim Jacket File Upon receipt of the notice of loss, the company should assign a claim number to the claim and establish a claim jacket file. This file will include diagrams, pictures, police reports, medical reports and bills, lost wage statements, repair estimates, and any other information that will have a bearing on the claim settlement.

Exhibit 3-3
Source Documents Flow

Claimant	Agent	Compay	Adjuster
Step 1 Claim	Notice of Loss	Claim Review Claim Jacket File Claim Coverage Form	
Step 2 Claim Adjustment			Claim Assignment Claim Adjustment Proof of Loss Draft Payment

Step 3 Claim Payment		Check Payment
		Payment Authorization
		  Form
		
		Claim Offset and
		  Correction Memo†
		Reinsurance Worksheet†	

†May be initiated upon claim review.

After the claim is settled, the claim jacket file may also contain a copy of the check or draft, any releases which the insured or claimant signed, and the documents used in the processing of the claim. In addition, the claim jacket file may also contain a loss history of the claim settlement. The loss history is a diary of the claim handling events along with a record of the payments rendered.

Claim Coverage Form At the time the claim jacket file is established, the policy coverage under which the claim demand is being made must be reviewed. This claim coverage confirmation may be made either manually from the policy file (daily report) or from a policy master computer file. In order to facilitate further handling, a claim coverage form is typed or computer printed and included in the claim jacket file. The claim coverage form will contain the insured information, policy coverage information, and serve as the data entry source for claim number and the other claim information the company deems necessary.

Proof of Loss After the adjuster has determined the amount due the claimant and the claimant agrees on the amount to be paid, a proof of loss statement may be obtained. The proof of loss is a sworn statement indicating that the claimant is the owner of the property, is covered by insurance, has sustained a loss of a specified amount, and discharges the company upon the payment of the stated amount from further liability in connection with this claim. After the proof of loss has been obtained, the payment mechanism is set in motion. In the case of third-party liability claims, the adjuster obtains a "release" from every claimant involved in the third-party claim. The release is signed by the third party, indicating that the company is released from all further liability.

Payment Authorization Form Losses are paid with either a check or draft. The claim payment authorization form is used in conjunction with the issuance of a loss check. The form will contain sufficient accounting and statistical information to permit issuance of the check, entry of necessary data, and approval by the adjuster.

Claim Offset and Correction Memo Under any system, a certain number of entries are required to maintain the system, to handle miscellaneous entries, or to correct error situations. These entries need to be documented so that good control is maintained. The larger a system, the greater the number of these types of transactions, and the greater the need for good control and proper documentation. In order to achieve this documentation, it is essential that a uniform method of initiating these entries be established. A uniform system of control and proper documentation can be established with the use of a form such as the claim offset and correction memo. The memo may be a multi-purpose form, used primarily to provide the data input operation for adding, changing, or deleting reserves, for correcting the coding of payments, and for entering claim offsets such as refunds, salvage, or subrogation. In addition to providing documentation and control, a copy of the memo may be retained by the accounting function to provide an audit trail of entries.

Reinsurance Worksheet The method of determining the impact of reinsurance recoveries on loss and loss expense will vary by company. As soon as practical the company should verify the existence or nonexistence of reinsurance. Estimated reinsurance recoveries on outstanding claims should be accurately classified and summarized. Reinsurers should be properly charged for their share of loss and loss expense paid, and such recoverable amounts should be accurately and promptly reported. As these entries are identified, either the claim offset and correction memo or a reinsurance worksheet, should be prepared to collect and input the required accounting and statistical data. Insurance companies use reinsurance to reduce exposure in certain lines of business. The reinsurance contracts serve no purpose if a company does not detect ceded losses and make the appropriate recoveries.

Data Bases

The records and files that might be maintained in performing the loss and loss expense cycle include both conventional accounting registers and computerized source of nonredundant and interrelated data readily available for use as the input to the user's application programs.

Claim Registers for Reported Claims   A claim register is a recording of a claim transaction received by an insurance company. The register can be either manually posted or computer produced. The register can be either a separate company record or in combination with another record, such as the cash disbursed journal or claim draft journal. If there are large volumes of claims, separate registers may be prepared by type of transaction, such as the outstanding claim register, claim register of refund and salvage, or the claim correction register. The register may contain claim number, policy number, loss date, cause of loss, and amount. Registers are usually prepared daily and maintained as a part of the insurance company's accounting information system.

Policy Master File   Depending on the company, the policy master file ranges from a skeleton policyholder name/coverage file to complex computer data base systems. The primary purpose of the file is to provide detailed policyholder and statistical data regarding current policies-in-force for use in policyholder service activities. The policy master file is a shared data file that is used in loss and loss adjustment expense processing to confirm coverage. In addition, the policy master file may contain a loss history that indicates the claims incurred on the file by recording the claim number, date of loss, type of claim, and amount.

Claim Master File   The claim master file, a working file of current claim activity, contains current open reserves, payment activity, reinsurance recoveries, and miscellaneous claim diary and management information. (The individual claim activity is contained in the claim jacket file.) As with other systems, the claim master file will vary in design from simple claim activity calendar systems to interactive claims data base systems. The claim reserve and payment entries usually are processed daily from the registers and journals to the claim master file to update the reserve data. Periodically, the reserve and paid data from the claim master file will be processed in the statistical summary data system to accumulate summary loss reserve and paid data by coverage.

Reinsurance recoveries may be identified and processed manually or through computer applications. If pro-rata reinsurance contracts exist, the reinsurer shares with the writing company in all premium and loss activity at a set percentage. In other contracts, the reinsurer participates in losses only on those policies in which premium was ceded. In these instances, a file of reinsurance ceded policies may be built; then monthly, the paid loss data processed through the claim master file is matched to the reinsurance ceded file to identify reinsurance recoveries.

Subrogation and salvage recoveries are an important offset to many property/liability insurance companies. Through the use of special codes, payment entries to the claim master file can be used to build subrogation and salvage recovery inventory records. As the recoveries are made, the inventory is adjusted to provide current status. The inventory may also be used to followup on items not collected on schedule.

Exhibit 3-4 summarizes the transactions, functions, source documents, data bases, and major accounts typical to the loss and loss expense cycle.

System Interfaces

In a computerized system, the interface medium is generally a file shared by several programs or a file that contains output from one system that can be used as input to another system. In a real-time system, the interface may be achieved within computer memory. For example, loss payments may cause the loss reserve, cash disbursement, and reinsurance programs to operate simultaneously without the transfer of a file. In a manual system, the sending of a document from one department to another is an interface.

Systems used to process loss and loss expense cycle transactions interface with systems identified with other cycles. The interaction of some of these interfaces is discussed below.

Policy Information and Reinsurance Activity from the Claim Master File to the Premium Cycle Typical activities in the premium cycle include policy underwriting, billing, cash receipts, and maintenance of policy master file data. Transactions created in the loss and loss expense cycle are vital in updating the current loss history experience, which indicates to the underwriter possible claim frequency or underwriting guidelines that are being exceeded. Based on this information, the underwriter may want to re-underwrite and determine

Exhibit 3-4
Loss and Loss Expense Cycle

Transactions	Claim Payments
	Reserves
	Salvage/Subrogation/Refunds
	Reinsurance
Functions	Claim Reporting, Processing and Payment
	Reserves
	Disbursements
	Cash Receipts
Source Documents	Notice of Loss
	Claim Jacket File
	Claim Coverage Form
	Proof of Loss
	Payment Authorization Form
	Claim Offset and Correction Memo
	Reinsurance Worksheet
Data Bases	Claim Registers
	Policy Master File
	Claim Master File
Major Accounts	Reserves
	Disbursements
	Cash Receipts

if the insured currently meets underwriting standards. The claim data on the policy master file includes a loss history, indicating claim number, date of loss, cause of loss, and amount of claim. In order to determine the policyholder's claim-reporting patterns, the closed-with-out-payment claim records should also be used to update policy master file.

Cash Disbursements to the Treasury Cycle An insurance company's treasury cycle includes functions concerned with the short and long-term planning of the company's sources and uses of funds. The largest single source of cost to an insurance company is the loss and loss expense function. As payments are made for loss and loss expenses, it is critical that the treasury function be notified of these disbursements. Some insurance companies make cash availability projections to plan the cash needs for operations and determine the funds that may be available for investment. The amount of cash needed to pay loss and loss expense has a great impact upon the priorities established by the treasury cycle. Due to the urgency of the disbursement information, the data needs to be available daily and perhaps, at certain times, even more frequently.

Cash Receipts from Claim Offsets to the Treasury Cycle Claim offsets result from the sale or salvage, subrogation, claim refunds on advances, and reinsurance recoveries. These cash receipts, particularly subrogation and reinsurance recoveries, can result in significant amounts of cash flow. When cash availability projections are made, claim offsets need to be considered. The information that results from entries to the claim master file should be provided to the treasury cycle on a daily basis.

General Ledger Entries to the Financial Reporting Cycle On a daily basis, general ledger entries for loss and loss expense items may be processed to the general ledger system. General ledger entries which reflect either individual transactions or summaries of similar transactions are received by the financial reporting cycle from the loss and loss expense transactional processing cycle and posted to the general ledger. General ledger accounts are reconciled to supporting loss and loss expense cycle information, analyzed, and adjusted when appropriate. The reports produced by this cycle may serve as either controls or as sources for general ledger entries. The loss and loss expense cycle transactions should flow to the financial reporting cycle as an integral part of loss processing.

Exhibit 3-5 illustrates the flow of loss and loss expense information in insurance operations.

RESERVE REPORTING CYCLE

The reserve reporting cycle activity is reflected in the liability section of the property and liability insurance company balance sheet. The company's financial progress is measured on an earned premium/incurred expense basis. This basis of accounting recognizes a matching of the earning of premium for service provided with the expenses that are chargeable to this accounting period. This matching establishes the proper picture of financial condition and the operating results of the accounting period.

Approximately 90 percent of the total liabilities of a property and liability insurance company consist of the unearned premium and loss and loss expense reserves. These liabilities are critical elements of an insurance company's condition and a knowledge of these reserves is a key factor in understanding statutory insurance accounting. Statutory insurance accounting requires the recognition of the conditional nature of insurance contracts. The primary consideration in insurance account-

Exhibit 3-5
Loss and Loss Expense Flow

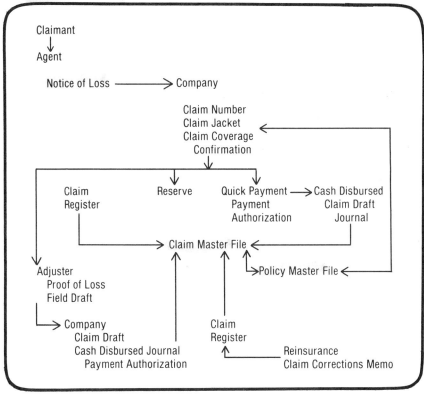

ing is to provide for the possible eventual obligations to the policyholders.

Property and liability insurance companies are required to establish liabilities for unearned premium, loss and loss expenses, and certain other liabilities. In addition, liabilities are usually established for taxes, underwriting expense, and other categories listed on Page 3 of the NAIC Annual Statement Blank. Depending on the accounting/statistical system used by an insurance company, the recognition of liabilities as ledger entries varies. Some liabilities, such as unearned premium, are determined from summary statistical files and the reserve amount may be entered directly to the financial statement. In these cases, the transaction is referred to as a nonledger liability. In other insurance companies, all transactions may be entered to the company's books and become a part of the insurance information system.

After the current period liabilities are determined, the change in the liability amounts for those liabilities affecting the operating results will be reflected in the insurance information system. These liability amounts for the unearned premium, loss and loss expense, and perhaps several other reserves will be determined from a summary data file with the detail required by the insurance information system.

Functions

The functions of the reserve reporting cycle include identification of liability requirements, selection of acceptable raw data, selection of the approved method of determining liability, and calculation of reserves.

Identification of Liability Requirements The identification of liability requirements is more a financial management matter than an insurance operations subject. The establishment of proper reserves is very important in the earning of premium and the incurring of expense. However, the primary emphasis on these reserve determinations is to find a method that effectively protects the interests of the policyholders and claimants by adequately restricting available surplus. Once acceptable methods of determining the liabilities to protect policyholders and claimants are established, then the effect of change in the liabilities during the accounting period can be reflected in the operation results. In addition to liabilities to protect the policyholders and claimants, normal business liabilities are established for such transactions as taxes, underwriting expense, and other liabilities.

In property and liability insurance companies, the NAIC Statutory Annual Statement requires the liabilities shown in Exhibit 3-6.

Selection of Acceptable Raw Data As shown in Exhibit 3-6, a number of liabilities are required for property and liability insurance companies. The five liabilities of loss, loss adjustment expense, other expenses, taxes, licenses, and fees, and unearned premiums will be covered here. The discussion is limited to these five areas because: (1) these are the majority of the liabilities included in operating results; (2) these liabilities can be supported by data base applications; and (3) the accounting and statistical data that result from these transactions may be used in the company's insurance information system.

For each of these five categories, there are certain criteria for selecting acceptable raw data.

Losses. The liabilities for loss-related amounts are either known individual case-related files or bulk amounts based on statistical/actuarial projections. Bulk reserves are also used for incurred but not reported losses. Companies view IBNR reserves in one of two ways:

Exhibit 3-6
Liabilities

*1. Losses

*2. Loss adjustment expenses

3. Contingent commissions and other similar charges

*4. Other expenses (excluding taxes, licenses and fees)

*5. Taxes, licenses and fees (excluding federal and foreign income taxes)

6. Federal and foreign income taxes (excluding deferred taxes)

7. Federal Income Tax Deferred

8. Borrowed money

9. Interest, including $_____ on borrowed money

*10. Unearned premiums

11. Dividends declared and unpaid:

(a) Stockholders

(b) Policyholders

12. Funds held by company under reinsurance treaties

13. Amounts withheld or retained by company for account of others

14a. Unearned premiums on reinsurance in authorized
companies $_____

b. Reinsurance on paid losses $_____ and on unpaid losses
$_____ due from unauthorized companies $_____

c. Total $_____

15. Less funds held or retained by company for account of
such unauthorized companies as per Schedule F, Part 2,
Column 6 $_____

16. Excess of statutory reserves over statement reserves

17. Net adjustments in assets and liabilities due to foreign exchange
rates

18. Ceded Reinsurance Balances Payable

19. Drafts outstanding

20. Payable to affiliates

21. Payable for securities

22. Other Liabilities

23. Total liabilities (Items 1 through 22)

1. A reserve for all incurred claims not recorded on the books ("pure" IBNR reserve).
2. A reserve for all incurred claims not recorded on the books, plus a reserve for deficiencies in case basis or pending reserves ("residual" IBNR reserve).

Both premium and loss data are used extensively as exposure bases for making IBNR loss reserve estimations. Most companies select either premiums or losses as the exposure bases, to the exclusion of the other; few compute and compare IBNR reserves using both exposure bases.

Loss Adjustment Expenses (LAE). Loss adjustment expenses reserves are directly related to loss reserve data. Many companies establish case reserves for allocated loss adjustment expenses. Most using case reserves for allocated loss adjustment expense (ALAE) supplement their loss reserves either through supplemental reserve provisions or with residual IBNR reserve provisions.

Other Expenses. Other expenses are those business expenses not covered in specific categories such as loss adjustment expenses, commissions, or taxes. The other-expense reserve is an annual statement statutory accounting reserve covering unpaid salary, rent, equipment, utilities, travel, and supplies. The data is determined from employee payroll records and unpaid invoice billings.

Taxes, Licenses and Fees. Taxes, licenses and fees are reserves for state and local tax obligations. The majority of the liability is composed of state premium taxes, fire marshal tax, fireman's relief, and policeman's relief. The reserve for licenses and fees includes privilege licenses and filing fees. Most insurance taxes are based on the premium written during the period, while license and fees are established by regulatory authorities.

Unearned Premium Reserve. Unearned premium for a policy is the premium applicable to the unexpired period of the policy. The unearned premium reserve is the sum of all the premiums representing the unexpired portions of the policies which the insurer or re-insurer has on the books as of the statement date. The unearned premium reserve is based on the premium for all policies which a company has in force. In-force premiums are the full-term premiums on all policies not yet expired. Unearned premiums represent the amount that would be due to the policyholders if all policies in force were canceled at a given reporting date.

Selection of Approved Method of Determining Liability

Guidelines for the determination of all statutory accounting reserves are established by the NAIC and by state and federal taxing authorities. Standards for the determination of approved method of reserving depend on the category.

Losses. Loss reserves, the largest and most complex of all reserves, are required by statutory accounting and are needed in the matching of income and expense. Statutory reserve minimums, also required for certain lines of business, are determined by the insurer and established in Schedule P, Part 1 and Schedule K of the Annual Statement Blank. The theory of the Schedule P formula is that, until loss experience has matured, the nonproperty case reserves determined by the company may not be completely reliable and should therefore at least equal a minimum ratio. In addition, some states have special reserve requirements. New York, for example, requires a reserve of 5 percent of the amount of surety premiums in force and 10 percent of fidelity premiums in force.

In selecting an acceptable loss reserve method, the impact of the zero tolerance allowed by the Internal Revenue Service when developing the ultimate cost of loss reserves is also an important consideration. Finally, due to the complex nature of the reserve and the importance of reserves in financial management, executive management judgment plays an important role in establishing the final reserve amounts. Although several departments provide input used in establishing loss reserves, many companies have formed loss reserve committees to centralize the general reserving responsibilities.

Loss Adjustment Expense. The general standards for loss adjustment expense will follow those for loss reserves. However, loss expense reserves usually have independent development patterns which should be recognized when reserves are established.

Other Expenses. Other expenses are reserved principally for the purpose of matching earnings and expenses. Statutory accounting of other expenses also requires the identification and reserving of the items for the annual statement. Except for salaries, which can be determined from payroll records, the establishment of guidelines for reserving other expense is a management responsibility.

Taxes, Licenses and Fees. Like other expenses, these items are reserved for the purpose of matching earnings and expenses and for statutory annual statement purposes. Taxes, licenses and fees are simple to identify and the basic nature of the subject identifies the items to be included in the reserve.

Unearned Premium Reserve. The unearned premium reserve concept deals with the recognition of revenue over the period of time for which a policy is in-force. In addition, state insurance laws require each insurer to establish a reserve equal to the company's unearned premium. For instance, present New York state law clearly states the statutory requirement for unearned premium reserves in Section 74 of its insurance code, entitled "Unearned Premium Reserve." In addition, insurance regulations generally indicate the method that must be followed in calculating the unearned premium reserve.

Calculation of Reserves After the proper base data is identified and guidelines for reserve calculation established, the reserves can be calculated. Reserves may be calculated in a number of ways.

Losses. Loss reserves are determined for case or pending claims and IBNR reserves.

Pending Reserves. Pending reserves are established by claim using actual reported amounts or using average minimum amounts. Average reserving systems generally relieve the examiner from establishing exact reserves until sufficient factual information is available and also avoid establishing exact reserves on property losses that settle rapidly and for which the range of exposure is relatively narrow.

IBNR. Incurred but not reported reserves may be developed in any number of ways. Some of the most common are based on:

- the number of claims reported—extended by an average severity,
- prior relationships of developed IBNR to premiums or policies-in-force,
- prior relationships of developed IBNR to premiums earned, and
- prior relationships of developed IBNR to paid, incurred, or outstanding losses.

Loss Adjustment Expense (LAE). Loss adjustment expense reserves may be determined for various categories of losses such as allocated LAE, incurred but not reported LAE, unallocated LAE, catastrophe LAE, or in-suit LAE. Loss adjustment expense can also be allocated by type of adjuster, such as company adjuster, agent, or independent adjuster. Regardless of the category or type of adjuster, loss adjustment expense reserves are usually calculated by applying a factor to the loss indemnity data.

Alternative methods used to provide allocated LAE are:

- Calculate ratio of paid ALAE to paid losses to apply to unpaid reserves.
- Calculate ratio of paid ALAE to paid losses, giving recognition to the increase in the ratio that occurs as claims become older.

Other Expenses. Other expenses are determined by reviewing the status of unpaid bills at the end of the accounting period. This review may be of actual unpaid invoices on hand or a review of purchase orders for items ordered but not yet received or invoiced. The reserve

Exhibit 3-7
Unearned Premium Reserve

	Premium In-Force	Pro-Rata Factor	Unearned Percentage	Unearned Premium
January	100.00	11/12	91.67	$91.67
February	100.00	9/12	75.00	$75.00
March	100.00	7/12	58.33	$58.33
April	100.00	5/12	41.67	$41.67
May	100.00	3/12	25.00	$25.00
June	100.00	1/12	8.33	$ 8.33
July	Expired		.00	.00

support may be an accumulation of items listed on an accounting worksheet.

Taxes, Licenses and Fees. This reserve may be estimated by applying the known tax rates to written premium. Most insurance taxes are based on the direct written premium amounts appearing on Page 14 of the Annual Statement. The system for calculating premium tax can be either manual or computer-based. Regardless of the system used, it is important to recognize pre-payments of premium tax and any of the various applicable credits such as dividends, guarantee fund offsets, and fire marshal credits.

Unearned Premium Reserve. The unearned premium reserve is determined by computing the reserve from the premium-in-force data using a pro-rata factor method. Pro-rata factors may be annual, semi-monthly, or daily. The most commonly used method is the semi-monthly method, which assumes that all policies written in a particular month are effective on the fifteenth, as shown in Exhibit 3-7.

Source Documents

Source documents of original entries are not as critical to the reserve reporting cycle as to other cycles. Once the criteria for the reserves are established, the processing of data is often a function of computer applications. Some source documents may be as follows:

Loss Factor Tables   The factors developed for the calculation of IBNR reserves should be developed on a standard worksheet and retained as a part of company accounting records.

Loss Adjustment Expense Factor Tables   Factor Tables may be developed by category of reserve, type of adjuster, and line of business. These factors should be developed on a standard worksheet and retained as a part of company accounting records.

Other Expenses   Other expenses are determined from payroll records, if salary is not paid through month-end, and from unpaid invoice or open purchase orders. The invoices and purchase orders serve as source documents in other systems, so the other-expense reserve amounts should be documented on a standard worksheet and retained as a part of company accounting records.

Taxes, Licenses and Fees   Tax rates applied to the direct written premium may have to be obtained from the various tax forms. The various license and fee amounts should be obtained from the same sources. These rates and license and fee amounts should be posted to a standard worksheet and retained as a part of company accounting records.

Unearned Premium Reserve   The pro-rata factors used in the unearned premium calculations should be posted on a standard worksheet and retained as a part of company accounting records.

Data Bases

The data bases for reserve information, with the exception of other expenses, are accounting and statistical computer files. These insurance information system data bases serve as the source of information for the required calculations and may also serve as the file for the computed reserves.

Claim History Master File   The loss and loss adjustment expense reserves will be determined from data on the claim history master file. A claim history master file is usually a summary file that contains the company's paid and reserve claim related information at the end of an accounting period. The file will contain not only amount but also the supporting statistical data, such as location, annual statement line, coverage, cause of loss, and loss count information.

A claim history master file is usually updated monthly by processing the effect of the current month's claim activity to the prior month-end master file. During this process of updating the master file, work files may be created by extracting the data that is required to process specific applications. In the case of loss and loss adjustment

Exhibit 3-8
Loss and Loss Adjustment Expense Reserve Processing

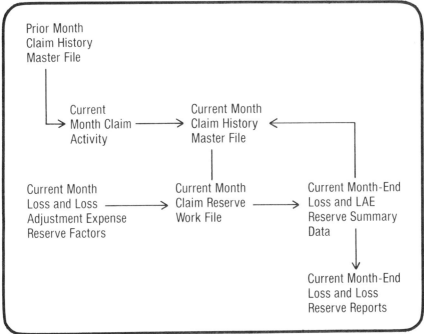

expense reserves, a work file may be created for the data required to determine the reserves. Work files are usually created to reduce the processing time and to maintain an environment for balancing and control. After the appropriate loss and loss adjustment expense factors are applied to the designated data, the master file will be updated to reflect the current month's status of the reserves. (See Exhibit 3-8).

Premium History Master File The premium taxes and unearned premium reserves will be determined from data on the premium history master file. A premium history master file is usually a summary file that contains the company's written, earned, unearned and in-force premium information at the end of an accounting period. The history file will contain not only amount, but also the supporting statistical data such as location, annual statement line, coverage, coverage period, and policy count information.

A premium history master file is usually updated monthly by processing the effect of the current month's premium activity to the prior month-end master file. During this process of updating the master file, work files may be created by extracting the data that is required to process specific applications. In the case of premium taxes and

Exhibit 3-9
Unearned Premium — Premium Tax Reserve Processing

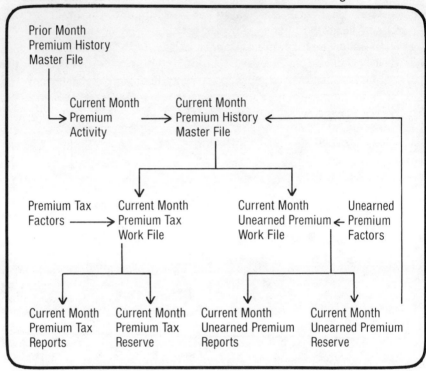

unearned premiums, two work files may be created for the data required for the two distinctly different reserves. Work files are usually created to reduce the processing time and to maintain an environment for balancing and control. In the case of premium taxes, a work file may be used in order to apply the premium tax rate factors to the applicable premium. After the tax amounts are determined, a separate file may be created for use in further processing. With unearned premium, after the appropriate pro-rata reserve factors are applied to the necessary in-force data, the master file will be updated to reflect the current month's status of the reserves (see Exhibit 3-9).

System Interfaces

Reserves are a unique category in insurance accounting systems. Many companies do not enter reserves on the company general ledger and reserves are often referred to as nonledger items. Other companies enter all transactions and do not have nonledger items. Regardless of the ledger transactions, all companies enter written/paid data and the change in reserves to the insurance information system. The written/paid data and the change in reserves provide the input for calculating the earned/incurred relationship and the underwriting results by location reflected in underwriting experience reports.

The reserve cycle interacts with other cycles to obtain raw data used in calculating reserves. The data will be obtained from the premium, loss and loss expense, payroll, and nonpayroll expense cycles.

If any general ledger entries are made for reserve transactions, the entries will flow to the financial reporting cycle. If ledger entries are not made, the reserve transactions will be manual nonledger postings to the financial statements. Nonledger results may be provided in special reports that are produced as output from the reserve computation routines.

REINSURANCE CYCLE

Reinsurance is the act of passing off, by one insurer to another, whole or some part of its exposure to loss. The purposes of reinsurance are:

- to reduce the amount of a loss on either a single risk or on a multitude of risks resulting from a single occurrence;
- to stabilize the underwriting results of the primary insurer by leveling off deviations from normal experience; and
- to protect the company's financial position against a weakening of its surplus by (1) too rapid a growth in premium volume, or (2) an accumulation of adverse results.

Reinsurance programs can be tailored specifically to suit the needs of the primary insurer. In contrast with direct insurance, reinsurance is not subject to the rate regulatory laws of the various states and the reinsurer has flexibility in negotiating commission terms.

Reinsurance is ceded under one of two methods. *Facultative* (specific risk) reinsurance involves a separate contract related to a particular risk or policy. *Treaty* (automatic) reinsurance is written under a comprehensive contract that requires the reinsurer to accept all cessions according to the terms of that contract.

Whether facultative or treaty, reinsurance can take one of two broad forms. With *pro-rata* (or share) reinsurance, the reinsurer shares losses in the same proportion as it shares premiums and policy amounts. Pro-rata reinsurance can be on a *quota share* basis, in which a fixed percentage of every risk is ceded; or on a *surplus share* basis, in which only those risks where the amount of insurance is greater than the retention are ceded.

Under a pro-rata treaty, the reinsurer agrees to accept a specified proportion of the ceding company's premiums and losses with respect to certain risks, or to a particular portion of the ceding company's business, under the specific terms and conditions of the treaty contract. The reinsurer receives a specified proportion of the ceding company's business, under the specific terms and conditions of the treaty contract. The reinsurer receives a specified proportion of the ceding company's gross original premium and agrees to pay a like proportion of every loss and loss expense incurred under the original policies of insurance involved. The reinsurer's premium is reduced by an agreed-on percentage of commission to reimburse the ceding company for its acquisition and overhead costs. The reinsurer also assumes its proportionate share of the unearned premium liability. Thus, the reinsurer's loss experience, as it relates to the business ceded on a pro-rata basis, is in direct proportion to that of the ceding company.

In the other major form of reinsurance, *excess of loss* reinsurance, the reinsurer makes loss payments to the insurer only when the latter's losses exceed a predetermined retention level. Excess reinsurance can be written as excess per loss, catastrophe excess, spread loss cover, and stop loss cover.

Certain combinations of pro-rata and excess of loss covers may be utilized, one supplementing the other, to reduce the loss exposure which one alone might leave.

Functions

The essential functions of the reinsurance cycle are paying the premium due for reinsurance ceded, processing reinsurance recoveries for claims, and reinsurance reporting.

Paying Premium Due for Reinsurance Ceded After the terms of the reinsurance contracts have been negotiated, the transactions necessary to settle the monthly activity must be created. In processing reinsurance premium ceded transactions, it is critical to identify properly the line of business, the coverage, or the policy for which the company is transferring all or part of its liability to another insurance company. Reinsurance premium cessions (see Exhibit 3-10) will vary by type of contract.

Facultative. The premium for the risk amount ceded is usually negotiated by the underwriter with the reinsurer on an individual policy basis. The reinsurance premium due is usually billed by the reinsurer on a policy basis. The ceding company verifies this billing to information

Exhibit 3-10
Reinsurance Premium Cession

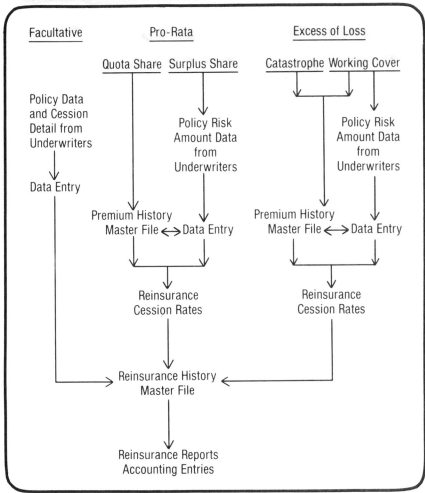

received from the company underwriter. Facultative coverage is usually primary to other reinsurance; that is, it will be processed first when making a premium cession or loss recovery. This fact needs to be considered when ceding automatic pro-rata treaty or excess of loss reinsurance.

Pro-Rata. Quota share cessions are the simplest to compute because a pre-agreed percentage is applied to all premiums. These cessions are usually made by coverage or annual statement line of business. The quota share transactions may or may not be supported with a list (bordereau) of policies involved.

Surplus share requires the identification of policies for the lines of business or coverage subject to the retention limits of the treaty and a factoring of the premium on the ratio of subject risk amount to total risk amount. Policies with limits below the retention or "line limit" are not included in the cession. The surplus share treaty transactions usually are supported with a bordereau listing providing accounting and statistical data. When individual policies are the basis of reinsurance cessions, a reinsurance master file can be built as a data source for premium cessions and claim recoveries.

Excess of Loss. This reinsurance coverage indemnifies the ceding company against all or a portion of the amount in excess of a specific retention. The premium paid for this reinsurance coverage is not a shared percentage of the policyholder premium, but rather a calculated rate determined by the reinsurer for the protection provided. The premium for the coverage can be based either on written premium or earned premium.

The premium due for some contracts, such as catastrophe contracts, may be determined by applying the reinsurance rate factor to written or earned premium by coverage or annual statement line. In some excess working cover contracts, the reinsurance premium calculations will include policy risk amount. As with surplus share pro-rata reinsurance, when individual policy data is used as the basis for working cover excess of loss reinsurance cessions, a reinsurance master file may be created for use as a data source for premium cessions and claim recoveries. If a reinsurance master file is created, all reinsurance transactions may be maintained on the file as a control.

The reinsurance settlement terms and reports will vary among reinsurers. In order to standardize reinsurance reporting, many reinsurers will request the primary company to use model or standard forms when reporting reinsurance transactions ceded.

Processing Reinsurance Recoveries for Claims After cover has been purchased, through the negotiation of a reinsurance contract, the claims subject to reinsurance protection must be recovered. In order to assist in reinsurance recoveries, a computer file of reinsurance ceded records may be maintained on a reinsurance history master file. If a computer application is maintained to identify losses recoverable by matching current month paid and outstanding case reserves to the master file, it is advisable to maintain a follow-up routine on certain types of losses. Reinsurance recovery routines (see Exhibit 3-11) need to identify those claims subject to recovery and may be handled as follows:

Facultative. The use of a reinsurance history master file to recover facultative claims will depend on the flexibility of the master

Exhibit 3-11
Reinsurance Loss Recovery

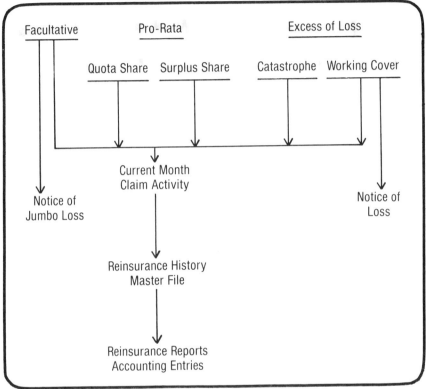

file. If the file contains detailed statistical policy records including the percent of facultative reinsurance, the recovery can be automated. In this case, the recovery reports can be produced along with the follow-up reports that should be sent to underwriting for confirmation of the transaction.

If the master file contains only the policy number for cessions, the current month's claim records containing policy number can be matched to the file to identify recoveries. The necessary policy data may be obtained from the underwriters and the recovery reports prepared manually. In most instances, some form of possible reinsurance recovery reports should be produced from the claim processing flow. These reports can be used for control and audit of reinsurance recovery transaction.

Pro-Rata. Pro-rata treaty recoveries will depend on the type of contract involved. Quota share pro-rata, in which the company and reinsurer share a contracted percentage of all premiums and losses, can be determined merely by applying the percentage to the monthly loss and loss adjustment expense data. When a reinsurance history master file is being used, the quota share loss recoveries may be recorded in summary by location and annual statement line of business rather than in policy number detail. Quota share contracts usually do not require detail matching for loss recovery, and summary data suffices for accounting purposes.

Surplus share contract recoveries may be identified by matching the current month's loss entries to the policies identified as surplus share on the reinsurance history master file. After the loss entries are identified, the cession criterion in the history file records can be applied to the eligible loss records to determine the surplus contract recoveries. After the recoveries are identified, reports can be prepared for use in ledger entries, control and follow-up.

Excess of Loss. Excess of loss recoveries will depend on the type of contract involved. Catastrophe excess of loss recoveries, in which the company usually recovers from the reinsurer for all losses in excess of the catastrophe occurrence limits, can be made by merely calculating the excess amount. When a reinsurance history master file is being used, catastrophe loss recoveries may be recorded in summary by location and annual statement line of business rather than in policy number detail. If more than one annual statement line of business is involved in a catastrophe recovery, the recovery can be assigned on paid data or allocated proportionately to the involved lines of business. Summary data will provide transactions for accounting purposes and the insurance information system.

Working excess of loss contract recoveries can be made by matching the current month's loss entries to the policies identified to the various excess of loss contracts on the reinsurance history master file. If reinsurance recoveries are made on a manual basis, the claim payments will need to be specifically identified by the claim examiner at the time of coverage confirmation. Using a reinsurance history system to select the applicable loss entries, the cession criterion in the history file records can be applied to the eligible loss records to determine the excess loss contract recoveries. It should be mentioned that a wide variety of excess of loss contracts exist and that specific system applications will differ by company. Under most systems, after the recoveries are identified reports can be prepared for use in ledger entries, control and follow-up.

Reinsurance Reporting The accounting and statistical needs of the ceding company and the assuming reinsurer are very similar, although the reinsurer does not usually require the detailed statistical information maintained by the primary company. Facultative reinsurance may be handled by policy, while other reinsurance transactions will be settled by contract. Some reinsurers will provide the primary company a model or standard form to be used in the reporting and settlement of reinsurance. A uniform settlement of reinsurance may include ceded written or earned premium, the applicable unearned premium, reinsurance commission, paid loss and loss adjustment expense, and outstanding loss reserves; accumulated into a net settlement of ceded premium less reinsurance commission and paid loss and loss adjustment expense. Due to the flow of information, reinsurance transactions are usually reported to the reinsurer after the primary company has closed for an accounting period.

In addition to the normal reporting of reinsurance transactions, most reinsurers require notice of large losses and catastrophe involvement upon occurrence of the event. The reinsurance history master file system is able to support the normal reporting of reinsurance transactions, but the claim function should provide notices of unusual losses. The master file may contain sufficient data to provide notice of specific types of claims.

Source Documents

Reinsurance source documents include reinsurance contracts, notices of loss, daily reports, and bordereaux.

Reinsurance Contracts These contracts are the agreements signed between the primary company and the reinsurers. The number of contracts will vary greatly among companies but will provide the legal agreement regarding the cession/assumption of premium, the losses that can be recovered, and other legal arrangements covering the administration of the contract. The contract itself may not be a source which supports ledger entries but will be the primary source of administrative direction. These contracts may also be the main source of information for the system analysis and programming of a reinsurance history master file.

Notice of Loss This form is usually considered a basic claims form but can also be used as a primary loss recovery notification form. The form can be used to provide information for facultative and surplus recoveries and be used to notify the reinsurer when jumbo claims occur on excess loss contracts.

Daily Report The daily report and the accompanying statistical data worksheet may be a source of coverage, location, and risk amount. The policy data may be important in determining the reinsurance to be ceded and in identifying the reinsurance recoveries on the claim confirmation form. The forms useful to the company in handling the insured's claims are usually applicable in processing reinsurance claims because similar information is required.

Bordereaux Bordereaux are lists of either premium or claim transactions involved in reinsurance contract settlements. A bordereau usually contains either the policy or claim identification along with the accompanying accounting and statistical data. The design of the bordereau will vary by reinsurance contract but will routinely serve as backing for reinsurance transactions.

Data Bases

For a computerized reinsurance processing system, data bases closely parallel the premium and loss systems of the primary company because the data needs of the company to process premium and losses and to handle reinsurance transactions are similar. Thus, reinsurance system data bases include the premium history master file, the loss history master file, and the reinsurance history master file.

Premium History Master File The premium history master file will contain sufficient accounting and statistical information to provide data for company needs. The file will generally be a summary file, but during update, sufficient detail may be collected to permit cession of ceded premium for applicable coverages. This file can serve as the basis of cessions when the reinsurance contract does not require detail policy information.

Loss History Master File Either during updating with the current month activity or after the current month update, the loss history master file will contain sufficient accounting and statistical information to initiate loss recoveries. The file will generally be a summary file, but during update, sufficient detail information may be collected to permit recovery of reinsured claims for applicable coverages. This file can be used as the basis of recovery for all contracts which do not require detail policy/claim information.

Reinsurance History Master File This file may contain the coverage and location summary data along with the accounting and statistical policy and claim information which served as the basis for premium cessions and claim recoveries. The reinsurance history may also serve as the source of information for the reports required for reinsurance reports. The design and use of the file varies by company. The use of a separate file of this type facilitates control and provides a convenient record of reinsurance information and statistics.

System Interfaces

The reinsurance cycle may contain data that has a significant impact on several other cycles of a company's insurance information system. Ceded transactions will reduce net premium and net losses, while assumed transactions will increase net premium and net losses. These transactions must be recognized in the treasury, premium loss, and reserve cycles of the company. These interfaces are described below.

Cash Payments on Receipts to/from the Treasury Cycle Each month, the reinsurance transactions should be forwarded to the reinsurers. Usually, the contracts are settled on a net basis with the premium payable (ceded) or receivable (assumed) offset by the losses, loss adjustment expense, and commission receivable (ceded) or payable (assumed). In certain contracts, only the premium transactions are involved until a significant event occurs such as a catastrophe or jumbo loss. These events must be a part of the cash flow/investment policy of the treasury cycle and the cash management function must be promptly informed of these activities.

Ceded or Assumed Reinsurance to/from the Premium (Revenue) and Loss Cycles The ceded or assumed reinsurance transactions can have a significant impact on the premium and loss cycles. Premium on a written or earned basis may be effected by reinsurance transaction, depending on the basis used for reinsurance calculation. Net loss paid and incurred will be effected by both ceded and assumed transactions. Net figures are usually direct business booked by the company less ceded and plus assumed transactions. The results of these transactions need to be reflected in the premium and loss cycles in the month in which the reinsurance entry is recorded.

Ceded or Assumed Reinsurance to/from the Reserve Cycle The effect of reinsurance needs to be reflected in the reserve cycle. Ceded premium will reduce the unearned premium reserve while assumed premium will increase the unearned premium reserve. Ceded losses receivable and assumed loss payable will have the same impact on loss reserves. The results of these transactions should be reflected in the month in which the transaction is entered.

Reinsurance Entries to the Financial Reporting Cycle The journal entries, either computer generated or posted manually from reinsurance transaction reports, will be entered in the general ledger and will flow into the financial reporting cycle. One of the principal reasons for reinsurance is to protect the company's financial surplus position. In order to properly reflect the effect of reinsurance, the transactions must be timely and accurately reflected in the current period financial reports.

SUMMARY

The individual cycles of activity in an insurance information system each encompass related logical steps that must be completed in an insurance operation, regardless of the configuration of the system or the organizational structure of the company.

An insurance company collects much of its initial data and generates the bulk of its revenues during the premium cycle. Typical functions of the premium cycle include quoting and rating, policy processing, premium processing, collections, master file maintenance, and journal preparation. Critical source documents in the premium cycle are policy applications, insurance policies, premium notices, and reinsurance agreements. Data bases affected in the premium cycle include the policy master file, the agents file, the policy statistical file, the premium rate book, the commission rate book, and the application file. The output of the premium cycle includes policies, endorsements, and bills, as well as premium data transmitted to the treasury cycle, the reserve reporting cycle, the general ledger, the statistical file, and the management information system.

The loss and loss expense cycle consists of those operations necessary to record, accumulate, and evaluate loss and loss adjustment expense reserves and payments. Its typical functions include initial reporting of claims, processing of claims, payment of claims, receiving cash for salvage, subrogation, refunds, and reinsurance, and establishing loss and loss expense liabilities. The critical source documents in this cycle are loss notices, claim jacket files, claim coverage forms, proofs of loss, payment authorization forms, claim offset and correction memos, and reinsurance worksheets. The usual data bases involved in the loss and loss expense cycle include claim registers for reported claims, the policy master file, and the claim master file. Policy term, coverage information, and possible reinsurance from the claim master file interface with the premium cycle, and cash disbursements and cash receipts from claim offsets interface with the treasury cycle. In addition, the cycle produces general ledger entries for loss and loss expense items.

The reserve reporting cycle consists of steps involved in establishing liabilities for an insurer. Typical functions in this cycle are the identification of reserve requirements, the selection of acceptable raw data, the selection of the approved method of determining liability, and the calculation of reserves. Although source documents are less critical in the reserve reporting cycle, input may come from loss factor tables, loss adjustment expense factor tables, other expense records, schedules of taxes, licenses, and fees, and pro-rata factors used in unearned premium calculations. The data bases for the reserve reporting cycle are the claim history master file and the premium history master file. Interfaces between the reserve reporting cycle and the premium, loss and loss expense, payroll, and nonpayroll expense cycles provide data for reserve reporting, and in some companies the reserve reporting cycle may also produce general ledger entries.

The volume and nature of reinsurance activity varies widely from company to company depending on the types of insurance coverages offered, the nature and size of risks underwritten, management philosophy, and the size of the company. Although occasional reinsurance activity could be processed within the premium, loss and loss expense, reserve reporting, and financial reporting cycles, the essential functions of the reinsurance cycle are paying the premium due for reinsurance ceded, processing reinsurance recoveries for claims, and reinsurance reporting. Critical source documents in the reinsurance cycle include reinsurance contracts, notices of loss, daily reports, and bordereaux. The cycle's principal data bases are the premium history master file, the loss history master file, and the reinsurance history master file. The reinsurance cycle's major interfaces are cash payments or receipts to or from the treasury cycle, assumed or ceded reinsurance to or from the revenue cycle, assumed or ceded reinsurance to or from the reserve cycle, and reinsurance entries to the financial reporting cycle.

In addition to the premium, loss and loss expense, reserve reporting, and reinsurance cycles discussed in this chapter, insurance information systems also include the treasury, investment, payroll, and nonpayroll expense cycles. Those four cycles are the subject of the next chapter.

Chapter Notes

1. Arthur Anderson & Co. developed this approach as a guide to evaluating internal controls for insurance companies. These two chapters present a similar view of the cycles of insurance activity, modified as appropriate. *A Guide for Studying and Evaluating Internal Accounting Controls—Insurance* (Chicago: Arthur Anderson & Co., 1981).
2. *Guide for Studying Internal Controls*, pp. 19–20.
3. *Examiners Handbook* (Kansas City, MI: National Association of Insurance Commissioners, 1985), Part 6, III, p. 247.

CHAPTER 4

Cycles of Insurance Activity: Treasury, Investments, Payroll, and Nonpayroll Expenditures

INTRODUCTION

This chapter concludes the presentation of the cycles of insurance activity begun in the previous chapter. The remaining cycles are the treasury, investments, payroll, and nonpayroll expenditure cycles.

TREASURY CYCLE

The treasury cycle involves those functions concerned with the short-term and long-term planning of the company's sources and uses of funds. Funds received as premiums and as investment income should be invested to obtain the maximum return, but should also be available when needed to meet the company's obligations. The treasury cycle typically includes overall asset and liability management, acquisition strategy and plans, and monitoring and controlling the company's liquidity position. Many of the functions associated with the treasury cycle in the insurance company are performed at the direction of a finance or management committee.

The treasury cycle functions are subject to great exposure. The cycle deals not only with the company's cash related transactions, but also with banking, stockholder, and investor relations. Accordingly, the treasury cycle should incorporate stringent controls to assure accuracy and reliability. They include authorization, transaction, classification, and physical safeguarding controls.

Authorization controls should be in place prior to the processing of transactions. The following transactions should be approved in accordance with management's criteria:

- sources of equity, debt, and other funds;
- the timing, conditions, and amounts of equity, debt, and other fund transactions;
- adjustments to treasury cycle accounts; and
- treasury cycle processing procedures.

Transaction controls assure that information is accurately processed. Treasury cycle transaction controls assure the following:

- Only requests to obtain or return equity or debt funds that meet management's criteria should be approved.
- Equity and debt funds should be promptly and accurately reported.
- Returns of and returns on equity and debt should be accurately and promptly calculated and reported.
- Disbursements or receipts of funds should be based on a recognized contractual obligation, and be accurately and promptly prepared and reported.
- Treasury cycle transactions and related adjustments should be accurately and promptly classified, summarized, and reported.
- Treasury cycle transactions and related adjustments should be accurately applied to the proper subsidiary ledger.

Classification controls assure that processed transactions are properly reported. The following are examples of treasury cycle classification controls:

- General ledger entries for treasury cycle transactions should be prepared on a timely basis and should classify and summarize economic activities in accordance to management's plan.
- Tax information stemming from treasury cycle transactions should be accurately and promptly reported.
- Balances recorded in treasury cycle accounts and related transaction activity should be periodically reconciled and evaluated.

Physical safeguarding controls relate to the safekeeping of securities and records to avoid unauthorized handling and misplacement. The following are the treasury cycle physical safeguarding controls:

- Access to securities should be permitted only as specified by management's criteria through the use of vaults and locked filing systems.
- Access to treasury cycle records, critical forms, processing areas and processing procedures should be permitted only in accordance with management's criteria.
- Access to checks and drafts and checksigner should be controlled.

Functions

The functions of the treasury cycle relate not only to monitoring and controlling the company's liquidity position, but also to overall asset and liability management. The treasury cycle plans the funding requirements for capital outlays, operational needs, and returns to investors. Functions of a typical treasury cycle include banking service analysis, cash management, stock issuance and retirement, and cash disbursement.

Banking Services Analysis The selection and analysis of a bank or banks is an integral treasury function. Responsibilities of the treasury cycle include securing letters and lines of credit, the continuous review of the banks' financial condition, maintaining zero balance accounts, and the integration of a lockbox collection network.

All banks do not provide equal services; some banks understand insurance operations better than others. The treasury area should communicate to the banks the needs of the insurance operation and work with the banks in developing cost effective services.

Letters of credit have become a popular security vehicle for insurance companies particularly from unauthorized reinsurance companies. A letter of credit transfers credit risk from another party to the bank issuing the letter of credit. The treasury area of an insurance company should be familiar with the banking industry and should be able to analyze a bank's credit risk and monitor the bank's financial condition. It is the treasury function that should offer guidance in approving banks for the issuance of letters of credit in which the insurance company is the beneficiary.

An important enhancement to any insurance company's collection system would be the utilization of a lockbox network. Under this system the receipt of all insurance and investment cash income is concentrated in several regional financial institutions. The financial institutions should be located in major cities with access to postal and airport facilities as well as exhibiting strong remittance banking operations. The average collection time at the regions could be reduced to less than one day. The funds deposited to the lockbox account can be quickly forwarded to the company's main operating account through wire or electronic fund transfers or depository transfer check where one day is needed by the bank to clear the checks deposited in the account. The accelerated receipt of cash represents a significant time savings over mailing checks directly to an insurance company's home office for processing. The cash receipt expediency results in greater investment income, as incoming "float" is reduced to a minimum.

An additional treasury cycle banking function is the accomplishment of "near zero" bank balances for all noninterest-bearing bank accounts. When analyzing the company's need for establishing zero-balance accounts, it is important to consider an alternate need for compensating balances. Certain fee reductions are given to accounts that maintain compensating balances. A cost benefit analysis should indicate which alternative—investment income with zero balance accounts or fee reduction with compensating balances—produces the greater income benefit.

Cash Management Possibly the most important function of the treasury cycle is to develop and implement a strong cash management system. A cash management and control system involves more than the bank services of collection, disbursement, and the reporting of balances. It is a fully integrated system that coordinates cash collection and disbursement, cash investing and borrowing, cash forecasting, and cash control and reporting.

Cash Receipts. In terms of management and control, cash receipts can result from three main sources—insurance operations, investments, and miscellaneous receipts.

Insurance cash flow typically can be divided into property and liability and life sources. Property and liability operations utilize two types of billing systems, agency and direct billings of insured. Both billing systems can utilize the lockbox collection network. Direct billing typically has a shorter remittance time since funds are received directly by the company as opposed to flowing through agencies.

Investment cash flow is comprised primarily of interest, dividends, real estate rental income, and mortgage payment receipts. The receipts can be deposited in a lockbox account. Proceeds received from the sale of stocks, bonds, and real estate are usually credited to the investment bank account by use of wire transfers.

Miscellaneous cash receipts include salvage recovery and subrogation. Salvage recovery involves the sale of real or personal property which becomes the property of an insurance company upon settlement of a claim. Subrogation involves funds received by the insurance company, after settlement of the claims with its insured, from third parties primarily liable for the claim. The funds from both salvage and subrogation should be deposited daily to the main operating account.

Cash Disbursements. An insurance company typically has four major sources of disbursements: (1) claims, (2) payroll, (3) investments, and (4) sundry expenses and purchases.

Regional claim offices can be authorized to settle small dollar claims (for a specified range). For claims in excess of the offices authorization, the information should be forwarded to the home office for disposition.

Payroll disbursements are usually made by check or electronic fund transfer to the employees' bank account. Since payroll accounts are noninterest bearing, the cash management function of the treasury cycle should project the period over which the checks will be cashed and consequently transfer the funds into the payroll account over this period to maximize investment income.

All disbursements for purchases of investments should be made by wire transfer or check on zero-balance account. Wire transfers should be made only upon written instructions issued to the bank with a few select people being approved to authorize these instructions. Checks can also be issued for other corporate purposes, such as loans to insurance agents and large claim settlements.

Sundry disbursements include items such as operating expense payments and commissions. All sundry expenses should be paid from centrally located disbursement accounts.

Cash Investing. One of the primary goals of an effective cash management system is to ensure prompt collection of cash receipts and to invest excess funds until they are needed to pay claims and other disbursements.

Cash Forecasting and Debt Management. Cash needs and availability should be forecast over both short-term and longer-term horizons. Net available cash for investment should be forecast in connection with the insurance company's operational plan or budget. These cash forecasts enable the investment department to determine appropriate investment alternatives given expected available cash. Accurate cash forecasting also facilitates debt management. Debt financing may be needed to fund a major capital expenditure, such as a real estate purchase, if the company does not want to liquidate investment assets, but accurate cash forecasting minimizes the outside financing required.

Cash forecasting is critical in periods of large insurance company losses. Insurance companies may be forced to liquidate their long-term bond portfolios at a market value less than their cost, resulting in investment losses. State regulatory and rating agencies and auditors are now examining the ability of insurance companies to hold their long-term bond portfolios to maturity.

Future Cash Management Opportunities. In an attempt to streamline the collection process, insurance companies are exploring the possibility of permitting insureds to pay their premiums by using "automated clearing house" deposits. An automated clearing house deposit is a form of electronic funds transfer that increases the efficiency of cash collection by giving the company the use of the funds on the next day and permits more timely investment of the funds.

Insurance companies are also studying the possibility of a direct terminal link to their major operating banks. This terminal would be used for most communications with the bank, reducing mail costs, paper flow, telephone time, and potential clerical processing errors.

Stock Issuance and Retirement Another major component of the treasury cycle responsibilities is the coordination of company stock issuance and retirements.

Stock Transfers. The treasury cycle is expected to provide reasonable assurance that only those requests to issue or retire equity that meet managements' criteria are approved and processed. It is the responsibility of the treasury function to assist the board of directors in establishing and implementing the policies relating to dividends, to stockholder records, and to stock option plans. In addition to assuring that stock transactions follow corporate guidelines, the treasury cycle is responsible for following two other stock transfer guidelines:

- assure that trade or broker instructions are properly implemented and documented, and
- determine that the S.E.C. and other regulatory or statutory requirements are met.

Dividend Requests. It is the treasury area of the company that is ultimately responsible for accruals and payment of stockholder and policyholder dividends. Treasury personnel reconcile total dividends payable with shares outstanding, as reported by registrars and transfer agents. The treasury cycle must assure that:

- only requests to pay dividends authorized by the board of directors are processed,
- dividends are being computed accurately and are promptly reported as a liability, and
- dividends paid are accurately and promptly reported.

Cash Disbursement The maintenance of the company's cashier's department also falls within the responsibilities of the treasury cycle. The cashier's department provides various employee services. Within an insurance company, the cashier may:

- accept employee insurance premium payments;
- disburse money for travel advances and expense accounts (also receives unused portion of travel advances);
- disburse funds for salary advances and vacation money; and
- cash personal checks, money orders, and drafts.

The cashier's department is also responsible for maintaining the company's cash books, which reflect bank balances and offsetting entries.

Source Documents

Critical source documents associated with an insurance company's treasury cycle include:

- cash,
- stock certificates,
- letters of credit,
- debt certificates, and
- interest and dividend checks.

The transactions that result from the above source documents are cash receipts and disbursements of income, debt financing, dividend and interest distributions, and the purchase and sale of investments. The processing of transactions may vary widely from company to company and for various types of transactions within the same insurance company. Dividend and interest distributions, sales and redemptions of commercial paper, and purchases and sales of short-term investments are usually frequent and routine transactions that receive standardized processing in the treasury cycle. On the other hand, certain treasury cycle transactions may be so infrequent that standardized procedures are not necessary; for example, a public offering of stock might be directly recorded in the company's general ledger.

Data Bases

A data base is a pool of stored information resulting from the processing of transactions. The records and books that might be maintained in performing treasury cycle functions include both static and dynamic data base elements. Transactions that change static data (additions, changes, and deletions) may occur less frequently than those that update dynamic data, but may be of even greater importance if they alter information that would be referenced in the processing of many transactions. Static data relating to the treasury cycle may be found in the following treasury data bases:

- master files of stockholders,
- commercial paper holders and investors listing,
- interest and dividend schedules,
- loan compliance checklists, and
- loans to affiliates.

The dynamic data for a treasury cycle may be included in these remaining treasury data bases:

- money market and commercial paper account balances,
- long-term debt subsidiary accounts,
- cash balances,
- stockholder subsidiary accounts, and
- intercompany account balances.

Outputs and Interfaces

Reports generated from treasury cycle transactions include reports on daily cash available for investments, stockholder listings, investor information, cash forecast reports, cash balance reports, and dividend and interest expense balances.

Because the nature of the treasury cycle involves the transfer of funds as required by the firm's operations, interfaces with other cycles are implicit. Cash management, for example, requires constant interaction with the investment cycle, the premium cycle, the loss and loss expense cycle, the payroll cycle, and the nonpayroll expenditure cycle. In addition, the treasury cycle produces general ledger entries for financial management reporting.

Investment Funds The purchase of investments requires the transfer of funds from the treasury cycle to settle the transaction. The sale of investments causes the proceeds to be transferred to the treasury cycle.

Premium Revenue The premium cycle generates funds collected as premium payments. The transfer of these funds requires an interface between the premium cycle and the treasury cycle.

Loss and Loss Expense Disbursements Funds must be transferred from the treasury cycle to the loss and loss expense cycle in order to pay claims and loss adjusting expenses.

Other Disbursements Similarly, funds must be transferred from the treasury cycle to the payroll cycle in order to issue paychecks and to the nonpayroll expenditure cycle to make other necessary disbursements.

General Ledger Entries The interfaces with the financial and management reporting cycles are in the form of general ledger entries reflecting either individual transactions or summaries of similar transactions.

INVESTMENT CYCLE

The investment cycle converts to earning assets the resources obtained primarily from the premium cycle. The investment philosophy and objectives established by management with respect to the overall financial planning and operations of the company determines the degree of commonality among investment functions. The investment cycle does not include the short-term investments included in the treasury cycle because they are related more closely to day-to-day cash management functions.

Internal control objectives for an insurance company investment cycle are similar to the objectives of other industries and of other cycles. These objectives are:

- capturing all the necessary information at the exchange or entrance point,
- processing accurately the above captured information in its entirety, and
- safeguarding the necessary assets, which in this case are stocks, bonds, mortgage notes, and any other type of negotiable investments.

Functions

The essential functions of the investment cycle relate to the authorization of investment transactions, the processing of principal and income, and the safekeeping of securities.

Authorization and Approval of Purchases and Sales Transactions Prior to any transaction entering the system, such transaction should be directly or indirectly approved by the board of directors. Directly means the board approves the individual transaction; indirectly means the board empowers management with the authority to approve the individual transactions. A common arrangement is to stagger authority levels by seniority. For example, assistant vice presidents may approve transactions up to $250,000, vice presidents up to $500,000, executive or senior vice presidents up to $1,000,000, and so on.

Statutory restrictions should be considered and board approval obtained before any large or unusual investment transaction is consummated. The board of directors may establish approved lists of securities and of brokers.

Internal controls consist of preventive and detective controls. Preventive controls are designed to capture transactions that do not follow the guidelines before such transaction takes place, while detective controls are designed to capture the same transaction after such transaction has taken place.

Specific preventive controls to achieve the objectives include, but are not limited to:

- documented procedures for reviewing and approving requests to buy and sell investment securities;
- written policy statements or procedures manuals detailing investment guidelines and limitations;
- investment/finance committee involving the board directors or officers of the corporation to identify specific investment activities before they occur; and
- lists of approved investments, authorized brokers, and authorized signature files.

Some specific detective controls to achieve the objectives are:

- reconciliations between investment income, accrued income, income received;
- comparisons of income accrued and income received;
- ratio analysis between expected investment yields and investment income earned;
- periodic reviews of investment transactions by the investment/finance committee; and
- the use and audit of forms such as trading advices, investment confirmations by an independent third party such as treasury, and the accountability of such forms.

Failure to achieve the objectives through the specific procedures could cause lack of compliance with statutory requirements and board directives. In early 1984, for example, the management of a major insurance broker circumvented trading controls, costing the company over $100 million aftertax. The trading of unauthorized bonds had occurred for a period of time. Gains were generated when such trading started, but when the bond market turned, losses occurred. These losses triggered questions which eventually discovered the circumvention of controls.

Controls can be circumvented. The ideal set of controls is segregated over a number of employees or departments, thus minimizing the odds that a dishonest or uninformed employee will successfully circumvent these controls. Additionally, such controls should be constantly reviewed for their appropriateness.

Transaction authorization and approval is a very critical component of this cycle because it is through this component that transactions enter the system and companies may incur liabilities or lose money.

Processing of Principal and Income Authorized purchases or sales of investments should be reported promptly. Upon placement of the order, which is usually an oral order with the broker, a signed prenumbered authorization ticket is prepared. This ticket is the source of information that is processed through the system. The broker then sends an advice to confirm the transaction which is matched to the authorization ticket. The advice includes an identifying code, or "CUSIP number," for each security.

The prenumbered tickets are important in implementing a population control. Such control is needed throughout the processing flow to assure that *all* the information is processed step after step. Batch total is an example of a population control which is used step after step. This control compares the total on a tape that summarizes all items being processed with an input total and ensures that all items were processed. The need for a population control after each step can be avoided if there is an overall compensating population control that assures all the information entered into the system has been processed throughout the system. The prenumbered authorization ticket creates a receivable or payable, depending upon whether the transaction is a sale or purchase. The offset should reduce or increase the investment account at both the general ledger and subsidiary ledger levels. Periodical reconciliations between these two ledgers are a good detective control to find out if the population is complete in both ledgers.

Another important control of the processing cycle is the accuracy control which assures that all the information is processed correctly (or accurately). For example, the authorization ticket shows ten shares of ARG Corporation purchased for $100 but such information enters the system as ten shares of DCW Corporation for $100. Balancing controls will not show the discrepancy since the $100 was entered correctly into the system, but in future periods when market prices are used to value this investment, the investment value will be misstated. Additionally, the company's detailed investment books will mislead the investment department since the books state that the company owns a security that it really does not own. This accuracy control could be performed by a separate department; for example, the treasury department receives confirmation of the transaction's critical characteristics while the investment department initiated the transaction. The use of separate departments strengthens controls by separating duties, making it harder to circumvent controls.

Accrual and Receipt of Bond Interest, Dividends, Rental Income, and Mortgage Interest. The accounting system should calculate the income accrual on a monthly basis. This calculation can be performed with the information contained in the data base which is provided by source documents such as authorization ticket/advice. Investment income cash receipts should be processed by the treasury department; hence, any discussion of the detailed cash receipts procedures is beyond the scope of this section. The investment accounting department should provide the treasury department with a listing of expected cash receipts for the period which would include any income items as well as maturing fixed income investments. This will help the treasury department's cash receipts area in deciding if the amount is received in its entirety and the account where such receipts should be recorded.

Changes in Carrying Value of Investments. Changes to investment values other than market value changes may occur for a number of reasons such as permanent impairment of an investment failure to pay interest on time or return of capital payments or affiliates based on audited equity. An impairment is a nonmonetary transaction that should only be processed after proper authorization forms should be approved. These authorization forms should follow the same flow through the system as the prenumbered (purchase/sale) authorization ticket. Return of capital transactions are a monetary exchange that should flow through the cash receipts system, therefore no special procedures are needed, other than recognizing that this payment is not an interest payment but a principal reduction. The values are determined by the Committee on Valuation of the NAIC.

Amortization of Premiums and Accrual of Discounts. Other nonmonetary exchanges that affect both principal and income are accrual of discount and amortization of premium. Most data processing systems calculate these amounts based on information provided from the source documents. The most common computerized methods are more scientific than straight-line amortization. The amounts are system generated and a reasonableness test such as a ratio or comparison with prior periods is the most practical control in this area.

It is important to record income in its proper accounts, since the accounting system usually provides the tax department with information needed to compute tax liabilities. Tax rates differ for various types of investment income. For example, return of capital and tax exempt coupon income are not taxed, domestic dividends are taxed at 6.9 percent, after considering the 85 percent dividend exclusion, foreign dividends and taxable interest income at 46 percent, and capital gains at 28 percent.

Additionally, an accounting system should keep management reporting objectives in perspective. The general ledger should be structured to assure that information required by management is readily available, rather than necessitating costly procedures to generate such information.

Physical Control and Safekeeping of Securities Safeguarding of securities is crucial, since bonds are the largest investment insurance companies own and bearer bonds could be a substantial amount of total bonds. Anyone possessing a bearer bond or a corresponding coupon may upon presentation to a bank receive cash upon maturity of this instrument or sell the instrument prior to maturity.

Other negotiable instruments besides bonds should be safeguarded. These instruments are stock, mortgage notes, property deeds, and any other instrument that might be easily converted into cash. The most likely place to store these securities is in a vault at the home office, although other alternatives are financial institutions, custodial accounts at banks, and the Depository Trust Company, an entity that safeguards bonds and stock securities and transfers them quickly upon purchase or sale. This service is especially convenient for transferring securities immediately, benefitting companies involved in securities lending or those who need to warehouse securities for a short period of time. Insurance companies planning to hold securities until maturity may keep these securities in their vault. A custodial account at a bank secured by a contract and insurance can also be used. Insurance companies usually have to maintain securities on deposit with different states. This deposit protects the company's policyholders residing in that state. These situations create the need to keep separate records to achieve the same objective—safeguarding of securities.

Controls over safeguarding of securities should start upon delivery of these instruments. The treasury department should compare the purchase authorization form to the security received to avoid problems as those previously discussed in the ARG and DCW Corporation example.

The treasury department should prepare a prenumbered vault deposit form or safekeeping receipt for every security that goes into the vault. This form would be the source that helps prepare a vault control listing. A similar prenumbered form should be prepared where the security is leaving the vault to update the vault control listing. The use and accessibility of these forms should be highly restricted.

Preventive controls are critical in this area to prevent the misplacement of securities. Some preventive controls follow:

- Always have two or more employees withdraw the security.
- Restrict the number of employees that are allowed in the vault area.
- Have two combinations to the vault.
- Rotate the duties of the employees.
- Install a timer on the vault so it can only be opened at certain times.
- Have an internal auditor, independent auditor, or Insurance Department examiner count the securities.

Detective controls are still useful in finding out if securities are missing. If such securities are registered the company may be able to recover the security. If the misplaced security is payable to the bearer, the company will most likely incur a loss and would tighten the preventive controls. A good detective control is a security count which compares the securities in inventory to the perpetual inventory record or vault control listing and then to the general ledger. An additional detective control is the listing of expected cash receipts previously discussed. If the company is not receiving the cash amounts the system predicted, this discrepancy may indicate that the securities were mis-coded into the accounting system, that the securities are registered under a different name, or that the bond issuer is having financial difficulties and a write-down due to permanent impairment might be needed.

These detective controls may not be effective with respect to zero coupon bonds. The risk involves counterfeit or fraudulent bonds. Zero coupon bonds do not pay interest; therefore, the second control would not be applicable and a cursory review of the first control might overlook any imperfections in the zero coupon investment. A company dealing with zero coupon bonds may want to strengthen its preventive control to ensure that a counterfeit bond does not enter the vault. A closer inspection during the security count may unveil any wrongdoing in case the bond does enter the vault.

A control similar to the vault control listing should be maintained for external depositories such as Depository Trust Company state depositories or bank custodians. Regular confirmation of their holdings with comparisons to the perpetual record should provide adequate control. Additionally, periodic internal control letters may be obtained from depositories.

Source Documents

Source documents contain information that flows through the system to generate the financial information needed for management reporting and outside reporting to shareholders and the investment community. These documents are fairly important since the information they contain generates the financial information and, as a result, bad source information will generate bad financial information. The most common source documents are buy/sell advices, buy/sell confirmations, safekeeping receipts, mortgage and loan service reports, and checks and drafts.

Buy/Sell Advices   A transaction usually starts with a trader placing a buy/sell order which is recorded on an authorization (purchase/sale) ticket. This ticket starts the process through the system by going through the treasury department, which confirms the information on the ticket with the broker. The broker advice usually arrives soon after and it serves as additional confirmation that the transaction has been executed. The advice usually contains the following information:

- description,
- maturity,
- par value or shares,
- coupon interest rate (or discount rate),
- trade date,
- CUSIP number,
- settlement date (for instruments other than short-term paper), and
- cost.

Buy/Sell Confirmations   Buy/sell confirmations can be written or oral. Based on the example described in the previous section, the treasury department orally confirms the information on the authorization ticket. Later the treasury department verifies the same information by comparing the authorization ticket to the broker advice. It is important that a different department, such as treasury, confirms the transaction. This is a clear situation of segregation of duties and makes it more difficult for any one person to circumvent controls and misappropriate funds.

Safekeeping Receipts   Receipts serve to create perpetual vault control records. The information needed on a safekeeping receipt is:

- maturity,
- par value or shares,
- coupon interest rate,

- name of security,
- CUSIP number, and
- vault location.

Mortgage and Loan Services Reports   When investing in mortgages and loans, the insurance company may consider using an outside servicing agent. The most common reason might be that the investment in these assets is too small to merit hiring personnel or accounting and data system implementation. This is also common with investments in real estate where regional property managers can be hired.

The important characteristic of these reports submitted by the servicing agent is that the information provided by them can be easily transferred into the company's reporting requirements.

Information desired in these reports is:

- mortgage balances,
- payment dates,
- original loan balance,
- value of property (collateral),
- latest appraisal of property (collateral), and
- any other significant information.

Checks and Drafts   Checks, drafts, wire transfers, and any other method of transferring funds such as electronic transfers may serve as source documents. Most likely these documents will not be source documents since the information on these instruments is rather limited, but they serve as verification of other information sources. As previously mentioned, the cash receipts area should have a listing of expected cash receipts. This listing should be generated by other sources such as investment ledgers which were generated through the buy/sell broker advices type of source documents. Any investment related cash receipts instrument not appearing on this list should be an exception until its proper account is identified. For this reason, these instruments serve as source documents.

Other Source Documents   Additional source documents are journal entries and contracts. Journal entries are source documents when accounting for situations such as permanent impairments. Contracts are the source document when interest rate swap agreements are consummated, mortgages are issued, and real estate is purchased or sold.

Source documents are very important since the information provided by these documents generates the financial data for various types of reporting. Source documents should provide information not only for the initial department using such information, but for all the departments that need the information. For example, the investment and treasury departments are usually the departments receiving the source documents, but when preparing or reviewing a source document, they should consider the investment accounting department reporting needs, especially since many of these reports go back to the investment and treasury departments.

Data Bases

The principal data bases for the investment cycle are the investment master files and the investment safekeeping records.

Investment Master Files The information provided by the source documents described in the previous section generates the data base. The information on this investment master file data base is processed to generate different reports that can be detailed by bonds, stocks, mortgage loans, real estate, and other investments. Investments in affiliated and in nonaffiliated companies must be distinguished in the master file. Similarly, taxable and tax exempt investments must be distinguished. In addition, the master file must include information showing the maturity dates and the book, tax, and market values of investments. The ex-dividend date of each security owned should also be in the master file, particularly if the company has an active securities lending program.

The reports generated from the investment master file include:

● investment subsidiary ledgers,
● accrued income reports,
● income received report,
● projected income reports,
● capital gains/losses report,
● investment receivable and payable report, and
● tax information reports.

Many other reports can be prepared from this data base. For example, sorts can be made by state to ensure that the company meets statutory requirements of investments in that particular state. The output of these reports should satisfy management and regulatory objectives and generate the information needed to create financial statements.

Reports generated from this data base are highly visible to upper management and potentially to the investment community; therefore, the company should ensure that the information contained in this data base is complete and accurate. Controls should exist that prevent individuals from changing the information in the data base and from changing the programs that generate the reports.

An EDP steering committee, as well as an approved EDP manual which includes system development, programming, and documentation standards, serves as a general preventive control. Some specific preventive controls that address the integrity of the data base are:

- the use of prenumbered forms for any changes which should be authorized by the appropriate supervisory employees, and
- limited access to on-line data through the use of passwords or physical controls over the terminals.

Some specific detective controls that should capture human error or unauthorized changes to the data base are:

- periodic reconciliations of used prenumbered forms to the data base actual changes,
- periodic tests of the data bases, such as the security count mentioned in a previous section,
- periodic reviews of the computer log searching for unauthorized users, and
- periodic reconciliation of the data base, such as beginning balance plus purchases and accretion of discount, less sales and amortization of premium, plus or minus any other authorized changes equals ending balance.

Some specific preventive controls that address the integrity of the programs that generate the reports are as follows:

- restricting access to programming areas and related documents, such as a computer software library that limits access to programs to authorized employees;
- informing appropriate supervisors of the library activity of the subordinate employees;
- testing programs and system before using production data; and
- requiring proper approval of any program changes by EDP department management and user department.

Some specific detective controls that may uncover unauthorized changes to the programs are:

- reconciliations between general ledger and subsidiary investment ledgers,
- ratio analysis, and
- comparing results to insurance industry results.

Investment Safekeeping Records   The previous section covered the protection of the data base from any changes, either to the programs accessing such data base or the data base information per se. This section covers the controls that should be considered to physically protect the storage of the data base. Controls similar to those used in safeguarding the investment securities should be considered.

Most companies probably have a centralized EDP section with similar controls for all cycles. Some companies are starting to process reports generated from this data base on personal computers through a process known as downloading. This movement will expand in the upcoming years as personal computers become more popular and storage capacities increase for floppy and hard disks. Therefore, the controls discussed in this section should be considered on the personal computers as well as on the EDP mainframe environment. In some situations, stricter controls should be observed in a personal computer environment since the atmosphere tends to be less restrictive than the atmosphere in an EDP mainframe environment. Employees in a nonEDP area have fewer restrictions than employees in an EDP area. Usually EDP areas are locked, off limits, and guarded while a production personal computer environment lacks these restrictions.

Other controls that may prevent unauthorized handling of information are:

- controlled custody and prenumbering of critical forms including periodic reviews by independent personnel;
- segregation of investment decisions from accounting activities and custodial responsibilities;
- provisions for reasonable protection against fire, explosion, and/or malicious destruction of records and processing facilities;
- work area layouts that permit maximum visibility by guards and fellow employees (including supervisors); and
- periodic compliance audits such as individual counts and inspection of tapes.

Inadequate controls in this area can lead to use of improper information in making critical decisions.

In the years to come not only will downloading from a mainframe computer to a personal computer proliferate but uploading will also increase. Uploading occurs when data produced in personal computers is transferred to a mainframe. Such data can then be downloaded to a different personal computer and processed into other reports.

Since computers, mainframes or personal, are so critical to most companies, these controls should not be overlooked.

Outputs and Interfaces

The principal interfaces of the investment cycle are with the treasury cycle to account for funds expended and received in investment activity and with the financial and management reporting cycle.

Proceeds from Sales and Payments for Purchases of Investments from/to the Treasury Cycle The investment accounting department periodically provides a listing of the expected cash receipts from sales principal and interest to the treasury department. In lieu of the listing, the investment accounting and treasury systems could interface to compare the data. Such interface should produce an exception report with any differences. These differences should be investigated on a timely basis. This procedure serves as a control to ensure that the investment accounting department has captured all the information of proceeds received by treasury.

When investments are purchased, the treasury department informs the investment accounting department of such purchases. Investment accounting uses this information to create the data base, which is then compared by investment accounting to the output generated by the treasury department to ensure a complete population in the investment accounting department files.

Proceeds from Receipts of Income to Treasury Cycle The projected income report is compared to the actual proceeds received. Any discrepancies should be investigated and may result in adjustments to the records. A system could be established that generates this projected income at the beginning of the month with an updated report at month end. This updated report would account for any cash receipts of investments purchased or sold throughout the month.

General Ledger Entries to the Financial Reporting Cycle The reports generated in this cycle can serve as either check controls or sources for general ledger entries in addition to generating other important reports for management. For example, a detailed purchases and sales of investment ledger may generate a journal entry for the assets. A subsidiary investment ledger should be reconciled to the general ledger.

Management Reporting A few years ago during periods of low interest rates and almost nonexisting interest rate volatility insurance companies were not likely to consider matching their assets with their liabilities. If an asset had to be sold before maturity, the market value was close to cost; therefore, the company's losses could be absorbed by surplus. This scenario changed during the 1970s, when interest rates fluctuated significantly. During the early 1980s the rates went from the low teens to the high teens and back down to the low teens in a matter of months. Many companies had to sell long-term, low yielding assets at a loss to satisfy liabilities.

In response to these changes, many insurance companies are changing the way in which their business is managed. The terms asset-liability management, duration, immunization, segregation of assets, and hedges are becoming popular. Although these concepts do not necessarily involve new types of investments, they do change the reporting requirements for present portfolios.

Asset-liability management attempts to match the maturity or duration of an investment to the maturity or duration of the liability. Duration is a calculation that attempts to measure the price sensitivity of a specific investment in relation to changes in market interest rates. Immunization is the point where assets and liabilities have the same duration and therefore any interest rate movement leaves the company's financial position unchanged, since the increase (decrease) of the liability is offset by an equal increase (decrease) of the asset.

A more refined goal of asset-liability matching is segregation of assets to find the true profitability of a line of business and therefore adequately pricing the products included in that line. Segregation creates a number of funds that are useful for management purposes but not necessarily needed for external reporting. Controls should be implemented to ensure that these segments are fairly stated since management is using this information for decision making. This entails procedures in addition to those stated throughout the cycle discussion. The objectives should be similar—the concern is in capturing the information and processing it properly.

Additional concerns are transfers between funds. These transfers should be made at market value, to properly measure the profitability of every fund. This "sale" creates gains (losses) in one fund and an increased (decreased) asset value in another fund. The result is a management reporting and GAAP/tax reporting difference that has to be monitored until an actual sale occurs. These transfers may be advantageous because individual fund investment objectives may be achieved without entering the market and incurring commission costs.

Hedges are not easy to account for by an EDP system. Futures are normally marked to market with a cash settlement to/from the broker daily, thereby creating significant additional transactions that need to be checked and balanced. Options carry expiration dates that should be monitored. Additionally, if the company has entered into an anticipatory hedge, the closing of the hedge does not generate an income statement item but creates a deferred balance sheet item that is amortized into income over the life to the hedged investments. Different state insurance departments have certain requirements that futures should meet before being considered a hedge. The system should address the requirements of hedging so management objectives are met (hedge instead of speculation).

Interest rate swaps cause additional concerns. Hedges are usually specifically identified with an underlying asset of liability since speculation is not permitted by state regulations. Swaps, on the other hand, do not have to be identified with underlying assets or liabilities. To complicate matters further, a swap involves no monetary exchange. Options are purchased as any bond is purchased, while futures usually start with a margin account in addition to the daily marked to market settlements. Swaps have a principal amount to which the interest rates are applied, but this principal amount does not exchange hands. The only exchange occurs at the end of the specified period when an interest payment has to be made or received. Since no payment is made when entering into the swap, such a swap could easily go unrecorded until a payment is required (which would be unknown) or until a payment is received. Special controls should be established to address this concern.

It is apparent that there are many new types of investments and changes to the traditional method of accounting for investments. The important aspect is that the information needs to be captured at the exchange point in its entirety and then processed accurately and completely. Negotiable investments need to be safeguarded, and the controls needed to achieve these objectives are both preventive and detective controls.

PAYROLL CYCLE

The payroll cycle includes functions that deal with payroll and payroll-related taxes such as federal and state unemployment taxes. This cycle interacts with several departments, especially personnel, payroll, treasury, and accounting.

Strong internal controls are essential in the payroll cycle to ensure accurate recording and reporting of information. Segregation of responsibilities between personnel functions and payroll responsibilities and segregation of check preparation from reconciliation of bank accounts help maintain integrity. Additionally, an imprest bank system should be used for the payroll account. Finally, the internal audit department should perform periodic internal compliance reviews. Critical forms, such as blank payroll checks, signature cards, master file change cards, and withholding forms should be prenumbered and stored in a safe and restricted location to enhance controls over these forms. Provisions should be made for reasonable protection of EDP records against fire, explosion, or malicious destruction of records and processing facilities. Offsite storage should be maintained for back-up tapes, records, files, programs, and related documentation for payroll transactions.

If the above controls are not followed, there is a risk that records may be destroyed or lost. Lost records could result in an inability to prepare reliable financial and operating reports. Also, records may be misused or altered by unauthorized personnel to the detriment of the company or its employees. Computer programs may also be altered by unauthorized persons.

Functions

The payroll cycle of an insurance information system resembles the payroll cycle in other industries. Its functions include hiring employees, monitoring attendance and salary changes, payroll distribution, and allocating salary and related expenses to the appropriate functions, cost centers, budget centers, offices, departments, and lines of business. The principal accounts affected are salary and salary related expenses (such as fringe benefits and payroll taxes) and liability accounts for payroll and employee requested deductions. The payroll cycle does not include the payment of commissions to independent agents, since this transaction is included in the premium cycle.

Hiring The personnel department is responsible for seeking and hiring qualified candidates for vacant positions. It selects candidates meeting predetermined standards such as technical skills, education, training, and job experience. Candidates can be sought internally and externally. Once candidates have been identified, the personnel department should conduct a prescreening interview before making recommendations to the department with the open position. Recommendations should be based not only on the interviews but also on reference checks and test of skills, if appropriate. The supervisor of the prospective employee then interviews recommended candidates and selects one as the best match between the requirements of the job and the qualifications of the candidate.

The personnel department is responsible for ensuring that all placement and rejection decisions are properly documented after a decision has been made. For example, all placement decisions should be specifically approved in writing by the appropriate supervisor. This rule controls unauthorized additions of personnel to the payroll listing. In addition, employment forms should be standardized and prenumbered so unauthorized changes can be easily identified.

Attendance and Time Reporting Guidelines and procedures should be established to assist supervisors and department heads in promoting regular attendance and in uniformly applying acceptable standards of attendance.

The following guidelines can assist supervisors in promoting good attendance:

- communicating to employees the required work schedule and the need for maintaining good attendance,
- making employees aware of acceptable standards of attendance,
- advising employees about their responsibility to report absences,
- quickly identifying the start of unacceptable attendance patterns,
- counseling employees as soon as a potential attendance problem is identified, and
- taking appropriate action when acceptable standards of attendance are not met.

It should be expected that all employees report to work every day and on time in accordance with the department or office schedule.

For hourly employees, certain techniques help to insure that attendance and time reporting objectives are met. Time cards and sign-in sheets for attendance reporting should be used, and they should be reviewed and approved by a supervisor. Overtime, vacations, and departmental personnel changes should be pre-approved. A checklist of employees should be prepared to ascertain that all the cards have been collected. A review and follow-up of budget variations in payroll expense by department monitors areas over or under budget.

Salaried employees are paid regardless of the hours worked. To ensure proper attendance, attendance cards should be maintained by each department supervisor. The department supervisor is responsible for ensuring that subordinates are working during scheduled hours and are completing all necessary work. These attendance cards are submitted to payroll periodically to update employee vacation, sick leave, and pension records.

Payroll Accounting The payroll department, the corporate accounting department, or the controller allocates payroll expense to individual departments to provide for budget comparisons and comparison between periods, and to allow for a detailed review of expenses. After employees are hired, personnel notifies payroll of the employee's name, department, and date of hire. This information is used to code the employee's pay to a particular department. Once this information enters the system, that employee's pay is charged to that department until personnel informs payroll of any further changes, such as transfer, salary increases, or termination. Payroll coding should facilitate cost allocation by line, by state, and by office. This information is essential for management control as well as for annual statement expense reporting. Some corporate budgeting systems may require both direct and secondary allocations of payroll expenses. To compare payroll expenses between accounting periods, adjusting entries must be made for work performed by employees but unpaid at the end of the accounting period. The general ledger accounts affected by the accrual are accrued payroll and payroll expense. Procedures should be established and documented to cutoff payroll at the end of the period. For example, a computer program could be established to identify payroll costs related to the period which is closing. Periodically, reasonableness tests should be prepared to ascertain all costs are properly being captured.

Most payroll costs are expensed in the period they are incurred. However, some employees may be involved in new product development or other activities generating new business. Generally accepted accounting principles allow their costs to be deferred and spread over the corresponding premium period although statutory accounting requires their costs to be expensed. A time study or other allocation method should be performed to determine deferrable costs and the length of the amortization period.

Payroll Adjustments The payroll department is responsible for adjustments to payroll disbursements, employee accounts, and account distributions. All adjustments should be authorized in accordance with management's criteria. For example:

- adjustment forms should be prenumbered and approved by the appropriate personnel,
- manual totals for approved adjustments should be compared to the actual adjustments for a pay period, and
- validity checks on adjustments should be used to detect unusual amounts.

When high volumes of a particular type of adjustment occur, the criteria for approval normally appears in statements of policy and procedures manual issued by management. Examples of common adjustments within the payroll cycle include:

- corrections to gross or net pay,
- termination payments, and
- special payments such as bonuses and advance payments.

Taxes Employers pay several different types of payroll taxes. The first tax is social security, commonly referred to as FICA tax. The employee contributes a set percentage of gross pay up to a stated maximum. Employers are required to contribute a similar percentage of the employee's salary. FICA taxes are remitted to the government periodically based on the payroll volume.

The second payroll tax is unemployment tax, paid solely by the employer. The federal unemployment tax is 3.5 percent of the first $7,000 in wages earned by each employee, although credits are allowed for state unemployment taxes. The amount paid for state unemployment taxes varies by state and reflects an experience rate determined by the company's history in the state and the number of workers currently employed. If a company has laid off many employees in the past and its former employees have collected unemployment benefits, the rate will be higher. The unemployment tax is generally paid quarterly.

Another deduction is for federal income tax. The amount is based on employees' wages and number of exemptions claimed. No expense is charged to the company since the company merely collects the tax. The amount withheld must be deposited in a Federal Reserve System bank three days after the end of the payroll period. If this is not done, the company is charged a penalty.

States or municipalities may impose local taxes. Thus, the company may be responsible for withholding taxes for these as well.

The payroll department is responsible for accounting for all these taxes. It is their responsibility to insure the company is paying the correct tax amounts and on a timely basis for each of the applicable taxes. As a result, the payroll department must keep abreast of changes in federal, state, and municipality tax laws which may require interfacing with the legal and tax departments.

Source Documents

Critical source documents in the payroll cycle include personnel action notices, time reports, and special payment authorizations.

Personnel Action Notices The payroll department can make changes to employees' pay records only from authorized documents. A salary increase should be approved by a department head and personnel. The payroll department then executes the changes from these approved documents. Employees may initiate changes in voluntary deductions such as:

- medical/dental,
- life and disability insurance,
- company savings and investment plans,
- U.S. Savings Bonds, and
- contributions to charitable organizations.

Employees may also change the number of exemptions claimed, altering the amount withheld for income tax. All of the above deductions should be supported by signed documents. Tax amounts withheld are supported by signed W-4 forms or state and local tax forms. Employee requested deductions are supported by signed authorization cards for each deduction.

Time Reports Approved time sheets or time cards should be submitted to the payroll department for hourly employees. Other payments, such as overtime, must be submitted on special approved documents in order for the payroll department to issue these checks.

Special Payment Authorizations Other special payments, such as bonuses, must have signed and approved documents in order for payment to occur. Advance pay requests may also be granted for vacation pay, business trips, and emergency advances. These requests should be approved by the employee's department head and a personnel officer.

Data Bases

The major data base for the payroll cycle is the employee master file. Additional data bases may include a current hours file and a tax table and deductions file.

Employee Master File When an employee is hired, employee data is collected and entered into the payroll data base. Usually both the personnel and payroll departments use a single payroll system, since both require similar information. For control purposes, however, only one department inputs data. The information entered consists of name, social security number, address, educational background, sex, number of exemptions, office location, spousal and beneficiary information, applicable benefit programs, and pay rates. Special payments or bonus payments for employee referral or service recognition awards are also recorded so costs for such programs can be monitored. The office location is needed to determine applicable state and local taxes. Spousal and beneficiary information may be required for settlements upon the death of an employee.

There may be more than one payroll/personnel system. The systems should be set up to handle efficiently the different disbursements, such as payout cycles, type of employees (salaried, hourly, executive, and officer), employees' country location, retirees, and so on. The data base information is also used to report other kinds of information. For instance, past earnings history is used to determine pension plan data and determine retirement pay. Finally, employees are informed periodically of any withholding deducted from their gross pay.

Current Hours File The current hours file contains the data needed to calculate each employee's gross pay for the current pay period. This data includes the number of hours worked, both regular and overtime, by each employee. It may also include a code for the nature or location of the work in order to facilitate expense allocation.

Tax Table and Deduction File Federal income tax withholding and other deductions information can be easily maintained in a separate data file, since this data changes infrequently. Combining this file with earnings, exemptions, and deductions information from the employee master file produces the actual deductions and makes it possible to calculate net pay.

Outputs and Interfaces

The major outputs of the payroll cycle are paychecks, payroll register and related reports, required government forms, general ledger entries, and budget reports.

Paychecks Depending on a company's payroll cycle, weekly, biweekly, semi-monthly, or monthly checks are prepared and issued. In the event of a payday falling on a holiday or weekend, the schedule is usually adjusted to pay employees on the preceding workday. The typical computer system prepares the checks and generates payroll ledgers which are reviewed to ensure that the proper amounts are paid. Employees may elect to have their paychecks deposited directly into their bank accounts if their banks belong to the National Clearing House Association. In this case, the employee would receive a receipt of deposit and a statement of earnings and deductions. Generally, paychecks or payroll stubs are delivered to employees by a designated employee other than the immediate supervisor. This procedure allows for a segregation of duties between check distribution and salary authorization.

There are a number of controls to assure that checks are disbursed for accurate amounts and only to authentic employees. These controls should include:

- establishment of check dollar limits,
- implementation of a computer generated exception report for excessive employee hours,
- segregation of duties between check preparation, check signing, and check distribution,
- use of prenumbered checks,

- reconciliation of checks signed to the payroll register before distribution,
- periodic check distributions by internal audit,
- reconciliation of a payroll imprest account, and
- employee verification when checks are disbursed.

Payroll Register and Reports   Amounts paid to employees and related payroll adjustments should be accurately and promptly summarized, classified, and reported. Summaries usually are in the form of a payroll register or journal. The amounts and hours worked are accumulated according to the company's chart of accounts. Payroll registers are the basis for the general ledger entries that are forwarded to the financial reporting cycle for posting to the general ledger. By means of the payroll register, selected data is extracted for individual employee reports, such as employee tax withholdings and contributions to savings plans.

Payroll registers are also used by management to control operations. Payroll costs are allocated to a number of different expense categories such as investments, underwriting expenses, and corporate expenses and reported in the results of operations. In addition, there are detailed reports that break out expenses by line of business or departments. Management uses these reports to analyze the results for the accounting period in comparison to prior years' results and budgeted goals.

Promptness as well as accuracy must be emphasized when summarization and reporting occurs. Promptness is necessary if all activities that occur in a particular reporting period are to be recognized in that period. The techniques that are employed in the payroll cycle to achieve proper recording of transactions should therefore address the completeness of what is classified, summarized, and reported, as well as the accuracy of information.

Required Government Forms   The payroll cycle also produces required government reports. All employers required to withhold income taxes or liable for social security taxes must file a quarterly return on Form 941. In January of each year, employers must furnish employees a record of taxes withheld (Form W-2), and this information must be transmitted to the Internal Revenue Service as well. Similarly, state payroll tax returns may be required. In addition, employers subject to Federal Unemployment Tax must file Form 940 showing their total payroll and tax liability for the year.

General Ledger Entries   Once payroll processing is completed, payroll transactions are summarized into general ledger entries. These general ledger entries should be coded to feed the expense allocation system.

Budget Reports The payroll cycle interacts with the budgeting system in monitoring payroll expense. The particular information needed from the payroll cycle depends in part on the nature of the company's budgeting system. Fundamental principles and common variations in budgeting are considered in Chapter 5.

NONPAYROLL EXPENDITURE CYCLE

The nonpayroll expenditure or purchasing cycle involves the acquisition of goods and services for use in the company's operations. The accounting information system classifies these transactions among various asset and expense accounts. These transactions include rental or purchase of office space and equipment, puchase of office and maintenance supplies, and the securing and payment of outside services, including most underwriting expenses except payroll and commission. The purchasing cycle transactions do not include investments in stocks, bonds, and real estate since these transactions are included in the investment cycle.

Various departments within an insurance company participate in the processing of nonpayroll expenditure cycle transactions. Accordingly, controls ensuring that the types and terms of the company expenditures are appropriately authorized and that the transactions are completely and accurately processed are an integral part of an effective nonpayroll expenditure cycle.

Functions

A number of departments process transactions related to the nonpayroll expenditure cycle. The requesting departments identify needs, request orders be placed, and may receive and inspect goods and services. The purchasing department places orders for goods and services required by all requesting departments in the company. Corporate accounting reviews vendor invoices, allocates expenses, prepares checks, summarizes detail in subsidiary ledgers, and records general ledger entries. Finally, the cashiers section of the treasury department reviews documentation supporting disbursements and signs checks.

Requesting Departments All departments within the company identify needs for goods and services. If those needs are included within the budget or proper authorization has been obtained, they prepare purchase order requests to notify the purchasing department of their needs. The supply department prepares purchase order requests for inventory items while the requesting departments prepare purchase order requests for noninventory items. The purchase order request notifies purchasing that goods or services are required. It details the requesting department, quantity and description of goods or services, and the date required.

The department preparing the purchase order request also receives the goods or services. Inventory items are sent directly to the supply department and noninventory items are sent to the requesting department. The receiving department's copy of the purchase order is used as the receiving report and should not include the price or the amount of goods requested. This department should be required to count the number of items received and include this number in the purchase order. This number will be compared to the invoice and original purchase order to ensure that the purchase order was processed accurately. Additionally, the receiving department should inspect the goods for any damage. The purchase order copy is then forwarded to corporate accounting.

If goods or services do not meet specifications, the purchasing department is notified and uses this information to update its authorized vendor list. When goods not meeting specifications are received, they may either be returned, or a price adjustment requested by corporate accounting through a debit memo. Receiving reports are forwarded to corporate accounting where they are used to verify that goods and services invoiced by vendors were received. Discrepancies between receiving reports and invoices are one source of debit memos requested by corporate accounting. Receiving reports for goods received but not invoiced at the close of an accounting period (the "open receiver file") are the basis for accrual entries.

Purchasing Department Most insurance companies have centralized purchasing departments which select vendors and contractors and order required goods and services. Vendor and contractor selection is based on the quality and price of required goods, delivery and payment terms, and reputation and prior experience.

Supplier and Contractor Selection. Dollar amount limits should be established to differentiate between items ordered through vendor listings or items where bids are required. For those purchases requiring bids, vendors are requested to submit bids detailing the price and terms under which they can provide the required goods or services. Bids are more frequently used when contracting services, since several criteria may be considered relevant, while price is the common criterion used to evaluate goods. The company should prepare requests for proposals specifying the criteria used to evaluate the bids. Additionally, the company may want to standardize the selection by assigning weights to the different criteria and then judging the criteria on a 1 to

10 point basis. The purchasing and requesting departments then select the vendor who scores the most favorably.

To facilitate vendor selection, purchasing generally maintains an approved vendor list. This list is updated periodically for new vendors and changes in the level of service provided by existing vendors. In other cases, purchasing agents consult vendor catalogs to obtain information on price, delivery, and payment terms. Information concerning the vendor's reputation and quality of his goods and services is obtained from industry publications and previous experience.

Purchasing of Goods.   Purchases made by an insurance company can be divided into two categories: inventory and noninventory. Noninventory items are purchased as needed rather than on a routine basis according to specifications provided by the department requiring the goods or service.

Noninventory items include but are not limited to, computer hardware and software, autos and other fixed asset additions. The single order purchase form is used for goods and services which are not routinely required. The single order purchase order details the description of goods or services, price, quantity of goods or duration of service, and special terms of the purchase, such as freight and delivery.

Inventory items are purchased routinely in large quantities, and they are often requested, received, stored, and distributed by a centralized supply department. Goods or services such as security, cleaning and maintenance services, small office equipment, and office supplies are usually purchased on a routine basis from pre-approved vendors. Rather than prepare a new purchase order each time the item is required, a blanket purchase order may be prepared. The blanket purchase order specifies the term over which service is to be provided, minimum/maximum quantity of goods to be purchased, and price. The delivery of goods covered by a blanket purchase order is authorized via a blanket purchase order release. The centralized supply department maintains records to internally allocate the supply costs to the user department. This supply department should establish an economic order quantity system. This system arrives at the best ordering point, which helps minimize expense. The advantage of a centralized supply department is that inventory will usually be lower and the company will not have money invested in non-earning assets. A disadvantage is that individual departments might feel the urge to maintain their own "mini-inventory" and thereby defeat the purpose of the centralized supply department. Analytical reviews provide controls that could avoid oversupply.

Purchase Orders.   Communication between the company and vendors or contractors begins with the purchasing department preparing a purchase order with copies distributed to the vendor or contractor, the requesting department, corporate accounting's open purchase order file, and purchasing's open purchase order file. Purchase order copies are used by receiving departments and corporate accounting to determine whether the goods or services received agree with those ordered and invoiced. Open purchase order files should be reviewed periodically to ensure receipt of items that may be important to the company. Additionally, this review would help in updating the approved vendor listing.

Services should be inspected on a regular basis with amounts retained to ensure service completion. Performance bonds may substitute such retentions. When a purchase order is prepared the purchasing department enters the expense classification. This account classification is checked and used by corporate accounting to allocate expenses.

Corporate Accounting The primary purchasing cycle functions performed by corporate accounting are invoice verification, maintenance of the expense allocation systems and capitalized asset systems, and budget reporting.

Corporate accounting matches receiving reports from requesting departments to invoices received from vendors to determine whether:

- the quantity, description, and terms of the invoice agree to the receiving reports,
- the invoice is mathematically accurate,
- the account classification is accurate, and
- the purchase was approved by an appropriate level of management.

These functions provide both preventive and detective controls. The accounting department should discover any discrepancies in the purchase order, and in the case of discrepancies, prevent the erroneous disbursement of funds. Corporate accounting matches approval signatures to an authorized approver signature file to determine whether purchases were approved by an appropriate level of management. This file contains the signatures of authorized approvers and indicates the type and amount of receipts they may approve.

Corporate accounting should prepare, but not sign, a check if the receiving report and invoice match, and the disbursement has been properly approved. Checks prepared by corporate accounting, along with the supporting invoices and receiving reports or other supporting documentation, are forwarded to the cashier's department for review and check signing.

Vendors do not always issue invoices for items paid on a periodic basis, such as monthly lease payments, consulting fees, and legal retainers. The amount and timing of these payments is established when the contract for the goods or services is negotiated. To expedite processing of these routine disbursements, check preparation may be automated through an automatic payment system, for which corporate accounting is responsible. When a contract is negotiated, corporate accounting records the amount, vendor, and payment terms on the automatic system. Each month, checks are prepared for all items on the system. As a preventive measure, corporate accounting should review the checks produced to ensure disbursements are prepared only for authorized items.

Corporate accounting must determine whether the goods or services purchased benefit more than one period, and if so, the items should be capitalized. The company should establish a policy to capitalize items over a specific dollar amount and expense items under such amount. This policy should reduce the bookkeeping of insignificant items and would not materially misstate financial information.

Normally, fixed assets are property and equipment used in the company's operations, such as furniture, office equipment, and office buildings. Corporate accounting computes and records depreciation and amortization to allocate the cost of long-term assets to expense over the periods they are expected to benefit.

In addition, corporate accounting is responsible for periodically reviewing the fixed asset system. Over time, the useful lives of fixed assets may change and therefore the amortization schedule should be revised. Also fixed assets may become obsolete and removed from service. Fixed assets should be written off when this happens.

Source Documents

Critical source documents in the nonpayroll expenditure cycle are purchase orders, vendor invoices, debit memos, payment requests, and expense checks.

Purchase Orders Purchase orders record the description, quantity, and related information concerning goods and services the company intends to purchase. Purchase orders indicate authorization to procure goods and services and document the details of each transaction. Purchase orders should be numbered consecutively for control purposes.

Vendor Invoices Vendor invoices normally show the description of the goods and services received, the price including freight, the cash discount terms, and the date of the billing. They are essential documents because each specifies the amount of money owed to a vendor for a particular acquisition.

Debit Memos When a company is invoiced for goods which were returned or received in damaged condition, corporate accounting prepares a debit memo to notify the vendor that the full amount invoiced will not be paid. The debit memo contains a reference to the original purchase order and vendor invoice, a description of the item, and the reason the item was unacceptable.

Payment Requests When payment to a vendor has been approved, the payment request documents the authorization and the account to be charged. This document, along with related invoices or other supporting documents, initiates the issuing of a check.

Expense Checks The checks issued to vendors are the actual payment for acquisitions. Normally computerized systems print checks and check stubs containing detailed information concerning the transaction. The information on the check stub can be traced back to the open payables file and to the original purchase order. When the vendor deposits the check and it clears the bank, the canceled check is returned. Those canceled checks serve to verify that payment was completed.

Data Bases

The principal data bases involved in the nonpayroll expenditure cycle are the vendor master file, the open and paid expense file, and the fixed asset inventory ledger.

Vendor Master File The vendor master file contains one record for each vendor. Each record shows a vendor's name, identifying number, address, telephone number, the name of the established contact with that vendor, and the normal discount provisions. In addition, the file maintains for each vendor a record of payments and discounts for the current period, for the year-to-date, and for the previous year. It is updated with each processing. Thus it provides the current balance by invoice for each vendor at any given time.

This file can also be used to record all payments to individuals during the year so that such information can be furnished on Form 1099, as required by the Internal Revenue Service.

Open and Paid Expense File All payables appear in this file with one record for each invoice. It links each invoice to a specific vendor in the vendor master file. This file allows the retrieval of any or all open payables. Together with the vendor master file it makes possible the determination of the total amount owed to any specific vendor.

Fixed Assets Inventory Ledger This file serves as a perpetual summary of fixed assets owned by the company. Fixed asset vendor invoices are the source documents for a detailed fixed asset subsidiary ledger. The ledger should include the following information:

- description,
- location,
- purchase date,
- salvage value,
- estimated life,
- category of asset for accelerated cost recovery system,
- accumulated depreciation (for book and tax),
- net book value for book and tax, and
- investment tax credit.

The additions and deletions should provide the general ledger entries. Additionally, depreciation expense can be calculated with the information stored in the data base. The resulting total generates the general ledger entry for depreciation expense. This ledger should also summarize the fixed assets held by location since it would facilitate the company's personal property tax calculation.

Periodically, a physical inventory of fixed assets should take place for control purposes and the file should be updated accordingly.

Outputs and Interfaces

The outputs and interfaces involved in the nonpayroll expenditure cycle are cash disbursements, general ledger entries, and cost accounting and budget reports.

Cash Disbursements The cashier's function is responsible for signing and mailing checks to vendors and contractors after the invoice and supporting documentation have been properly approved. The primary documents generated by cashiers are vouchers to record disbursements issued in payment of purchasing cycle transactions. The entries made by cashiers affect cash and expense accounts as well as accounts payable and fixed assets.

The timing of cash disbursements is established according to the company's cash management policy. This policy coordinates cash receipts and disbursements to provide optimum use of cash balances and should be an objective of the treasury cycle.

General Ledger Entries General ledger entries to record purchases and accounts payable are prepared by corporate accounting based on input from purchasing, requesting departments, and vendors.

The entries made by corporate accounting generally affect the following accounts:

- fixed assets,
- expense accounts,
- accounts payable, and
- other assets such as prepaids.

Fixed assets are allocated to expense through periodic depreciation and amortization entries. When corporate accounting computes and records depreciation and amortization, these amounts are then allocated through the expense allocation system to the appropriate departments.

Cost Accounting and Budget Reports To establish a basis for comparison between years, purchasing cycle transactions must be allocated to expense on a consistent basis, in accordance with uniform accounting instructions. State insurance department regulations provide instructions for the allocation of expense by basic operating expense classification, company (if more than one insurance company is operated jointly), functional expense group, and line of business. There are a number of principles used to allocate expenses to the appropriate categories. Expenses incurred for a specific company, function, or line of business are allocated directly. Expenses not directly allocable that are related to certain direct expenses are allocated in the same proportion as the direct expense to which they relate. Expenses unrelated to any direct expense may be allocated based on time studies or any other reasonable method, such as premium volume.

To compare expenditures between accounting periods, accrual entries must be made to account for purchases received but unpaid for at the end of the period. There are two sources for the accrual entries. Accounting vouchers all vendor invoices received and unpaid. The open receiver file contains receiving reports for goods and services received but not yet invoiced by the vendor.

Management monitors the progress of an organization towards goals and objectives by comparing costs between accounting periods and by comparing actual to budgeted results. Before an accounting period starts, management should prepare measurable goals such as sales and expense volume by department. At the end of each accounting period, actual results are compared to the budget. Variations are highlighted so corrective actions can be taken. A number of budget performance reports are prepared in varying length of detail for use by operating, middle, and senior level management.

SUMMARY

This chapter reviewed the treasury, investment, payroll, and nonpayroll expenditure cycles. Together with the cycles reviewed in Chapter 3, these cycles encompass the essential processing activity for an insurance company.

The treasury cycle coordinates the receipt and application of funds. Its functions typically include banking services analysis, cash management, stock issuance and retirement, and cash disbursement. The critical source documents are cash, stock certificates, letters of credit, debt certificates, and interest and dividend checks. Data bases may include a master file of stockholders, a listing of commercial paperholders and investors interest and dividend schedules, loan compliance checklists, records of loans to affiliates, balances of cash, money market and commercial paper accounts, long-term debt subsidiary accounts, stockholder subsidiary accounts, and intercompany accounts. The treasury cycle generates daily reports for cash management and interfaces with the investment, premium, loss and loss expense, payroll, and nonpayroll expenditure cycles to transfer funds for company operations and with the financial reporting cycle to make general ledger entries.

The investment cycle uses the funds generated in company operations for income producing purposes. Its essential functions are the authorization of investment transactions, the processing of principal and income, and the safekeeping of securities. Source documents for the investment cycle include buy-sell advices, buy-sell confirmations, safekeeping receipts, mortgage and loan service reports, and checks and drafts. These documents generate the principal data bases, the investment master file, and the investment safekeeping records. Interface with the treasury cycle accounts for funds expended and received in investment activity and with the financial and management reporting cycle produces general ledger entries and management reports.

The payroll cycle encompasses all the activities involved in paying employees and accounting for that expenditure. Functions of the payroll cycle include hiring, attendance and time reporting, payroll accounting, payroll adjustments, and tax reports. The critical source documents are personnel action notices, time reports, and special payment authorizations. The employee master file constitutes the primary data base for the payroll cycle although it may also draw on a current hours file and a tax table and deductions file. The output of the payroll cycle includes paychecks, payroll registers and related reports, required government forms, general ledger entries, and budget reports.

The nonpayroll expenditure or purchasing cycle acquires goods and services needed in the company's operations. Its typical functions include identifying needs and requesting purchase orders, selecting vendors, purchasing goods, receiving and inspecting goods, accounting for transactions, and making payments. Critical source documents are purchase orders, vendor invoices, debit memos, payment requests, and expense checks. Data bases used in the nonpayroll expenditure cycle may include a vendor master file, an open and paid expense file, and a fixed asset inventory ledger. The cycle's output includes cash disbursements, general ledger entries, and cost accounting and budget reports.

In addition to the eight cycles presented in these two chapters, insurance information systems also incorporate a financial reporting and control cycle. The financial reporting cycle of an insurance company normally does not process transactions as other cycles do. Rather, it obtains accounting and operating information from other cycles and analyzes, evaluates, summarizes, reconciles, adjusts, and reclassifies the information so that it can be reported to management and outsiders.

The next chapter develops the essential budgeting concepts that underlie the design of major planning and control processes for an insurance company.

CHAPTER 5

Budgeting and Planning

INTRODUCTION

An insurance company, like any other firm, is a complex *system;* that is, a collection of individuals, offices, and functions working together to achieve a common objective. The major purposes of an organization's planning and control processes are to align all of the resources, talents, and energies of the firm in the direction desired by management, to measure progress toward company goals, and to identify, where necessary, the need for corrective actions.

Planning for any firm is a complex process involving a very long-range mission, long-range strategies and short-run goals and objectives. The short-run operational plan usually results, in part, in a budget as an integral part of the plan. The discussion here will be limited to budgets or the translation of other forms of planning into documents which use numbers as both goals for the planning period and yardsticks to measure results.

Whether it is called annual business planning, tactical planning, operational planning, or some other name, most companies undertake some sort of annual process that includes a budget. In fact, many companies prepare a variety of annual budgets for planning purposes, including cash budgets, capital budgets, and human resource budgets, which one author has called the "capital budgets of service companies."[1] Nevertheless, for the purposes of this chapter, the term "budget" will be understood to mean a *short-term operating plan for an insurance organization which contains detailed premium, loss, expense, or other financial operating information grouped by company, profit center, or functional responsibility.*

189

Although prepared in a variety of different formats, with different time horizons, and using different processes, the purposes served by the preparation of detailed annual operating budgets generally include one or more of the objectives discussed below.

Coordinate Actions of Diverse Organizational Units

Planning, negotiation, and inter-departmental communications involved in the development of annual budgets help insure that each operating unit or function has a clear picture of short-run corporate objectives and the contribution each division must make in order to achieve the budget targets. For example, as a part of its annual planning process, management may decide to introduce a new product or coverage not previously written directly by the company. Such a decision would have an impact on a variety of functional or profit center budgets, each of which would have to consider the impact of the new product on its own operations. Sales, for instance, would have to consider the new product's potential effects on agency production quotas, sales commissions, advertising, and promotional expenses. Claims would have to review claim volume projections for the new product, and budget for the anticipated changes in the number, training, and locations of adjuster personnel. Underwriting would have to consider the rating, classification, and pricing demands to be created by the new product. Data administration, accounting, and a variety of other support functions would assess their own budget impacts.

The budgeting process should force the consideration of all these impacts in a coordinated fashion and cause resource needs (and possibly resource constraints) to be identified before the plan becomes operational.

Communication

Both initial budgeting targets and the final budget document are important communication devices. The initial goals or budgeting objectives which are established provide a clear indication of the expectations, desires, and outlook for the future held by top management, and may significantly affect (either positively or negatively) the outlooks of middle and firstline managers. Similarly, the final budget or operating plan represents the major blueprint for the firm's activities over the indicated time horizon, and should be viewed as a critical communication document for guidance and direction to management throughout the period.

Motivate Performance

Carefully constructed budget targets can give managers incentives to strive for results beyond those they would normally seek. Budgets which contain such "stretch" objectives may cause the organization to work harder, longer, or more productively than would be true without the existence of the budget goals (particularly when a significant portion of compensation is dependent upon their achievement). However, targets perceived as impossible to achieve may cause managers of operating units to give up any attempt to achieve, or even come close to, the stated budget targets. Early communication of targets before the final budget is generated helps to mitigate this potential problem.

Evaluate Performance

Many companies use annual budget goals as performance measures. They may even tie a sizable fraction of an agent's or employee's annual compensation to the level of actual performance versus annual plan or budget. This particular use of the budget may provide motivation to some managers to "game-play" with the establishment of budget targets by attempting to establish easily achievable targets. This factor should be considered in evaluating the reasonableness of individual departmental or profit-center budget submissions, particularly in a budget process that begins at the bottom levels of the organization.

Support Delegation of Authority

Top-level managers will be more willing to delegate day-to-day operational decision-making authority to subordinates and line units if managers (1) have a clear understanding of the objectives and detailed action plans of the individual units, and (2) are confident that a timely and responsive reporting process will identify significant deviations from expected results. A comprehensive annual budgeting cycle that creates a clear understanding of unit operating objectives among top management as well as meaningful financial or operational targets for subordinate managers will permit top management to delegate the authority necessary to accomplish the plan farther down the organizational structure than would otherwise be possible.

Link Strategic and "Tactical" Planning

This discussion of the annual planning or budgeting process presupposes the existence of longer-term corporate goals, objectives, and strategies as normally encompassed in a *strategic plan.* The yearly budgets, therefore, become "the vehicle for the near-term implementation of the ongoing strategy."[2] Alternatively, we can view the long-term strategy as "composed of a series of short-term plans or strategies. Each of these short-term plans builds upon the one before it."[3] Whichever view is held, it is vital that annual plans or budgets be linked to longer-term corporate objectives, and that these annual plans provide a means to accomplish broader strategic programs and action plans through current operations.

A company's budget, along with an associated reporting system to identify actual versus expected results, supports both the *planning* and *control* functions within an organization. The activities associated with developing an annual budget may, in fact, represent the majority of the planning effort which a company and its managers expend during a typical year. Thus, the requirement to prepare an annual budget is the catalyst which forces managers to consider their own long and short-run objectives and the kinds of activities required within their own organizations to support corporate goals. Once in place, however, the purpose of the budget shifts to that of *control,* with constant monitoring and reporting of actual results measuring the company's progress toward established targets and identifying the need for corrective actions. Thus, just as a linkage must exist between strategic and operational plans, so must a close relationship exist between the budgeting system and the systems developed to monitor and control company activities. In essence, the budgeting and reporting systems are "two sides of the same coin," since:

1. the establishment of appropriate budget targets or performance standards is largely based on historic data, derived from a company's reporting process; while
2. performance measurement (reporting) systems must be closely linked to budget targets and parameters in order to provide management with relevant performance measures.

ESSENTIALS OF BUDGETING AND REPORTING SYSTEM DESIGN

Each company creates its own unique budgeting and reporting system. To do so, it must first resolve certain fundamental issues concerning the dominant objectives of the system. In addition to those objectives, the system should meet accepted criteria for budgeting and reporting systems.

Fundamental Issues

The company can resolve the fundamental issues by reaching agreement on a series of essential questions. When should budgeting start, and what time period should the budget cover? Should a "top-down" or "bottom-up" budget process be established? Should the budget be fixed, or should it be revised periodically to incorporate actual results or activity levels? How much "stretch" should be introduced into budgets, and to what extent (if any) should management compensation be based on actual versus budgeted performance? There are no universally correct answers to these questions. Each company must consider the advantages and disadvantages discussed below and determine its own priorities.

Time Period In general, budgeting should commence as close to the start of the budget period as possible, yet early enough to insure a thorough and conscientious job. The precise timing of the budget preparation cycle will be a function of a number of factors, including the size and complexity of the organization, the nature of the process itself, and the nature of the planning environment and product markets (stable or dynamic, stage of product life cycle, and so on).

The time period budgeted may also vary widely among companies, ranging from daily cash budgets to the more standard monthly, quarterly, or annual basis for operational budgets. In order to accommodate the Annual Statement reporting requirements, however, most insurance companies use a calendar-year basis for budget and reporting systems.

Top-down or Bottom-up Approach A critical issue in the development of a budgeting process is the extent to which all levels of management will participate in the establishment of initial budget targets and final budget amounts.

A top-down approach permits senior management to establish corporate operating goals in line with its assessments of the company's strengths, weaknesses, resources, organizational structure, and economic and competitive environments. Top-down approaches are particularly relevant in times of dynamic changes or crises within the company's existing product markets, when the nature of the business demands close coordination among diverse operating or functional units, or when unit managers lack the perspectives, skills, or training to participate in budget setting.

A bottom-up approach, however, takes advantage of operating management's daily interaction with and knowledge of the company's marketplace, products, and customers. Furthermore, budget targets and objectives developed with strong input from affected unit managers are far more likely to evoke commitment than those imposed from above.

Fixed or Revised Many companies, particularly those which emphasize the *planning* (as opposed to "control") use of the budgeting process, periodically revise or update budgets as time passes or as actual results differ from planned. Some companies utilize *rolling* budgets, which constantly project nine to twelve months ahead, and which add an additional quarter to existing budgets each time a quarter is completed. Other companies revise budgets periodically throughout the budget period as conditions change or new information becomes available. One common approach is to use a *flexible budget* concept, which ties most or all budget parameters to amounts per unit sold or produced, thus insulating management's evaluations of performance from errors in volume forecasts.

Whatever approach is used, modifications or revisions to budgets can be used to communicate and reinforce necessary changes to company operating plans and procedures in response to economic, competitive, or environment conditions different from those assumed in budget preparation. Nevertheless, budget revisions may be highly controversial. Periodic budget revision activities may take up a considerable amount of management time. More basic, however, is the question of whether a "rubber yardstick" is being created that cannot effectively measure company or managerial performance. This issue highlights the dual (and, sometimes, contradictory) nature of the planning versus control purposes served by company or operating unit budgets.

Actual versus Budgeted Results The uses of the budget as a catalyst for management *planning* responsibilities have been discussed earlier, as has the operation of a budget/reporting system as a *control* mechanism for the company. Budgets and budgeting targets can also be used to *motivate* the organization to achieve results beyond what would be attained without these goals. Often, budget targets for individuals or units are established at levels somewhat *beyond* what may be readily accepted as achievable, with the anticipation that extraordinary efforts will be made to attain the goals, resulting in exceptional performance for the organization. The risk in this approach is that goals will be set so high that they are perceived as impossible, thus producing no additional effort and, in extreme cases, poorer results than would have been achieved with more realistic targets.

This situation may be further complicated when actual as opposed to budgeted results are used as a major tool in a manager's performance evaluation, compensation, or both. Under these circumstances, the conflicts between top management's desires for "stretch" budget targets and middle managers' attempts to negotiate feasible goals may inject controversy into the determination of annual planning targets.

Budgeting Systems

Regardless of the approach a company takes in resolving these issues, two principles of budget and reporting system construction are applicable to virtually any firm.

First, a budget is more than simply a forecast or extrapolation of historic trends into the future. One of the purposes of planning is to "impact" or influence the organization, marketplace, or competitive environment such that corporate goals are obtained. In short, a forecast is a prediction of what may happen, while a budget involves a commitment to a forecast to make an agreed outcome occur. In contrast to a forecast of "where will we be," a budget includes "where we are, where we want to go, how we want to get there, when we want to arrive, and how much we want to pay for the trip."

Second, budgets should focus on critical success parameters for an organization. Depending on the nature of the operation or organization, the most critical parameters for planning and control purposes may be either financial or operational in nature. For instance, planning and reporting systems at the corporate level of an insurance company emphasize financial measures and systems aimed at measuring the financial impacts of planned actions. Such measures are appropriate for *profit and service centers* within the company, which may encompass the organization as a whole or various individual operating units under the corporate umbrella.

Budgeting and reporting systems and data bases, particularly at the corporate level, are often adjuncts to those required to support statutory and regulatory financial reporting requirements. The product groupings, accounting techniques employed, and measures developed in this manner *may or may not* be optimal for planning and reporting. Management should recognize the possibility that modifying a statutory-based information system may be necessary for internal planning.

Although financial targets and reporting in dollar units may be suitable for many budgeting entities, nonfinancial or operational planning parameters may be more relevant in many situations, particularly those involving functional organizations or sub-units within a profit center. A regional claims operation, for instance, may consider such items as number of adjusters, claims per adjuster, or numbers of suits, far more critical to the unit's success than numerous financially-oriented performance measures. Thus, it is important that any budgeting and reporting system addresses and measures the most critical performance parameters for the corporate level or unit it intends to serve whether those parameters are financial or operational in nature.

Reporting Essentials

A sound reporting system is an inseparable part of the budgeting process because it enables management to use the budget for *control* purposes. The design of such a system must incorporate devices that allow time for corrective action, provide information useful for decision making, and assure that the information appears in an understandable format.

Time for Corrective Action   Using the budgeting and reporting process for control purposes within an organization depends on receiving feedback concerning the actual results in relation to plan *in time to implement appropriate corrective actions*. The more closely an information or reporting system can operate to "real-time," the more valuable the resultant information will be. There are trade-offs, of course, between the timeliness of the feedback and both the accuracy and cost of the reporting system. Thus, management must constantly evaluate the cost/benefit relationships associated with the development of faster, more precise information systems.

Decision Support   The output of a reporting system must be "information," not simply "data." A key test of the success of a reporting system is whether it supports decision-making and corrective action programs through the generation of actionable information. For instance, knowledge that losses are high in a given state or geographic territory may be available to management, but this data may provide little guidance in the formulation of proper corrective action programs. A breakdown of losses by line of business or coverage, a review of loss ratios by county or rating territory, the identification of the relative influence of catastrophe losses compared to prior years, or the distinction between paid loss data and incurred losses (which incorporate loss reserving effects) may all provide clues to the *action* required to correct a significant deviation between actual and planned losses.

One means of insuring that major variances between actual and planned results are highlighted is via a technique termed *exception reporting*. Under exception reporting, *only those parameters for which results deviate from plan by an amount greater than some pre-determined level are routinely displayed*. All other results are assumed to be tracking closely with plan, thereby precluding the need for explicit management consideration. The purpose of this technique is to extract from the thousands of bits of information which *could* be provided to management only those items which may require greater attention and, very possibly, the development of explicit corrective action programs.

Understandable Format Finally, reporting systems built initially for other purposes, such as statutory reporting, may not provide information in the desired format or detail to support management decision-making or corrective action programs. Where appropriate, product definitions and product groups, expense and investment income allocation practices, and basic accounting techniques all may be different within management's information and reporting systems from those used to support regulatory reporting needs.

BUDGETING

As the introduction to this chapter explained, budgeting and reporting are "two sides of the same coin." Companies must budget as part of the planning process, and they must report in order to exercise control. The reporting and controlling activities will be explained in detail in the next chapter. For now, the details involved in the budgeting process will be reviewed.

This discussion of budgeting covers all facets of property and liability underwriting operations: income, losses, expenses, and underwriting gain or loss. The techniques employed to arrive at budget objectives will vary from company to company depending on many factors: the legal form of the entity (stock, mutual, or reciprocal); the producers involved (independent agents, direct writer agents, or "no-agent-telemarketing operations"), personal lines versus commercial lines emphasis, and so on.

Budgeting Principles

Certain general budgeting practices should be explained before turning to the major issues of income, losses, expenses, and underwriting gain. These general practices involve forecasts, schedules, forms, the controller's role, reconciliations, critiques, and techniques.

Forecasts The budget-year objectives in most instances are based on a desired improvement or change from current year levels. For example, desirable income growth may be 12 percent; expenses are to be held to an increase of no more than 5 percent; loss ratios are to improve two points (for example, from 70 percent to 68 percent).

Thus, in order to set objectives for the budget year, the current year results must first be identified. However, usually the current year is still unfolding since budgeting is usually done in the September-November period. Consequently, it is necessary to *forecast* the current year results. This is an important step, since the forecast provides the "jumping-off" point for the following budget year. As an example, if a forecast of policies-in-force is too optimistic, premium objectives for the budget year will be more difficult to attain.

Conversely, an overly pessimistic forecast involving current year sales production levels could mean that the quotas for the following budget year will contain less stretch than desired. Instead of budget-year sales increase of 11 percent planned in September, the January comparison of a quota to prior year actual may reveal only an 8 percent improvement objective (i.e., forecast year $100 versus budget year $111 = 11 percent; actual year $102.8 versus budget year $111 = 8 percent).

Thus, along with the other elements discussed, a sound budgeting process must also contain well-developed forecasting and estimation procedures. The later discussions of specific budgeting techniques applicable to each major area of an insurer's operations (agency strength, premium income, losses, and expenses) will, therefore, review both forecasting procedures useful for estimating current period results, as well as those procedures used to establish budgets for future time periods.

Schedules The budgetary schedule is the basic tool on which to plan the coordinating activities. All parties affected by the budget must agree to specific completion dates. The data requirements must be known. Simply stated, the schedule indicates "who does what ... and when." With this knowledge, no unanswered questions should exist.

An abbreviated example of a budget schedule appears in Exhibit 5-1.

Forms The forms used impose constraints on the budgeting process. Thus simplicity is desirable. The forms should not be complicated, and there should not be too many of them. The overriding concern has to be one of accuracy and completeness so that the final budget is one that is reliable (that is, it must contain no errors of omission or commission.)

For example, on one form (shown in Exhibit 5-2) a profit center displays its actual results through August, the forecast for the current year and a comparison to the current year budget, the proposed budget for the upcoming year, and a comparison of the proposed budget to the current year forecasts.

Controller's Budgetary Role Managerial judgment is paramount in budgeting. It must be exercised at all decision-making points to ensure not only understanding of the budget but acceptance as well. Normally, the individual with the controllership role acts as the "devil's advocate" for management, making certain that the budget is realistic and contains achievable goals. When the final product is completed, it

Exhibit 5-1
Budget Schedule—IIA Insurance Company

President prepares a Letter of Direction to the vice-presidents of operations and other presidential cabinet officers. —Complete by September 2.

Each property/casualty line unit, including Reinsurance, and all staff offices develop operating plans in accordance with their Letter of Direction. —Complete by October 28.

Budgets and Costs Department meets with the Staff Offices to review and reaffirm their expense plans. —Complete by November 25.

Financial Analysis Department presents the Operating Plan to the Board in light of 1985 major changes and the 1986 Strategic Plan goals. —Complete by December 11.

should bear a striking resemblance to and be consistent with the desired results, policies, and practices of the organization.

Budget Reconciliations   The ideal budgeting process also involves a recognition of the "reconciliation" need. Budgeting begins with direction from the top indicating what the executive group would like to see in the budget itself. The line unit planning its budget builds what it thinks are achievable goals. Frequently the top-down direction and the bottom-up planning conflict and require a reconciliation of both viewpoints. When this reconciliation occurs, the best of both worlds results, with each side understanding the other's position.

One technique for a budget reconciliation is to convene a meeting between line and staff.

The line managers present their plans and budgets for the coming year. If these plans and budgets do not adhere to direction from the top, they provide explanations.

The controller's staff reviews the results, compares the line's proposed budget to the desired company direction, and arrives at a consensus, if at all possible. During a concluding session, the top staff officer summarizes the points of disparity between the line and staff positions and provides the final budget agreements to the line management group.

Critiques   Any budget critique should involve a review or post-mortem of the budget schedules, forms, meetings, data, and so on. This procedure should constantly be raising the question, "How could we

Exhibit 5-2
Region Operating Results—1986 Budget

R-1

	August Year to Date	Current Year Forecast	Current Year Budget	()=Unfavorable Variance	Proposed Budget	Unit Changes Over Current Year Forecast	() = Decrease Percent Changes Over Current Year Forecast
Total Direct Written Premium	$47,110.3	$71,153.0	$ 72,574.7	$(1,421.7)	$79,192.3	$8,039.3	% 11.3
Decentralized Direct Written Premium	40,130.7	60,134.6	61,122.6	(988.0)	67,192.0	7,057.4	11.7
Decentralized Net Earned Premium	37,737.4	57,836.3	58,804.7	(968.4)	64,491.2	6,654.9	11.5
Decent. Losses Incurred	27,581.9	40,410.0	38,173.3	(2,236.7)	44,081.7	3,671.7	9.1
Total Regional Expenses—Related	14,031.5	21,060.6	22,921.5	1,860.9	23,148.5	2,088.0	9.9
Regional Related Gain/(Loss)	(3,867.0)	(3,634.3)	(2,290.1)	(1,344.2)	(2,739.0)	(895.3)	(24.6)
Loss Ratio	73.1%	69.9%	64.9%	(5.0)%	68.4%	(1.5)%	—
Expense Ratio—Related	37.2%	36.4%	39.0%	2.6 %	35.9%	(0.4)%	—
Reg. Related Gain/(Loss) Ratio	(10.3%)	(6.3%)	(3.9%)	(2.4)%	(4.3%)	(2.0)%	—
Other Charges Ratio	(8.2%)	(8.2%)	(8.6%)	0.4 %	(7.4%)	(0.8)%	—
Operating Gain/(Loss) Ratio	(18.5%)	(14.5%)	(12.5%)	(2.0)%	(11.7%)	(2.8)%	—

Departmental Expenses

Amount	$10,214.5	$15,624.5	$ 16,563.1	$ 938.6	$ 17,101.2	$1,476.7	% 9.5
Percent of Decentralized Direct Written Premium	25.4%	26.0%	27.1%	1.1%	25.5%	(0.5)%	
Cost per Policy	$ 77.08	$ 77.70	$ 80.46	$ 2.76	$ 76.80	$ (0.90)	% (1.2)
Total Policy In Force—December	228.480	235.635	245.270	(9.635)	262.745	27.110	11.5
Decentralized Policy In Force—December	202.287	209.283	217.892	(8.609)	236.033	26.750	12.8
Full Time Equivalence—December	293.6	293.4	294.8	1.4	301.7	8.3	2.8
Policies per Full Time Equivalence (Avg.)	679	689	697	(8)	739	50	7.3
Life Volume Production (000.0)	$63,271.0	$95,000.0	$104,777.0	$ (9,777.0)	$109,340.0	$14,340.0	% 15.1

have done it better?" The answer to this question means that intelligent plans for improvements will emerge in the next budgeting cycle.

Budgeting Techniques The process of budgeting has existed long enough for many variations to emerge. *Zero-based budgeting* is one. Zero-based budgeting involves building each year's budget from scratch, ignoring prior years and simply indicating what is needed during the next budgetary period without regard to the current one. This approach requires a justification for each proposed expenditure, including the staff needed to accomplish each task or goal.

Another technique is *variable budgeting*, which involves building a budget based on expense per unit. For a property and liability insurer, it might be a budget built on so many policies in force or so many claims incurred.

Flexible budgeting is yet another process in which a budget is adjusted throughout the budgetary period as new developments emerge that make an adjustment necessary.

Adjustments are made for three basic reasons:

1. Home office management actions—such as the approval of new goals or changes affecting products.
2. Centrally budgeted expense for projects to be implemented in operating units. As these projects are implemented, the funds are released to the involved unit.
3. Rate adjustments—increases or decreases of approved rate changes not appearing in the original budget.

Adjustments are *not* made for errors in management judgment. For example, if an expense estimate is budgeted at a 5 percent increase but actual experience reaches 7 percent, objectives are not adjusted for this development.

Any of these budgeting techniques may be successful. The choice depends simply on which technique suits management.

Budgeting Procedures

The previous sections have described general principles applicable to the budgeting process. The following discussion illustrates specific budgeting approaches or procedures applicable to the major elements of an insurer's operation and financial statements.

Income—General Before the income budgeting process commences, the top management of an organization will have indicated its desired direction for the budget year: income growth, policy in force gain, agency size, and so on. The detailed planning efforts that follow will reveal whether the executive direction is viable or not.

Quotas Budgeting for a property and liability insurer usually begins with a projection of sales production expectations for the coming year. Quotas for different lines of insurance are established so that the marketing department has targets (or guides) for its operation in the coming year. These sales quotas should be compatible with the premium income level desired as well as with the unit growth objectives that have been established for the budgetary period. Assuming the operation has a strategic plan in place, the sales production objectives should support the strategy developed for the operation. For example, in an unprofitable line of business, the objective might be to hold sales volume constant or even to decrease it in the coming year.

A normal process in establishing quotas is, first, to forecast the current period's sales results and then establish quotas for the budgetary period based on these current period's anticipated developments. For example, new homeowner policy sales for the budget year might be targeted at 14 percent above the current level (i.e., current/forecast year level—400,000 plus 14 percent or 56,000—equals next year's quota—456,000).

Agency. After the sales objectives for the budgetary period have been established, the sales organization must be examined to determine what is required of it in order to achieve the sales quotas. Agency strength at the district, sales region, or regional levels must be determined. Agent terminations, promotions, and retirements as well as recruiting and licensing of new agents must be planned.

As with sales objectives, a normal process involves forecasting the size of the agency force during the current year and the required number of producers for the budgetary period to support the desired sales production effort.

Having set the sales objectives and determined the numbers of producers, the productivity per producer or agency can be determined both for the current year and the budget year. Then, the desired improvement in productivity by line of insurance can be modified or approved. For example, commercial production per producer might be indicated at an ambitious increase of 25 percent.

This objective may be unrealistic in the light of underwriting or financial conditions. At this point two options are open: either increase the size of the agency force or reduce the size of the productivity increase for the budget year. The latter action will, of course, reduce the sales quota for the current year.

Units in Force. The number of policies that will be in existence, requiring both policyholder and claimant service, should be determined next. Different lines of insurance require unique approaches. For example, consider personal automobile. Actual results are the starting points—knowing the size of today's existing portfolio. The next step is to determine the number of policies-in-force at the end of the current period by forecasting the total new writings for the year and the expected terminations for the same period. (It is best to employ more than one forecasting technique. For example, through the current mid-year, personal auto may be growing at a rate of six percent. How does this rate compare with the result from forecasting new writings and expected terminations?)

The budget year begins with the quota (units) that has been established for personal auto and it takes into consideration the terminations or cancellations expected during the budgetary year. The difference represents a "net gain" or loss of policies. This gain or loss, added to (or subtracted from) the prior year projected in-force, emerges as the budget year-end in-force.

Homeowners budgeting is identical. The in-force for both the current year and the budget year must be determined in the same way as for personal auto.

The commercial lines require a different budgeting approach for units in force. Since premium per policy/vehicle relationships are an important consideration when developing commercial policies/vehicles in force, it is recommended that commercial premium forecasts be completed before the forecasting of Commercial policies/vehicles in force begins.

The first step is to analyze the historical trend of premiums. This provides a base from which to forecast average premium per new policy for the current year. The third step is to divide the forecasted premium per new policy into the current year forecasted new premium to arrive at the current year new writings.

Historical trends also provide a basis for forecasting the termination ratios against the beginning policies/vehicles in force to generate the current year terminations. The final step is to add the forecasted new writings to the beginning policies/vehicles in force and subtract the forecasted terminations to arrive at the current year ending policies/vehicles in force.

Income—Direct Written Premium   The planning or budgeting of direct written premiums begins with an overview, of the total income picture for the current year and what is expected in the budgetary period. The overview can consist of an examination of income levels by state, by line of business, by either personal or commercial classification.

The importance of accurate forecasts cannot be overemphasized. The average premium per policy must be precisely estimated since this figure multiplied by the average units in force produces the income expectations for both the current year and the budgetary year.

Personal Automobile. The current year premium is determined by multiplying the average premium per policy by the average in force and adding any rate developments anticipated in the current year. (For example, an approved rate increase effective November 1 of the current year might be expected to produce $1,200,000 annually but only $200,000—one-sixth—in the current year.) Budget year premium is also based on average premium but many other factors must also be considered such as the anticipated changes either in coverages (such as higher deductibles) or in the mix of automobile types (such as high performance cars) insured. Average in-force times the average premium produces the unadjusted premium. "Unadjusted" means the premium that exists before any rate adjustments assumed in the budgetary period are taken into consideration. When these are added to the unadjusted premium, the budget year premium is determined. (For example, a rate increase planned for April 1 of the budget year estimated to be worth $400,000 annually would produce $300,000—75 percent—in the budget year.)

Other Personal Lines Other personal lines, such as homeowners and personal inland marine, are budgeted in a similar fashion as personal auto, but each is budgeted separately. This is necessary because each line of insurance has a different premium level. The forecast average annual premium is determined, and it is multiplied by the forecasted in force premium at year-end. For the budget year, the average premium per policy, which is usually the prior year's forecasted level, plus any anticipated rate adjustments and the budgetary unit in force will produce the personal fire premiums.

Commercial Lines. Commercial lines require a different procedure because premium per policy can be $1,000 or $1,000,000 in size.

"New" premium is calculated separately from renewal premium. To determine the new premium it is at first necessary to refer to the quotas established for the budgetary period. For large companies, the commercial lines such as workers' compensation, general liability, and multi-peril can be budgeted individually. Smaller companies tend to budget the commercial lines in total and from that determine the new direct written premium anticipated for the budget year.

The commercial historical relationships between sales and new premiums are important. For various reasons, 100 percent of sales do not translate into premiums. The most common example is a new three-year commercial multi-peril policy. Only the first-year premium will be recorded, yet the immediate sales production credit will be for all three years. By reviewing sales production and the amount of new premium, a forecast for the current year is made.

The budget year is determined from the sales quotas and estimating a new premium relationship. For example, 96 percent of a commercial quota of $2,000,000 would produce $1,920,000 in new premium. If each line has not been budgeted separately, premium income should be split by line of commercial insurance. This is usually based on past levels and relationships (for example, general liability may usually be 30-32 percent of commercial total).

The calculation of renewal premium is made by forecasting the renewal ratios by line of insurance. In other words, how much of the prior year total premiums will be renewed in the current year? What is the historical relationship? What does the current trend data reveal? Finally, forecast the current year renewal ratio (for example, 89 percent of the total general liability premium for *last* year is *forecasted* to renew this year).

The renewal premium for the commercial lines budget year begins by determining what the anticipated renewal ratio will be for the budget year. Both better persistency and more premium per policy would favorably affect this renewal estimate. The renewal ratio times the current forecasted year of direct written premium will produce the renewal direct written premium. For example, if the total direct written premium for the current year is $100 million and the renewal ratio selected was 82.5 percent then the renewal premium for the budget year would be $82,500,000. This figure plus the new direct written premium and any anticipated rate developments equals the total commercial direct written premium for the budget year.

Seasonal Distribution. After determining the premium forecast for the current year and that planned for the budget year, the next step requires a distribution of the budgetary premium by quarter or by month. This distribution is best accomplished by taking into consideration several years of seasonal developments. Property and liability operations tend to produce a rather consistent seasonal picture. Sales of automobile policies, for example, are higher in the spring. A mature organization that is not growing or contracting very rapidly can expect these seasonal patterns.

The distribution by either month or quarter provides interim targets by which results can be measured. Management reporting can present actual results in comparison to the budget objectives, as in the statement: "Commercial premiums through August are 116 percent of budget."

As a final step in determining the seasonal distribution of direct written premium, management must modify any proposed distribution based on the knowledge of anticipated rate adjustments, processing days, holidays, or other unique factors in the budgeting period.

Other Factors. This process produces a seasonally distributed forecast of direct written premium. Also reinsurance treaties might be considered to develop forecasts of net premium.

Loss Budgeting Prior to reviewing the specifics involved in loss budgeting, a definition of some of the terms involved is in order—loss frequencies are used to determine the anticipated claims developing from the policyholder portfolio. Frequencies represent the number of claims per units in force. How many automobile claims are expected from the number of coverages on the books? How many homeowners policies will produce claims? Average incurred cost on the other hand measures the size of the claims. What is the average cost of medical payment claims? What is the settlement value of property fire claims?

Frequency and average incurred cost will produce "incurred loss dollars" which, divided by earned premium, produces a "loss ratio." For example, a company with a $50 million earned premium budget and $32 million in incurred losses planned would have a budgeted loss ratio of 64 percent.

As with other budgetary steps, special considerations must be made for reliable indicators. What have been the trends in the number and size of claims? Is frequency deteriorating? Or is there improvement? What about average incurred cost? Is inflation driving up the costs of claims? What is the anticipated level of settlements for a bodily injury claim in the coming year?

Loss budgeting techniques are not usually complicated. The beginning point is a review of historical data. What does it reveal to management? Is winter driving consistently producing heavier claims volume? What about jury awards? Are they becoming burdensome? Are some lines of insurance producing abnormally high loss ratios? Are provisions for catastrophic losses needed?

A completion of the loss budgeting process may reflect an anticipated unprofitable operation. If so, corrective action programs must be developed by management in order to get the operational profit centers back into the black. These action programs may be designed to improve frequency, such as a reunderwriting of an insurance line or average incurred cost, such as changing from "outside" attorneys to house counsel. The important thing is once these action programs have been devised, total commitment must be obtained by management so that the programs are successfully executed.

Frequency Budgeting. The definition of frequency is the ratio of reported claims to units of loss exposure. In some lines the exposure is tantamount to the policies or coverages in force. This is true of personal automobile and the fire lines of insurance. Frequency is generally expressed as the number of claims per 100 units of exposure. For example, if there were 7,365 claims, per each 100,000 units in force, the frequency would be expressed as 7.365.

Commercial liability insurance frequency must be determined in a different fashion, since the size of the commercial policies range from the very small to the very large. Policies in force do not correctly reflect the amount of exposure that the property and liability company must consider. Instead, earned premium is used to reflect the frequency in some commercial liability claims handling and claims are considered in relation to each $1,000 of earned premium. For example, if three workers' compensation claims occurred, for each $1,000 of earned premium, frequency would be expressed as .300 frequency.

Forecasts.   After reviewing past and current frequency levels, a forecast or a modification of the projected results is made. This forecast is based on assumptions regarding any anticipated social or economic change that would affect current frequency levels. For example, a new regulation requiring a change in an automobile coverage might knowingly result in fewer or more claims.

Budget.   The frequency for the forthcoming year is determined by adjusting the forecasted levels based upon developments anticipated in the budget year. These developments might be the discontinuance of management programs or the alteration of such management programs. For example, the claims department may have determined that its claims settlement activities have been unsatisfactorily slow and have agreed to plans which will accelerate the handling of claims in the budget period. Higher frequency may result as a consequence.

Frequency budgeting reflects the "health" of a policy portfolio and an excessive number of claims is usually indicative of a portfolio mix that is not going to produce a profitable result. However, before this conclusion can be drawn, the other side of the coin, average incurred cost, must be examined. This is because even though a high number of claims may be anticipated it could very well be that the lower average incurred cost of these claims offsets the high number of claims by producing fewer incurred loss dollars.

For example, a state may change its automobile liability insurance laws, reducing the size of the expense "threshold" (that is, the level of expenses, due to an automobile accident, which must be reached or exceeded before the insured person is entitled to sue under tort liability). This change would result in more average bodily injury claims but at an average lower level.

Average Incurred Cost.   Average incurred cost (or severity) is defined as incurred losses for a period divided by the number of reported claims. To illustrate, $100,000 in losses resulting from 500 claims would mean that the average incurred cost for those claims, the severity, would be $200.

As with frequency, historical data is extremely valuable in budgeting average incurred cost. Up to five years of historical trends should be examined to reveal what the annual changes in severity are. Once this has been accomplished, the average incurred cost budget involves the forecasting of the current year to form the base for the budgeting of the next year. As with other budgetary components, trends are considered and a forecast is made of the current year average incurred cost levels for each of the major lines of insurance. This forms the basis for building the average incurred cost budgets for the forthcoming budgetary period.

After reviewing the trends, a determination is made of the average annual increases in average incurred cost for each of the lines. Are they increasing at a rate of 3 percent annually? 5 percent? Or is a leveling indicated? And, any adjustments first must be considered in the light of known distortions. For example, windstorms can produce an unusually high number of claims which drive up the homeowner frequency level but by the same token, this type of claim—wind damage to the roofs of homes—usually costs much less than a fire claim. In a given period, automobile comprehensive average incurred cost could be abnormally high due to a hail storm. Unusual developments have to be taken into consideration when budgeting the average incurred cost for a line for the coming year.

The economic and legislative activity must be reviewed. Such matters as compulsory insurance, uninsured motorist coverage, and no-fault—all affect average incurred cost in one form or another.

Reserves. Claim reserve levels must also be reviewed to determine the proper levels for the budget period. For example, an evaluation recently performed on bodily injury reserves may have indicated an "inadequate" (that is, insufficient dollars to settle the claim—perhaps due to inflation) situation during the current year. Management may have since decided to "strengthen" or increase these reserves. If this strengthening is done during the budget year, it will increase average incurred cost. For example, a case reserved at $35,000 that has $10,000 added to it for a revised reserve level of $45,000 causes $10,000 to be charged to incurred losses in the budget year.

Any change in coverage must also be taken into consideration when budgeting severity. For example, new and higher automobile deductibles may be introduced that would affect the size of collision claims in the budget period.

Incurred Losses—Loss Ratio. The main objective of loss ratio budgeting is to determine the anticipated loss ratio for each of the major lines of insurance and to communicate to management whether unsatisfactory or profitable levels are likely to be experienced in the coming year.

The loss ratio formula is simply the number of claims times the average incurred cost to produce the total losses divided by the earned premium. As an illustration, assume for a particular line of insurance that the earned premium anticipated is $40,000 and the frequency budget indicates that ninety claims can be anticipated in the budget year. The severity budgeting determines an average incurred cost budget of $300. The product of ninety claims at $300 produces an incurred loss dollar of $27,000. The loss ratio resulting from dividing incurred loss dollars by the earned premium ($27,000 divided by $40,000) is 67.5 percent.

A budgeted loss ratio could very well be at an unprofitable level requiring each of the three components (that is, earned premium, average incurred cost, and frequency) to be reexamined. Perhaps management action (for example, reunderwriting) could produce fewer than ninety claims in the budget period or steps taken within the claims function might lower the anticipated $300 average incurred cost to a lesser level. Or the earned premium might be increased by determining methods to raise the level of premium per unit in-force.

This process may suffice for an insurer, such as a predominantly personal lines company, with a stable pattern of average incurred cost data. When the effects of large losses can be substantial, as in commercial lines, it may be necessary to segregate incurred losses into outstanding case losses, changes in incurred but not reported losses, and paid losses. Each of these components can then be budgeted separately.

The results of the many steps required to budget premiums and losses may be summarized on one simple form. Note that the display in Exhibit 5-3 illustrates the budgeted written premiums (DWP), earned premiums (NEP), incurred losses, and loss ratios for all of the personal and commercial property and liability lines.

Expense Budgeting Expenses, as with all businesses, must be budgeted. Property and liability insurers usually budget expenses according to the classifications contained in the Annual Statement Underwriting and Investment Exhibit, Part 4—Expenses. Expenses, however, must also be classified according to management categories, since their nature determines the degree of control that management may exercise. One classification technique for budgeting and reporting

Exhibit 5-3
1986 Objectives Premium and Losses by Line-B

	DWP	NEP	Losses	Loss Ratio
Region _____ Date _____				
Family				
Personal Auto	$ 88,431.2	$ 89,902.0	$61,588.4	68.5%
Residual	3,305.1	3,305.1	3,079.4	93.2
Voluntary	85,089.9	86,596.9	58,509.0	67.6
Tier I	84,723.4	85,137.2	56,636.7	66.5
Tier II	1,640.9	1,528.3	1,872.3	122.5
Homeowners	16,537.3	15,710.4	11,154.9	71.0
Pers. Property Fire	2,426.7	2,257.1	1,197.9	53.1
Personal I.M.	769.5	711.0	532.2	74.9
CFL, Polio, TA, FA	113.0	112.6	151.0	134.1
Personal Total	$108,277.7	$108,693.1	$74,624.4	68.7%
Business				
Fleets	$ 8,428.7	$ 8,513.0	$ 7,032.4	82.6%
Worker's Comp.	3,968.9	4,032.4	2,570.7	63.8
Garage Liability	747.9	730.7	388.7	53.2
General Liability	2,012.7	1,934.2	707.0	36.6
Bonds and BR&T	56.4	57.9	81.6	140.9
Glass	17.7	18.6	12.7	68.3
Farm Fire	148.4	144.8	73.0	50.4
Commercial Fire	730.6	740.1	364.0	49.2
Farmowners	47.9	43.8	82.4	188.1
SMP	1,824.2	1,847.9	609.8	33.0
Commercial I.M.	423.3	417.0	208.5	50.0
BOPP	1,866.0	1,621.6	1,714.8	105.7
Commercial Total	$ 20,272.7	$ 20,102.0	$13,845.6	68.9%
Decentralized Lines Total	$128,550.4	$128,795.1	$88,470.0	68.7%

is to identify property and liability expenses under one of three categories: departmental, project, and nondepartmental.

Departmental Expenses. Certain expenses are considered to be "controllable"—that is, management is able to determine how much will be spent. The most obvious departmental expenses are salaries (How many people will be employed? At what salary levels?). Also

Exhibit 5-4
Proposed Budget for the Year 1986—Supporting Detail

REGION or OFFICE _____ Central _____ DEPARTMENT _____

CODE _____ 4683 _____

Expenses	Current Year 9 Mos. Actual	Current Year 12 Month Forecast	Budget Year	Budget Year Under (Over) Current Forecast Amount	Percent
AVERAGE ANNUAL SALARY	XXXXX	18,569	19,592	1,023	(5.5)
AVERAGE PERSONNEL	816.2	820.4	828.4	(8.0)	(1.0)
ENDING PERSONNEL	818.0	827.2	824.6	2.6	0.3
Salaries	$12,427,616	18,774,300	19,933,500	(1,159,200)	(6.2)
Salary Benefits	2,710,392	4,091,400	4,341,400	(250,400)	(6.1)
Outside Claims Expense	2,246,757	3,391,200	3,102,000	289,200	8.5
Travel	525,021	888,700	955,700	(67,000)	(7.5)
Rent	1,294,759	1,952,200	1,978,800	(26,600)	(1.4)
Postage Express Telephone, Telegraph and Exchange	1,793,470	2,646,600	2,914,200	(267,600)	(10.1)
Equipment	557,696	973,100	1,143,700	(170,600)	(17.5)
Survey and Und. Reports	452,032	691,900	927,300	(235,400)	(34.0)
Printing and Supplies	543,524	900,000	987,700	(87,700)	(9.7)
Advertising	145,269	212,200	248,400	(36,200)	(17.1)
Personal Computing	57	200	1,500	(1,300)	(650.0)
Other Expenses — Total	$201,232	382,700	378,600	4,100	1.1
TOTAL	$22,897,825	34,904,500	36,913,200	(2,008,700)	(5.8)

significant are travel expenses. (How many sales meetings to be scheduled? What should be budgeted for repairs and operating expenses of company cars?) Equipment, telephone, and postage are still other departmental expense types.

One company's list of departmental expenses is illustrated in Exhibit 5-4. A manager must indicate current expenses by type, forecasts for the current year, and the amount of the proposed budget.

Departmental expense budgets represent the anticipated needs of management for resources either in the form of money or personnel in order to get the job done. Resources are nearly always limited and consequently, the executive management group in any organization will establish permissible limits to guide the budgeting of management at all levels.

Before departmental budgets can be constructed, the plans and programs that have been established for the operational unit must be known so that the anticipated resource needs can be identified. For example, an unusually ambitious commercial sales campaign during the budget year translates into at least these needs for additional resources inside the underwriting unit—more underwriters, more raters, and more coders to process the business.

Salary dollars play a large role in the establishment of any departmental budget and could represent from 50 to 70 percent of a given department's needs. Consequently, an analysis of future personnel requirements must be made before the budget can be determined. In addition, the salary administration plans should be established for the remainder of the current year and for the budget year to follow. Then, by knowing the human resource situation and the salary administration plans, the salary dollars and the salary benefits can be planned for the budget year.

A major consideration in establishing the number of personnel required to efficiently staff an organization requires a review of employee productivity levels. (Within a property/liability operation, productivity might be measured by the number of policies per employee; a claims manager would be more interested in claims per adjuster.) The current year must be forecasted and any desired improvement will result in a productivity objective for the forthcoming year. Knowing these objectives, the personnel requirements can then be ascertained in order to eventually build the salary budget for the coming year. To illustrate, a 6 percent budgeted improvement in employee productivity and an 8 percent growth in policies-in-force may require hiring twenty-five new employees during the budget year.

Other expense considerations must be reviewed in order to build the total departmental expense budget. The amount of travel that will be done in the budget period, any new equipment purchases, changes in telephone techniques requiring fewer or more instruments, postage requirements, printing and supplies, and so on. Each of these budgetary requirements should be fully supported in order to obtain approval for their funding in the budget year.

Project Expenses. Project expense budgeting represents a desire on the part of management to carry out unique plans or programs that have been proposed and approved. For example, a new data processing system that could affect several functions such as underwriting, sales, and administration may require setting aside project funds to ensure successful introduction and monitoring of the systems changeover. The project funds might represent the cost of new electronic data processing equipment, supplies, travel, training rooms—all the costs associated with the project.

The project budgeting procedure will involve the consideration of many projects. Several will be proposed requiring both approval and funding. It is for top management to determine which projects will be funded and which will be disapproved or delayed. Criteria first have to be determined that reflect harmony with the company's long- and short-range goals. A company that desires growth, for example, may assign a low priority to a new payroll system and a high priority to a special advertising campaign. An essential final step in project expense budgeting is monitoring results. How is the project proceeding? Are the budgeted funds proving to be adequate, or inadequate? Should the project funding require excessive amounts over the approved amount, other areas of the operation may be adversely affected since a project once launched will rarely be aborted.

In project budgeting, it is important to consider personal resources required. A systems project, for example, requires not only data processing equipment and people, but also the support of end users in specifying data requirements, definitions, and sources, in specifying report formats and frequency, and in testing the adequacy of the final system. For major projects, this support can require a significant commitment of time from senior level people.

Nondepartmental Expenses. Certain expenses, such as state premium and local taxes and uncollectible agents balances charged off, cannot be specifically identified with a designated department such as claims, sales, or underwriting. They are therefore defined as "nondepartmental." The property and liability controller usually assumes responsibility for the budgeting and reporting of these expenses. Premium taxes, commissions, the write-offs of uncollectible premium due, and so on, should be budgeted with diligence, however, since they, too, affect the "bottom line."

Budgeting nondepartmental expenses begins with the review of the historical data. Of particular interest is the relationship of the various nondepartmental expense items compared to direct written premium. For example, commissions usually hold as a steady percentage of direct written premium unless the company's strategy has resulted in a change in the product mix. Premium taxes are usually a constant percentage of premium volume.

The nondepartmental expense budgeted ratios will mirror the current year's results unless of course changes are to be introduced in the budget year, such as commission schedule revisions or premium tax modifications.

STRATEGIC PLANNING

The preceding discussion of budgeting assumes that the annual budgeting activities are part of a longer range strategic planning process. This process links the annual plans to clearly defined, long-term strategic goals.

Strategic planning can be defined as a systematic and ongoing process directed towards developing the company's future. Strategic planning considers issues such as:

- What type of business are we in?
- Where will we be several years from now?
- How will we grow?
- How much risk will we take?

The strategic planning process includes the analysis and decision making necessary to define objectives, establish the timetable, organize resources, and measure progress. Strategic planning emphasizes control of the company's future through today's systematic decisions.

The Need for Strategic Planning

The key function of insurance in our society is to reduce economic uncertainty and provide economic stability. Stability of the institutions offering insurance can be threatened unless they continue to grow and achieve an acceptable return on investments. Change, whether from social trends or regulation, potentially disturbs existing stability in the insurance environment.

In recent years the pace of change in the industry has accelerated. Insurance companies and their managers are challenged to meet the demands of change. In itself, change is not harmful. Change is potentially harmful only for those who fail to recognize its signs and are, in the end, unprepared. Change can spell opportunity for those who do prepare.

There is little prospect for the type of stable, long-term growth known to the insurance business prior to the 1970s. Opportunities may become lost if management becomes preoccupied with the magnitude of today's problems, near-term events, or the internal operating problems of running the business each day. For this reason, insurance company planning needs an in-depth future orientation. Strategic planning is the structured approach which embraces this future orientation.

Strategic Planning in the Insurance Industry The accelerating rate of change in the insurance environment and the popularity of strategic planning in management circles have combined, resulting in the increasingly widespread adoption of formal planning programs, most often called long-range or strategic planning.

Today, formal planning systems are pervasive in the insurance industry. In 1981, an industry association stated that "long-range planning has become a formal process used in most medium and large companies."[4] A survey of strategic planning as it exists today in the insurance industry finds that it is widely established, but also that ongoing improvement in the process may be needed to achieve its goals.

Strategic Planning versus Operational Planning It is important to note the distinction between strategic and operational planning. As defined above, strategic planning is directed at defining and determining the company's future. Strategic planning focuses on tomorrow. Operational planning and budgeting have a more immediate focus on today. Given these different perspectives, operational planning is responsible for accomplishing the performance requirements of the strategic plan. In this sense, operational planning is subordinate to strategic planning.

The two processes have contrasting planning horizons. Strategic planning addresses issues confronting the company three to five years (or even ten years for some companies) in the future, while operational or budget planning addresses operations within the next one or two years. Thus the logical intersection of operational and strategic planning would be in the medium-term span.

Strategic planning analyzes both the internal and external environment. Preparing the company for the future must take into consideration the entire business environment. The operational plan, by contrast, tends to reflect the way the company does business today. The main focus of operational planning is on effective internal corporate performance.

As these intersecting time horizons suggest, linkage between strategic and operational plans is essential for both to be effective. Operational planning is a valuable and necessary management tool. It represents the unit-by-unit plan of activity that is responsible for maintaining a smooth work flow. It is intended to achieve efficiencies in systems and procedures. However, as a company's only planning technique, operational planning would be very limiting. When operational and strategic planning are coupled, the combined planning effort supports top management direction. Effective linkage between the two dimensions of planning results in successfully translating strategy into action.

The Strategic Planning Process

The literature of strategic planning includes the contributions of many writers, and there are some variations in the terminology each uses to describe the major steps of the strategic planning process. This discussion will use the following five phases to describe the strategic planning process:

1. definition of the company's mission and objectives,
2. position assessment
3. strategy development
4. action planning, and
5. plan monitoring.

Company Mission and Objectives An organization develops and grows to accomplish a specific purpose. A starting point for strategic planning is the development of formal mission statements to answer questions such as: "What business are we in?" and "What will our business be?" For instance, a farm bureau mutual insurance company might define its company mission as "to provide low cost automobile insurance to farmers."[5]

The mission statement should serve the company for many years. It should not be changed frequently. On the other hand, if the original statement becomes inadequate, revision is appropriate. For instance, the business of the insurance company cited above might evolve to the point that the following might be a more appropriate statement of mission:

> To provide people—individually and in groups—with the highest quality insurance and financial services for their economic and personal welfare; and to provide these services at the lowest possible cost consistent with the maintenance of efficiently operated, financially sound, growing companies.

The mission statement should suggest a set of supporting objectives for each level of management. Common objectives focus on profitability, sales growth, market share improvement, and diversification. The objectives should be prioritized, and they should be specific, quantified, realistic, and internally consistent. A goal such as "maximizing premium and underwriting gain" is not specific, quantified, nor necessarily internally consistent, since it ignores a possible strategic trade-off.

Position Assessment The position assessment or situation analysis step is intended to understand and outline the present position of the company. This assessment includes both an internal analysis of company factors and an analysis of the external environment.

The position assessment begins with a background section summarizing recent operating results for the company or product line. This information is followed by a review of facts and trends relative to customers, market segments, market growth, distribution channels, and competitors. This background is often followed by the "normal forecast" which projects results assuming no major changes in the external environment or the firm's marketing strategies.

The position assessment also includes a list of strengths and weaknesses. This list must be developed critically to be worthwhile in the planning process. The weaknesses should be harshly realistic, and the strengths should be confirmed, perhaps by industry experts. Workable strategies should exploit strengths, or large investments may be required to overcome weaknesses.

Analysis of the external environment is an important aspect of the position assessment. The perspective should be wide-ranging and might include some of the following questions.

- What is our place among our competition?
- What is our market share? What is our potential for capturing more of the market?
- Are there emerging trends? How do they influence our products and services?
- Are there new or potential technological innovations in the future?
- What are the external barriers to growth?

The goal of the position assessment is to arrive at an understanding of the present position by considering both internal and external influences.

Strategy Development After completing the position assessment, key issues will tend to be obvious as areas of weakness in the present position, or areas in which the company has no position. The number of issues so identified may be rather large in the first planning effort. A few critical issues should be isolated for concentrated consideration.

The difference between the company's objectives and its present position, as outlined in the position statement, can be thought of as a "strategic gap." Once strategic issues have been identified, management must develop appropriate strategies for closing the strategic gap.

The strategy statement should be a coherent statement directing major efforts towards the stated goals. The strategy statement should be both clear and succinct. For example:

Our basic strategy for achieving our goals will include building on our established expertise in the association marketplace. We will introduce a new small businessowner's product line that will be sold with endorsement by direct response. We will increase our premium volume in the Quality Agents Program through aggressive support, including provision for personal computers in their offices and special continuing education training programs, such as the Accredited Adviser in Insurance (AAI) Program, targeted at achievement of higher levels of production. Our expense management program will continue with full support, including the conversion of personal lines auto underwriting to a fully automated system effective mid-year.

The strategy adopted should be selected from several alternatives. Management should be certain to consider the several alternatives which emerge with knowledge of the company's strengths and weaknesses, potential problem areas, and areas of strength. The strategies should be tested with scenarios depicting the most likely potential adversities. The strategic planning process should provide the methodology to ensure that the most promising and innovative alternatives have been considered.

Action Planning   The planning effort comes to closure through development of practical programs for action. The programs explain the actual steps by which the strategy will be implemented to reach the established objectives. A typical action program includes specifics such as "how to," "by whom," "by when," "with what help," "at what cost," and "with what priority." For the sample strategic statement presented earlier, there would be an action program for each strategic goal. For instance, the introduction of a new business owner's policy targeted to small businesses would have an action program detailing the steps involved, the accountable individuals, timing, and cost factors.

Plan Monitoring   The strategic planning process is ongoing. Action steps towards each goal should be regularly monitored. As operational targets are hit or missed, the corporate strategy constantly reacts.

Control systems should be developed to assure this monitoring. Reporting systems should be closely related to the company's planning system. This close relationship must exist with reference to strategic planning as well as to operational planning.

Failure to achieve operational goals may indicate that a strategic objective may be inappropriate or ill-timed. This monitoring and feedback process should generally be performed at least quarterly; however, significant changes in strategic objectives generally should not be made more often than once a year. The documentation in the formal plan of factors such as key assumptions should prove useful when readjusting strategies and measuring progress toward objectives.

Progress in Strategic Planning

Long-range planning is being adopted more and more widely in the insurance industry. Despite this pervasiveness, however, some prominent experts question whether strategic planning actually plays such a key role in managing insurance companies. For example, Peter Walker, Director of the well-known consulting firm, McKinsey & Co., has stated, "Strategic thinking, which was largely a management buzzword in the 1950s and 1960s, became a reality for many companies in the 1970s. The property/casualty insurance industry, however, has not stepped forward and embraced these concepts and put them into practice...."[6] In Walker's opinion, some companies' actual strategic planning efforts tend to be ritualistic and numbers-driven at the expense of creativity. Such a process tends to generate more paper and more meetings, but leaves less room for new ideas.[7]

Walker defines the following four stages in the evolution of strategic management:

Stage 1—Budget Planning
Stage 2—Forecast Based Planning
Stage 3—Externally Oriented Planning
Stage 4—Strategic Management[8]

In Walker's opinion, most major insurance companies are in Stage 2, which includes a more formal aproach to planning, multi-year forecasts, and explicit assessment of economic, regulatory, and social forces likely to affect results. However, since Stage 2 planning is essentially static and heavily focused on short- to medium-term results, it does not fully meet the objectives of strategic planning.

By Walker's definition, Stage 3 is the first phase of strategic, as opposed to operational or tactical, management. As such, it represents a major step from sophisticated, but internally oriented, financial planning to truly externally oriented planning. From this viewpoint, the accelerating rate of change in the external environment triggers a need which challenges insurance companies to move further towards strategic planning.

The strategic planning process is complex. As a company implements formal planning, it experiences a learning curve with respect to the planning process, and it often makes modifications to the process in its next cycle. Strategic planning is relatively new to most companies in the insurance industry. Accordingly, the level of sophistication in planning is increasing as planning experience grows.

Many benefits are expected from strategic planning. We expect planning to contribute to:

● clear direction for the organization,

- anticipation of opportunities,
- improved control over operations,
- identification of areas needing improvement, and
- development of planning as an essential part of the organization and its day-to-day operations.

It would be an overstatement to claim that these goals have been fully realized in the insurance industry. However, it does seem clear that most companies have seen a need to adopt strategic planning and are working to master its implementation.

CAPITAL PLANNING

A crucial linkage between budgeting and strategic planning is capital planning. This process coordinates the use and the availability of the organization's financial resources.

Capital planning includes not only planning for such major capital projects as new computer systems or data centers, but also may include planning for adequate premium to surplus ratios and dividends to shareholders. Capital planning, while closely linked to operating plans, is often treated as a separate process. Major capital projects often require a longer planning horizon than the one to three years typically used in operational plans. In this way it is linked more to strategic planning, but it will also affect budget year operational plans. Another reason for this separation is that many capital items can be "capitalized" on both statutory and GAAP statements. That is, the cost will be amortized or depreciated over time rather than expensed as incurred. Profits for the budget year will be affected only by capital expenses actually flowing through the budget-year income statement, typically the costs for using internal resources. If there are start-up or development projects with little current return, major capital projects can depress current year income, but they should improve future years' earnings as efficiency, new product lines, or other projects result in improved operations.

While capital planning involves concepts of financial management beyond the scope of this course, it should be noted that the information system must provide adequate input for the capital planning process. Critical information for this purpose includes forecasted premium, surplus, policyholder dividends, stockholder dividends, funding required for current and projected projects, and sources of funds. The budgeting and reporting system should be designed to support an effective capital planning process.

SUMMARY

Effective planning and control of an insurance company's operations requires a continuous cycle of budgeting and reporting activities. Although each company must design a unique system that fits its own priorities, the tasks incorporated into the system should flow in a continuous cycle, such as the one depicted in Exhibit 5-5.

In designing its specific budgeting system, a company should decide the appropriate time period for the budget, the desired level of management participation in the budgeting process, the degree to which established budgets can be revised to accommodate changes in plans, and the amount of "stretch" that can be included in the budget to motivate higher levels of performance. In any case, however, a sound budgeting system provides specific targets for the organization and focuses on the critical success factors of the organization. Sound budgeting also requires an effective reporting system that allows time for corrective action, provides information to support critical decisions, and presents that information in an understandable format.

The budgeting process should incorporate general budgeting practices regarding forecasts, schedules, forms, the controller's role, reconciliations, critiques, and particular budgeting techniques. An insurer's budgeting process develops specific targets for each of the interrelated variables. A projection of general income leads to the establishment of appropriate production quotas and the corresponding agency force, policy units, and direct written premium for each line of insurance. Loss budgeting involves an analysis of frequency and severity of past losses and a projection into the budget year that corresponds to the expected sales volume. Expense budgeting requires both a projection of the expected expenses and their classification into appropriate categories for management control.

The targets established in the budgeting process should follow from the long-term strategic objectives of the company. Without an effective linkage between the budgeting process and the strategic planning process, the effort to guide the organization through an uncertain future is more likely to fail. The strategic planning process defines the company's mission and objectives, assesses its current position, develops an appropriate strategy, plans the required action, and monitors the results.

A crucial linkage between budgeting and strategic planning is capital planning. Since the strategic plan may call for investments over a longer time horizon than the budget period, capital planning coordinates the major capital projects required by the strategic plan and the regular budgeting process.

Exhibit 5-5
The Budgeting/Reporting Cycle

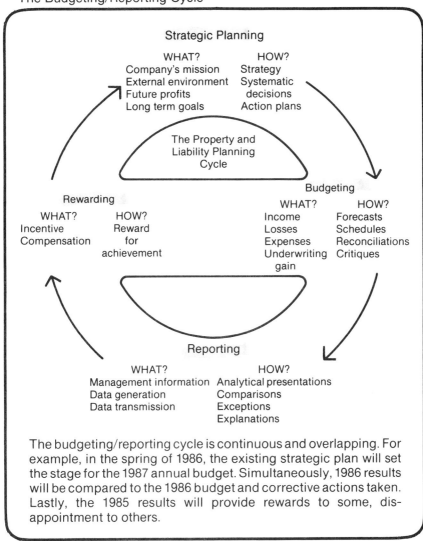

The budgeting/reporting cycle is continuous and overlapping. For example, in the spring of 1986, the existing strategic plan will set the stage for the 1987 annual budget. Simultaneously, 1986 results will be compared to the 1986 budget and corrective actions taken. Lastly, the 1985 results will provide rewards to some, disappointment to others.

As this chapter has emphasized, coordination of all forms of planning and budgeting is essential. It is also essential that results be reported effectively so that the plan can be monitored and improved in the next cycle. The design of an effective reporting system is considered in the next chapter.

Chapter Notes

1. Neil C. Churchill, "Budget Choice: Planning vs Control," *Harvard Business Review*, July–August 1984, p. 150.
2. Philip H. Thurston, "Should Smaller Companies Make Formal Plans," *Harvard Business Review*, September–October 1983, p. 168.
3. Steven D. Grossman and Richard Lindhe, "Important Considerations in the Budgeting Process," *Managerial Planning*, September/October 1982, p. 24.
4. Life Office Management Association, *Financial Planning and Controlling* (Financial Planning and Control Report No. 52), May 1981, p. 15.
5. Robert J. Gibbons, editor, *Dimensions of Corporate Strategy: Selected Readings* (Malvern, PA: Insurance Institute of America, 1983). The examples of mission statement, objectives, and strategy statement presented here are drawn from "Strategic Marketing" by Larry M. Robinson from this text used in the Associate in Research and Planning (ARP) program. Other chapters also deal with topics of relevance to strategic planning.
6. Peter B. Walker, "Strategic Management—New Tool for Insurers—Part I," *Best's Review*, March 1982, p. 34.
7. Walker, p. 109.
8. Peter B. Walker, "Strategic Management—New Tool for Insurers—Part II," *Best's Review*, April 1982, p. 26.

CHAPTER **6**

Management Reporting

INTRODUCTION

Management reporting is the communication process that provides the corporate decision makers with brief, concise, analytical presentations of key operating information for use in planning, directing, managing, and measuring progress toward corporate and operational goals. This *attention-directing information* should be consolidated at the same levels at which management responsibilities are consolidated. This allows easy comparison of the actual monthly, quarterly, or year-to-date data to the corporate plan. In addition, the actual results for the respective periods can be compared with the results of the corresponding period in the prior year. The quality, timeliness, and comparability of data are all essential ingredients for a successful, credible, reporting process.

Management communication is often structured on an *exception* basis. Thus it omits misleading and insignificant data and directs attention to exceptional aspects of the results that are significantly better or worse than expected. Signs of progress, or lack of it, should be highlighted. The analysis will be most effective when attention is directed to what has happened, where it has happened, why it has happened, and what the implications are if the situation continues. By avoiding a data recitation, or merely a comparison of actual to budget, management attention can be directed to specific areas or situations that may require correction, a new approach, or additional efforts to accomplish the goals. Management reports should provide sufficient detail to illustrate the desired points, but excessive detail rapidly reduces the effectiveness of the communication.

Data should be analyzed before reports are prepared. Due to the importance of taking corrective action as quickly as possible, it is critical that management not be misled by incomplete or inaccurate reporting. Raw data can often be misleading and must be scrutinized carefully to gain a true understanding of results. Circumstances such as sales promotions, "jumbo" cases, timing differences, and organizational realignments can distort results, and their effects should be taken into consideration. If a product's content or measurement has changed or an unequal number of days of activity are compared, incorrect conclusions will likely result. It is therefore important to restate the prior period on a basis comparable to the current one; for example, adjusting to an equivalent workday basis.

Thorough analysis will improve identification and reporting of trends. In addition, historical and supplemental background information will add relevance and lend credence to observations and conclusions. Care must be taken that current external influences equate with the past. Conditions, such as economic climate, interest rates, automobile usage, catastrophic weather, and a company's competitive standing may have changed so that previous historical relationships no longer apply.

Reporting formats may include narrative, exhibits, charts, graphs, and tables. The overriding consideration in reporting is choosing what form will most clearly and succinctly convey the desired message. Questions must continually address whether information could be reported in a more meaningful manner. Be creative—a chart or graph often conveys a message much more easily and effectively than a long narrative. Do not be afraid to experiment. While not all trials succeed, reflecting data in a different manner or form often brings facts to light that would not ordinarily be seen.

REGULAR MANAGEMENT REPORTS

The organizational structure, corporate culture, and management style dictate acceptable and effective formats for management reports in different organizations. Even though variation occurs between companies, most management reports include the following categories:

1. sales activity,
2. underwriting activity,
3. claims activity,
4. loss control activity,
5. administrative and human resources activities,
6. investment performance, and
7. profitability.

Sales Activity

Sales activity can be considered the heart of any business. Without new sales to sustain and provide growth, a company will not prosper. It is important, therefore, to monitor the marketing function continuously to be sure that there is progress towards the company's sales and growth goals. Management reporting of sales activity should highlight both key issues of current interest and problem areas.

What Sales Information Should Be Reported   The end result of a successful sales effort is an expanded policyholder base. That means retaining current customers and bringing new policyholders to the company. Information of potential interest to management could be broken down into: (1) sales activity, (2) production, and (3) productivity.

Measurements of Sales Activity.   While normally sales activity suggests new sales, the marketing function also encompasses retention and renewal of existing policyholders. Thus the marketing function has a major role in the total results of the company. If either new sales or retention receives priority, the other suffers and the overall company plan may be missed. Some additional measurements of sales activity are:

1. direct written premium,
2. net earned premium,
3. new premium,
4. renewal premium, and
5. persistency or terminations.

Direct written premium includes both new and renewal premiums. It reflects gross premiums received by a company from policyowners less those amounts refunded because of cancellation or adjustment.

Earned premium is that part of the premium applicable to the expired part of the policy period. It includes the short-rate premium on cancellation and the entire premium on the contract at the expiration of the policy period. Net earned premium includes reinsured premiums assumed and excludes premiums ceded to other companies. New premiums are revenues from additions to the policyholder base while renewal premiums come from the existing policyholder base.

Persistency measures that portion of the portfolio which remains in force during a given period of time. Terminations are those policies lost from the portfolio.

Production Measurements.   Measurements of production frequently vary among products. The more common measures are:

1. production premium,

2. policy/vehicle counts, and
3. face amounts of life sales.

For a given line of business, the production measurement may consist of any one or more of the above or it may be a special calculated figure.

Production premium may vary from new direct written premium in that it may reflect annualized premium for life insurance; new direct written premium reflects only those premiums actually received by the company. Production credit normally does not apply to rejected, not taken, assigned, replacement, and conversion business in order to restrict adverse selection and to reflect only producer generated new sales.

In order to accentuate a given line of business or to equate sales of different products, production may be expressed in terms of calculated figures. For example, to encourage selling of whole life rather than term life, volume production credit could be expressed as a derivative of premium, such as annualized premium, rather than the normal face amount. Since whole life premiums are normally higher than term premiums, producers would receive more production credit for selling whole life than they would for term.

Productivity Measures. Agent strength and productivity should be monitored to determine whether agent productivity is improving or if production gains are the result of additions to the agency force. Agent productivity may be calculated by dividing sales production by the average number of agents over a given time period. In evaluating agent productivity, like periods of time should be compared and some consideration should be given as to whether the level of agent experience has changed significantly.

Monitoring the sales management span of control can also be beneficial. The sales management span of control is the number of agents per manager. If a manager supervises too many agents, lack of training and instruction may result. Conversely, supervising too few agents causes higher than necessary expense levels.

How Is Reporting Accomplished? The effective communication of sales activity must consider the following aspects:

1. At what level should sales information be reported?
2. How should the information be presented?

At What Level Should Sales Information Be Reported? While management reporting is primarily concerned with companywide results, it may become necessary to examine results at lower levels, including, on occasion, the individual producer level in order to identify specific problem areas and to gain insight and understanding. A

Exhibit 6-1
1984 Sales Production Summary

	10 Mos. 1984	Percent Change From 1983	Annual Planned Percent Change	Percent Above (Below) Seasonal Quota		
				Eastern	Central	Western
Tier I & II Vehicles	845,372	1.0%	10.3%	(8.8)%	(7.2)	(2.4)%
Fire Policies	238,280	1.5	11.8	(6.7)	(11.6)	(9.1)
Health Premium	14,945.7	(14.9)	(11.7)	20.9	6.5	—
Commercial Premium	101,071.7	55.5	30.4	27.0	7.7	3.6
Group Premium	58,865.4	(16.3)	(6.9)	1.8	34.5	(76.6)
Life Volume	1,606,159.0	(6.1)	12.2	(12.7)	(15.4)	(44.7)
Mutual Funds	48,700.5	8.4	4.4	6.6	(2.3)	—

standard format may be established in order to communicate details of continuing interest on a recurring basis. In addition, ad hoc reporting segments can be used to point out items of current concern. Exhibit 6-1 provides an example of possible format.

How Should Sales Information Be Presented? Data normally reported to management are:

1. comparison of actual to planned results,
2. comparison of actual to prior year results,
3. results from specific channels of distribution,
4. results from different strategies,
5. product and geographic mix results,
6. trends and fluctuations that may be early indicators of changes occurring in the environment, and
7. other specific items of management interest.

When comparing actual to planned or prior year results, both amount of change and percentage of change should be examined. An item reflecting a significant percentage change may not be that important to the overall results if the number is small in comparison to others. Comparison of actual to planned or prior year results on both a monthly and year-to-date or quarterly basis facilitates identification of changes in trends.

Care should be taken when attempting to compare one month's results with the previous month. Sales activity often reflects seasonality. Past or current sales contests, for instance, may cause significant variation from one month to the next. Therefore, when comparing one month to another, past relationships should be considered.

Seasonal distribution patterns often remain relatively stable from one year to the next and can be used with some degree of accuracy to predict activity for a given period of time. For example, if at the end of six months, auto production equaled 120 policies and it was known that in recent years 60 percent of total production was produced in the first half of the year, total production could be estimated by dividing 120 by 0.6 to obtain an annual sales projection of 200 policies.

Underwriting Activity

Underwriting is the most fundamental function of any insurance company. Management's financial control of the company depends on communicating the status of underwriting activity to the corporate decision makers. Routine underwriting decisions concerning the acceptance or rejection of various submissions directly affect the profitability of the company. Through an effective management reporting function, decision makers can monitor the underwriter's degree of success in avoiding adverse selection and track the nature of the exposures assumed through comparisons of risk measurement characteristics such as motor vehicle reports, age, sex, previous claims, experience modifiers, hazard group, and risk size. The rate-making process strives to establish premium levels adequate to provide profitable results when potential policyholders, in the aggregate, possess certain assumed risk characteristics. By monitoring the underwriting function, management can observe the actual results and compare them to the anticipated results.

Monitoring the Results Several methods are commonly employed to present underwriting results. The *calendar-year* basis typically reflects premiums earned and incurred losses that occur between January 1 and December 31 of the reporting year but may use any twelve-month period. The accrued methodology used includes all incurred losses (including IBNR) and loss expenses in the calendar year. This method has the advantages of timely availability after the close of the reporting period and easy comparison to the industry average as well as to the results of selected competitors.

Another method used to measure underwriting performance is *policy-year* results. Using this method, premium is considered earned from inception and all losses, loss expenses, and adjustments within the year of the policy issue date are charged to a particular year. In this case, a policy may be issued in December 1985 and an accident could occur in November of the following year and still be included in 1985 policy-year results. Liability claims from this accident may stretch on for several years, but would still be charged to policy year 1985. Therefore, final development for 1985 could extend as long as seven or eight years.

Since the computer has all pertinent policy and claims information, an insurer can track the development of all business placed with that company during a given calendar year. By using an input coding system, the computer can develop underwriting experience by risk characteristic on an inception-year basis. For personal automobile insurance, for example, the data from the application, motor vehicle report, and inspection report are coded to identify a number of risk characteristics, such as "licensed less than one year." An inception-year report then relates earned premium to incurred losses by risk characteristic. Thus, underwriters can compare claim frequency on any group of new business written in a given year with the claim frequency of any other group that has been coded by risk characteristic. This information may be analyzed by territory, by state, by regional office, and companywide. It is useful in modifying the underwriting guide to reflect current conditions and as an indicator of rate adequacy. Such reports assist management in analyzing the degree to which certain underwriting management decisions influenced the final loss ratio of that year of business.

The *accident-year* method resembles the policy-year method, except that accident-year data is entered on the year in the which the loss occurred. Thus it also takes several years to develop a complete accident year.

What Underwriting Information Should Be Reported Underwriting information should indicate the combined ratio, loss ratios, expense ratios, frequency and severity, new business, inspection activity, underwriting terminations, product mix, rate deviations, accommodations, and assigned risks.

Combined Ratio. One of the best gauges of underwriting results is the combined ratio, which reflects the ratio of incurred losses and loss adjustment expenses and other underwriting expenses to total net premiums earned. Underwriting profits (combined ratios under 100 percent) have evaporated in recent years, and for 1984 the property and liability industry experienced, on the average, combined ratios estimated between 112 and 118 percent. Even with underwriting losses of this magnitude, the combined ratio remains the best statistic to communicate underwriting results to management as well as to compare one company's results with another.

Loss Ratios. The individual component ratios of the combined ratio are also routinely used in management reporting. The pure loss

Exhibit 6-2
Loss Ratios

3rd Quarter			9 Months		
1984	1983		1984	Plan	1983
71.5%	67.7%	Total Company	71.1%	71.0%	69.0%
		Direct Lines:			
65.8	63.9	Personal Auto	65.9	70.6	66.7
60.7	56.5	Homeowners	67.8	62.7	54.9
60.4	55.4	Personal Fire and Property	55.0	60.8	50.8
67.7	86.1	Individual Health	69.7	73.7	90.0
97.7	74.7	Business Auto	88.1	74.1	71.3
125.1	65.8	Workers' Compensation	86.9	63.1	64.2
65.8	54.3	Business, Fire and Property	58.6	67.7	53.6
78.1	81.5	SMP	82.5	73.6	74.0
		Reinsured Lines:			
75.5	86.0	Group Health	83.3	83.3	92.1
73.8	71.3	Affiliate XYZ	71.2	63.5	68.3
86.1	91.5	Reinsurance Dept.	85.3	77.8	86.9

ratio, which is incurred losses divided by net earned premiums, is often presented as an overall company total, but it also can be used to reflect line-by-line results. Exhibit 6-2 shows one way loss ratios can be presented to management. Loss ratios often raise questions which lead to further analysis. Some aspects and circumstances which could be analyzed to help explain the trends in the reported loss ratios include:

1. Reviewing large favorable or unfavorable settlements.
2. Impact of a severe storm.
3. Increases in reserves: IBNR (incurred but not reported), case (individual estimate method), and formula (average value method).
4. Change in procedure for opening claims.
5. Change in claim severity.
6. Change in claim frequency.
7. Change in mix of business.

Expense Ratios. Expense ratios, the second component of a combined ratio, appear in two general forms—the financial or statutory basis and the trade basis. Both forms can appear in several variations.

The financial basis expense ratio is frequently calculated using all expenses divided by net earned premium.

Some organizations modify the calculation to exclude allocated loss

Exhibit 6-3
Actual and Planned Expense Ratios

Third Quarter			Nine Months		
1984	1983		1984	Plan	1983
17.2	18.3	Expense — Dept. Ratio	17.6	18.1	19.1
18.6	18.7	— Nondept. Ratio	18.6	18.8	18.7
35.8	37.0	Total Expense Ratio	36.2	36.9	37.8

adjustment expenses or both allocated and unallocated loss expenses when determining their expense total to use as the numerator.

The trade basis expense ratio is similar but uses the net written premiums rather than net earned premiums for the underwriting portion of expenses. The trade basis ratio can be a more meaningful measure when premium volume is increasing or decreasing.

Two examples of commonly used trade basis expense ratio formulas are:

1. Underwriting expense ratio (trade basis)—expenses incurred (less loss expenses) divided by net written premiums.
2. Total expense ratio (trade basis)—underwriting expenses incurred divided by written premium, plus loss adjustment expense divided by earned premium.

The expense ratio is a meaningful portion of any effective management reporting function. Anticipated results and actual results can be compared with prior periods as well as with industry averages to give management a good picture of the company's results. An example of a different presentation which could further enlighten management is shown in Exhibit 6-3. Notice the example classifies expenses in a completely different breakdown. Nondepartmental expenses include such items as agent commissions, taxes, change in loss expense reserves, and general expenses; while the departmental expense category would include salaries, telephone, depreciation, and other items directly connected to a particular and identifiable operating unit of the organization.

Frequency and Severity Reports. Exhibit 6-4 illustrates a type of underwriting management report that separates personal auto loss experience by type of coverage.[1] It compares the loss ratio for the current year to the two preceding years to show if a trend is developing. The reported claim frequency per 100 cars brings out some important facts to consider in the decision-making process. For example, the claim frequency on medical payments was about 0.07 per 100 cars for the first preceding year. The claim frequency on comprehensive losses during the same period was 9.37 per 100 cars. Of course, this must be adjusted for the lack of full credibility on this book of business. Exhibit 6-5 presents the same type of underwriting management information on homeowners business.

Reported claim frequencies per 100 houses and average paid claims are computed by *cause of loss*. Although the peril of fire had the highest claim severity by far, fire losses were less frequent than theft or liability losses. Analysis of recent loss experience should be made available to line underwriters to assist in new business selection and in monitoring.

Inspection Reporting Activity. By placing into the data processing system the name of the inspection company from which an inspection was ordered, a coded reason for the ordering of the report, the data ordered, and the policy number (which would then make all other data regarding that policy number available), the system could:

1. be used as a suspense file to alert the underwriter if the requested report were not received, and
2. produce data by producer, by inspection company, or by underwriter regarding the frequency of reports and reason ordered.

Underwriting Terminations. When an underwriter terminates a policy, a coded reason for termination could be entered that would permit the computer (with proper programming) to compile certain known policy information and create output indicating such things as:

1. the amount of business terminated by an underwriter, where it was terminated, and why;
2. comparison with inspection reporting information to determine what inspection companies were involved with termination, and the resulting percentage compared to number ordered; and
3. timeliness of initial underwriting terminations.

New Business Obtained. Another ratio, the written to quoted ratio (the percent of the cases quoted that are accepted), indicates the degree of success in writing new business. If the ratio is increasing, it might suggest lessening of competition, poor pricing (too low), or general deterioration in the quality of underwriting. Conversely, a ratio suspiciously low might indicate rates that are too high, increasing competition, or coverages that are too restrictive.

Exhibit 6-4
Personal Auto Underwriting Experience

PERSONAL AUTO
IIA INSURANCE COMPANY
UNDERWRITING EXPERIENCE, REPORTED CLAIM FREQUENCY & AVERAGE PAID CLAIM
PERIOD ENDING 12-31-X1

UNDERWRITING EXPERIENCE

CAUSE OF LOSS	EARNED PREMIUM	INCURRED LOSS & ADJ. EXP.	I.L.A.E.† RATIO		
			CURRENT YEAR	FIRST PRECED.	SECOND PRECED.
BI	2,260,411	1,090,456	48.2	66.1	69.3
PD	1,372,009	776,804	56.6	79.4	65.5
MED PAY	178,647	5,384–	CR	CR	CR
PIP	617,604	245,173	39.7	94.9	89.6
COMP	692,647	429,890	62.1	65.9	65.2
COLL	1,231,194	759,536	61.7	93.0	68.2
TOTAL	6,352,512	3,296,475	51.9	78.7	64.6

REPORTED CLAIM FREQUENCY/PER 100 CARS

EXPOSURE UNITS OR PAID CLAIMS	CURRENT YEAR	FIRST PRECED.	SECOND PRECED.	CURRENT YEAR/FIRST PRECED.		CURRENT YEAR/SECOND PRECED.	
				AMOUNT	PERCENT	AMOUNT	PERCENT
BI 27,331	1.70	2.06	1.57	.36–	17.48–	.13	8.28
PD 27,324	6.72	8.38	6.83	1.66–	19.81–	.11–	1.61–
MED PAY 16,112	.02	.07	.12	.05–	71.43–	.10–	83.33–
PIP 26,591	1.93	2.48	2.40	.55–	22.18–	.47–	19.58–
COMP 24,898	9.79	9.83	8.59	.04–	.41–	1.20	13.97
COLL 19,398	7.36	8.97	7.22	1.61–	17.95–	.14	1.94

AVERAGE PAID CLAIM

	CURRENT YEAR	FIRST PRECED.	SECOND PRECED.	CURRENT YEAR/FIRST PRECED.		CURRENT YEAR/SECOND PRECED.	
				AMOUNT	PERCENT	AMOUNT	PERCENT
BI 515	2,891	2,369	3,443	522	22.03	552–	16.03–
PD 1,940	417	375	320	42	11.20	97	30.31
MED PAY 4	357–	212–	219	145–	68.40	576–	263.01–
PIP 442	654	719	667	65–	9.04–	13–	1.95–
COMP 2,994	140	138	125	2	1.45	15	12.00
COLL 1,602	486	511	417	25–	4.89–	69	16.55

† INCURRED LOSS AND ADJUSTMENT EXPENSE

Exhibit 6-5
Homeowners Underwriting Experience

HOMEOWNERS
IIA INSURANCE COMPANY
UNDERWRITING EXPERIENCE, REPORTED CLAIM FREQUENCY & AVERAGE PAID CLAIM
PERIOD ENDING 12-31-X1

UNDERWRITING EXPERIENCE

	EARNED PREMIUM	INCURRED LOSS & ADJ. EXP.	I.L.A.E. RATIO CURRENT YEAR	I.L.A.E. RATIO FIRST PRECED.	I.L.A.E. RATIO SECOND PRECED.
TOTAL	3,053,088	1,303,107	42.7	49.7	67.2

REPORTED CLAIM FREQUENCY/PER 100 HOUSES

CAUSE OF LOSS	EXPOSURE UNITS OR PAID CLAIMS	CURRENT YEAR	FIRST PRECED.	SECOND PRECED.	CURRENT YEAR/FIRST PRECED. AMOUNT	CURRENT YEAR/FIRST PRECED. PERCENT	CURRENT YEAR/SECOND PRECED. AMOUNT	CURRENT YEAR/SECOND PRECED. PERCENT
FIRE	28,948	.94	1.31	1.39	.37-	28.24-	.45-	32.37-
W & H†	28,948	.59	.67	.66	.08-	11.94-	.07-	10.61-
WAT DAM††	28,948	.67	.76	.74	.09-	11.84-	.07-	9.46-
THEFT	28,948	2.87	3.78	3.90	.91-	24.07-	1.03-	26.41-
VAND	28,948	.13	.18	.24	.05-	27.78-	.11-	45.83-
MYS DIS	28,948	.00	.00	.01	.00	.00	.01-	100.00-
ALL OTHER	28,948	.89	1.55	1.20	.66-	42.58-	.31-	25.83-
LIAB & MP	28,948	1.43	1.70	1.61	.27-	15.88-	.18-	11.18-
C C	28,948	.00	.00	.00	.00	.00	.00	.00

AVERAGE PAID CLAIM

CAUSE OF LOSS	EXPOSURE UNITS OR PAID CLAIMS	CURRENT YEAR	FIRST PRECED.	SECOND PRECED.	CURRENT YEAR/FIRST PRECED. AMOUNT	CURRENT YEAR/FIRST PRECED. PERCENT	CURRENT YEAR/SECOND PRECED. AMOUNT	CURRENT YEAR/SECOND PRECED. PERCENT
FIRE	256	2,134	1,253	1,829	881	70.31	305	16.68
W & H	164	332	332	394		.00	62-	15.74-
WAT DAM	157	448	440	446	8	1.62	2	.45
THEFT	759	503	411	364	92	22.38	139	38.19
VAND	36	271	364	203	93-	25.55-	68	33.50
MYS DIS				354			354-	100.00-
ALL OTHER	252	247	285	263	38-	13.33-	16-	6.08-
LIAB & MP	352	662	457	451	205	44.86	211	46.78
C C						.00		.00

†WIND AND HAIL
††WATER DAMAGE

Product Mix. Reports indicating product mix enable management to see more readily the company's distribution of business written. Thus they can be a stepping stone for developing strategic plans.

Rate Deviations. Reports showing deviations from manual rates and underwriter's performance for a book of business may indicate the effectiveness of pricing decisions.

Accommodation Writings. An underwriter may agree to write an otherwise undesirable account as a concession when a good producer indicates that other profitable business will also be written. A condensed report could be issued to management which would indicate the frequency of these writings and the results on accommodation accounts.

Assigned Risks. A report showing involuntary or assigned business may be of interest to management. These risks are not voluntarily accepted by the company but rather are assigned by a state insurance plan or reinsured under the Fair Access to Insurance Requirements (FAIR) plans, which were developed though state or federal regulation in order to make insurance available to those otherwise unable to obtain it. The results from these blocks of business may not be as manageable as the business voluntarily accepted by the underwriter and are often broken out as a separate category for management reporting purposes.

How the Reported Information Is Used Ongoing management of an insurance company as well as operational and long-range planning require accurate underwriting information. Historical trends are often an effective starting point. Charts and schedules showing employee counts, productivity, loss ratios, expense ratios, and mix of business are all helpful when reviewing results and building next year's operational budget.

Claims Activity

The largest single category of routine insurance company expense is claim settlements. Processing fluctuations in the claims functions cause immediate and sometimes severe consequences to the company's financial picture. In addition, larger losses must be reported promptly for reinsurance purposes as well as internal financial and cash flow needs. Lastly, the current loss ratio trend and its individual components of loss severity and frequency are normally of interest in comparison to anticipated and historical results. The annual financial plan depends on assumptions concerning claims experience, and as results become available, management can reevaluate the assumptions to better project progress toward the year-end goal.

What Claims Information Should Be Reported Company decision makers will generally be interested in (1) monitoring claims activity, (2) evaluating the quality and timeliness of claims service, (3) tracking loss reserves, and (4) monitoring loss adjustment expense reserves.

Monitoring Claims Activity. The traditional way to monitor claims activity involves analysis of the loss ratio and its component parts. Loss ratio could be presented by line, by coverage, or by peril and become meaningful to decision makers when proper trends and comparisons were shown. Such things as large claims, catastrophe activity, and so on should be identified since this unusual claim activity could disturb trends and historical analyses. Exhibit 6-6 illustrates an in-depth analysis of the pure loss ratio for personal auto insurance.

A chart such as Exhibit 6-6 allows comparison of the favorable or unfavorable conditions from year to year, but further detailed analysis of frequency, severity, average net claim payment, and premiums by coverage could reveal specific situations of interest. The chart in Exhibit 6-7 plotting these items illustrates percent changes. Notice 1984 loss ratios have been consistently above those for 1983. The frequency and severity experience when compared to the premium per policy helps explain this result. The cost for settling each claim has increased from the 1983 level and, in addition, the number of claim payments has increased. Since the average earned premium per policy did not increase as fast, the loss ratio is higher in 1984 than in 1983.

Evaluating Claims Performance. Management will also be interested in monitoring the level of services provided to policyholders and claimants. One way to track the quality of a company's claim handling is to observe the workload fluctuations within the claims function. Some measurements of service include:

1. number of investigations per claims reported,
2. number of settlements,
3. number of claims per adjuster,
4. number of claims adjusters per claims manager, and
5. contact time from time reported.

Loss Reserves. Loss reserves play an important part in determining the financial position of the company since the estimate of all future costs for settling all currently incurred claims is required for proper reporting. Management reports should contain references to any changes in reserving practices and reserve adequacy.

If, for instance, the number of IBNR claims is known to be changing, the reserves for this type of anticipated loss will change. Likewise, if reserves for pending claims that were established through either a formula or case reserve are revised, it may indicate a change in

Exhibit 6-6
Auto Loss Ratio

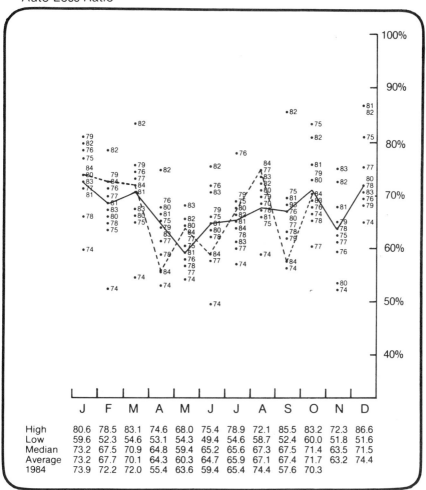

	J	F	M	A	M	J	J	A	S	O	N	D
High	80.6	78.5	83.1	74.6	68.0	75.4	78.9	72.1	85.5	83.2	72.3	86.6
Low	59.6	52.3	54.6	53.1	54.3	49.4	54.6	58.7	52.4	60.0	51.8	51.6
Median	73.2	67.5	70.9	64.8	59.4	65.2	65.6	67.3	67.5	71.4	63.5	71.5
Average	73.2	67.7	70.1	64.3	60.3	64.7	65.9	67.1	67.4	71.7	63.2	74.4
1984	73.9	72.2	72.0	55.4	63.6	59.4	65.4	74.4	57.6	70.3		

reserve adequacy and require a detailed analysis to determine cause and effect. Management will be interested in knowing of changes in adequacy and its effect on current operating experience.

Loss Adjustment Expense (LAE) Reserves. As with loss reserves, the LAE reserve established as a liability representing future expenses for settling incurred claims, is of interest to company decision makers due to the immediate financial impact of changes in reserving practices or reserve levels. Management reports should include information pertaining to reserve changes and their impact. The component parts of the loss adjustment reserving process (allocated versus unallocated

Exhibit 6-7
Collision — 3 Month Moving — End Plotted

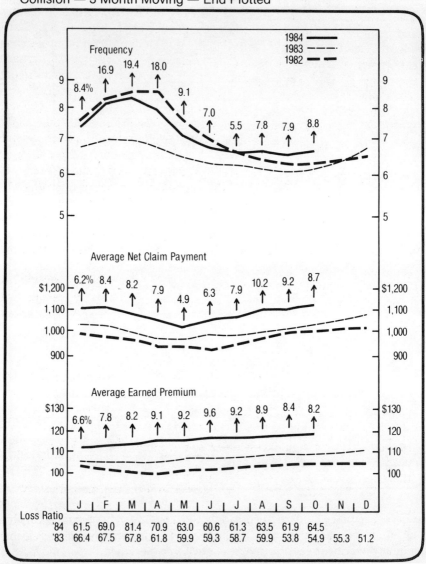

expenses, salvage and subrogation as well as reinsurance/catastrophe situations) may become relevant to the management reporting of LAE as their level of importance grows to the point at which financial results are impacted.

Uses of Reported Claims Information   In addition to the need to monitor the claims function from the financial management perspective, claims information may influence corporate strategic planning and, specifically, the marketing and underwriting aspects of insurance operations. Particularly favorable or particularly unfavorable loss experience in either a portion of the operating territory or throughout the company may point up a need to alter marketing or underwriting plans and programs.

Information on the claims activities may also be of greater importance to management than data from other functions due to the interest directed toward this area by external factors. State insurance examiners are very much interested in claim information and, in particular, loss and LAE reserving adequacy. The major cause of insurance company insolvencies originates with reserve inadequacies. Likewise, for stock companies, the Securities and Exchange Commission as well as the brokerage house financial analysts focus attention on claim and reserve data found in corporate statements. Management must be kept informed of any changes in the status of claims that will generate questions or comments from outside sources.

Also, from an industry perspective, the Insurance Services Office takes notice of claims status and disasters. Industry results are monitored to detect changing trends.

Loss Control Services

The traditional view of the loss control function is changing. While safety and health maintenance services are still provided to policyholders, an additional emphasis involves aggressive pursuit of loss control activity in conjunction with the marketing and public relations functions. For example, the public discussion of air bags and other passive passenger restraints, as well as the price discounts offered for their installation, point out the multi-faceted impact.

One of management's concerns for loss control activities focuses on the cost effectiveness of the investment of corporate resources in this area. The support for industry associations designed to reduce theft or arson losses is an example of a corporate investment in loss control. Likewise, safety and health services provided to policyholders must be evaluated for cost effectiveness. Marketing strategies and public awareness of the company name can often be combined with loss control services or activities since the policyholder as well as the company generally benefits from risk reduction. If the loss control activity in question can justify a rate reduction or discount, the combined effort could result in more sales to better risks.

Thus the management reporting system should provide the

information required to evaluate such activities and to recommend new directives.

For companies with large commercial portfolios, the loss control function is still more significant. Commercial marketing often emphasizes the loss control services available to the client. The loss control information contained in management reports should reflect the level, timeliness, and quality of the service provided to the customer as well as a comparison to the level of services provided by competitors. Although it is not possible to measure losses that did not occur because of loss control activities, measures of service standards do facilitate an evaluation of the costs and benefits of loss control activities.

Administrative and Human Resources

The measurements of administrative effectiveness are numerous and sometimes not recognized as a part of management reporting. Normally, administrative reporting is included in corporate level reports only when variances are significant to overall results. These reports fall into several classifications such as human resources, accounting, policyholder services, field office activities, expense management reports, and other statutory reports. Many are housekeeping reports. Although not reported at companywide levels, they are essential to the day-to-day operation of the business.

Human resources administration is one of the most important areas, since employee salaries and related costs represent the largest expense which the company can control. Because of the expense and the effect on employees, many internal records and reports must be maintained to ensure that proper amounts are paid, turnover is kept at the desired level, and total corporate expense is in the proper relationship to income. The human resource reports of most companies include the following:

1. salary administration records,
2. comparisons with national, local, and industry salary levels,
3. employee training and development,
4. employee controls and employee productivity measures,
5. employee benefits costs and programs,
6. average salary per employee compared to past periods and to indicators of the proper current level such as the consumer price index, and
7. governmental reports dealing with such subjects as compliance with minority hiring, EEO, and safety.

Accounting administrative activities include:

1. processing activities and time service,
2. coding and policyholder service activities,
3. statutory accounting reporting, and
4. internal management reporting of premiums, losses, and expenses.

Although many of the above reports are routine and used by only a few specialized functions or management groups, as exception situations occur, they may become important and require reporting at high levels.

For example, companies in compliance with minority hiring requirements will find no need for extensive management reporting. But companies in danger of governmental sanctions and loss of government contracts will emphasize reporting at a much higher level. Much of the administrative reporting will be dictated by management's desire, interest, and needs. Statutory or mandated governmental reports often do not answer the question—what does this imply for the future? What has happened in the past is of little value if it fails to indicate what is to be expected in the future. Administrative reporting should be designed to facilitate planning as well as to satisfy current reporting requirements.

Investment Performance

Investment income has become a significant factor in the overall profitability of property and liability insurance companies. As underwriting gains recede, the portion of total operating gain related solely to the investment function continues to grow. In adverse market situations, insurers may rely on investment income to offset underwriting losses. Often, the viability of the company hinges on the effectiveness of the investment function.

The investment strategies for a property and liability insurance company are designed to respond to prevailing and forecasted economic conditions as well as to internal factors such as budgeted operating results, cash flow projections, and current and expected tax status. Using this information, a company establishes an acceptable balance of risk factors and desired yields for each class of investment and the entire investment portfolio. In some companies, prior approval is required before any investment transaction can be made. This approval is typically provided by an investment committee comprising members of the board of directors and top management. In other companies, investment transactions are carried out and later reported to an investment committee for ratification.

Investment reporting is the process of comparing actual investment performance to budgeted investment performance. Significant variations in any of the factors used in developing the investment strategies should be the primary emphasis of periodic investment performance reporting. In the absence of any such significant variations, the investment reporting process would include presentation of investment activity data similar to that shown in Exhibit 6-8. Realized capital gain or loss data would be presented to provide the results of the investment activity to date. Other investment information reported would be the change in unrealized gain or loss in the carrying values of assets valued at market prices. This information provides insight into the general market conditions for those stocks within the company's portfolio.

Profitability

Each of the operating and administrative areas of a property and liability insurance company (sales, underwriting, claims, human resources, investments, and finance) is involved in making daily management decisions that are likely to have an impact on the revenues and expenses of the company. Periodic measurement and reporting of a company's revenues and expenses are necessary to monitor the progress toward profitability goals. While each of the operating and administrative areas has goals that are monitored periodically, the profitability goals probably represent the most widely used measurement of a company's overall success.

Profitability can be measured and reported at various organizational levels—general management, officers, and board of directors; and operational hierarchies—company, regional, or branch office, line of business, and policy coverage. However, before profitability can be measured, it must be defined. Each of these reporting levels has defined specific information needs to monitor performance. In all cases, the profitability reporting process would be structured to highlight variations from expected results. It is imperative that financial results be analyzed and that an appropriate narrative accompanies financial results to avoid misinterpretation by the reader. Exhibit 6-9 is an example of the financial statement detail that might be presented to officers or the Board of Directors.

General management would have analyzed the basic financial data behind these statements and briefed the officers on significant items. Any narrative accompanying the financial statements to the board could be supplemented by the information obtained by the officers during the briefing held with general management.

General management financial statements might be similar to the one shown in Exhibit 6-10.

Exhibit 6-8
Report of Office of Investments

First Quarter, 19XX

Investment Changes — Shown in the following schedules are acquisitions, eliminations, net gain, or "net new money," and investment holdings at March 31, 19XX ($000's).

	First Quarter 19XX — Book Values			Statement Values
	Acquired	Eliminated	Net New Money	Holdings 3/31/XX
Bonds				
Short-Term	$132,176	$201,715	$(69,539)	$ 43,875
U.S. Government/Agency	86,521	26,866	59,655	511,711
Foreign	2,537	—	2,537	33,164
State, County, and Municipal	—	16,179	(16,179)	316,790
Special Revision, Tax-Exempt	19,353	10,013	9,340	724,567
IRB/Pollution Control	—	397	(397)	179,006
Railroad	—	—	—	—
Public Utility	13,000	173	12,827	22,446
Industrial and Miscellaneous	—	95	(95)	13,093
Total	$253,587	$255,438	$ (1,851)	$1,844,652
Stocks				
Preferred	$ 2,446	$ 3,628	$ (1,182)	$ 153,080
General Market Common	54,767	33,249	21,518	722,991
Other Common	1	1	—	477,246
Total	$ 57,214	$ 36,878	$ 20,336	$1,353,317
Other Investments	$ —	$ —	$ —	$ 1,082
Mortgage Loans	$ —	$ 334	$ (334)	$ 11,140
Real Estate-Owned	$ 290	$ —	$ 290	$ 135,901
Real Estate-Partner Interest	$ 272	$ —	$ 272	$ 3,222
Home Purchases	$ 2,752	$ 3,438	$ (686)	$ 4,890
Grand Total-Investments	$314,115	$296,088	$ 18,027	$3,354,204

These management statements can be used to illustrate several important profitability measures within a property and liability insurance company. The most common measure of profitability for an insurer is the combined ratio, which measures the profitability of the underwriting (or insurance-related) operations of the company. This measure of a property and liability company's profitability does not

Exhibit 6-9
Operating Results ($ in Millions)

Annual Plan		1984	9 Months Plan	1983
$2,557.0	Net Earned Premium	$1,884.9	$1,891.4	$1,694.5
70.6%	Loss Ratio	71.1%	71.0%	69.0%
36.6	Expense Ratio	34.7%	37.0%	37.1%
19.1	Departmental	17.6	19.2	19.2
17.5%	Nondepartmental	17.1	17.8	17.9
$ (183.6)	Operating Gain (Loss)	$ (108.5)	$ (152.1)	$ (103.1)
(7.2)%	Percent of Earned Premium	(5.8)%	(8.0)%	(6.1)%
$ 249.8	Investment Income	$ 197.2	$ 181.3	$ 170.9
$ 66.2	Operating and Investment Income	$ 88.7	$ 29.2	$ 67.8
2.6%	Percent of Earned Premium	4.7%	1.5%	4.0%

include the impact of investment earnings on the premium writings. Extreme price competition and high interest rates have resulted in less profitable underwriting operations and more profitable investment operations. Perhaps a more comprehensive measure of an insurance company's profitability would be the operating and investment gain (line 16 of Exhibit 6-10). This measure has become extremely popular in the past few years.

The large underwriting losses that currently pervade the industry have resulted in most companies paying little or no federal income taxes. Many companies have recovered all available past taxes and are currently carrying losses forward to offset future tax liabilities. The tax position of the company, which may have a significant bearing on investment strategies and capital budgeting, may not be readily determinable from management statements.

A standard financial management measure of a property and liability insurer's financial strength is the premium to surplus ratio. Since a solid surplus base protects against large losses and provides for growth, line 22 of Exhibit 6-10 should also be examined. In this case, the total change in surplus resulted largely from changes in the market values of the investment portfolio (securities not sold during the period). As line 20 of Exhibit 6-10 shows, these values can fluctuate significantly from year to year or quarter to quarter.

The management statement shown in Exhibit 6-10 reports results for the entire company. Other organizational units within the company may measure profitability differently. For example, assume that a property and liability insurer has several decentralized regional offices, but the reinsurance operations (for ceded and assumed business) and investment functions remain in the home office. Profitability by region would be reported on a direct basis (excluding reinsurance). Profitability measures would probably exclude home office overhead expenses, which would be allocated to each regional office subsequently. In other words, profitability would be measured for those income and expense items under the regional management's control.

As the reporting levels become more narrowly defined, the need to allocate costs and expenses becomes more prominent, since a sophisticated cost accounting system may not be cost justified. Premium and loss data and some expense data can be accumulated according to lines of business or coverage levels. However, certain allocations of overhead expenses may make measurement of profitability at these levels somewhat imprecise. Many companies are currently pursuing ways to allocate investment income to lines of business to provide another meaningful profitability measure for the industry. The methodologies used by the different companies vary, and it will probably be some time before a standard investment allocation method is adopted by most companies.

In summary, profitability must be defined so that it can be measured. The definition of profitability can vary at different organizational levels and operational hierarchies. In any case, however, it should include consideration of underwriting results, investment results, expenses, and taxes.[2] The reporting of profitability should concentrate on variations from expected performance and all financial statements should be accompanied by an appropriate analytical narrative to avoid misrepresentation by the reader.

RESPONSIBILITY ACCOUNTING

The phrase "responsibility accounting" is somewhat self-defining. Responsibility accounting theory says that performance should be reported based on placement of responsibility and authority to make result-influencing decisions. Those who have responsibility and authority to make decisions should be accountable for the results of their decisions.

This last sentence provides three bases for determining accountability and measuring performance under responsibility accounting. The *first* is responsibility to make decisions which affect results. The *second* is authority to carry out the plans and programs necessary to support the decisions made. The *third* is the results. Without both

Exhibit 6-10
Management Statements, June 30, 1984 ($ in Thousands)

SUMMARY OF OPERATIONS

	(1)	(2)	(3)	(4)	(5)	(6)	(7)	(8)
	Second Quarter, 1984		First Half, 1984				First Half, 1983	
	Actual	Percent of Net Earned Premiums	Actual	Plan	Percent of Net Earned Premiums Actual	Plan	Actual	Percent of Net Earned Premiums
Operating								
1. Net Written Premiums (B)	$557,452		$1,084,473	$1,118,841			$ 994,255	
2. Earned Premiums	$537,035		$1,057,828				$ 953,444	
3. Less: Dividends to Policyholders	1,089		2,286				863	
4. Net Earned Premiums	$535,946	100.0%	$1,055,542	$1,050,694	100.0%	100.0%	$ 952,581	100.0%
5. Losses Incurred	$349,416	65.2%	$ 747,946	$ 749,895	70.9%	71.4%	$ 662,940	69.6%
6. Operating Expenses — Departmental	$ 94,795	17.7%	$ 188,328	$ 200,522	17.8%	19.1%	$ 187,568	19.7%
7. — Non Departmental	89,242	16.6	171,832	184,505	16.3	17.5	162,568	17.1
8. Total Operating Expenses	$184,037	34.3%	$ 360,160	$ 385,027	34.1%	36.6%	$ 350,136	36.8%
9. Total Losses and Expenses	$533,453	99.5%	$1,108,106	$1,134,922	105.0%	108.0%	$1,013,076	106.4%
10. Operating Gain (Loss)	$ 2,493	0.5%	$ (52,564)	$ (84,228)	(5.0)%	(8.0)%	$ (60,495)	(6.4)%
11. Commission on UPR — 1/1/84	-0-	-0-	1,528	-0-	0.2	-0-	-0-	-0-
12. Adjusted Operating Gain (Loss)	$ 2,493	0.5%	$ (51,036)	$ (84,228)	(4.8)%	(8.0)%	$ (60,495)	(6.4)%

Investment								
13. Net Investment Income	$ 53,084	9.9%	$ 106,230	$ 99,590	10.0%	9.5%	$ 94,014	9.9%
14. Capital Gains (Losses)	22,263	4.1	27,277	-0-	2.6	-0-	10,327	1.1
15. Investment Gain (Loss)	$ 75,347	14.0%	$ 133,507	$ 99,590	12.6%	9.5%	$ 104,341	11.0%
16. Operating and Investment Gain (Loss)	$ 77,840	14.5%	$ 82,471	$ 15,362	7.8%	1.5%	$ 43,846	4.6%
17. Federal and Foreign Income Tax	1,398	0.3	1,449	4,950	0.1	0.4	(289)	—
18. Net Operation and Investment Gain (Loss)	$ 79,238	14.8%	$ 83,920	$ 20,312	7.9%	1.9%	$ 43,557	4.6%
Surplus Adjustments								
19. Change in Valuation of Association Costs	1,117	0.3	9,246	9,400	0.9	0.9	18,585	2.0
20. Change in Valuation of Other Investments	(50,636)	(9.5)	(90,871)	32,611	(8.6)	3.1	119,496	12.5
21. Other Changes	(3,939)	(0.7)	(5,112)	(3,189)	(0.5)	(0.3)	(677)	(0.1)
22. Increase (Decrease) in Surplus for Policyholders' Protection	$ 26,374	4.9%	$ (2,817)	$ 59,134	(0.3)%	5.6%	$ 180,961	19.0%
23. Premium/Surplus Ratio			1.62				1.44	

responsibility and authority for decisions, decision-makers should not be held accountable for the results.

Responsibility accounting frequently exists in decentralized organizations where responsibility and authority are delegated to divisions or regional offices. In these structures, fairness requires that performance be measured only on those results under management's total control. For example, one regional office should not be measured by the impact of a second regional office on corporate results.

Responsibility accounting places accountability at the source of the decision, leading to potentially better decisions. The decisions are more likely to consider corporate goals and plans, since the decision-maker must account for the effect of the decision on the total corporation. This is done by accumulating results from line levels to higher management levels. Decisions are reviewed at each management level for positive and negative results.

Organizational Structure

Responsibility accounting may not measure performance by profits earned because management at each level may not control all expenses or income-generating decisions. For example, a regional office must generate income (premium) and control its expenses to realize a profit. But the central corporate office may make decisions affecting profits by which regional management should not be measured. For example, a centralized investment function may contribute greatly to corporate profits but these results will be outside regional control. Therefore, the region should not be measured by these profits (or losses). Responsibility accounting may not measure performance by number of dollars either. For example, a claims processing unit may be measured by the number of claims processed in a standard time period. As the claims processing supervisor reports performance to the claims processing manager, and to higher levels of management, results are eventually converted to the dollar cost of claims handling. Different measures of performance allow each level of management to analyze what is happening.

Decentralization The degree of decentralization in an organization will affect the use of responsibility accounting. Totally centralized organizations have a chief executive officer (CEO) who is accountable to the corporation owners for results. The CEO may delegate responsibility to functional office heads (such as sales, marketing, and systems) who are then accountable to the CEO. Responsibility accounting can be used by the CEO to measure the performance of the office heads and their ability to work as one unit. Responsibility and profitability accounting can be used by the corporation owners to measure the performance of the CEO in running the corporation.

Many organizations have several decentralized offices reporting to a central home office. An extremely decentralized organization may not have a central home office which makes decisions but would allow each decentralized office to be a completely autonomous business center. An example might be a holding company which purchases businesses and retains the original management, allowing them all prior authority. Since management has authority to make decisions, they will be held responsible for all results. If the holding company dislikes the results, it can exercise its right to change management. The held company's strategy is decided by its management. The holding company's strategy is determined by the companies it buys and holds.

Centralization   In operating companies as opposed to holding companies, the services provided by the central home office depend on cost effectiveness. For example, data processing services may cost less if operated centrally than if each office operates its own data center. Decentralized management is accountable for the results of decisions and plans under their control and centralized management is accountable for results of decisions and plans made by the centralized offices. The CEO is accountable to the corporation owners for total operations and corporate strategic plans.

Each decentralized unit is considered a profit center. Costs for services provided by the central office may be charged to the decentralized results but decentralized managements should not be measured by these costs unless they can also control them. Responsibility accounting would be concerned only with gains or losses resulting from decentralized operations exclusive of uncontrollable charges for centralized services.

Dual Responsibility   Matrix structures classify personnel according to both functional and line responsibility. Organizations with matrix structures have decentralized offices with functional, usually centralized, staff offices. Decentralized personnel are accountable to both decentralized management and functional office management. Employees have a dual responsibility to their immediate line supervisor and to home office staff. For example, an adjuster may be accountable to the regional manager for the results of his or her actions and also responsible for following directions set by the home office claims staff management.

When using responsibility accounting to measure performance, the possibility of joint responsibility should be considered. If more than one business center is responsible for results, procedures should be implemented to report the full responsibility. An example would be selling group homeowners insurance through a regional office when group insurance processing and underwriting is centralized. Regional management makes decisions that affect the amount of group insurance sold. Group management makes underwriting decisions that affect the amount of business accepted and finally are reflected in regional and group results. The results of both decisions must therefore be reported and measured, since they impact each other and final results.

Goal Planning

Four factors must be considered when planning goals under responsibility accounting. First, the responsibility and authority of each person or group must be defined. Second, the measures of performance must be defined to ensure that the corporate strategic goals will be supported by the operations. For example, if high persistency ratios were an important corporate goal, performance should not be measured by the lowest possible expense ratio if the expense ratio can only be achieved at the cost of policyholder service. Third, goals must be agreed upon by both line and corporate management. And, fourth, performance measures must support both strategic and operational plans.

Responsibility Centers

A responsibility center has the responsibility and authority to decide business direction. Responsibility accounting can then be used as a performance measurement system.

Four types of responsibility centers can be observed. *Profit centers*, such as subsidiaries or regional offices, must generate income and control expenses to net a profit. *Cost centers* have authority to decide how money is spent to provide services to other responsibility centers and must remain within their budget while providing an adequate level of support. An example would be a centralized data processing office. *Revenue centers* generate income and probably reside within profit centers. An example would be a sales district responsible for generating insurance sales leading to premium. The sales district may report to a regional office, the profit center. *Investment centers* are responsible for investing in profitable ventures such as subsidiaries, stocks, bonds, mortgages, or real estate to generate investment income. An example would be the centralized money management office, directed by the CEO and Board of Directors.

Planning for the responsibility center depends on the type of center. Types of plans which may be developed include revenues, expenses, strategic, operational, and support levels.

DECISION SUPPORT

An entirely different type of management reporting occurs in decision support situations. Decision support requires *decision making* information rather than *attention directing* or *scorekeeping* information. Instead of standard reports on a periodic basis, decision support requires information that relates to a unique question or situation.

One authority distinguishes decision support from other management reporting as follows:

> Oversimplifying a bit, we can say that the basic philosophy of most EDP systems is to automate the storage and retrieval of data, thereby reducing costs, improving accuracy, and allowing quicker access to data concerning day-to-day operations. The philosophy underlying decision support systems is that it is every bit as legitimate to use computers to improve or expedite the processes by which people make and communicate decisions. Thus the emphasis of decision support systems is on increased individual and organizational effectiveness rather than on increased efficiency in processing masses of data.[3]

Decision support does not necessarily mean reporting aggregate results, since information reflecting a representative sample may provide an adequate basis for a decision far more conveniently.[4] Flexibility is important in responding to requests for information needed for a special analysis or other decision support.

From a management information perspective, what qualifies as special analysis? It is generally thought to be a request for information in a form not currently provided although in many situations the data necessary to support the information request may already exist. Special analysis can be an analysis of a potential strategic or operational opportunity, or it can be an analysis of a strategic or, more likely, an operational problem. If the analysis relates to an operational problem, it might require information to determine what is wrong or what went wrong or, perhaps, whether anything is actually wrong.

Usually special analysis is highly focused on a specific issue or question. It may result in the reporting of information on a "one-shot" basis or the continued reporting of information on a periodic basis until management is certain that the problem has been satisfactorily resolved. Even in the latter case, management may desire ongoing information reporting to assure that the problem never arises again; or if it does, it can be acted upon quickly.

Often, developing management information in support of special analysis can be costly. These incremental costs must be understood in order to determine if it is worthwhile for the organization to pursue the special analysis. The additional costs associated with special analysis may include those incurred for specially trained analysts; the costs of unique data collection efforts, special data access, and manipulation capabilities; and the cost of unique data processing hardware and software acquisitions including models.

Before going to the expense of providing management information in support of special analysis, the company should address the four key management questions presented in Chapter 1:

- How is the desired information to be used?
- How much information is required and how often must it be produced?
- Does the data necessary to support the information request exist within the organization and, if so, is it readily accessible?
- What is the cost or loss to the organization to go without the requested information?

Answers to these questions will assure that management information reports produced for special analyses are worth the cost involved.

SUMMARY

The competitive nature of the insurance business necessitates insurance information systems that are responsive, flexible, accessible, and cost-effective. Information must be reported in a manner that directs the attention of management toward situations requiring corrective action for the company to remain competitive in its desired markets.

Although the specific reporting system should be adapted to the company's objectives and management styles, certain fundamentals of management reporting provide a framework for designing the company's unique reporting system. Sales reports should highlight sales activity, production, and productivity for the benefit of marketing managers. Timely reporting of loss, expense, and combined ratios as well as other underwriting information enables management to monitor the success of its underwriting policy. In addition to reporting loss experience, claims reports should also indicate the quality and timeliness of claims service, track loss reserves, and monitor loss adjustment expense reserves. Loss control reports should reflect the level, timeliness, and quality of service; and provide a basis for evaluating the costs and benefits of loss control activity. Although much administrative reporting consists of required reports for personnel and accounting purposes, it also includes incidental record keeping for routine office administration. Investment performance is a specialized, but highly

significant, factor in an insurer's profitability; thus reports of investment performance should emphasize variations from the results
expected in the planned investment strategy. Investment gain and
underwriting gain can be combined into a measure of overall
profitability, but an insurer should take care that its profitability
measures allocate income and expenses in a manner consistent with the
management structure.

An effective reporting system facilitates responsibility accounting
within the company. Managers have information indicating the results
of their decisions and can be held accountable for those decisions. If
they do not have responsibility and authority for decisions, however,
they should not be held accountable for the results. Responsibility
accounting places accountability at the source of the decision. Thus, the
management structure, the corporate goals, and the responsibility
centers should all be considered in a designed responsibility accounting
system.

In addition to regular management reporting and responsibility
accounting, an insurance information system must occasionally provide
management reports for special analyses. Such reports may be
important because of a strategic opportunity or a major problem, but
they can also be costly. Thus the costs and benefits of such special
management reports should be considered before they are generated.

These fundamental principles of management reporting should
guide an insurance organization in developing an information reporting
system that responds effectively to management needs.

Chapter Notes

1. This discussion of frequency and severity reports, inspection reporting activity, and underwriting terminations has been adapted from G. William Glendenning and Robert B. Holtom, *Personal Lines Underwriting*, 2nd ed. (Malvern, PA: Insurance Institute of America, 1982), pp. 494–498.
2. IASA Accounting Research Committee, "Profitability: Management's Need for Information," *The Interpreter* (June 1985), pp. 5–32.
3. Steven Alter, *Decision Support Systems: Current Practice and Continuing Challenges* (Reading, MA: Addison-Wesley Publishing Company, 1980), pp. 2-3.
4. Dale R. Schissler, "Organizing an Insurance Company Research Unit," *Research Philosophy and Techniques: Selected Readings*, ed. Robert J. Gibbons (Malvern, PA: Insurance Institute of America, 1983), pp. 70-71.

CHAPTER 7

Statistical Reporting

INTRODUCTION

In addition to the management uses described in the previous chapter, statistical reporting provides the information needed to determine and to justify insurance rates. Historically, statistical reports furnished essentially *scorekeeping* information. Insurers calculated and justified their rates for the coming period simply on the basis of their premiums, losses, and expenses for the past period. The increasing complexity of ratemaking, however, has imposed new demands on the statistical reporting process. *Decision-making* information is now required to project the future impact of loss development factors and other trends affecting premiums, losses, and expenses.[1]

Insurance pricing, called ratemaking, is the calculation of each policyholder's fair share of losses and expenses. This calculation involves the evaluation of premium and loss statistics collected when insurance policies are written and processed by an insurance company and when claims are adjusted. This retrospective testing of data is used in modifying the underlining rate structure. As business volumes have increased and deficiencies in initial rating procedures have become apparent, new and more sophisticated, equitable, and economical ratemaking methods have evolved.

To apply accepted ratemaking methods, there must be a creditable data base from which to extract experience. This means that the experience should be from a large homogeneous group of insureds. This data must have detailed exposure, loss, and expense information to satisfy the needs of the ratemaking methodology used.

Insurance rate filings require extensive statistical documentation to justify rate requests. While at one time the data might have been accepted readily, public concern over rising rates has focused the regulatory spotlight on the accuracy of ratemaking statistics. In justifying higher rates, the burden of proof rests with the insurers. Any gaps or errors in the data presented, therefore, undermine the entire rate case. Unless convinced of the data's unimpeachable accuracy, the insurance commissioner may not approve a requested rate increase. Thus insurance organizations face a significant statistical reporting burden.

STATISTICS AND RATEMAKING

The entire concept of ratemaking requires that each rate must be the correct price per unit of exposure. The correct price is the amount just adequate to cover losses and the insurer's expenses and to provide sufficient profit to attract capital to the insurance industry. If the rate is too low to provide an adequate profit, it will result in inadequate capital to meet the insurance needs of the public. If it is too high, it will result in dissatisfied customers, investigations by governmental agencies, and the attraction of excessive capital (with resulting excessive competition) to the industry. Before examining the rules of various parties in providing statistics for ratemaking, a closer look at fundamental ratemaking concepts is in order.

Ratemaking Concepts

An insurance rate consists of three components: (1) an expected loss component, (2) an expense component, and (3) an allowance for profit and contingencies. In practice, the expense component and the allowance for profit and contingencies are usually combined into a single element, usually called an expense loading.

The determination of the expected loss component, frequently referred to as the *pure premium*, is the most difficult part of the ratemaking process and the part involving the greatest amount of uncertainty.

The amount needed for expected losses is estimated on the basis of past loss experience, adjusted to reflect probable future trends in inflation, accident frequency, and other factors that may cause future losses to differ from those incurred in the past. The pure premium is usually calculated by dividing the number of earned units of exposure into the dollar amount of losses incurred for some period of years, known as the experience period. The pure premium can be expressed by the following formula:

$$\text{Pure premium} = \frac{\text{Dollar amount of losses}}{\text{Number of units of exposure}}$$

Thus, if the losses and loss adjustment expenses incurred during the experience period (after adjustment for inflation and other factors) amounted to \$5,710,000 and there were 1,000,000 earned units of exposure (for example, \$100,000,000 of payroll), the pure premium would be

$$\text{Pure premium} = \frac{\$5,710,000}{1,000,000} = \$5.71$$

The length of the experience period may vary from one year to five years or more, depending upon the characteristics of the line of insurance and the size of the premium volume. A line such as windstorm insurance, for which the losses fluctuate substantially from year to year, may require an experience period of ten or fifteen years in order to level out the fluctuations. For a line with little loss fluctuation, an experience period of one or two years may be sufficient. All else being equal, a line with a small premium volume requires a longer experience period than one with a large premium volume.

Because insurance rates depend so heavily on the loss statistics and the exposure unit statistics, it is essential that those statistics be gathered and reported with utmost accuracy. An error in either the loss data or the exposure data will cause the resulting rates to be incorrect for the exposures assumed.

The insurer's loss adjustment expenses are usually included in the pure premium for ratemaking purposes, but all other expenses are included in the expense loading. The size of the total expense loading and the exact nature of expense categories vary by line of insurance. For example, in boiler and machinery insurance, 36.7 percent of the premium is allocated to general administrative and loss control expenses. Only 9.0 percent of the premium is allocated to those expenses for commercial fire insurance. The difference is due largely to the greater expenses incurred for loss control inspections under boiler insurance.

The *gross rate*, which includes all three of the rate components mentioned above, is usually calculated by dividing the expected loss percentage into the pure premium. For example, if the pure premium is \$1.27 per \$100 of payroll, and the expected loss percentage is 57.1 percent, then the gross rate will be:

$$\text{Gross rate} \ = \ \frac{\text{Pure premium}}{\text{Expected loss percentage}} \ = \ \frac{\$1.27}{.571} \ = \ \$2.22$$

The expected loss percentage equals 100 percent minus the percentage loading for expenses, profit, and contingencies.

The loading for underwriting profit and contingencies has been standardized at 5 percent for most lines of insurance since the 1920s. The major exception is workers' compensation insurance, for which a loading of 2.5 percent has been used in many states. The inclusion of a 5 percent loading for underwriting profit and contingencies does not mean that insurers always earn exactly 5 percent. In fact, they seldom do. Insurers also rely on investment income on the funds they hold for the time between collecting premiums and paying losses. Historical data indicate that actual underwriting profit has been less than 5 percent much more often than it has equaled or exceeded 5 percent. This fact accords with the designation of the loading as "underwriting profit and contingencies." The principal contingency is the possibility that the actual amount needed for losses incurred will exceed the amount included in the rate to pay them.

In insurance terminology, the *law of large numbers* says that the accuracy with which losses can be predicted improves as the number of exposure units increases. For example, a firm that owns only one car cannot predict with acceptable accuracy the dollar amount of liability claims which will arise from the use of the car in any one year. However, an insurer that insures ten million cars can predict its annual losses with much greater accuracy. Thus, by pooling the loss exposures of many insureds, an insurer increases the predictability of losses.

Of course, an insurer is able to perform this function effectively only if it can properly allocate the cost of loss among its various insureds. The equitable allocation of the cost of loss is the function of insurance rating plans.

An insurance rating plan provides an objective means for determining insurance premiums. The terms *insurance rate* and *insurance premium* are sometimes used synonymously. However, they have distinctly different meanings. An insurance rate is the price charged for each unit of exposure. The insurance premium is the total charge for all of the units of exposure insured under a given policy.

Thus a rating plan must specify the *exposure base* (or premium base) used as well as stipulate a precise rate per unit of exposure. Most rating plans also define distinct classifications of insureds and stipulate a different rate for each classification, reflecting the different loss exposures involved.

Exposure Bases An *exposure unit* is a measure of the loss exposure an insurer has assumed. The *exposure base* is the denomination in which the exposure units are expressed. The exposure base for workers' compensation insurance is payroll. The exposure unit is $100 of payroll. Liability coverages may also be based on payroll, receipts, or other units of exposure. The exposure base for fire insurance is the amount of insurance, and the exposure unit is $100 of insurance. In automobile insurance, a unit of exposure is one car insured for one year, usually called one car-year.

Rating Classes One of the major goals of ratemaking is to spread the cost of insurance equitably over all of those insured. Three methods of spreading the cost have been used or suggested: (1) charge all insureds the same rate for each line of insurance; (2) set a different rate for each insured based on that insured's own characteristics; and (3) divide all insureds into relatively homogeneous classes and charge the same rate to each insured in a given class based on the average loss exposure of the class.

The first approach, the same rate for all insureds, has been used in some lines of insurance for which the loss exposure does not vary greatly among insureds, when sufficient information is not available to determine the extent of variation among insureds, or when the premium for each insured is too small to justify the expense of either of the other two methods.

However, when substantial variation exists among the loss costs of various classes of insureds, the single rate approach can lead to substantial problems. In such cases, the single rate is too high for some insureds and too low for others. Unless insurance is compulsory, there will be a tendency for those in the high loss classes to buy insurance, while those in the classes with low loss cost will not. This adverse selection results in underwriting losses for unwary insurers.

In order to avoid losses, insurers may tend to seek out the insureds with low loss exposures and to refuse coverage to those with high loss exposures. Of course, this approach leaves many people without insurance.

The second rating approach, an individually determined rate for each insured, would seem to solve the problems caused by charging the same rate for all insureds. However, it creates some problems of its own. First, individual rating is an expensive process so it would not be economically feasible except for those loss exposures which involve a substantial amount of premium. Second, individual rates would necessarily be judgment rates for a great many kinds of insurance, since present knowledge does not permit exact evaluation of individual loss exposures. Judgment rates leave much room for unfair discrimination, either intentional or unintentional.

Class rating is a compromise between a single-rate system and individual rating. If the classification criteria are properly selected and applied, class rating has most of the advantages of both of the other systems and few of the disadvantages of either.

Classification criteria vary with the loss exposure insured, and a wide variety of such criteria are used in commercial lines insurance. For example, the business of the insured is the principal rating criterion for workers' compensation insurance. The workers' compensation manual shows rates for approximately 600 rating classes. They range from clerical workers, with rates that are among the lowest, to such hazardous and high-rated occupations as steeplejacks. Commercial fire insurance loss exposures are classified by construction, kind of business (occupancy), and public fire protection. The classification criteria for most commercial crime coverages include kind of business, territory, and the alarms or other protective devices in use. The use of protective devices as classification criteria in crime insurance is an excellent example of encouraging loss control through the classification system.

Class rating is less expensive to apply than individual rating and only slightly more expensive than a single-rate system. Class rating is not as prone to adverse selection as a single-rate system, since there is a narrower range between the least hazardous and most hazardous exposures within a class. For the same reason, there are likely to be fewer exposures for which insurance will not be available because of rate inadequacy.

It should be noted that rating classifications also involve the use of an average rate for the class, with the rate being too high for some and too low for others. However, a proper classification system limits the variation about the average rate, thus reducing the range for adverse selection by the insured.

A further refinement toward this end uses merit rating techniques to reward insureds with below average losses and penalize those above the average. Experience rating plans, for example, include an adjustment in the premium determination called an experience modification factor. This factor reflects the insured's actual loss experience, usually over the last three years.

Rate Regulation and Statistical Requirements

From a legal aspect, certain distinctive features of the insurance business justify close public supervision. The insured must be guaranteed, to the fullest extent possible, that in the event of a loss covered by an insurance policy, funds will be available to indemnify the insured. Since the usual insurance policy is a long and detailed contract, it must be reviewed to see that its provisions conform to its generally intended purposes and the policyholder's understanding. By regulating the rates charged for insurance, the states also strive to maintain an orderly market for the insurance protection the public needs. The three essential legal requirements for insurance rates are that rates must be (1) adequate, (2) not excessive, and (3) not unfairly discriminatory.

The Merritt Committee Report of 1910 showed that uncontrolled competition could not assure a quality product at reasonable prices. Because of its concern over possible conflagrations and the resulting impact on insurance solvency, it recommended that statistical data be combined. By combining data, insurance companies would be able to develop adequate rates and thus provide needed insurance. Statistical bureaus were considered best able to perform this function because of the expense savings that result by eliminating duplication of effort.

A 1922 amendment to the New York Insurance Law required insurers to file premium and loss experience annually in conformance with approved classifications. Through the formation of statistical agencies, insurers were able to comply with this law.

In 1925, the United States Supreme Court affirmed that in certain areas, public policy favors the exchange of cost and pricing information in a competitive environment:

> The public interest is served by the gathering and dissemination, in the widest possible manner, of information with respect to the production and distribution, cost and prices in actual sales of market commodities, because the making available of such information tends to stabilize trade and industry, to produce fairer price levels and to avoid the waste which inevitably attends the unintelligent conduct of economic enterprise.[2]

Thus, a bureau, viewed as a trade association that collects and disseminates cost and price information for the insurance industry, was considered an efficient support function for its members in the pricing of their insurance services.

The Southeastern Underwriters case of 1944, however, held that rating bureaus were illegal because they violated antitrust laws. The Supreme Court found that the insurance industry was engaged in commerce and, as such, was governed by the federal laws regulating interstate commerce. The Supreme Court based its decision on the findings that rating bureaus were making rates for the insurance industry by unlawful combination. The insurance industry maintained that this was necessary in order for the law of large numbers to work properly. Small insurance companies especially did not have sufficiently large groupings of similar insureds to enable them to develop accurate rates unless they combined their data with the data from other insurance companies. As a result of the Court's decision, Congress enacted Public Law 15, also called the McCarran-Ferguson Act. This legislation exempted the insurance business from the anti-trust laws, to the extent that the states regulated the industry.

By 1948 every state had accepted the invitation of Congress to pass a rate regulatory law permitting joint action in establishing rates. These laws were patterned after the model law adopted in 1946 by the National Association of Insurance Commissioners.

The All-Industry Bill was designed to give the insurance business a type of regulation which would exempt it from certain parts of the antitrust and monopoly legislation. It also required all insurance companies to report statistical premium and loss experiences annually. This is in addition to the filing of the annual statement and independent of rate filings which would assist the states' insurance commissioners in the regulatory function.

The five sentences in the model bill drafted by the All-Industry Committee that govern recording and reporting of loss and expense experience are as follows:

(a) The commissioner shall promulgate reasonable rules and statistical plans, reasonably adapted to each of the rating systems on file with him which may be modified from time to time and which shall be used thereafter by each insurer in the recording and reporting of its loss, and countrywide expense experiences, in order that the experience of all insurers may be made available at least annually in such form and detail as may be necessary to aid him in determining whether rating systems comply with the standards set forth. . . .

(b) Such rules and plans may also provide for the recording and reporting of expense experience items which are specially applicable to this state and are not susceptible of determination by a prorating of countrywide expense experience.

(c) In promulgating such rules and plans, the commissioner shall give due consideration to the rating systems on file with him and, in order that such rules and plans may be as uniform as is practicable among the several states, to the rules and to the form of the plans used for such rating systems in other states.

(d) No insurer shall be required to record or report its loss experience on a classification basis that is inconsistent with the rating system filed by it.

(e) The commissioner may designate one or more rating organizations or other agencies to assist him in gathering such experience and making compilations thereof, and such compilations shall be made available, subject to reasonable rules promulgated by the commissioner, to insurers and rating organizations.[3]

Although all states have enacted legislation requiring the supervision and proper control of the ratemaking process in the insurance business, this legislation varies from state to state. Some states are more stringent in their requirements and reviews than others. Some states set the rates while other states rely on the competitive nature of the business to set the rates for particular types of insurance. In order to ensure control when required, all companies must file their rates with the state commissioner in each state in which they write business. All companies must file their statistics with the state's insurance departments either through a rating bureau, through an advisory organization, or directly. Some states will not accept direct filings, in which case, a company must belong to a rating bureau or an advisory organization. Furthermore, the commissioners must approve the method by which the statistics are compiled. These are called *statistical plans* and apply to both premiums and losses. These statistical plans must be adhered to if the company writes business in the state.

State Insurance Departments State insurance departments are responsible for administering insurance regulations. They supervise the organization, management, and examination of insurance companies and other companies doing business or having a corporate existence in that state and create rules known as "administrative laws." The official in charge is known as the commissioner, superintendent, or director. The commissioner generally is appointed by the state governor but in a few states is elected.

In regulating the solvency of insurance companies, the commissioner has the power to (1) license insurers that meet the state's financial requirements, (2) revoke licenses of insurers with impaired finances, (3) examine insurers periodically, (4) require adequate valuation of reserve liabilities, (5) require reasonable valuation of assets, (6) approve classes of investments, (7) require adequate rates, (8) require filing of annual statements, (9) regulate insurer expenditures, (10) act as a depository of securities in those states with depository laws, and (11) liquidate insolvent insurers. In regulating trade practices, the commissioner normally has the power to (1) approve policy contracts, (2) require that rates be neither unfairly discriminatory, inadequate, nor excessive, (3) investigate complaints of policyholders and others, and (4) serve as the agent accepting service of process from domicile insureds on unlicensed insurers operating a mail-order business in the state. In the area of marketing insurance, the commissioner can license agents, brokers, adjusters, and, in some cases, counselors.

The commissioner is a member of the National Association of Insurance Commissioners (NAIC), a voluntary organization that seeks and has achieved uniformity in insurance practices and laws. Through its various committee hearings and conferences with industry representatives and supervisory authorities, legislative subjects are reviewed and model bills are prepared, which the commissioners often present to their respective legislatures.

Virtually all states require insurers to make rate filings with the state regulatory authorities for at least some lines of insurance. The filings must include the rate schedules but also must include an explanation of the method by which the rates were determined and sufficient statistical data to show that the requested rate change is necessitated by loss experience, law changes, or other factors.

The calculation of actuarially credible class rates depends on accurate data regarding claims payments, earned premiums, and insured exposures for each class. The detailed class-by-class breakdown of exposures is necessary for the company's statistical report to the rating bureaus as well as for billing purposes. When the insurer or the rating bureau has accumulated statistics showing the premium volume, the loss experience, and the total insured exposures for each class, the actuaries can calculate appropriate rates. The rate filing is based on this information.

A *rate filing* is an application to the state commissioner requesting a change in rates or revision in the rules. In many cases, the request is substantiated by the statistical analysis of experience covering the last several years. In the case of private passenger automobile coverage, the most recent experience is usually given more weight since the rates are to be applied in the future. The rate change may become effective after a specified length of time after the application has been made. In some cases, rates are allowed to be effective immediately upon the filing or even before the filing of the rate changes. Regardless of the procedure allowed by the various states, the states can deny a rate filing or grant a lesser increase than requested. Once the rate filing has been approved, it becomes a part of public record.

When the rates are excessive, the insurance commissioner, after reviewing the loss statistics, may ask for a rate reduction. If the insurers are unable to justify the rate for that particular line of insurance and excessive profits are resulting, the reduction will be promulgated.

A rate filing may consist of only a few pages or may be many pages in length, depending largely on the financial and political importance of the line of insurance. A recent workers' compensation rate filing in one state was approximately 260 pages in length, including fifteen exhibits and appendixes.

An insurer may choose to prepare its own rate filings, and many insurers do so for at least some lines of insurance. However, many insurers prefer to share the cost of filings with other insurers through membership in or subscription to a rating bureau.

Rating Bureaus   A rating bureau is an organization of insurance companies formed to assist its member and subscriber companies in the gathering of statistics and the calculation and filing of rates. It may also perform other functions. Rating bureaus are owned by their member companies. Day-to-day management is usually conducted by bureau employees, but committees composed of employees of member companies usually establish policy and exercise general supervision over the bureau staff.

Companies that do not want to become members of the bureau, or do not qualify for membership, may obtain the bureau's services by becoming subscribers. In that capacity, they receive bureau services but do not exercise any management control over the bureau.

Rating bureaus are subject to regulation by the states in much the same manner as insurance companies. They are audited periodically by examiners from the state insurance departments to confirm that they are performing their functions in accordance with the appropriate laws and regulations.

In order to determine rates, a rating bureau must collect statistics on a uniform basis. Consequently, it must develop uniform statistical plans and communicate them to members and subscribers. Such statistical plans spell out in detail the nature of the statistics to be reported, the rating classifications into which they must be categorized, and so forth. At one time, it was customary for bureaus to accept statistics reported by members and subscribers without questioning their accuracy. However, it is now common for bureaus to edit statistical reports carefully in order to find and correct as many reporting errors as possible.

Rating organizations use statistics as the basis for the development of advisory rates and rate filing activities, which include preparing rate schedules for approved policy forms. They also standardize insurance policies and aid insurers in preparing merit rates for individual exposures. They have been designated by state insurance commissioners to assist in the gathering of such experience for the state. They also furnish, at prescribed intervals, statistical information which encompasses premium and loss data, either in summary or in detail form.

In general, they provide a wide range of advisory, actuarial rating, statistical, research, and other related types of services to the affiliated insurance companies and to the government regulatory agencies and state insurance departments for which they are licensed. They file rates, rating plans, rules and policy forms, and endorsements with the state insurance departments, when such filings are required by law, and to the extent authorized by the insurer. In those states where rates are advisory by law, rating organizations provide the advisory rate schedules to state regulatory authorities, and if requested, provide an insurer with any or all of the advisory pricing information, including supporting data to the insurers.

If rates are inadequate, insurers would be susceptible to insolvency. In determining the adequacy of a rate, rating organizations compare the assumed loss ratio (a percentage of the earned premiums needed to pay incurred losses, including loss-adjustment expenses) to the actual loss ratio compiled by statistical experience.

If an insurer elects not to join or subscribe to a rating bureau, it must then calculate and file its own rates. In doing so, it is required to furnish the regulatory authorities with sufficient data to demonstrate that its rates comply with the statutory requirements, just as a rating bureau does.

Some large insurers have sufficient data from their own experience to satisfy regulatory requirements. New or small insurers must use experience data from other insurers either combined with or instead of their own data. Data from other insurers may be obtained directly from insurers or from a rating bureau or an advisory organization licensed to perform data-gathering functions similar to those performed by rating bureaus. If the line of insurance is new, there may not be any insurance data available. Data gathered by other industries or by governmental agencies may be used in such cases.

The independent filer must bear the entire cost of the necessary technical personnel to calculate its rates, prepare filings, and maintain the necessary contacts with regulatory authorities. Bureau members and subscribers share such costs among themselves, reducing the expense to be borne by any one insurer.

In spite of the indicated disadvantages, independent filings have become increasingly important in recent years in some major lines of insurance, especially private passenger automobile insurance. However, they are not nearly as common in fire insurance partially because of the need for rating engineers to inspect commercial buildings for rating purposes. Also, the lower frequency of loss in fire and allied lines insurance requires a much larger body of data for sufficient credibility for ratemaking purposes. Few insurers could accumulate sufficient fire insurance data solely from their own experience.

Statistical Agents   Rating organizations and statistical agents perform different functions, although in many cases a ratemaking organization also acts as a statistical agent in the lines of business for which it makes rates. Statistical agents may or may not be affiliated with a rating organization or trade association.

Statistical agents are also independent bodies, and they perform two important functions. They develop and submit to each state insurance department statistical plans that meet their statistical requirements. These plans, for each line of insurance, are published and distributed to insurance companies for their use in recording and reporting of data. They outline in detail the technical rules and data elements required and are constantly reviewed in order to reflect the needs of changing environments in the market and statutory requirements.

Statistical agents collect statistical data on behalf of the member insurance companies and submit the results to the insurance department. This data supports rate filings and provides a basis for a general review of the experience. These statistics are compiled to assist the regulator in determining whether the existing rates in rating systems are compatible with the insurance statutes of a particular state. While the data within the submission is not directly suitable for ratemaking purposes, it provides significant insights for the evaluation of the insurance situations within various territories and classifications during a selected time period.

It is often necessary to change statistial plans due to changing environments and requirements. Frequently, there are territory or classification changes that result in corresponding statistical changes. An example of a major change was the new data requirements needed in the 1970s to accommodate the pricing of no-fault laws.

In addition to publishing statistical plans, statistical agents issue *calls for experience.* These calls to insurers specify the technical requirements for the submission of data, including the required content, time schedules, error detection and correction procedures, and the requirements for the cover form. The cover form or transmittal letter serves as a control on insurer data submissions. Upon receipt of the data, statistical agents perform extensive and comprehensive checks on the accuracy and completeness of the data. All invalid data is returned to the insurer for correction and resubmission.

A statistical agent who collects and disseminates cost and price information for the insurance industry performs an efficient support function for its members in the pricing of their insurance business. This is confirmed in a study of governmental regulation of the insurance industry which noted the special importance of gathering past experience and the necessity of pooling and projecting loss experience. Since consolidated data is often needed across state boundaries on a regional or national basis, national organizations were considered to be best able to perform this function.

Through the formation of statistical agents, insurers are able to comply with the directions of the statutory regulators in relation to scheduled filings of statistics. These agents eliminate the potentially burdensome activities of both the companies and the various state insurance departments. Annually, the statistical agents send to the states data for each line of business, for all of the companies combined. The states receive a uniform final product, instead of the hundreds of reports in varying formats and are thus relieved from performing highly technical, time consuming and costly statistical functions. The statistical agents develop the technical reporting instructions and the complex verification and compilation tasks, saving the states from this detailed task.

Data Administrators Most companies employ a group of statisticians or data administrators who oversee, receive computer output, and periodically report the corporate statistics to rating bureaus. It is their responsibility to interpret bulletins and calls from the regulators and to provide specifications for programs and coding technicians.

Additionally, as well as responding to regulatory requests and schedules, the data administrators must maintain an inventory of these corporate assets with respect to:

1. where the data is stored,
2. what systems process the data, and
3. how the raw data (from applications or claim reports) is transferred by these systems.

With this knowledge, it becomes much easier to respond to most requests for data. It is critical that this data is not accidentally or fraudulently changed or misused. Therefore, the data administrators must also exercise control over the data and allow access to only authorized persons.

In order to ensure the integrity of this data, the following specific, fundamental approaches should be taken.

Establish an Error Identification System. In order to establish an effective error identification system, two things must be accomplished. First, the system must pinpoint the type of errors commonly occurring. They could be the result of the lack of knowledge on the part of the individual who is manually coding the policy information or incorrect specifications in the compiler programs that develop the coded values.

Secondly, an immediate feedback system for errors should be developed for the codes or data processing systems. A one-day turnaround document should be produced for manual risks in a batch environment or if there is a rejection in an online environment. Coding generated by computer processing of transactions that do not meet editing criteria could be recycled and returned through an interfacing system step with the system generating the error.

Establish a Controlling or Monitoring Function. The processing of business in the insurance industry is subject to almost constant change. Rules and regulations are passed and statistical plans or data requirements are in a constant state of flux. These changes must be monitored by responsible individuals and prompt instructions given to those liable for producing data.

Establish a Quality Control Audit Program. A periodic self-review of statistical data should be made to determine an accurate error percentage on a line of business and also to point out areas where errors are repeatedly occurring but have not been detected.

Quality control assists management in making crucial business decisions as well as complying with the data requirements of regulatory bodies. If statistics are not accurate, the ratemaking process could seriously be jeopardized, affecting premium dollars and company assets. Delays and subsequent fines assessed by regulators could result, and error correction procedures for data reported to bureaus could become costly.

MAJOR STATISTICAL ORGANIZATIONS

Statistical organizations provide the insurance industry with many necessary services. They help reduce redundancies and costs associated with statistical information compilation as well as with mandated state and local reporting and filings. Most of these organizations are nonprofit, established by the insurance industry in an attempt to serve their needs and reduce costs. Membership is voluntary, but generally an insurer benefits by enrolling in as many statistical organizations as necessary to service all the lines of insurance it writes. While many of these organizations service multiple lines, some specialize in a particular line of insurance such as workers' compensation or surety bonding.

These statistical organizations also aid the industry in rate setting by compiling industry-wide statistics for individual lines of insurance. This helps with state regulatory agencies by providing a clearer picture of the industry's exposure to potential loss as well as the costs of operations, thus justifying more equitable and competitive rates and educating the legislatures, news media, and general public. A majority of these statistical organizations also act as advisors to the insurers, keeping the industry abreast of changes in legal requirements, pending laws, public opinion, and general trends pertinent to the insurance industry.

Rating Bureaus for Workers' Compensation Insurance

Most states require insurers to belong to the approved rating organization in order to write workers' compensation and employers' liability insurance in that state. These bureaus are the statistical gathering organizations for workers' compensation in all states where private insurers are authorized to underwrite this coverage. The bureau files with supervisory authorities the manual for classifications, rules, rates, rating plans, and policy forms on behalf of its members. Although in many states rating laws encouraging open competition have eliminated the uniform application of rates, rating bureaus continue to serve an important role in the administration of workers' compensation insurance.

The bureaus employ actuaries and statisticians who compile experience, promulgate rates, and develop experience and retrospective rating plans. The underwriting committee of the bureau establishes classifications and determines the rules and procedures for the administration of the rating system.

National Council on Compensation Insurance The National Council on Compensation Insurance is the preeminent influence in the administration of workers' compensation insurance. It is an unincorporated association of companies writing workers' compensation insurance. In thirty-two states and the District of Columbia, the National Council is the licensed rating bureau operating under the laws of the state. Other states have independent bureaus which rely on actuarial and statistical services provided by the National Council or which closely follow the methods of the National Council. Even in the states with monopolistic state funds for workers' compensation insurance, the National Council may provide advisory services.

By means of the Unit Statistical Plan the member companies provide the National Council with payroll, premium, and loss information for each insured. By studying the statistical trends developing in each jurisdiction for which it is the licensed ratemaking organization, the National Council determines when rate revisions are necessary. Some revisions result from amendments to the state workers' compensation law changing the benefits provided injured employees. Other revisions are needed occasionally to keep pace with inflation. Still others may be prompted by technological or social developments significantly altering the loss experience for a particular rating classification. In any case, the rate revisions are to provide insurers sufficient premium income to pay all workers' compensation claims and expenses. When revisions are necessary in a particular state, the National Council or appropriate rating organization often files the necessary data with the insurance department. In other states the bureau filing may be a model from which individual insurers are permitted, or even required, to deviate. It is also possible for the National Council to provide pure premium data only, to which insurers may add expense data in their individual rate filings.

The National Council underwriting department continually reviews classification problems. With the benefit of its extensive research information, the underwriting department can resolve difficult classification problems regarding individual insureds. As changes occur within an industry, this department is also able to study the situation and recommend the proper classification procedure. If necessary, it can establish a new classification for a unique new industry group, which, if approved by the underwriting committee, can then be filed for approval by the state insurance department.

The National Council also monitors social, economic, and regulatory trends to analyze the potential impact on the workers' compensation system. Its activities in these areas enable the National Council to undertake research and to offer advice to other organizations where warranted.

Independent Bureaus Several states have independent rating bureaus for workers' compensation insurance. Some of these use the services of the National Council. Others make their own rates and issue their own rules and manuals. In Texas, the State Board of Insurance promulgates rates on the basis of statistics gathered by the National Council. In all of these cases, however, the procedures generally resemble those of the National Council. While premium auditors, of course, must be thoroughly familiar with the various state exceptions, the essential principles of premium determination and classification apply in independent bureau states just as they do in National Council states.

The independent bureaus consist of those insurance companies which write workers' compensation insurance in the state. They are controlled by a governing committee of representatives elected by the member companies. Most bureaus, in addition to the governing committee, have a classification and rates committee and an actuarial and statistical committee. The actuarial committee reviews the statistical information compiled by the bureau staff and makes rate recommendations to the classification and rates committee for rate filings. After its review and consideration, the rates committee instructs the bureau staff to make appropriate rate filings with the state regulatory body responsible for approving workers' compensation insurance rates.

The Unit Statistical Plan The unit statistical plan is used in reporting workers' compensation experience. Every state rating organi-

Exhibit 7-1
First Report*

REPORT	POLICY NUMBER			STATE	STATE NO.	CARRIER	CARRIER NO.	CARD SERIAL NO.	ADM. FILE NO.
1	WC 54321			Any	55	X.Y.Z. Insurance Co.	49999		(Leave Blank)

EFFECTIVE DATE	TERM	EXPIRATION DATE	INSURED		
04/01/82		03/31/83	P.A.Z. Industries Corp. (Address Optional)		
			OTHER		

COND.	91	92	93	94	95	96	97	98

EXP. COV.	CLASS CODE	EXPOSURE	MANUAL RATE	PREMIUM	CLAIM NUMBER	ACCIDENT DATE OR NO. OF CLAIMS	CLASS CODE	INJ	INCURRED LOSSES INDEMNITY	INCURRED LOSSES MEDICAL		LOSS COV	CAT NO.
11	2003	1,214,435	7.11	86,346	46096	07/26/82	2003	9	3,465	1,035	1	18	
11	2014	10,400	11.54	1,200	46114	08/05/82	2003	5	1,323	137	1	11	
					46122	07/12/82	2014	2	140,053	13,000	0	11	
					7		2003	6	–	200	1	11	
					1		2003	6	–	20	1	12	

		PREMIUM
A — TOTAL SUBJECT PREMIUM		87,546
B — EXPERIENCE MODIFICATION		1.62
C — TOTAL MODIFIED PREMIUM (A) X (B)		141,825
D		
E		
F		
G		

TOTALS													
STD	1,224,835	x x x	141,825										
OTHER		x x x	x x x										
006	PREMIUM DISCOUNT	x x x	(21,158)										
0900	EXPENSE CONSTANT		60	TOTALS	11	x x x x	x		144,841	14,392	x	x x	x

DO NOT USE	PREM SIZE	INDUSTRY GROUP	TYPE	INDUSTRY SCHED

KEYPUNCH #

FORM 21 — 80

VERIFIER #

*Includes material of the National Council on Compensation Insurance, copyright 1983, 1984. Used with permission.

zation, whether independent or part of the National Council on Compensation Insurance, requires the use of the unit statistical plan.

The unit statistical plan provides for the reporting of payroll, manual premium, and incurred loss data by classification code by state for each insured. Incurred losses as used in ratemaking include amounts paid plus the amounts at which losses are reserved. Losses are valued as of eighteen months after the effective date of the policy and are due to be reported to the rating organization twenty months from the effective date of the policy. If any of the losses reported at that time is open or if a closed case has been reopened and settled for an amount different from that shown in the evaluation eighteen months after the effective date of the policy, a subsequent report must be made to the respective rating bureau. This procedure is continued for five annual sequences, if required. The data contained in these individual statistical reports are sent on a monthly basis to the respective rating bureau. Exhibit 7-1 is an example of one of these reports.

Losses are identified by type of injury. The major categories are death, medical only, permanent total, permanent partial, and temporary total disability. Permanent partial disability cases are further divided into major or minor cases. In each instance involving the previous types of injuries, medical costs are shown separately from the disability (indemnity) benefit.

Even on minimum premium policies, the payrolls reported must be audited payrolls. Whenever there is a change in experience modification, the payrolls must be separated as of the effective date of the change. The report must also show the premium for each classification. The premium is obtained by multiplying the amount shown in the exposure column by the manual rate. This information on payrolls and premiums by classification codes comes from premium audit reports.

The Unit Statistical Plan has been in effect since 1940. A change during the 1960s expanded the loss updating from three reports to five reports. This change increased the development from 30 months after expiration to 54 months after expiration.

However, some actuaries still suspected that there were additional losses not included in the experience used in calculating the rate changes. These omissions resulted from a combination of late development of known claims, the difference between case reserves shown on unit reports and financial reserves used in the annual statement, and incurred but not reported claims.

Aggregate Financial Calls Thus two calls were designed to collect data regarding these additional loss amounts. These are named the aggregate financial calls because they are produced from accounting type data and the timing coincides with the financial reporting. The first of these calls is the Annual Call for Compensation Experience by State. This call is completed as of the end of each year and is to be submitted by March 15 of the following year. It is a summary report by state which provides earned premiums on a standard and net basis, as well as incurred losses for the calendar year being reported. This standard earned premium is the entire earned premium for the state resulting from standard rating procedures, prior to the application of premium discounts, prior to the expense modification program where applicable, and excluding any retrospective rating plan.

To provide additional detail, insurers also complete the Supplementary Call for Compensation Experience by Policy Year. This call is completed as of the end of each year and is to be completed by March 15 of the following year. This report was completed for the first time for calendar 1966 as of December 31, 1966. This report gives a more detailed breakdown of the amounts shown on the Annual Call. The Policy Year Call has a separate form for each state. This form is designed to provide a means to display the experience for all prior experience distributed by policy year. The form requires the premium to be filed on both a standard and net basis. The incurred losses are separated between indemnity, medical, and total. These losses are separated between paid, outstanding, and IBNR.

A subsequent modification of these two reports excluded experience for the 27 "F" classifications from the Annual Call and the Supplementary Call for policies effective January 1, 1974 and thereafter. "F" classifications apply to operations inherently subject to exposure under the United States Longshore and Harbor Workers' Compensation Act. The experience for these classifications, which might distort the indicated rate changes for the non "F" classifications, is reported on the Annual Call for *"F" Classifications* Compensation Experience by State and the Supplementary Call for *"F" Classifications* Compensation Experience by Policy Year. The layout and content of these two calls is the same as the two calls for non "F" classification experience.

An additional report provides financial data split by accident year. In its present form, the annual call for compensation calendar-accident year experience by state is very similar to the policy year call in the way it assigns the calendar year results to the appropriate accident year. The accident year call was completed for the first time as of December 31, 1976. The accident year call for the current year-end should, in total, be greater than the total from the prior year-end by an amount reconcilable to the current calendar year experience. In the future, the accident year call should have the same check-out to the Annual Statement as the supplementary call.

A form submitted to the National Council by April 15 of each year helps with this reconciliation process. The first part provides a place to indicate the net premiums and incurred losses reported. The second part provides for those items that are not considered a part of the experience to be reported. This exposure is not a part of the regular workers compensation writings of a company. If these two categories do not equal columns two and three of Part IV of the Insurance Expense Exhibit, the form requires an explanation. This step addresses the concern of the National Council and the regulators that all reportable experience be used in the ratemaking process.

Insurance Services Office

The Insurance Services Office (ISO) is a national organization established by the property and liability insurance industry to provide a full range of insurance services, with maximum flexibility and economy to affiliated insurers.

ISO was formed January 1, 1971, through the consolidation of several national insurance industry service organizations: the Fire Insurance Research and Actuarial Association, the Inland Marine

Insurance Bureau, the Insurance Rating Board, the Multi-Line Insurance Rating Bureau, and the National Insurance Actuarial and Statistical Association. Also included in that consolidation was the Insurance Data Processing Center, a joint computer facility of two of the predecessor organizations. By January 1, 1972, most of the former state and regional fire rating organizations in the United States had also become a part of ISO.

ISO is licensed in all fifty states and has assumed the functions of its predecessor organizations in those states. It is licensed as a fire rating organization in most of the jurisdictions, and it operates as an advisory organization to state fire organizations in the others. ISO also acts as an advisory organization for other property and liability lines of insurance in those states with statutory rating bureaus.

Services are provided for thirteen lines of insurance:

1. boiler and machinery
2. commercial automobile
3. commercial fire and allied lines
4. commercial multiple line
5. crime
6. dwelling fire & allied lines
7. general liability
8. glass
9. homeowners
10. inland marine
11. nuclear energy liability & property
12. private passenger automobile
13. workers' compensation and employers' liability

ISO renders a wide range of advisory, actuarial, rating, statistical, research, and other services. ISO also develops manuals to provide for the implementation of various programs it offers. The specific functions of ISO are to:

1. collect insurance statistics on a single-line or a multiple-line basis;
2. classify and process the data to produce usable information;
3. do actuarial research;
4. make advisory rates for affiliates;
5. provide statistical and actuarial data for companies to make their own rates;
6. develop standard forms of policies and coverages;
7. act as an agency for filing forms, rules, and rates with state insurance departments;

8. act as a statistical agent for the submission of experience data to regulatory authorities as required by law;
9. publish and distribute manuals of rules, rates, and standard forms for all the lines of insurance it handles;
10. act in an advisory capacity to independent state rating bureaus where they exist;
11. create and apply, through inspection of insureds, property rating schedules that reflect safety features and hazards of occupancy and use; and
12. calculate and review policy pricing.

Equipped with a professional staff as well as a sizable computer installation, ISO performs many of the vital support functions that the insurance industry requires.

Insurance companies may affiliate with ISO in varying degrees. They may use the organization's services as members, as subscribers, or as service purchasers.

Any insurer—stock, mutual, or reciprocal—can become a member or subscriber for any one or more of the thirteen lines of insurance handled by ISO, or for any subdivision of those lines. Affiliation, whether as a member or a subscriber, may apply in one or more states and territories in accordance with the needs and expressed desires of each insurer. Affiliated insurers under the same ownership, control, or management are eligible for membership whether or not all the companies of a given insurance group are members. Also, individual companies in an insurance group may become subscribers whether or not other insurers in the same group are associated with ISO. Any insurer, or any other persons or organization, may become a service purchaser for one or more of ISO's specific services.

An insurer affiliated with ISO as a member or a subscriber has available to it the extensive statistical and actuarial data underlying the development of rates, policies, coverages, and programs meeting the requirements of the various state regulatory laws. It also has access to other technical information prepared by ISO.

ISO also acts as a local service outlet for its members, thus providing all the necessary field services, which include policy review, inspections and specific rating, engineering reports, town grading, fire protection engineering consultations, and sprinkler system and other fire protection evaluations.

ISO provides its membership and the various state regulators with manual rules, territorial, and other classifications for those companies which give authorization. Keeping companies abreast of the latest trends and pending legislation is another of ISO's important contributions to the insurance industry. It accomplishes this through the publication of a "circular letter," which is ISO's primary means of communications with its subscribers. This letter might relate pertinent information on rate filings, rule changes, procedure changes, or almost any conceivable development deemed important to the industry.

National Association of Independent Insurers

The National Association of Independent Insurers (NAII) is a voluntary nonprofit trade association and the largest insurance trade organization in the world.

The NAII's stated objectives, as listed in its by-laws, are as follows:

1. to preserve reasonable competition within the insurance industry,
2. to support legislation which is consistent with these objectives and purposes,
3. to work with legislators to ensure these objectives and purposes,
4. to research matters of common interest to its membership,
5. to provide its members with a forum for discussion, study, and solution to common problems,
6. to collect and compile statistical information, and
7. to protect the interests of the insurance companies in every proper way.

The member companies of NAII, approximately 460, are provided with a vital source of information which is generally unavailable to them. The association also works with the various local, state, and federal legislative bodies, and insurance regulatory agencies to foster a better understanding of its members' positions on related issues and laws. Legislators, regulators, and news media usually listen to the opinions of the NAII because of its extensive membership, which compromises companies of various types and sizes.

The major services provided are in the fields of legal-legislative ratemaking, advisory and technical services, regulatory liaison, annual meetings and workshops, public affairs, research, property insurance, casualty insurance, workers' compensation, personnel, traffic safety, and surplus lines.

While the organization does not develop or file rates, it is an approved advisor and supplies its membership with data for ratemaking decisions. It also counsels its member companies regarding rates, emerging trends, and regulatory proposals. The NAII works on the principle of one vote per member company for matters requiring a vote. Its ruling body is elected by its membership.

American Association of Insurance Services

The American Association of Insurance Services (AAIS) is an unincorporated association of insurance companies. It is a countrywide licensed rating organization and an official statistical agency. It offers services for the following lines of insurance:

- personal
- dwelling
- farm property
- farmowners
- homeowners
- inland marine
- mobile homes
- personal farm
- personal liability
- commercial
- property
- general liability
- glass
- inland marine
- manufacturer's output
- commercial packages
- burglary

The AAIS receives loss and premium statistics from its member companies and files the aggregate statistics with the various state regulatory agencies. This enables the association to develop and maintain equitable rates for the lines of insurance services. The rate-making procedures are complex and encompass many descriptions. These include:

1. classification homogeneity,
2. the effect of deviation on premiums,
3. credibility,
4. the effect of rate level adjustments,
5. the incidence of unusual catastrophies,
6. the impact of inflation,
7. investment income, and
8. trends.

Neither membership nor filing authorizations are mandated by law, but it is beneficial for insurers to join the association because when the AAIS files for rate revisions it does so on behalf of all its affiliates; thus realizing substantial savings for the member companies by reducing redundancies. Also, AAIS strives to attain rates which are competitive and equitable. Affiliation also enables an insurer to satisfy most of the statutory reporting requirements.

The association also offers assistance in interpretation of new or pending state and local insurance regulations. It publishes insurance bulletins and manuals periodically. These are designed to aid in explaining rule revisions as well as evaluating pending legislation.

National Independent Statistical Service

The National Independent Statistical Service (NISS), incorporated in Illinois as a nonprofit organization, provides independent insurers with advisory and statistical services. It compiles countrywide statistics for the preparation of statutory reports to state regulatory insurance departments. It maintains its independence from all trade associations and legislative, or lobbying groups to provide its members and subscribers with equal and fair representation. NISS also provides simplified statistical plans, equal representation for its membership, open membership, and management assistance, which includes specialized insurance, data processing, auditing and office services.

Its Articles of Incorporation state the reasons NISS was established as follows: "...to assist in promoting the public welfare by aiding in the making of insurance rates by insurers which shall not be excessive, inadequate or unfairly discriminatory, without restricting reasonable competition."[4]

NISS's basic statistical plans are for the following lines:

1. automobile
2. automobile assigned risk
3. general liability
4. burglary
5. glass, and
6. inland marine.

NISS also employs a modified version of the ISO statistical plans for homeowners, dwelling, and commercial fire insurance. As a statistical agent, NISS cooperates fully with the insurance authorities at every level and with other advisory organizations in the gathering and supplying of statistical information.

Automobile Insurance Plan Service Office

The Automobile Insurance Plan Service Office (AIPSO) is an insurance service organization for the shared automobile insurance market. This market serves those insurance consumers who do not find a company which believes it can include them in its book of business at its rate level. In more than forty states, automobile insurance plans distribute the business of these consumers among insurance companies in proportion to the amount of insurance each insurer writes in the state. In still other states, the results of experience of a pool of consumers are allocated through joint underwriting associations, reinsurance facilities, or state funds. The shared market represents a significant segment of the insurance business since about 6 million motorists obtain their automobile insurance coverage in this way.

The major purpose of AIPSO is to serve the entire shared market in streamlining these operations and in developing appropriate rate levels.

AIPSO is an incorporated nonprofit service association of over 900 companies writing automobile insurance in the country. Almost all companies subscribe to AIPSO in at least one state.

AIPSO's governing board, the National Industry Committee, was established in 1947 under the auspices of the National Association of Insurance Commissioners and was initially known as the National Advisory Committee on Automobile Insurance Plans. Today, it consists of twelve member company officials who represent the three national trade associations as well as companies not affiliated with any trade association.

AIPSO is a licensed rating organization in forty-three states and the District of Columbia. In these jurisdictions, all subscribers to the plan are also direct subscribers to AIPSO and must use the rates and rating rules filed on their behalf by AIPSO. Each company, or each statistical agent designated by the company, must furnish AIPSO with all of the statistical data required to perform this function. In three additional states, AIPSO prepares rate filings as a service to a licensed rate filing organization.

AIPSO also collects, processes, and distributes other information needed by the shared market mechanisms. In addition to data related to management and ratemaking, these needs include quota sharing, assessment, and processing. Equitable sharing of applications or operating results among companies requires determination and adjustment of ratios for each organization by subline, year, and company. The Uniform Automobile Insurance Plan provides that all the data necessary to comply with the distribution procedures shall be reported to AIPSO, either directly, or through a statistical agent designated by the company.

Since insurers share the expenses of operating shared market organizations, AIPSO determines each company's share of budgeted expenses, bills each company on behalf of all shared market organizations using AIPSO's assessment service, and collects and disburses fund. In addition, AIPSO provides data processing services for the compilation of ratemaking exhibits, as a central processor of alternative mechanisms, and for conducting research studies.

STATISTICAL REPORTING REQUIREMENTS

Statistical plans serve to obtain the data necessary to calculate rates. A statistical plan is a manual containing reporting instructions or rules, record formats, codes, and interpretations with examples. Statistical calls specify when the data is due, how it should be labeled and transmitted, and how corrections should be processed. All statistical plans deal with premiums and losses, but differ in nature, method, and period of statistical breakdown. Experience statistics are compiled according to a detailed breakdown of premiums and losses by the rate classifications on which the premiums are based. Most detailed experience is compiled by classification and territory within the state and type of insurance business. These are further subdivided by the creation of rate groups. Depending on the line of business, statistical experience may be analyzed by calendar year, policy year, or accident year. Although there are many variations, there are also many similarities in the statistical reporting requirements of rating bureaus and statistical agencies. In this discussion, ISO requirements serve to illustrate what is expected from insurers.

Scope

Statistical plans used by rating bureaus and advisory associations vary in nature, method, and period of statistical breakdown. All of them, however, collect detailed information concerning premiums and losses.

Generally, in fire and allied lines and all other property insurance in which the settlement of claims is made quickly and the payment is made directly to the insured, the statistical analysis is on a calendar-year basis. The calendar-year basis is an analysis of premiums and losses paid or incurred within a year, without following them through subsequent periods if they extend beyond the period of one year.

Casualty lines, which involve bodily injury or property damage to persons other than the insured, such as automobile, general liability, and workers' compensation insurance, use policy-year or accident-year statistics. Policy-year statistics are those in which all premiums and losses refer to the date of inception of the policy. It does not matter when the premiums were earned or when the losses were incurred or actually paid. On the accident-year basis, losses are related to the premiums earned in the calendar-year during which the loss-incurring accident took place, the date when the losses were paid, or liquidated in any other way.

Insurance companies compile all experience statistics according to a detailed breakdown of the premiums and losses by the rate classifications on which premiums are based. These breakdowns go far beyond those for the various coverages that are contained in the annual statements of the company. For the purpose of eventual rate adjustments and for research purposes, rating bureaus may need further breakdowns. These breakdowns chiefly show the territorial distribution of premiums and losses to provide data for adjustments based on geographical changes in hazards.

When analyzed by sound actuarial techniques, the statistical data must indicate that rates are not inadequate, excessive, or unfairly discriminatory. In some states the insurance commissioners have prescribed special forms for rate filings and their statistical justification; others make no such provision. The data required usually follows the statistical exhibits developed by the various rating bureaus.

Frequency and Timeliness

Companies must prepare and file statistical data with the bureaus, advisory organizations, or insurance departments on specified dates, usually three to six months after the filing of annual statements. The figures on the annual statement are the control figures for all such filings. Bureaus require various reconciliations to demonstrate the completeness of these statistics. Generally, an office audit of these statistics is made before accepting and merging the statistics of any company into the composite reports. While companies only make voluntary rate filings when they desire changes in the rates or rules, all companies are required to make periodic statistical filings. Statistical filings may be made with rating bureaus or advisory organizations if the companies are members or subscribers to such organization. They are made directly with the insurance departments by those companies that do not belong or do not subscribe to any such organizations. These experience filings are made on forms prescribed by the organization or various insurance departments. They can be made either by filling out these forms or by submitting appropriate data processing media from which the data can be developed. Some insurance departments and organizations require the filing of such media for specific statistical data and will accept no forms with respect to such data. After they are accepted, all rate filings become a matter of public record. This is true of all other filings by insurance companies. This means that anyone desiring to see a copy can go to the insurance departments and obtain one for review. Individual statistical agents do not become a matter of public domain. They are private documents, available only with the express consent of the companies involved. After they have been filed with the various insurance departments, only the composite compilations prepared by the bureaus and statistical agents become a matter of public record.

Data Required

Until 1966, the statistical plan used by statistical agents was relatively simple in its detail. The data submitted by rate filers in support of rate revisions was fundamentally identical to the statistical information, for instance the fire line of business, collected under the statistical plan. The statistical agent, in effect, gave the state and rate filer all the information available under the statistical plan. However, in 1966 this identity ceased to exist under the National Insurance Actuarial and Statistical Association Personal Lines Statistical Plan. The primary objective for supplying data to the state regulatory authorities would remain the same but now additional information has to be collected beyond that needed for preparing the regular statistical compilation.

Supervisory officials are presented with a problem when the commissioner requests additional data, if the statistical agent is different from the rate filer, because the rate filer utilizes the data of the statistical agent in establishing rates. Should the additional data not be available through the statistical plan, the rate filer could have difficulty meeting the commissioner's needs. The commissioner is also inhibited from directing the statistical agent because this may involve asking 100 companies to modify their information-gathering systems to meet the needs of a rate filing of a single company. While this situation presents something of a dilemma, it must be recognized that there are at least three information levels in question. The first is the amount of information necessary in order for the regulatory officials to be able to test the general rate level in a state. This information must be provided by all agencies equally.

The second level of data collected by the statistical agent may in some cases exceed the information provided to the regulatory officials. This additional information is equivalent to the output of a research organization and reflects the costs that the companies are willing to incur in the way of research. This level gives us the required complexity of information the companies must submit to the statistical agency; it usually appears in the form of a statistical plan which the agency employs.

The third level of information gathering is conducted by the companies themselves. In many cases, the companies go beyond the requirements of the statistical agency and introduce research or experimental coding for their own purposes.

The extensive use of computers and the thousands of programs utilized to capture and make statistical data available has made the job of supplying information to statistical agencies and to state regulators a little less hectic. In today's environment, the insurance companies, regardless of size, have the capability of retaining data on each policy, including the smallest detail. They can utilize retrieval methods and scan years of data history in order to provide information of an analysis nature for company management to experience data for rate filings. They can be members of various rating organizations and statistical agents and still submit individual data requirements. These data requirements may range from a mini statistical plan requiring limited data on a line of business to a maxi statistical plan requiring extensive statistics.

As an example of the data that must be furnished by an insurer, Exhibit 7-2 shows Part I of ISO's 1984 Auto Full Plan Calls for Liability and Physical Damage.

Reporting Media and Methods

Statistical reports can be transmitted in various ways. The statistical agent receiving the data specifies the acceptable forms. Usually the data is required on magnetic tape, diskette, punch cards or listings. There are exceptions to this, however, such as for workers' compensation. There is a Workers' Compensation call when the National Council on Compensation Insurance (NCCI) accepts copies of the policy's daily report. The information is then extracted from the daily report and assembled for the insurer onto one of the previously mentioned mediums. There may be an additional fee charged to the insurance company for reporting data in this way. It is important to have uniformity in reporting data. A bureau or state agency receives thousands of submissions and must be able to process the data quickly and accurately. This is not possible without rules.

Periodically notices are released by the bureaus and agencies which specify all of the details necessary to meet their reporting forms. For instance, Insurance Services Office usually sends its reporting requirements annually to the insurance companies using its services. This circular includes separate sections describing the detailed requirements for magnetic tape, diskette, and punched card. The requirements must be adhered to under normal circumstances. Prior approval has to be given by ISO for any company to deviate from their rules.

The actual instructions from the ISO circular for 1984 for personal

Exhibit 7-2
1984 Auto Full Plan Calls for Liability and Physical Damage

Part I

(A) INSTRUCTIONS FOR THE REPORTING OF CALENDAR YEAR 1984 EXPOSURE AND PREMIUM TRANSACTIONS IN MONTHLY OR QUARTERLY SHIPMENTS.

1. Exposures and premiums shall be reported monthly or quarterly in the form of unit transaction reports and such unit reports shall show full coding detail. Companies which elect the quarterly reporting option shall enter the last account month of the quarter on all unit transactions for the quarter.

2. Reporting instructions for exposures and premiums are contained in the Private Passenger Non-Fleet Automobile Statistical Plan.

3. Transmittal letter forms ISO 1044 contains instructions for the preparation of summary totals and for the forwarding of the transmittal letter to ISO. Transmittal letters and separate summary state totals must be furnished for each "Line of Business" code. For each line of business, the transmittal letters shall show *separate exposure* totals for *Bodily Injury, Property Damage, and Personal Injury Protection.* See "General Instructions" for additional information on completion of the Transmittal letters.

4. The exposure and premium records shall be received by the statistical agent at its receiving location *within 45 days* after the close of the accounting month or accounting quarter.

5. Punch cards submitted to ISO *must be punched in perfect alignment.*

6. Prior to submission of statistics to ISO the carrier SHALL make an audit of the statistics being reported to detect and correct any errors in the *recording of the exposures* and in the assignment of classification and territory.

7. ISO's Premium records contain one (1) exposure field and two (2) Premium amount fields. If only one (1) Premium amount field is being used, then the other amount field must be blank or zero filled. In either case, the units position of the blank or zero filled field should be unsigned. A sign in this position could

generate an exposure for a non-existing premium, and will subsequently cause an out of balance and invalid record condition.

8. The procedure for handling inquiries received from ISO is given in the "General Instructions" of this Call.

(B) INSTRUCTIONS FOR THE REPORTING OF CALENDAR YEAR 1984 PAID LOSSES AND ALLOCATED LOSS ADJUSTMENT EXPENSES TRANSACTIONS IN MONTHLY OR QUARTERLY SHIPMENTS.

1. Reporting instructions paid losses and allocated loss adjustment expenses are contained in the Private Passenger Non-Fleet Automobile Statistical Plan.

2. Transmittal letter form ISO 1033 contains instructions for the preparation of summary totals and for the forwarding of the transmittal letter to ISO. Transmittal letters and separate summary state totals must be furnished for each "Line of Business" code. See "General Instructions" for additional information on completion of the transmittal letter.

3. The loss records shall be received by the statistical agent at its receiving location *within 45 days* after the close of the accounting month or accounting quarter.

4. Prior to submission of experience to ISO, the carrier *SHALL* make an audit of the statistics being reported to detect and correct any errors in the assignment to classification and territory.

5. Punch cards submitted to ISO *must be punched in perfect alignment.*

6. The procedure for handling inquiries received from ISO is given in the "General Instructions" of this Call.

(C) INSTRUCTIONS FOR THE REPORTING OF LOSSES AND ALLOCATED LOSS ADJUSTMENT EXPENSES OUTSTANDING:

a. March 31, 1984
b. June 30, 1984,
c. September 30, 1984,
d. December 31, 1984
on *ALL* Accident Years for Private Passenger Non-Fleets, Special Automobile Policy and No-Fault

Losses. Substandard (LOB 03, and 71) may optionally be reported as of 6/30, 9/30 and 12/31. Required for the 3/31 report.

1. Reporting instructions for outstanding losses and allocated loss adjustment expenses are contained in the Private Passenger Non-Fleet Automobile Statistical Plan.

2. The records for the losses and allocated loss adjustment expenses outstanding as of March 31, 1984, as of June 30, 1984, as of September 30, 1984 and as of December 31,1984 shall be identified in positions 6 and 7 respectively by the values "34," "64", "94" and "(ampersand) & 4" (card code 12, Hex Code 50) for the month of December.

3. Transmittal letter form ISO 1033 contains instructions for the preparation of summary totals and for the forwarding of the transmittal letter to ISO. Transmittal letters and separate summary state totals must be furnished for each "Line of Business" code. See "General Instructions" for additional information on completion of the transmittal letter.

4. Prior to submission of statistics to ISO, the carriers *SHALL* make an audit of the statistics being reported to detect and correct any errors in the assignment to classification and territory.

5. Punch cards submitted to ISO *must be punched in perfect alignment.*

6. The procedure for handling inquiries received from ISO is given in the "General Instructions" of this Call.

7. The losses and allocated loss adjustment expenses outstanding shall be received by the statistical agent at its receiving location *on or before* the following dates:

Outstanding as of	*Due*
March 31, 1984	May 15, 1984
June 30, 1984	August 15, 1984
September 30, 1984	November 15, 1984
December 31, 1984	February 15, 1984

PART II — INSTRUCTIONS FOR THE REPORTING OF EXCESS
   LOSSES

Those companies not meeting the requirements for
calculation of their excess losses by ISO must continue
to file excess loss reports in accordance with the
following instructions.

SECTION 1. Excess Losses on *Accidents*:

a.   Closed ("F") during the period of October 1,
1983 through March 31, 1984 — accidents that
occurred during the period of January 1, 1974
through March, 1984.

b.   Open ("O") as of March 31, 1984 — Accidents
occurring January 1, 1974 through December
1983.

A.   *Policies other than the "Special Automobile
Policy" and the "Personal Auto Policy"*

A separate report of Bodily Injury and Property
Damage Liability Excess Losses for each Line of
Business Code shall be filed for each state.

©ISO

and commercial lines include the following rules for reporting on
magnetic tape:

1. Specifications are given for the length and width of a tape (i.e.,
   width: one-half inch; length: between 50 and 2,400 feet).
2. The tape should be clearly marked with a "reflective spot" at
   the beginning and at the end of a tape.
3. Tapes should be carefully and sufficiently packed to avoid
   damage in transit.
4. External labels must be on each reel. They must specify the
   company or group name, company or group number, reporting
   period, type of business (such as private passenger automobile),
   density, parity, track, record length, volume serial, data set
   name and the type of submission and statistics contained on the
   tape (such as original submission for premium data).
5. The format of the data to be reported, as far as the maximum
   number of records allowed per block, is specified. For ISO, the
   maximum records per block is 200, or it can be unblocked.

6. Nine track tapes must be used for reporting data with 1,600 or 6,250 density and odd parity.
7. Internal labels are required. They can be second or third generation, although third generation labels are preferable.
8. Field by field detail descriptions of the allowable header and trailer records are provided showing fields that may be used for the individual company's use.

Rules for reporting data on diskettes include the following:

1. The physical characteristics must meet specifications as to the size, format, bytes and the capacity of the diskette.
2. Proper packing is needed to avoid damage in transit.
3. External labels are required on both the diskette and its envelope showing the company or group name and number, the accounting date, diskette number, sequence number in case of multivolume files, type of insurance, type of submission, and type of statistics.
4. Characteristics of the label when initializing volume label and when creating a header label are specified.

Insurers report data on punch cards only when they cannot use magnetic tape or diskettes. The requirements are similar to those for diskettes or magnetic tapes, and there are also rules governing shipping, external labeling, and the type of cards to be used.

The reporting forms are very stringent, and companies are not given much leeway. Without this uniformity, ISO or other bureaus and agencies would not be able to process the data accurately or on a timely basis.

Another reporting form that is required is the *transmittal*. Sometimes transmittals are computer printouts showing totals for the data being submitted. These totals are prescribed by the bureau or agency as to the required format and content. The data submitted on tape, diskette, or cards must equal the transmittals, and the transmittals must be delivered with the data.

Many times, as in the case with ISO submissions, the computer printout transmittal is attached to a preprinted transmittal form. These may be color coded by type of insurance. Exhibit 7-3 shows an example of an ISO transmittal for the Commercial Statistical Plan.

The following information is provided on most transmittals.

1. The company or group name.
2. The company or group number.
3. The accounting period.

4. The type of statistics, such as premiums or outstanding losses.
5. The type of submissions. This specifies whether the data is an original submission, resubmission, or error correction.
6. The type of submission count which shows the sequence number in the case of multiple submissions of the same type. This also indicates whether or not it is the final submission of its type.
7. If there is a transmittal letter correction.
8. Technical information dealing with the tape such as density, track, parity, block size, label, and volume serial numbers.
9. Notes if the data being submitted was run on their ISO's edit program.
10. Totals for the amount of dollars and record counts being submitted. There are grand totals and totals by line of business.

DATA QUALITY

The accuracy and timeliness of statistical reports are major concerns of statistical agents. Upon receipt of data, statistical agents perform extensive and comprehensive checks of its accuracy and completeness. Several key steps in the process include the following:

- *Absolute Edits*—A data item that does not contain appropriate specified codes.
- *Inconsistent Coding*—A data record that contains an invalid code in relation to another valid code.
- *Distributional Editing*—An examination of company and industry profiles.
- *Annual Statement Page 14*—Reconciliation of statistical data to Annual Statement Page 14 data to ensure the completeness of data.
- *Field Relationship Edits*—An example would be a review of the average rate.

Other extensive automated and manual checks are performed. All invalid data is returned to the insurer for correction and resubmission.

These procedures, however, discover only a portion of the errors that can occur in statistical reports. Insurers must take further steps to assure the quality of the data they report. The requirements of both the statistical agencies and the regulators include a number of devices intended to promote data quality.

Exhibit 7-3
Notice of Transmittal of Data Under ISO Commercial Statistical Plan

IMPORTANT NOTES:

a. Statistics are to be reported on DIRECT BUSINESS ONLY. Paid Allocated Loss Adjustment Expenses Data, where required, are to be included in the same submission(s) with Paid Loss Data. Outstanding Allocated Loss Adjustment Expenses Data, where required, are to be included in the same submission(s) with Outstanding Loss Data. Amounts for Allocated Loss Adjustment Expenses are to be included in the Grand Totals in items 11 and 12.

b. A separate Notice of Transmittal shall be filed for each of Premiums, Paid Losses and Paid Allocated Loss Adjustment Expenses, where required, and Outstanding Losses and Outstanding Loss Adjustment Expenses, where required.

c. An affidavit shall be filed at the end of each Accounting Year attesting to the truth and accuracy of experience reported during the year with respect to the Company or Group Records for that year.

d. All appropriate information must be completed on this form.

1. Company/Group Name: _____

2. Company/Group Number: _____

3. Accounting Month: _____ Year: _____

4. Type of Statistics:

   Enter Number in ⟶ ▢

   Premiums 1
   Paid Losses and Paid Allocated Loss Adjustment Expenses, where required 2

Outstanding Losses and Outstanding Allocated Loss Adjustment Expenses, where required 3

5. Type of Submission:

   Enter Number in ☐

   No Statistics to Report 0
   Full Original 1
   Partial Original 2
   Resubmission 3
   (Specify)

   Type of Sub ☐
   TOS Cnt ☐

   Error Correction 5
   Supplemental 6

6. Type of Submission Count:

   Enter Number in ☐

7. If this is your Final Partial Original Submission for this Type of Statistics and Accounting Period and completes your Transmittal of Data to ISO for this Type of Statistics and Accounting Period then enter "X" in ☐

8. Transmittal Letter Correction

   Enter "X" in ☐
   (Copy of Original Transmittal Letter must be attached.)

9. EDP Technical Requirements:

Enter "X" in each appropriate box

a. Track — 9: ☐ — or — 7: ☐

b. Density — 6250: ☐ 1600: ☐ 800: ☐ 556: ☐

c. Parity — Even: ☐ — or — Odd: ☐

d. Label (Specify): _____

e. Block Size (Specify): _____

f. Volume Serial #: ___ ___ ___ ___ : Reel ___ of ___
                    ___ ___ ___ ___ : Reel ___ of ___
                    ___ ___ ___ ___ : Reel ___ of ___
                    ___ ___ ___ ___ : Reel ___ of ___
                                             ___ of ___

g. Error Correction Submission *only*:
   Type of Card when applicable   80 column: ☐☐

                                    System 3: ___ of ___

   Version Number: _____
   Table Number: _____

10. CEP used?   Yes: ☐   No: ☐

11. Grand Total Dollars: _____   Place X if Credit ☐
    (Exclude Submission Control Records. For Error Correction Submissions leave this item blank.)

12. Grand Total Records: _____
    (Exclude Submission Control Records. For Error Correction Submissions enter the number of Parameter Records.)

Date Shipped to ISO: _____ 19 _____

Signature _____ Date _____ 19 _____

Title* _____

*Signatory must be company official responsible for compilation of statistical data.

Data Received ISO Receiving Location: _____

1. Company/Group Name: _____

2. Company/Group Number: _____

Optional CSP Module Identification of Data Included in this Submission

Place number from table below in "Type" box next to each appropriate CSP Module. Total amounts should be filled in where shown. THESE TOTALS DO NOT REPLACE THE SUBMISSION CONTROL RECORDS REPORTED WITH THE EXPERIENCE.

0 .... No Statistics to Report
1 .... Full Module Original
2 .... Partial Module Original
3 .... Full Module Resubmission
4 .... Partial Module Resubmission
5 .... Error Correction
6 .... Supplemental
7 .... Out of Balance Correction

CSP Module	Type	Dollar Amount(s)/Record Count (#)		X Credit
		$	#	
1. Commercial Fire & Allied Lines	☐			☐
2. Farmowners—Ranchowners	☐			☐
3. Inland Marine	☐			☐
4. Medical Professional Liability	☐			☐
5. General Liability	☐			☐
7. Commercial Auto	☐			☐
8. Fidelity and Forgery (written as part of a package policy)	☐			☐
9. Glass	☐			☐
10. Burglary and Theft	☐			☐
11. Boiler and Machinery	☐			☐
12. Earthquake	☐			☐
13. Businessowners	☐			☐
14. Non-Bureau	☐			☐

ISO Data Quality Programs

In 1976, ISO commissioned a study of the data gathering, processing, and reporting systems. The study indicated a critical need for improved control over the accuracy of data. As a result, ISO took several major steps to strengthen its commitment to the quality of data. Current ISO data quality programs include company edit packages, an audit guide, the annual verification call, performance evaluation report cards, and the incentive assessment program.

Edit Packages   ISO has developed edit packages for company use. The Company Edit Packages and the Multiple Line Edit Package provide insurers with a means to edit data using the same edit criteria as ISO uses. The use of these packages increases the timeliness and accuracy of the reported statistics, since it enables companies to process their insurance experience prior to its submission. As a result, in many cases, the data received at ISO requires no error corrections, and the insurer eliminates costly reprocessing of data from rejected submissions.

Audit Guide   Another ISO step to improve the quality of data was the development of *The Data Quality Audit Guide*. This publication provides guidelines for the conduct of a comprehensive audit of data quality. These guidelines are designed to assure the accuracy, completeness, and timeliness of an insurer's data. The Guide outlines the audit process which, if performed regularly, enables an insurer to state conclusively that its data complies with established standards for accuracy.

Annual Verification   ISO's annual verification requirements provide another assurance of data quality. Under this program, insurers must reconcile data in their statistical reports with the data shown in their Annual Statements for the same lines of business. This requirement provides a check on the completeness of the data.

Performance Evaluation Program   The Performance Evaluation Program, implemented in 1978, issues report cards to company data quality and chief executive officers. It has been a very effective tool in providing feedback to insurers at a senior level, which can greatly enhance a company's endeavor to improve the quality of its data. Aggregate evaluations are provided for the last six-month period. An evaluation is made and a letter grade is assigned separately for timeliness and quality. Grades are provided for essentially each line of insurance. The grades take into consideration all types of statistics, all resubmissions and error correction activity and also may reflect subjective adjustments as a result of reporting problems identified by insurers or ISO staff. Exhibit 7-4 shows an actual report card received by a major insurer from ISO.

Incentive Assessment Program   In April 1972 the ISO Board of Directors established the Incentive Assessment Program to provide incentives for timely reporting of statistics. The program was modified in 1979 to provide additional incentives for reporting quality statistical data.

This program proved effective in enhancing insurer data quality. Since 1979, the number of insurer error corrections annually processed by ISO declined by 75 percent, producing savings for both ISO and individual insurers.

In 1983 the ISO Board of Directors approved a new Incentive Assessment Program which focuses on critical dates supporting ISO's processing of insurer's statistics towards the ultimate consolidation of experience for statistical and ratemaking reports. Because these dates are fixed, a company can exercise greater control on its allocation of time for the initial reporting of data and any subsequent error correction activity. The actual assessment amounts vary by company size, and so as not to make the program unreasonable, there are minimum and maximum amounts by line of insurance.

ISO's Incentive Assessment Program assesses an insurer for all rejected submissions and all submissions of statistics which require error correction. These are assessed on a schedule which provides for greater assessments as the volume in error increases. These assessments are tempered by the implementation of minimum cutoffs, and in addition, there is a ten-record waiver for all such transgressions. The turnaround time evidenced by an insurer in submitting resubmissions or error corrections are monitored. If it is unacceptable for more than thirty calendar days, assessments will accrue. If error corrections are required by a submission failure for a line/state error tolerance, then additional assessment free time is provided to the insurer to comply. At this time, each type of statistics is assessed separately for each line of insurance. The assessments are performed on an individual account period basis so that monthly reporting insurers have greater exposure to these assessments than those who report on a quarterly or annual basis.

Statistical Data Monitoring System

On November 18, 1982 the New York Superintendent of Insurance promulgated Regulation 103. This announcement marked the completion of a two-year project to develop a Statistical Data Monitoring System (SDMS). The project was a joint effort of an NAIC Zone 1 Task

Exhibit 7-4

Performance Evaluation — Alphabet Insurance Company Data Reported to ISO for 3rd Quarter 1983 Through 4th Quarter 1983

Line of Business	Company A				Company B				Company C			
	Latest Quarter		Latest Half Year		Latest Quarter		Latest Half Year		Latest Quarter		Latest Half Year	
	Time-liness	Quality	Time-liness	Quality	Time-liness	Quality	Time-liness	Quality	Time-liness	Quality	Time-liness	Quality
Private Passenger Auto Liability	A	B†	A	A	A	A	A	A	A	A	A	A
Private Passenger Auto Physical Damage	A	A	A	A	A	A	A	F	A	A	A	B
Homeowners, Tenants & Condominiums	A	A	A	A					A	A	A	A
Dwelling Fire & Allied Lines	A	A	A	A					A	A	A	A
(Personal) Inland Marine	A	A	A	A					A	A	A	A
Commercial Automobile	A	A	A	A					A	A	A	A
Commercial Fires & Allied Lines	A	A	A	A					A	A	A	A
General Liability	A	A	A	A					A	A	A	A
(Commercial) Inland Marine	A	A	A	A					A	A	A	A
(Commercial) Glass	A	A	A	A					A	A	A	A

(Commercial) Burglary & Theft	A	A	A	A	A	A
Farmowners-Ranchowners	A	A	A			
Boiler & Machinery	A	A	A			
Medical Professional Liability	A	A	A			
Businessowners		A	A	A	A	A

Grade:
A=Excellent, meets or exceeds current timeliness or quality standards
B=Good, meets most timeliness or quality standards but needs some improvement
C=Fair, needs improvement to meet timeliness or quality standards
D=Poor, needs substantial improvement to meet timeliness or quality standards
F=Very poor, severe problems in reporting data

The lower of the timeliness and quality grades most accurately reflects overall performance.
† Quality grade of "B" assigned due to major data problem.

Account Period 10/83 - 12/83 (Qtr) 07/83 - 12/83 (Half Yr)

Personal Lines
Private Passenger Auto Liability

	Submissions Received	Delinquent Submissions[1]		Average Days	Average Error Turn Around[2]	Overall Timeliness Grade[1]	% Errors[1]		Number of Submissions Failure Line State[4]	Average Submission Quality Grade[1]	Number Rejected Resubmissions	Number Submissions Out of Balance[1]	Overall Quality Grade
		Number	Percent				Record Count	Dollar Amount					
Premium (Qtr)	3		0%			100%	1%	1%		98%			98%
† Loss (Qtr)	4		0			100	1	2		97			97
Combined (Qtr)	7		0			100				98			98

continued on next page

	Submissions Received	Delinquent Submissions		Average Days	Average Error Turn Around	Overall Timeliness Grade	% Errors		Number of Submissions Failure Line State[4]	Average Submission Quality Grade[3]	Number Rejected Resubmissions	Number Submissions Out of Balance[2]	Overall Quality Grade
		Number	Percent				Record Count	Dollar Amount					
Premium (Half Yr)	6		0%			100%	1%	0%		99%			99%
Loss (Half Yr)	8		0			100	1	3		97			97
Combined (Half Yr)	14		0			100				98			98
Private Passenger Auto Physical Damage													
Premium (Qtr)	3		0%			100%	1%	1%		98%			98%
Loss (Qtr)	3		0			100	1	3		97			97
Combined (Qtr)	6		0			100				97			97
Premium (Half Yr)	6		0%			100%	1%	1%		99%			99%
Loss (Half Yr)	6		0			100	1	1		97			97
Combined (Half Yr)	12		0			100				98			98
Homeowners, Tenants, And Condominiums													
Premium (Qtr)	3		0%			100%	9%	2%	1	91%			91%
Loss (Qtr)	4		0			100	0	0		100			100
Combined (Qtr)	7		0			100			1	97			97
Premium (Half Yr)	6		0%			100%	6%	1%	1	94%			94%
Loss (Half Yr)	8		0			100	0	0		100			100
Combined (Half Yr)	14		0			100			1	97			97

1. Original, partial and supplemental submissions only.
2. The average time it took your company to file error corrections which brought your submissions (See Footnote 1) below error tolerances or to file submissions for rejected submissions.
3. The average submission quality grade does not follow from information on this report. Refer to grading criteria circular.
4. Number of submissions (See Footnote 1) which met countrywide tolerances but failed line (module) state tolerances.

† Quality grade of "B" assigned due to major data problem.

Force and Arthur Anderson & Co. and also involved an Industry Advisory Board composed of representatives from ISO, NAII, and six of their member companies. The regulation applies to companies writing private passenger, nonfleet, automobile insurance in the state of New York and requires both insurers and statistical agents to implement certain controls and monitoring procedures included in the Statistical Data Monitoring System. Collectively, these procedures are designed to assure the reliability of the data collection process which provides statistical data for statistical filings and for ratemaking purposes. While SMDS is designed to be self-monitoring, it anticipates regulatory review for compliance. The significance of SMDS may be inferred from the following preamble to the New York State Insurance Department Regulation 103.

> The purpose...is to assure the accuracy and reliability of private passenger automobile statistical data reported to the Insurance Department by its licensed statistical agents. The statistical data provides part of the general support for insurers' rate and classification filings and supply important information with respect to the character and composition of the market. In addition, in most companies, the raw data utilized in a company's statistical reporting system are essentially the same data as those utilized in its rate making system. The accuracy and reliability of these data are of fundamental importance to the Insurance Department.[5]

This regulation is described in three volumes of instructions; Volumes I and II apply to companies; Volume III to statistical agents. In summary, SDMS consists of five major requirements:

1. Description of Company Systems and Procedural Controls
2. Sample Testing
3. Reasonability Testing
4. Financial Reconciliation
5. Annual Review and Certification

Description of Company Systems and Procedural Controls
The primary purpose of this requirement is to provide insurance examiners with a concise summary of an individual company's data flow. For each system version narratives, schematics, and checklists must be prepared and available on request.

Sample Testings Statistically repairable transactions are to be sampled and tested for each system version. Data elements are to be compared at different stages in the processing mechanism to assure the data handling process. The sources for data errors should be identified and the causes corrected. The results of the sampling in terms of error rates must be reported to the statistical agents.

Reasonability Testing The accuracy of summarized data is tested by comparing current data to data from prior periods. The categories examined should include territories within the state, coverages within the state, and major classes within the state. The twenty-five most questionable items must be investigated and documented. The results are to be retained by the company for five years. No external reporting is made.

Financial Reconciliation Data reported to the statistical agents must be reconciled to the financial data, Page 14 of the company's Annual Statement. A specific reconciliation format was devised.

Annual Review and Certification Each company is required to conduct annual reviews of its compliance with SDMS. The reviewers must be independent from the production and use of the statistical data. Annually, an officer of the company must certify that the company has complied with SDMS.

How a company conforms to these regulations and what internal procedures are utilized to comply with SDMS can vary from company to company, but the final results must be verifiable by examiners as outlined above. Although the regulation applies only to private passenger automobile insurance, it is possible that the requirements will be extended to other lines of business.

The testing and checks required by SDMS probably should be viewed as an extension of the internal controls as they apply to statistical data. Since such information is used for ratemaking analysis, it is constantly being challenged. The insurance industry can now point to a set of uniform procedures, which will be nationally known as substantiation for the soundness of the systems used in generating this statistical information.

In essence, SDMS presents the insurers with the challenge of providing a road map through the complexity of processing technology in the form of standardized documentation of systems and controls data verification, financial reconciliation, and self-certification. They should now have the tools to withstand close scrutiny by the examiners and supply accurate data to the statistical agents.

SUMMARY

The unique ratemaking needs of the insurance business impose extensive statistical reporting requirements. The objective of insurance ratemaking is to establish rates that cover the cost of losses, expenses, profits, and contingencies. The rate is an amount charged for each unit of exposure to loss. To determine the premium charged a particular insured, the rate is multiplied by the number of exposure units involved. To produce an accurate rate, the experience analyzed must cover a sufficient number of insureds with a similar likelihood of loss and cover an adequate period of time.

Rates must be submitted or filed with the state commissioner in all states in which the insurance company writes business. Rates and rules are regulated by all states, but changes can be requested by submitting a rate filing. Statistical agents collect the statistical data state regulators require of insurers and submit it in the forms acceptable to the various state insurance departments. Some organizations combine the functions of rating bureaus and statistical agents for some lines of insurance.

Of all lines of insurance, workers' compensation is one of the most extensively regulated. Most states require workers' compensation insurers to belong to a designated rating bureau and to adhere to the rules, forms, classification plans, and possibly rates filed by that bureau. The National Council on Compensation Insurance is the designated bureau in over thirty states; other states have independent bureaus that follow similar procedures. The Insurance Services Office is the largest statistical organization; it functions as an advisory and rating organization for most lines of property and liability insurance in all fifty states. Other organizations, however, perform similar functions in some states for some lines of insurance. These include the National Association of Independent Insurers, the American Association of Insurance Services, and the National Independent Statistical Service. The Automobile Insurance Plan Service Office is also an important statistical organization, since it compiles data for the shared automobile insurance market of most states.

Statistical reporting requirements are set forth in the particular statistical plans of the organizations involved. Statistical plans include detailed instructions regarding the scope of the data required, the frequency and timeliness of reports, the specific data items to be reported, and the forms in which the reports may be transmitted.

Statistical reporting is also subject to certain data quality standards. These standards improve the efficiency of the statistical collection and reporting process for both insurers and statistical organizations as well as improve the accuracy of ratemaking data. ISO's initiatives toward improving data quality include company edit packages, an audit guide, annual verification, performance evaluation report cards, and the incentive assessment program. The Statistical Data

Monitoring System promulgated by the New York Superintendent of Insurance for private passenger automobile insurance provides another example of data quality requirements in statistical reporting. Other bureaus and other regulators have implemented or at least proposed similar steps to control data quality. Accordingly, maintaining the integrity of data processed in an insurance information system is the subject of the next chapter.

Chapter Notes

1. Bernard H. Battaglin, "A Changing Role—Insurance Statistical Agencies," *The Interpreter* (December 1984), p. 17.
2. *Maple Flooring Association v. United States*, 268 U.S. 564, 45 S. Ct. 582 (1925).
3. National Association of Insurance Commissioners, *All-Industry Rating Bills*, June 12, 1946.
4. *Membership Information Fact Sheet* (Chicago, IL: National Independent Statistical Service, n.d.), pp. 10–11.
5. New York Superintendent of Insurance, *Regulation 103*, "Implementation of Private Passenger Automobile Insurance Statistical Data Monitoring System (SDMS)," November 18, 1982.

CHAPTER 8

Data Integrity

INTRODUCTION

In today's business environment, insurance organizations naturally are concerned about the quality and integrity of the vast amounts of data on which they depend heavily. One of the first to make extensive use of computer processing, the insurance industry recognizes that effective management and control over company electronic data processing (EDP) has become all the more important as these operations have grown.

Simultaneous with an ever-increasing volume of data have been revolutionary developments in EDP technology. Modern systems often comprise many components, including telecommunications networks; online, realtime systems that perform immediate, potentially destructive updates of data on file; locally linked computers; and data base management systems. Many of these are paperless systems that do not automatically provide a visible audit trail, so that, by necessity, management's attention focuses on the need for controls over various aspects of computer processing.

In order to maintain overall data integrity, different controls are required. Part of the ability to maintain data integrity depends on the function of the programmed procedures, or steps that the computer performs on the data. In modern insurance company operations, these procedures can be extremely complicated, involving calculations, such as automatic policy rating, and summarizations of massive quantities of data, such as loss reserve triangles.

This chapter defines the controls that ensure the completeness, accuracy, validity, authorization, continuity, and maintenance of the data. These are called application controls, usually classified by the control objectives that they fulfill.

Control techniques commonly used to achieve these objectives are explained, including both the manual and computerized, or programmed, procedures. How to apply these techniques so that an organization's computer-processed data is reliable, meets management's expectations, and continues to do so is discussed in detail. Controls over EDP itself, called general or integrity controls, are discussed in Chapter 9, Systems Controls.

Potential Significance of Errors

A major factor in the design and evaluation of application controls is the potential impact of various types of errors on statistical reports and financial statements. Consider the significance of errors in transaction data, master file data, and programmed procedures.

Errors in individual *transaction data* have a limited impact because they affect one transaction at a time. Transaction files are usually not a major audit concern, since transaction data is normally transferred to master files at the completion of the job. Thus errors in transaction data are often detected by subsequent manual or programmed procedures. However, a significant error may result from a single wrong transaction, and there is also the danger of bogus transactions.

Errors in *master file data* may affect many transactions in a particular account, such as the insured, agent, policy type, company, and so forth. Furthermore, these errors may not be detected by manual procedures, since master file information is not printed and checked frequently. Programs are less likely to be designed to detect errors in low-volume master file data (such as a reinsurance company's net return, which is entered once) than in high-volume transaction data (such as losses). As an example of such an error, imagine what the repercussions would be if a reinsurance company's net retention were entered as $1,000 instead of $1,000,000.

Program errors have the potential to affect all transaction and master file data. These errors may not be detected by manual procedures because of a lack of visible evidence, and user assumptions that the system is functioning properly. Programmed procedures that do not function properly and other related errors may accumulate over time; they may not be noticeable at first, but eventually they can materially distort the financial records. For example, an erroneous calculation of loss reserves or unearned premiums for a property and liability insurance company can have a major impact on the company's financial statements.

In addition to controls on transaction data, master file data, and programmed procedures, adequate manual procedures, designed to provide the procedures needed for people to use the system properly, are needed. An example is the manual investigation and follow-up on items rejected and reported by the computer.

Financial Systems Procedures

Financial systems procedures consist of a combination of manual and programmed procedures. Their relative mix and importance varies, depending on the complexity and type of system in use.

Manual Procedures in Computerized Financial Systems In this environment these are similar to those used in a noncomputerized system. They are frequently described in written instructions, as they are in a noncomputerized environment. Some differences follow:

- Specific procedures are required both to prepare data for computer processing and to act on the results of computer processing, as shown by printed reports or displays on a terminal screen. For example, to prepare a claim for a loss system, there must be a special type of loss code that is related to the claim description. Those codes have a specific meaning to the computer and are the key to how it stores the information.
- There are often fewer manual procedures, with the result that data receives less manual scrutiny and review. For example, investment income and commission calculations are done by the computer, not by hand.

Programmed Procedures in Computerized Financial Systems These are used to perform many routine calculations, information storage, and decision functions of an accounting system. For convenience, these procedures may be divided into the following categories:

- Bookkeeping functions such as calculating, summarizing, categorizing, and updating procedures that are applied to data. For example, an upgrade in an agent's commission rate would require an update of the agent's rate table to calculate the commission accurately.
- Procedures relating to control over the completeness, accuracy, validity, and maintenance of data. These normally consist of edit tests, accumulation of totals, reconciliations, and identification and reporting of incorrect, exceptional, or missing data. Just as data entry clerks must use valid transaction codes for premium transactions, and all policy entries should require

policy numbers, procedures must ensure an accurate, complete, and effective data control system.

- The automatic generation of accounting data or paperwork following the occurrence of another transaction, such as the automatic creation of statistical files when premiums and claims are processed, or the timely billing of premiums.

Obviously, these programs must contain, in specific detail, all the processing steps required for the computer to accomplish the desired results.

Importance of Controls

As explained in Chapter 2, computer processing of data differs from manual processing in two significant respects. Traditionally, accounting information was recorded on visible accounting documents (such as agents' account currents, direct bills, and claim checks) and in ledgers and journals. In a computerized system, data is recorded and held in machine-readable form, which may be referred to as an "invisible" record. In paperless systems, there may be no hardcopy documents involved with input of transactions at all. Furthermore, not all data held in the computer is printed; only summaries and exception reports may be printed unless the data is required for a particular function. Thus, both the data that makes up the financial records and the intermediate results of computer processing may not be available for review.

Automated systems that communicate, process, and store data must incorporate adequate controls. Data is a vital resource that needs protection. When uncontrolled, its exposure to neglect, carelessness, catastrophe, or an overt act (which might range from improper copying of data to divulging confidential information to competitors) can seriously impair an entire organization and result in a loss of assets, both tangible and intangible.

In a computer system, the information needed to exercise control over data is produced by programmed procedures. The logical question is then: How are these procedures controlled?

In some basic computer systems, the details of all application data processed are printed out. As a result, the programmed procedures performed by the computer can be controlled by duplicating the computer's operations through manual reperformance.

In more complex systems, it becomes impracticable, and sometimes impossible, to reperform manually the programmed procedures for applications performed by the computer. For example, a computer checking the sequence of prenumbered claim drafts may be programmed to print only an exception report. There is no way that the user can reperform all the intermediate steps that the computer has taken to account for all prenumbered drafts. Thus another set of controls must be established over the programmed procedures to ensure their consistent and proper operation. These controls, normally known as *general controls*, are controls over the data processing environment as a whole.

General controls usually cover all programmed procedures and applications. In contrast, *application controls* are controls over specific applications; they consist of both manual procedures and programmed procedures. General controls ensure that the programmed procedures continue to operate properly. If there are weaknesses in the general controls, there is no assurance that the programmed procedures will continue to be effective.

APPLICATION CONTROL OBJECTIVES

Application controls are controls in a computerized system that relate to specific applications that accomplish particular tasks. The objectives of application controls include:

- completeness of input,
- accuracy of input,
- completeness and accuracy of update,
- validity and authorization,
- maintenance and continuity, and
- calculating, summarizing, and categorizing procedures.

Completeness of Input

Completeness of input is concerned with the recording and entering of transactions. This objective has two aspects. The first is to ensure that all transactions are initially recorded, entered into the computer, and accepted by the computer. The most difficult transaction to detect is a missing transaction. For one example, document control numbers can assist ensuring that all transactions are entered.

The second aspect relates to the following properties of completeness:

- *All rejected transactions should be reported.* For example, if the policy number on a policyholder's claim is invalid, the program should reject and report that invalid number. If such exceptions are not reported, erroneous claims might be paid automatically.

- *Each transaction should be processed only once.* For example, if controls over claims are ineffective, payments might be duplicated. For retrospective policies, this duplication could also distort the company's premiums-written account and could prompt an unwarranted increase in loss reserves.
- *Duplicate transactions should be rejected and reported.* If there is a weakness in reporting duplicate transactions, erroneous payments might be made. Controls over completeness should also include controls designed to ensure that rejected data is resubmitted after the problem has been resolved.

Accuracy of Input

While completeness of input ensures that all relevant data is entered, accuracy of input ensures the correctness of that data on transactions being processed. The objective of controls over accuracy is to ensure that the initial recording of data is correct. Where applicable, the data is transcribed accurately from source documents to input documents and data is converted accurately into machine-readable form.

Controls over accuracy need to be stronger at the data entry stage than during processing and updating. For example, a premium payment might be erroneously recorded during key entry and rejected during subsequent edit checks because it failed to match any premium amount billed. Or, a key-stroke error might transpose two digits in a policy number, inadvertently matching it to another number in the master file. This type of error might be caught by an edit program validating check digits, or by a manual control such as a review by a premium input clerk to ensure that each input sheet matches the update report.

Completeness and Accuracy of Update

A major concern in computer-based systems is ensuring that data already in the computer is updated completely and accurately.

Completeness and accuracy of update involves controls over data inside the computer, including the internal processes carried out by programmed procedures.

The input controls take the data to the point of acceptance by the computer. Once accepted, the data undergoes a series of processing steps, which may include sorting and calculation by programmed procedures; analysis and accumulation; and updating a master file.

Several things can interfere with the integrity of data once it has been entered for processing. Programming errors, or programmed procedures that do not perform as expected or desired, can obviously affect much data. For the most part, programs are designed, written, tested, and then put into production to handle common types of transactions in a particular system. Consequently, these standard, day-to-day procedures are usually well tested. Unforeseen events, errors, or exceptions may occur that the programmed procedures cannot process correctly. Programs may also include logic errors that escaped detection in testing. It is also possible for a program to be accurate when implemented, but develop errors when new procedures are added without sufficient testing. Such errors may occur in the way the data is processed, without obvious, immediate ramifications so that the errors may go undetected for long periods of time.

Operational errors can also affect data. During the operation of standard computer procedures, an operator may make a mistake, such as not marking an output file for future use in the next processing cycle. Computer operations manuals may become out-of-date or contain errors, computer operators may need retraining, or equipment may fail. For example:

- The wrong record may be updated. This may happen when there is no built-in check over the record selected for updating. A control over accuracy, such as dependency checking, should detect such an error in processing.
- Calculations may be wrong. Either the formula for the calculations may be in error or the variable and table data used in the calculation may be incorrect. Calculations that involve decimal values stated beyond the hundreds often have the decimal value in error since most people think in two-digit decimals and will enter them that way.
- Analysis and accumulation errors may result from either incorrect programmed procedures or incorrect logic. If data analysis is based on matching data to another file and the wrong file is selected, the resulting analysis will be incorrect. Accumulation errors are infrequent when figures can be added to a total. They do often occur when the numbers are categorized into accumulations that are not easily footed.

Controls are needed to ensure that when computer files are updated, the new input is accurately carried through intermediate processing and accurately updated to the correct data on the correct generation of the master file. As with controls over input, master file data and reference data must be accurately updated.

One method of controlling accuracy of update (and of input) that is commonly used for the control of master file data amendments is as follows:

- The new data to be processed is entered together with the old data. For example, if the reserve amount of an outstanding claim is to be amended, the claim number is entered with both the new reserve amount and the previous reserve amount.
- The computer matches the claim number and the previous reserve amount entered to those held on the file. If a match is obtained, the new reserve amount updates the file.
- If a match is not obtained, the item is reported for investigation.

Validity and Authorization

It is essential that only valid data, authorized by management and representing economic events that actually occurred, be written to master files, printed on reports, or incorporated into records. Thus, all data should be appropriately authorized or checked.

Sometimes validity of transactions can be ensured by matching an organization's data to other data, such as when an outside agent uses the company's online computer system to check the status of a policy against the agent's own files.

In many cases, the authorization programmed procedures are similar to those used in noncomputerized systems. There are, however, the following important differences in authorizing data in computer systems:

- Data is often authorized at the beginning of processing, at the time it is entered into the computer system, rather than when the resulting output is produced or used.
- Instead of authorizing data prior to entry for processing, the computer may be programmed, in accordance with management's specifications, to identify and report items that fail certain edit checks or define items for manual authorization (for example, in a claim system, excessive late charges to reserve amount).
- In some cases, the programs test an item's validity so precisely that manual authorization is no longer required.

Maintenance and Continuity

Controls that ensure that data remains correct are called controls for the maintenance of data. Maintenance controls are required for both transaction data and master file data, and are designed to provide controls over the following:

- Correctness of data—To ensure that the data stored on the file cannot be changed other than through the normal, controlled processing cycle.
- Currency of data—To ensure that data is kept up-to-date and that unusual data requiring action is identified.

A date mark is one way to indicate when data was last amended. However, if the system does not create date marks, master file data from a prior period can be matched to the master file data of the current period. Records that are identical for both periods may be considered exceptions that require investigation.

In addition, maintenance controls should provide assurance that the correct generation of the file has been used each time it is updated.

Data can be changed by programs written and processed quickly in a crisis to correct other program errors or operational errors. Care must be taken in using such programs, however. For example, in a particular claim payment system, the current date was entered as a batch parameter each day. At the start of the new year, the computer operator kept entering the month and date correctly, but forgot to change the year. The first aged outstanding draft report for the year showed that drafts outstanding over ninety days had increased dramatically. An investigation uncovered the error. To correct the payment records, the date had to be changed for all the drafts processed during the first four days of the year. Since the drafts themselves had already been mailed, a "quick and dirty" program was used to change only the last digit of the year. It seemed to be such a simple solution that the program was not even tested. Unfortunately, it had a logic error that caused it to fail to write the last record read, dropping the last payment record on the file while still adding it to the totals. Thus, the draft was deleted from the records. When the check was later processed in the bank reconciliation process, it did not match the record on the outstanding drafts file.

Calculating, Summarizing, and Categorizing Procedures

When the computer performs operations such as calculating, summarizing, and categorizing, controls over those procedures are needed to prevent the generation of erroneous data.

Calculating Calculating consists of matching two sets of data and performing an operation using them to produce a third. For example, a program calculating reserves multiplies the face amount of each policy by the appropriate factor to produce the reserve value. The calculations typically consist of marrying:

- master file data (such as the policy amount), which is held permanently on a master file and may include table files and other reference data, with
- transaction data (such as as a notice of loss), which is entered and used only once.

The following conditions are necessary for accurate calculating:

- The master file data must be reliable. This involves all controls over amending and maintaining the data on the file.
- There should be controls to ensure that the correct generation of the file containing the data is used.
- The transaction data must be entered completely and accurately.
- The method used in the program to carry out the calculation must be logically sound and approved by management.
- There should be some means to check the accuracy of the calculations. This may be a manual review of exceptions (such as excessive claim payments produced and reported by the computer). A manual review of the results of the calculations can also be done, in the form of an overall reconciliation.
- Computations that could result in an overflow condition in the data field, or in an intermediate field, should be checked for the potential overflow condition and a report produced, or other appropriate action taken.

Summarizing and Categorizing Summarizing is accumulating all transactions, often after calculating, and producing a total (such as the total premiums written for the period).

Categorizing consists of analyzing a summarized total, such as premiums written analyzed by line of business classification. Categorizing is normally performed by referring to a code that is included in the details entered for each transaction.

For summarizing and categorizing to be effective, the following user controls and programmed procedures are necessary:

- The codes on which summarization and categorization are based must be accurately determined and entered.
- There must be adequate controls over the completeness of summarization.
- The basis on which the program carries out the categorization must be sound.

CONTROL TECHNIQUES

Various techniques are available to control data integrity. These techniques, together with tasks that need to be done in the case of rejections, are discussed in the following paragraphs.

Control Techniques for Completeness of Input

The most commonly encountered techniques to control the completeness of input are:

- computer sequence check of serially numbered documents,
- computer matching with previously processed data,
- agreement of manually established batch controls, and
- one-for-one checking of reports.

Computer Sequence Check In this technique, the computer checks the preprinted or entered serial numbers of input transactions, and reports missing or duplicate numbers for manual investigation. Ideally, transactions should be recorded on serially prenumbered documents; alternatively, they can be sequenced after preparation. The first method is preferred, but is not possible if a document originates outside the organization (for example, a supplier's invoice).

In paperless systems, transactions are often sequenced after entry by the system in order to provide a means of tracking these transactions through the system. In these online systems, transactions are assigned sequence numbers by the edit program upon entry. Computer-assigned sequence numbers can be highly effective in tracing the exact cutoff point after a processing failure. If such a failure necessitates a restart farther back in the processing cycle, it is easier to locate the appropriate restart location.

There are different ways to carry out a sequence check. Two of the most widely used are the cumulative sequence check and the batch sequence check.

Cumulative Sequence Check. A cumulative sequence check typically operates in this way. A table file is created of all document numbers that have been issued. This file may be created by entering the numbers of the documents to be issued or it may be computer-generated as a product of a previous accounting process. Transactions are recorded on standard, serially numbered documents, or are serially numbered on receipt. The transactions are entered and items on the file are flagged to indicate that the transaction has been processed. Any arriving transactions that have already been flagged as processed are rejected and reported as "duplicates." Periodically, reports of missing numbers are produced for manual follow-up.

Batch Sequence Check. In a batch sequence check, the sequence of transactions within a batch or file is checked as follows. The serially numbered transactions are entered together with the range of the numbers to be checked (the range is the first and last numbers in the particular sequence). The computer program sorts the transactions into numerical order, checks the documents against the sequence number range, and reports missing, duplicate, and out-of-range transactions.

For computer sequence checking to be effective as a control technique, the following user controls and programmed procedures must be present. There must be adequate procedures to ensure that all forms are numbered after completion or, if practical, that all transactions are recorded on serially prenumbered forms.

The method used in the program for checking the numerical sequence must be logically appropriate and understood by the user department. In this context, procedures are required to deal with:

- changes or breaks in sequence,
- more than one sequence running concurrently (such as when different locations use different blocks of numbers), and
- identification and reporting of duplicate numbers.

When a suspense file of missing numbers is maintained, there should be adequate controls to ensure that unauthorized adjustments are not made to this file. Reports of missing and duplicate numbers must be produced frequently to allow for prompt follow-up action to correct the error. There must be adequate manual procedures to investigate missing numbers. Any rejected duplicates must be manually checked; they are then canceled or re-entered, depending on the outcome of the investigation.

A cumulative sequence check is easier to operate since it rejects all duplicates and keeps reporting overdue items. If the sequence check is not cumulative, then specific manual procedures will be needed to check for duplicates in different runs and to ensure that each item reported as missing is followed up. Changes or breaks in sequence for the batch-type sequence check ranges should also be verified, manually or by a computer program, to ensure that sequence continuity is maintained from computer run to run, subject only to new sequences issued.

Computer Matching Computer matching consists of matching of input data with information held on master or suspense files. Unmatched items are reported for manual investigation. As an example, the computer might match the policy numbers of all claims to the policies in force file; if there is no match, either the claim policy number is wrong or there is no coverage.

Computer matching is especially useful in online systems that have the ability to match with up-to-date master or suspense files during editing.

For this control technique to be effective, the following user controls and programmed procedures must be present. There must be adequate controls over the file holding details of items to be matched. This will usually be achieved by a regular agreement of file totals to an independent control account. All adjustments to the data on file should be properly authorized. For example, higher claim reserves (cash basis) will need special authorization.

The method used in the program for matching must be logically appropriate and approved by the system users. The number of data elements matched must be sufficient to make the transaction unique. For example, matching a date is usually inappropriate since many transactions can have the same date. Even matching a policy number may be inappropriate if the company has many lines of business, all of which use the same range of policy numbers. In this instance a possible solution is to add the code for the line of business to the invoice number, thus creating a unique transaction number.

The matched items must be appropriately indicated on the reference file to permit production of a report listing unmatched items. Manual procedures must be adequate to follow up outstanding and mismatched items. If reports contain a cumulative list of outstanding items, control over investigation is easier.

The current generation of the file holding details of items to be matched must be used. If an older file is used, many mismatches will turn up, merely because the file is out-of-date.

Batch Totals The batch control technique involves manually grouping transactions at the input stage and establishing a control total over the group. This control total can be based on document count, item count, dollar totals, or hash totals.

Document Counts. A simple count of the number of documents entered can be agreed to the number of documents processed. This is normally the minimum level required to control completeness of input. It will not be sufficient, however, if more than one transaction can appear on a document.

Item or Line Counts. A count of the number of items or lines of data entered (such as a count of the number of items or lines on an invoice) can be agreed to the number processed.

Dollar Totals. An addition of the dollar value of items in the batch can be agreed to the dollar value of items processed.

Hash Totals. An addition of any numeric data existing for all documents in the batch can be checked against the total of the same numeric data fields for items processed (such as total of quantities, total of policy numbers, or total of all numeric fields entered).

Batch Totals in Online Systems The use of batch totals is common in batch processing systems. It has also proven effective in on-line systems where documents are entered as received. A batch concept is created by choosing a time frame in which transactions are entered and treating those transactions as a batch. There are a number of different ways batch totaling may be carried out.

Manual Agreement of a Batch Register. This technique is used in the following manner:

- The batch total is established manually and recorded in a register or batch control book.
- The batch is entered into the computer, accumulated, and the batch total is printed.
- The total printed is manually agreed to the total recorded in the register or control book.
- The batch totals in the register or control book are adjusted for rejected items.

Computer Agreement of Batch Totals. This technique is used in the following manner:

- The batch total is established manually and entered on a batch header slip with the batch.
- The application program accumulates the batch total and compares it with the total entered. (This technique is sometimes referred to as zero-batch balancing, since the total of the batch minus the total on the batch header should be zero).
- A report is produced that will normally contain details of each batch, together with an indication of whether the totals agreed or disagreed.
- Batches that do not balance are normally rejected. Some applications write the batch to a suspense file pending the reentry of corrected items.

Manual Agreement of a Control Account. This method is a variation on the use of a batch register and works in the following manner:

- Total of all types of transactions that update the master file (such as endorsements, cancellations, credits and payments) are established during an initial edit program before processing to update the master file. These totals are established in the same way for manual agreement of a batch register.

- The totals are recorded in a control account.
- Transactions are entered and processed in the master file.
- Periodically, the balance on the control account is agreed manually to an accumulation of all individual balances on the master file. For example, in a casualty claims system, each outstanding claim on the claim master file might have a data element designated as amount paid. A total of all the claim amounts paid during the month should agree to the total claim disbursements, calculated from the claim processing system.

This method, as well as ensuring completeness of input, also ensures completeness of update, which is discussed in the following section.

For the batch totaling technique to be effective, the following user controls and programmed procedures must be present:

- There should be adequate controls to ensure that a document is created for each transaction.
- There should be adequate controls to ensure that all documents are batched.
- There should be adequate controls to ensure that all batches are submitted for processing (such as a manual or computer sequence check on batch numbers).
- The user must determine that all batches have been accepted by the computer.
- When computer agreement of batch totals is used, there should be adequate evidence printed that the checking was carried out.
- There should be adequate procedures for the investigation and correction of differences disclosed by the input reconciliations. These procedures must be performed on a timely basis.
- There should be adequate procedures for the resubmission of all rejections.

One-for-One Checking This technique consists of checking each individual document or source document with a detailed listing of items processed by the computer. To rely on this technique, it is necessary to ensure that all documents are submitted for processing. This is usually achieved by retaining in the originating department a copy of all documents sent for processing. The report is then checked with the retained copy, and missing items are followed up. Checking against copies returned from data processing does not guard against forms being mislaid before they are entered, and cannot therefore be considered a satisfactory control for completeness.

Reconciling the number of documents sent for processing with the number actually processed and accounting for differences is another method.

The report produced and checked contains items that have updated the files. This will provide control over both completeness of input and update. Alternatively, the report may be produced at the edit stage. In this instance, it will contain items that have been accepted but not updated, providing adequate control only over completeness of input.

If carried out effectively, checking of detail reports is a powerful control. It is, however, time-consuming and costly. It is normally used as a technique to control important low-volume transactions, including master file data amendments and other adjustments.

For checking of reports to be effective as a control technique, the following user controls and programmed procedures must be present:

- There must be adequate controls to ensure that all documents are submitted for processing (such as checking output with retained copies by sequence checking or by document counts).
- There should be a regular review of source documents to detect unprocessed items.
- Missing or duplicate items disclosed by the checking process should be promptly identified and followed up. Such followup is essential to the control.

Control Techniques for Completeness of Update

There are two basic ways to ensure that files are updated completely:

- introduce controls for completeness of data entry that can also apply to updating, and
- institute specific updating controls.

Sometimes controls over completeness of input also control the completeness of updating. When controls can do both, the input controls described earlier are reviewed, as is a description of the circumstances in which they can be used to control updating. Several techniques used to control completeness are described below.

Computer Sequence Check Normally, a computer sequence check is performed when data is entered; however, it does not ensure completeness of update. The following situations are found in many systems, particularly in online and realtime environments:

- A sequence check and identification of missing or duplicate transactions are performed on the updated master file after the transactions have updated the file.
- The file that maintains the sequence numbers is not flagged until after the master file has been updated.

In these instances, computer sequence checking provides a control over the completeness of update.

In online systems, the sequence check often operates along with procedures to update the master file. This ensures the completeness of input and update; any duplicates will probably be rejected at the input stage, because the computer will not allow a terminal operator to reuse a previously entered number.

Some systems carry out a sequence check by flagging the sequence number file as the last step prior to updating the master file. Since this normally does not provide sufficient control over updating of the master file, it is important to know how a particular system operates before deciding to rely on this control.

Computer Matching As with sequence checking, computer matching is normally carried out as data is entered. In certain circumstances, the matching process also provides a control over the completeness of update. Matching is then conducted against:

- A master file (as opposed to a suspense file)—The missing data report is produced by reading the master file after the matching process has been completed.
- A suspense file that is not updated until after the master file has been updated—As with sequence checking, care is required, since some systems update the suspense file immediately before updating the master file. In the latter case, the matching normally does not provide control over updating of the master file.

Batch Totals The computer agreement of batch totals never ensures completeness of update, since the technique checks totals only at the input stage. If this is the technique used to control input, specific updating controls will be required.

The manual agreement of a batch register sometimes ensures completeness of update, depending on what sort of report is checked to the register. Checking a report that lists items that have been written to the file will guarantee completeness of update. Checking batch totals against reports produced at the edit stage does not ensure completeness of update, so specific updating controls are required. Manual agreement of a control account usually ensures completeness of updating, because the control account is checked against an accumulation of the balances on file.

Manual agreement of a batch register or control account can usually be applied only where there is little or no intermediate processing and the data updating the file is identical in form to that orginally entered (such as processing details of cash received).

More often, the data entered will be subject to further processing before updating. During this time, the form of the data may change (for example, figures for number of claims paid may be converted to total losses in dollars). When this happens, batch totals cannot be checked manually against the updated totals, and specific updating controls are required.

One-for-One Checking of Detail Reports This technique ensures completeness of update in situations where the report checked contains items that have been used to update the file. If such reports are produced at the edit stage, they will not control updating.

Checking reports is not an effective control technique unless an appropriate method is used in the program that updates transactions to a master file. If the user checks the source documents for a report that shows the record after update, this check will also control the reliability and logic of the programmed procedure. The user must clearly understand this method for it to work effectively.

Specific Updating Controls

When an input control does not also apply to completeness of update, updating is usually controlled by the agreement of control totals. These are generated by computer programs during or prior to operation of the input control. The control totals are the totals of items that have updated the file.

However, totals cannot always be checked directly to see that they agree for the following reasons:

- Control totals may be summarized (such as when several input batches are combined for subsequent processing).
- The type of control total used may change as a result of an intermediate processing step (for example, controls over the reserve valuation normally start at the policy level but end up with aggregated values by kind, age, and year).
- Items may be, or may have been, rejected at an intermediate step.

In those situations, reconciliation procedures may be relied on. The totals of accepted items can be reconciled either manually or by computer.

Techniques that can be used to control updating are described in the following paragraphs, and different methods for accumulating the totals of accepted items are explained.

Manual Reconciliation of Accepted Item Totals In manual reconciliation of accepted item totals, the computer program accumulates and reports the total of items accepted when the input control was exercised. The computer then processes items through a series of programs. Reports that include the relevant control totals are produced, usually at the conclusion of each program in a series. When totals are summarized or changed, the new control totals are printed at the end of the computer run. The old totals are usually printed as well and may be carried through all later processing. After updating, the totals of items updated to the master file are reported. The totals of accepted items are manually reconciled to the updated totals, using any summarization or change in totals that has taken place. Any rejections are also taken into account.

When there is no change in the totals, the accepted item totals may be recorded in a manual control account or cumulative register. The balance in the control account or register can then be periodically agreed to an accumulation of the total balances on file to prove completeness of update.

Computer Reconciliation of Accepted Totals In computer reconciliation of accepted item totals, the computer program accumulates the totals of accepted items in the same way as the totals are accumulated in manual reconciliation. After all data has been entered and processed, the control totals are recorded on a control record in the file of accepted items. In sequential tape files, the totals are added to the trailer label; in disk files that are indexed sequentially or can be accessed randomly, the control record information is usually contained as a header record or the first record of the file. The opening control total on the file should be checked to the previous closing total to determine that the correct generation of the file was used. During each subsequent program run in the series, the computer accumulates the totals of transactions that have been processed and reconciles them to the total forwarded from the previous program run. This technique is often called "run-to-run control totals." At each stage in the reconciliation process, the program produces evidence that the reconciliation has taken place—usually the totals themselves—and a message stating whether the totals agree or disagree. The computer-produced reconciliations are then manually checked and any differences are investigated.

Another method of control that uses computer reconciliation of accepted item totals works as follows. In computer systems where all transactions are first summarized on independent control files, the totals are balanced by a set of programs. In some cases, these are independent programs. This set of programs makes certain that the correct files have been used and that all transaction files have been combined for processing. Manual intervention ensures that programmed reconciliations are not bypassed as a result of unusual events, such as a system failure. It is also necessary to make sure that control totals are brought forward each time the system is closed down and restarted.

Establishment of Totals of Accepted Items   The way the total of accepted items is established depends on whether transactions are entered and processed in batches or individually, as in many online systems. Depending on the method used, the following procedures are employed:

- Batch systems—The total of accepted items should be accumulated during or prior to the program run in which the computer sequence check, computer matching, or other input control is carried out.
- Online systems—Transactions are entered one by one and trigger whichever programs are required to process them. Transaction totals are progressively accumulated at intervals during processing and are periodically reported or reconciled by the computer. These totals may be generated daily or more frequently if there are many transactions. It is important for accepted item totals to be accumulated during or prior to operation of the input control, if that control is effective.

Reliance on Controls over a Previous Application   When systems are integrated, a file produced by one application is used for another application. In this instance, completeness of input to the first application should be controlled to ensure completeness of input to the next application.

Specific update controls, as described in this section, are necessary to ensure that all transactions accepted by the first application are passed through to the second. In addition, if two or more files are updated at the same point in the processing cycle, the same input and update controls may be effective over all files.

Online Sequence Controls   This method of control operates as follows:

- Transactions are assigned a sequence number as they are entered.

- A report of missing and duplicate numbers is produced after all transactions have updated the master file.

Online sequence control is similar to a batch sequence check. This type of control also helps to prevent unusual events, such as the possible loss of transactions from a system failure, since transactions can be identified and recovered at the proper point in processing.

In a sequential update, the sequence of both the transaction file and the master file should be specifically checked, and out-of-sequence records should be reported. If duplicates are found, they should be investigated and dealt with according to the system design.

Master data records usually should have a date mark to indicate when the record was first entered or last amended; guidelines should be set for review of any data not amended for a certain period of time (such as one year) to ensure that it is current. If data is untouched for long periods, it should be reviewed to ascertain that records were not lost in the interim. An insurance company that had not performed such reviews discovered recently that it was using a 1975 actuarial table to calculate life expectancy and the reserves on hand.

Duplicate Processing Memos Duplicate processing is common in an online data base environment. When transactions are entered in this type of operation, a memo update is usually made to the data base. This memo update enables the current updated status to be checked at any time. The data base, however, is not actually updated until overnight processing is done. At that time, the transactions are rechecked against the memo update and a report is produced that lists the differences between the memo update and the overnight update.

Control Techniques for Accuracy of Input

Various techniques are used to control the accuracy of data input. The most widely used are discussed under the following headings:

- Completeness Control Techniques Used for Accuracy
- Programmed Edit Checks
- Prerecorded Input
- Key Verification.

Completeness Control Techniques Used for Accuracy Although the objective of controlling accuracy of input is different from that of controlling completeness of input, some of the techniques used are the same. The applicable completeness of input controls described earlier are listed below, together with a description of the circumstances in which they can control accuracy.

- Computer matching—Computer matching can be effective as a control for accuracy, but it establishes the accuracy of only those elements matched by the program. Often several fields are matched by the program, each of which is therefore controlled in this way.
- Batch totals—The agreement of manually established batch totals can control the accuracy of those data fields that are totaled and agreed. This does not, however, guard against the possibility of compensating errors in one or more individual items. It is unusual, because of the time that would be involved, to establish batch totals over a large number of fields. Batch totals of numbers of documents or item lines do not control accuracy.
- Checking of detail reports—The checking of detail reports can control the accuracy of those fields covered in the detailed checking. Often several data fields are covered by the checking and can be controlled in this way. Data should be checked against the originial input documents retained by the user department. This provides the only adequate control over accuracy of entry and update.

Because completeness control techniques do not ordinarily cover all significant data elements, programmed procedures often check the accuracy of other data, as described in the next section.

Programmed Edit Checks   Programmed procedures that check the accuracy of data are usually called edit checks. Edit programs often include several checks, which when well-designed can be ingenious and powerful. At the program specification stage, it is important to ensure that all appropriate checks are included in the program and that the logic of the checks is correct. Powerful editing is usually easier to achieve in online systems, since a wide variety of data is available for reference for the checking.

In many cases, edit checks cannot provide conclusive proof that only accurate data is accepted. However, a suitable combination of edit checks may be very helpful in reducing the likelihood of error.

Sometimes data may be entered online by someone who is not from the originating department. In these circumstances, there is a danger that the person will incorrectly adjust a transaction that fails an edit test, so close supervision may be required.

It may also be possible to override edit checks. If so, the system should be designed to ensure that all instances of override are suitably reported for investigation by users. The reasons that an override was used should be included in the system use documentation.

The most common types of programmed edit checks include

reasonableness checks, dependency checks, existence checks, format checks, mathematical accuracy checks, range checks, check digit verification, alphanumeric codes, document reconciliation, and prior data matching.

Reasonableness Checks. These are checks to test whether the contents of the data entered fall within predetermined limits. The limits may describe a standard range or may be determined in relation to previous input. Such data is not necessarily wrong, but is considered sufficiently suspicious to require further investigation. For example, a computer program includes a range check that identifies a claim with a settlement amount that is unusually high. If the settlement amount is equal to or greater than $50,000, the transaction is printed on a "claims $50,000 or greater" report.

Reasonableness checks can often be applied to data fields (such as dates and indicators) that are difficult or impractical to control in any other manner.

The use of a standard range is frequently encountered in a claim processing system when a new claim is opened. The computer program identifies and reports reserve estimates, by type of coverage, that exceed or fall short of the norms for those coverage types.

Similarly, a reasonableness check by reference to previous input might be found in a claims processing system. A computer program might identify changes to the estimated reserve in cases where the new estimated amount is unusually high or low in relation to the previous estimate. In general, the data referred to for a reasonableness check may be held on a file (as with the reserve change example above), included in the computer program (as in the range limits in the preceding example), or input at run time.

For reasonableness checks to be effective as a control for accuracy, the following user controls and programmed procedures should be present:

- The method used in the program for identifying exceptional items should be logically sound and should ensure that neither too few nor too many items are identified. This requires care in setting ranges.
- Periodically, the parameters used should be reviewed by the user department. This is particularly true when the parameters are variables.
- If data referred to in a reasonableness check is entered by means of parameters, adequate controls are required to ensure that the correct parameter data is used each time.

Exhibit 8-1
Example of Edit Checks (Programmed Validation)

	Input Data	Reasons For Failing Validity Check	Stored Data
Reasonableness			
	Effective Date 021185 (MMDDYY)	Must be today or before	System date 021284
	BI/PD Reserve 100	Reserve less than normal minimum	Minimum BI/PD Reserve 500
	New Reserve $10,000	New reserve exceeds previous reserve by more than 50%	Previous Reserve $5,000
Dependency Check			
	Effective Date 84067 (yyddd)	Expiration date exceeds date received by more than the term of the policy	Policy Term 6 months
	Expiration Date 85067(yyddd)		
Existence Check	Policy Numbers Entered		Valid Policy Numbers
(Matching)	38169		38169
	38224	Policy 38224 is	
	38598	invalid	38598
	38624		38624

Note: 1. Stored data must be correct.
2. Program must be logically correct and must report all failures.

- Reports of transactions failing the edit must be produced at regular intervals. Positive reporting methods should be employed so that the user knows that all such reports are received.
- There should be adequate procedures for the investigation of the exceptional items reported.

Reasonableness checks are illustrated in Exhibit 8-1.

Dependency Checks. These are checks to test whether the contents of two or more data elements or fields on a transaction bear the correct logical relationship. Considerable ingenuity can be required in devising checks of this nature. Properly designed and implemented, they can provide a strong control over the accuracy of the fields concerned.

As an example, there should be a logical relationship among the premium amount, the number of installments to be made, and the installment amounts as entered for an installment policy. As with reasonableness checks, dependency checks are often applied to dates and indicators.

For dependency checks to be effective as an accuracy control, the following user controls and programmed procedures should be present:

- The method used in the program for relating the data concerned must be logically appropriate.
- There should be adequate procedures for investigating items reported as failing the checks.

Dependency checks are also illustrated in Exhibit 8-1.

Existence Checks. These are checks to test that the data codes entered agree with valid codes held on the file or in the program. For example, when premium payments received are processed, they require a valid agent code and a valid policy number. On input, the program checks that the codes allocated are valid account numbers. Items that do not match (for example, invalid or nonexistent agent codes or policy numbers) will be reported.

Existence checking is usually limited to the control of reference numbers or, occasionally, indicators. It is not, in itself, a complete control, since it will not detect the entry of an incorrect but valid code; accordingly, further controls are required. Careful construction of codes, however, can reduce the possibility of erroneous but valid codes being entered. As explained below, the use of check digits or alphanumeric codes may help in this regard. Check digits are often used in conjunction with existence checks; their use complements the existence check by making the number more complex. As a result it is more likely that an incorrect number will be identified, especially when the error is a transposition of numbers.

For existence checks to be effective as a control, the following user controls and programmed procedures should be present:

- The allocation of codes to transactions should be checked.
- The method used in the program for validating the input data must be logically appropriate.
- The file holding the code table must itself be adequately controlled.

- There should be adequate procedures for investigating items reported as a result of the check.

Existence checks are also illustrated in Exhibit 8-1.

Format Checks. These check the format (existence of expected numeric or alphabetic characters) of a transaction, thus ensuring that all required data is present. Checks of this nature are often included for operational reasons and may assist in ensuring that reference data, such as dates and indicators, is present.

All numeric data should be properly subjected to format checks. However, since format checks usually determine only that data complies with certain broad rules, it is unlikely that they will be of much assistance in controlling the accuracy of data. Format checks are illustrated in Exhibit 8-2.

Mathematical Accuracy Checks. Mathematical accuracy checks check the calculations performed, as shown in Exhibit 8-2.

Range Checks. These check to see whether a number falls within a predefined range, and are illustrated in Exhibit 8-2.

Check Digit Verification. This technique is used to control the accuracy of input of reference numbers. A check digit is designed to prevent an incorrect but valid match. The numbers are constructed so that the last digit bears a mathematical relationship to the preceding digits. As transactions are entered, the computer checks that the reference number contains this relationship. Check digits provide a stronger control over accuracy of input than do existence or format checks.

For check digit verification to be effective as a control, the following user controls and programmed procedures should be present:

- The method used in the program for calculating the check digit should be logically appropriate.
- There should be adequate procedures for the investigation of items reported because of an incorrect check digit.

Check digit verification is also illustrated in Exhibit 8-2.

Alphanumeric Codes. These are combinations of letters and digits and can function in a manner similar to check digits. The use of check digits, however, is a stronger control.

Document Reconciliation. This technique, which is common in on-line systems, involves checking the mathematical accuracy of the entry of numeric data on transactions.

Each transaction, in effect, is treated as a batch. Prior to entry, a hash total is established of all, or all important, numeric data elements on the document. The total is recorded on the document and the

Exhibit 8-2
Examples of Programmed Edit Checks

		Input Data	Reasons for Failing Edit Check
Format	Reference Number:	122 476	Embedded blank
	Dollar Value:	00013A4	Non-numeric
	Name:	_____	Must enter (cannot be blank)

Mathematical Accuracy		$ Value	
Invoice:	Premium	2000.00	
	Membership	10.00	Does not foot
	Total:	2100.00	

Range Check			Month 13 is illegal (out of
	Date:	131385	range)

Check Digit

Employee Numbers: 046176

Modulus 11 check digit

6x1 = 6
7x2 = 14
1x3 = 3
6x4 = 24
4x5 = 20
0x6 = 0

Answer not divisible by 11
Should be 046167

Document Reconciliation

Document Number:	1394	
Code:	17	
Value:	1732.59	
Hash total:	2144.59	Hash total does not foot

Note: Program must be logically correct and must report all failures.

document entered, usually through a terminal. The program totals the data and checks the result with the hash total. Transactions that do not balance are not accepted. The terminal operator can see on the terminal screen if an input error was made and, if so, correct it. If the error is the result of an incorrect hash total, the document should be returned to the originating department for correction. Document reconciliation is also illustrated in Exhibit 8-2.

Prior Data Matching. Neither existence checks nor check digit verification will detect entry of an incorrect but valid reference number. To overcome this drawback, prior data matching is utilized.

This technique is commonly used for the control of master file data amendments and works in the following way:

- The new data to be processed is entered, together with the old data to be superseded. For example, if a rating table is to be amended, the state and territory reference numbers are entered with both the new rates and the rates to be replaced.
- The computer matches the reference numbers and the old rates as entered with those held on the file. If a match is obtained, the new data is updated to the file.
- If a match is not obtained, the item is reported for investigation.

This technique ensures that the correct rate table is updated. It controls the accuracy of the reference field entered, but not the new information being put on the file. In the example just given, it cannot ensure that the new rates are accurate, only that the correct items received new rates.

For prior data matching to be effective as a control technique, the following user controls and programmed procedures should be present:

- The method used in the program to match the prior data must be logically sound. In general, the more prior fields that are matched, the stronger the control. The possibility of a chance match of an incorrect record with identical prior data is reduced as more fields are matched.
- There should be adequate manual procedures to follow up mismatched items.

Prior data matching is illustrated in Exhibit 8-3.

Prerecorded Input Errors frequently arise during the initial recording of transactions. These errors can be reduced by preprinting certain information fields on blank document forms. Of course, there should be strict control over the accuracy of the initial design of prerecorded data. Optical character recognition, mark sensitive, or

Exhibit 8-3
Prior Data Matching

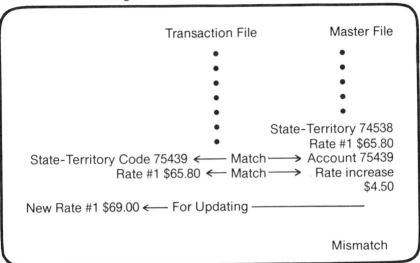

magnetic ink character forms are commonly used. Because they are machine-readable, they avoid the errors that occur in keying.

When the above types of prerecorded input are used, the following conditions must be met for control over both initial recording and conversion to machine-readable form to be adequate:

- The edit software used must be appropriate to identify, report, and reject incorrect input forms.
- User procedures must include investigation, correction, and reentry of rejected data. If documents are damaged, which precludes use of the original input technique, there must be alternative procedures to ensure the accuracy of input.

Examples of prerecorded information include:

- Preprinted policy numbers used in a computer sequence check.
- Magnetically encoded credit cards used to identify customers at bank terminals or retail point of sale terminals.
- Preprinted premium notices, which are sent to policyholders with a request that they be returned with the payments. If an amount different from the preprinted amount is paid, the payment requires special handling.

The premium notice sent to policyholders is a familiar example of what is often called a "turnaround document." It is a document produced by the computer for subsequent entry to its own or a related system.

Turnaround documents can also be used to amend master file data. When the master file data is first set up, the complete contents of the record are printed, and the output document is filed. When an amendment is necessary, the data to be changed is crossed out, and the new values are entered.

The changed fields are keyed for entry to the computer, and the new output document is checked one-for-one with the input and filed for subsequent use. The program can also indicate on the report which data was changed, thus increasing the effectiveness of the one-for-one check.

Key Verification Key verification is a common technique for controlling the conversion of information from input documents into machine-readable form. It is normally used for key entry, and involves a repetition of the keying-in process by a different individual to check the results with what was originally keyed. The technique is usually of limited use, however, in the absence of the other techniques discussed above.

Control Techniques for Maintenance

In order to ensure the integrity of data in the system, adequate maintenance controls are needed. They require the application of the relevant control techniques, described earlier, to both master file data and transaction data. Separate control techniques may be required to satisfy the two aspects of maintenance—correctness and currency.

Controls over Reference Data The accurate updating of reference data means ensuring that correct accounts are updated, and table files, dates, and indicators are accurately updated. Control techniques that may insure that reference data is updated accurately are one-for-one checking of detail reports and programmed edit checks.

In practice, reliance is likely to be placed on a combination of the following to ensure the accurate updating of reference data: the proper operation of the computer programs; the controls over accuracy of input; and other procedures (such as checking of policy endorsements by the agents who service the policies). Generally, programmed procedures are relied on to ensure that some or all of the significant data fields are accurately updated.

Controls over Master File Generations Master files are processed according to generations. The previous master file is run with the input transactions to create a new master file. In subsequent runs, the new master file will become the old master file, and so on. If the most recent master file is not used, all transactions processed since the last correctly updated master file will be lost.

When a control account technique is used at input, no additional control is necessary to ensure that updating has been performed on the correct generation of the master file. The control account technique records in a control account all types of transactions that should eventually reach the master file; the cumulative totals of these transactions are carried forward from period to period. At intervals, the balance of the control account is compared to the accumulated individual balances on the master file to see if they are the same. If the wrong generation of the master file has been used for an update, the control account and master file balance will disagree.

Detailed Checking of Data on File   Controls for the maintenance of master file data can also be exercised by regularly checking data on the file against authorized source documentation. It is usual to check only a portion of the file at a time, so that the whole file is regularly checked on a cyclical basis. This technique is often referred to as "cyclical checking." The frequency of checking depends largely on the importance of the data and the existence and strength of other controls (such as the checking of agents' accounts).

The selection of portions of files for cyclical checking should be unannounced or at random. Otherwise, the opportunity would exist to manipulate data just prior to or just after the check.

Controls over Computer-Generated Data

A computer can be programmed to initiate data. Data may be generated when the processing of a transaction may create the condition that triggers the generation of data. For example, adding a new vehicle to an automobile insurance policy causes a new endorsement and premium notice to be produced. In this instance, the conditions that cause the new data to be generated are normally identified by comparison with master file data.

As an alternative, a signal to initiate transactions may be entered. For example, the entry of a certain date initiates the production of premium notices for all policies with expiration dates within a certain number of days of that date. Subsequently, if no payment is received by the expiration date, a lapse notice will be generated; if payment is still not received within the grace period, a cancellation will result.

Generated data requires controls over completeness and accuracy. These controls should cover the generation process and, sometimes, the updating of the data produced. If data is to be produced by the computer completely and accurately, the following user controls and progammed procedures are necessary:

- The data (such as dates) that triggers the generation of other data must be entered completely and accurately.
- The steps carried out by the program in generating the data must be logically sound.
- The master file data that is referred to or used as the basis for generating the new data must be reliable. This involves all the controls over the amendment and maintenance of master file data, because such data may not be manually checked on the documents as it is in noncomputerized systems.
- The generated data should be controlled for accuracy, either by a manual review (such as a scrutiny of CMRs) or by programmed procedures, such as reporting all claims over a certain dollar amount so that they can be investigated.

After the data has been produced by the computer, it may need to be subjected to updating controls. These are similar to the controls already outlined for entered data and are based on the control totals accumulated while the data is being generated. In practice, updating often takes place prior to or at the time of production of the data.

Control of Rejections

Rejections may arise at the update stage as well as at input. Rejections at the update stage usually occur because a transaction cannot find a matching master file record.

Rejections at the update stage are much less common in online systems, because the system can match the transaction against a master file record on input and establish that a matching record exists.

The procedures and techniques required to control rejections arising at the update stage are similar to those required for rejections produced at the data entry stage.

Data entered for processing in a computer system often contains incorrect items. Particularly in batch processing, it is not possible or practical to investigate and adjust each incorrect item as it occurs during processing. It is usually faster to have the computer continue processing the batches on hand as it handles input errors. This is often done in one of two ways:

1. The computer will reject the items or particular batch from further processing, with no record other than a report of the rejections.

2. The computer will reject the items or particular batch from further processing, but maintain error suspense files of items awaiting correction. It will then produce cumulative reports of all uncleared items on the error files.

Detailed procedures are required to ensure that rejection reports and items held on error files are promptly investigated and rejections corrected and resubmitted, and that previously established control totals are adjusted in relation to the rejected data.

The timely correction of rejections is important in realtime systems where input data is matched with master files for validity. If rejections are left uncorrected, the master files will not be up-to-date when the validity of subsequent input is checked. This is of particular significance for financial transactions such as the application of cash, which can impact the magnitude of accounts receivable and the status of a particular policy. The timeliness of correction procedures may also be important when data base organization is used, since several users may depend on common input and other users are not likely to be kept aware of outstanding rejections from a particular user's area.

Rejections in Online Systems   When an online system is used and computer matching is the input control technique, operators can correct rejections as they occur by amending the entered data on the terminal screen.

Specific procedures to deal with rejections are normally needed when a suspense file is not used to control rejections in computer sequence and matching techniques or when batch totals form the input control. Checking of detail reports, computer sequence checking, or computer matching techniques that use a suspense file of accumulated rejections are adequate controls over rejections because these techniques usually continue to identify items that are unprocessed, missing, or unmatched. This may not be the case when other techniques form the control, however, because the computer may not store and continue to report details of rejected items or batches.

Monitoring Rejection Procedures   How rejection procedures are monitored depends on whether the batch totals are checked manually or by computer. In manual checking of totals, there will be a register or batch control book. Rejections should be recorded when the control totals are adjusted. In computer checking of totals, there will be no predetermined record of the batch totals and no record of the adjustment. There is less visible evidence of the volume of rejections and a greater reliance on exercising and supervising the detailed procedures for dealing with rejections reported by the computer program.

Action Taken on Erroneous Data   Edit checks identify erroneous or suspect data. In batch systems, it is printed out on a report for
manual action. Data failing edit checks may be handled in any one, or a
combination, of the following ways:

- Data is rejected and dropped from subsequent processing. The
  data then requires correction and reentry.
- Data is rejected and held in suspense. The data then requires
  either an amendment to the suspense file for any errors or a
  manual override of the edit check if the transaction is correct.
- Data is not rejected but is identified, reported, and carried
  through processing in the normal way. In these circumstances,
  the report must be investigated; corrective action is necessary
  only if the transaction was in fact wrong. This method is not
  preferred. It is usually not good system design to identify
  problems and continue processing, unless the problems are
  minor. If there is a serious problem, another transaction has to
  be entered to back out the transaction in error before the
  correct transaction can be reentered.

In online systems, edit checks are usually applied as data is
entered. Erroneous data may be highlighted on the terminal screen to
allow the operator to take corrective action.

Many online systems permit the operator to override edit checks.
For example, an item may fail a reasonableness check. The operator,
after scrutinizing the data input and deciding that it is correct, can
override to process the data in the normal way. For control to be
adequate, operator overrides should be more selective. The operator
should be allowed to override only by using a password or supervisor's
key. In systems where the operator has the discretion to override edit
checks, it is important that a record of every override be maintained
and printed for subsequent approval. If no record of overrides is
provided, checks that can be overridden should not be relied on to
provide adequate control.

PROCESS DOCUMENTATION

Documentation is a necessary part of all systems. In systems
involving computers, it is extremely important to management, user
departments, the data processing department, and the auditor that the
systems be in conformity with well-defined written standards. Ideally,
documentation is initially developed during the programming, testing,
and implementation phase. Then it is reviewed and approved as part of

the systems acceptance function. Documentation should provide the following:

- An understanding of the objectives of the system, the concepts and methodologies employed, and the output of the system
- A source of information for all personnel responsible for maintaining and enhancing the system
- Information necessary for supervisory review
- A basis for training new personnel
- A source of information about the controls in the system
- Adequate user manuals and information needed to use the system
- Information needed by computer operators to run the system

Documentation provides a basis for gaining an accurate understanding of the computer processing phases of the system. It also serves as a source of information for the study and evaluation of controls.

Documentation should include all of the following:

Systems Documentation
- Systems narrative
- Flowcharts of:
  - Systems architecture
  - Organization of programs
  - Procedures and usage
- Input description (source documents, parameters, etc.)
- Output descriptions (printed reports, data files, turnaround documents)
- File descriptions
- Data capture instructions
- Descriptions of controls (batch, manual, and computer) embodied in the report distribution and data file retention requirements
- Copies of written change requests showing authorization for each change, the programs and files involved in the modification or enhancement, approvals of the test results, and the effective date of implementation of the change

Program Documentation

- Detailed program narratives
- Decision tables and flowcharts
- Detailed file formats and record layouts
- Data element descriptions
- Report layouts

- Operation flowcharts showing input and output of the programs
- A listing of program processing parameters
- Source program compilation listings
- Record of changes, their authorizations, and effective dates

Operations Documentation

- Operations flowchart
- Operating instructions, including:
  - Frequency, operating system requirements, job set-up instructions, sequence of input files, listing of program messages and responses, program halts and remedial action, restart and recovery procedures
  - Estimated normal and maximum running times per program
  - Emergency procedures

User Documentation

- Description of the system
- Graphic representations of the systems structure and of the sequence of activities involving both the system and manual operations
- Description of the source documents for the system and procedures for their preparation
- Description of the output of the system and the procedures governing its use, security, review, disposition, and retention
- Control procedures, including cutoff requirements, controls to be established and maintained, reconciliation procedures, error correction, and resubmission
- Titles of individuals responsible for all control functions

SUMMARY

Just as computer technology has multiplied information processing capacity, it has also multiplied the potential for errors. To protect the integrity of its data, an insurance information system must incorporate appropriate controls. These controls include both application controls and general controls.

Application controls can be categorized by their objectives. Completeness of input insures that all transactions are entered once and only once. Accuracy of input means entering correct data for each transaction. A third control objective is similar completeness and accuracy of all updates. Still another control objective is to ensure the validity and proper authorization of all data. Maintenance and continuity controls ensure that data is kept current and not changed in any unintended manner. Controls over calculating, summarizing, and categorizing procedures prevent the generation of erroneous data by operations programmed in to the system.

Techniques to control completeness of input include computer sequence checks, computer matching, batch control totals, and one-for-one checking. These techniques may also be used to control completeness of update. In addition, specific updating controls include manual reconciliation of accepted totals, establishment of totals of accepted items, reliance on controls over a previous application, online sequence controls, and duplicate processing memos. Completeness control techniques may also be used to control accuracy of input, which may also be controlled by programmed edit checks, prerecorded input, and key verification. Separate techniques for maintenance controls may involve controls over reference data, controls over master file generations, and detailed checking of data on file. Controls over generated data depend on the same techniques that ensure completeness and accuracy of input and updates, as well as on a review of the program logic that generates the data. Specific procedures are also needed to control rejections so that rejected transactions do not escape the system.

The final assurance of data integrity comes from process documentation. Documentation facilitates an understanding of the processing phases of the system and assists in the evaluation of controls.

In addition to the application controls discussed in this chapter, the system should also incorporate general controls. The next chapter explains the appropriate general controls for an insurance information system.

CHAPTER 9

System Controls

INTRODUCTION

This chapter continues the discussion of controls in EDP systems. Internal control and its components — administrative controls, the conditions of control, and accounting controls — are defined. Then categories of general, or integrity, controls are described. These are the controls over the EDP environment and are necessary in a computerized system to ensure that the programmed procedures carried out by the computer are performed properly. The effects of weaknesses in general controls are explored, and various forms of computer abuse, such as fraud, vandalism, and human error are described. The chapter continues with an illustration of converting a manual system to a computerized one, examines the control concerns involved, and then closes with a discussion of types of control reviews.

THE NATURE OF INTERNAL CONTROL

Internal control refers to all the methods, policies, and procedures adopted within an organization to ensure the safeguarding of assets, the accuracy and reliability of financial records, the promotion of administrative efficiency, and adherence to management standards.

Internal control deals with the processes and practices by which management attempts to ensure that approved and appropriate decisions are made and activities are carried out. These decisions and activities may be governed by external forces: regulatory requirements, professional ethics, and accounting practices. Internal factors

347

also influence how controls may be implemented to ensure management that the business operates as expected.

In addition, internal control strives to prevent officers, employees, and outsiders from engaging in prohibited and inappropriate activities. In this way, internal control provides the mechanism for preventing chaos, crisis management, and other abnormal events that interfere with the smooth operation of an organization. As with all standardized procedures, controls must be regularly reviewed and reaffirmed to be effective.

Controls have not always been widely implemented in the data processing community. Although they may be standard for the rest of the departments, the EDP department may not be controlled in the same way as the rest of the organization; it has its own controls. The controls that exist within the data processing department are often specifically tailored to that department. The more mature the EDP department is within a business environment, the more likely it is to have a standard structure of controls.

Uncontrolled computer processing can have serious financial repercussions for any organization. It can also have a negative effect on employees when the staff has to work long hours to recreate data that is destroyed due to lack of control. For example, consider the effects of the loss of a week's worth of premium transactions. All of the source documents would have to be requested and reentered into the system. While many organizations experience occasional difficulties created by computer systems, an out-of-control system can actually ruin a business that depends on its output.

Administrative Controls

Administrative, or operational, control has a primary operating purpose that may be different from that of internal accounting control. It is usually exercised by the operating management over all departments, including management control over the financial and accounting departments. Administrative controls are the procedures necessary to ensure that an organization's resources are used effectively and efficiently to keep it functioning according to management's intentions.

As a result, administrative controls may be separate from internal accounting controls. For example, quality control may focus on the policy service function to make sure that all policyholder inquiries are properly handled and that customers are satisfied. This is an administrative control procedure that has little to do with safeguarding assets or maintaining reliable financial records, except indirectly.

In other situations, administrative controls and internal accounting controls are not mutually exclusive. Procedures and records used to ensure that administrative controls are operating effectively can simultaneously ensure that internal accounting controls are adequate. For example, a failure to calculate loss reserves correctly could result in errors in investment strategy, underwriting policies, and general financial forecasts. This situation involves both kinds of control. Management should make sure that any accounting implications of such administrative control weaknesses are evaluated by the auditors; the evaluation should be acted on appropriately by management.

Auditors frequently recommend that management include administrative controls in the review of internal controls, even though an evaluation of administrative controls may not be required by applicable professional auditing standards.

Administrative controls are concerned with management's overall business perspective: increasing efficiency, revenues, and the effectiveness of the managerial decision-making process. These concerns include the following:

- The reliability of management information, which is broader than financial information.
- The timeliness of management information.
- The detection and correction of errors and exceptions on a timely basis.
- The efficiency of administration in general, and of control procedures in particular.
- The nature of information available to management.
- The response of operating units and their performance in carrying out management's intentions.
- The appropriateness of major decisions made by management or their delegates.

Requirements for establishing effective and efficient administrative or operational procedures usually involve a high level of technical skill, including awareness, knowledge of alternative operating methods, and sound business sense.

Administrative controls are designed to ensure that an organization's information structure functions in accordance with management's intentions. They ensure the timeliness of information, the efficiency of control procedures, and the quality of processing in general. They also relate to the effectiveness of management decisions. The reliability of the information on which management decisions are based and the procedures for implementing those decisions are usually linked. During a review of administrative controls, the appropriateness of management's decisions in relation to the objectives of the organization might also be considered.

Efficiency Efficiency refers to the costs incurred in processing and controlling the systems within an organization. A review of administrative controls typically includes the efficiency of internal accounting control procedures, as well as consideration of efficiencies in all parts of the system. Knowledge of the most cost-efficient techniques is particularly valuable when designing or modifying systems. In some case, more effective control procedures are also less costly. An example is replacing time-consuming, detailed clerical checks with accurate EDP reporting procedures, which are usually more precise and less expensive to operate.

Timeliness Organizations operate more effectively when essential information is up-to-date. Possible ways to reduce the age of the information are to shorten the period involved, increase the frequency of the reports, or switch from batch processing to an on-line realtime system that includes immediate update capabilities.

The time taken to detect errors, exceptions, and control failures is significant. Timely detection of errors has the following advantages:

- Further errors, or repetition of the same mistakes, may be prevented by changing the procedures that allowed the errors to take place.
- Investigating the cause of an error is usually easier when it is a recent occurrence.
- Reversing the effect of an error is simpler if it has not yet affected other information in the system.
- If the error is caught early in the transaction processing cycle, only the early stages will have to be repeated, avoiding duplicate processing through the later stages of the cycle.

Management Information Obviously, management needs more than financial information, as evidenced by the fact that many accounting information systems are only a part of the overall management information system. Much management information is derived from processing similar to that occurring in a financial information system. A major difference is the required precision of the results. Information that is accurate to within 5 percent may be sufficient for many management purposes and may also be acceptable when precise information is too expensive or would take too much time to prepare.

Other features of management information systems include:

- The need for up-to-date information.
- The greater need for specialized inquiry and reports, as contrasted with the routine reports produced by financial information systems.

- The need to produce summary reports, exception reports, or graphic representations in a form that management can use easily.
- The possible unfamiliarity of senior management with the capabilities of the management information system. This is particularly true of a technologically advanced EDP system. Management may not realize, and therefore not request, the detailed information available that would be of greatest assistance.

Control techniques for nonfinancial transactions and data are similar to those used in financial systems. As in those systems, management information system controls are concerned with completeness, accuracy, authorization, continuity, and maintenance of data. In addition, controls are needed over the efficiency of processing and the timeliness, quality, and usefulness of management information.

Quality of Information   A review of administrative controls may suggest improvements to the information received by management. Those suggestions may be particularly valuable when senior management is not conversant with details or capacities of the management information system. Such suggestions might include adding information to a report that would make it more useful; resequencing a report so that the most significant items appear at the front; restructuring reports for clarity and ease of use; producing better summaries and subtotals so that management can review information at an overview level; increasing the use of exception reports, thereby decreasing the cost of producing reports and concentrating management's attention on those items that require action; and producing additional reports for management, using data that already exists within the system.

Management Decisions   Many control procedures are designed to ensure compliance with management's expressed or implied intentions, which are sometimes incorporated into company policy or standards. If these required procedures are not followed, an administrative control deficiency results. Senior management also delegates authority to other individuals. How those individuals exercise the authority is also an aspect of operational controls.

Conditions of Control

Before control is possible, there must be:

- some degree of systemization,

- documentation of that system, including transactions and their disposition,
- competent, honest people to operate the system, and
- sufficient resources to maintain the system.

These conditions are necessary for the implementation and functioning of appropriate controls.

Systemization An organized plan is fundamental to the control of any operation. The more explicit the definition of an operation, the easier it is to perform and control. At best, those involved in an operational area should know the procedures to follow in all circumstances. Since this is unlikely, individuals should know the specifications for their own jobs. An example is a data entry operator who knows how to handle all types of transactions—unauthorized, incomplete, or erroneous—as well as normal transactions.

If a system has not been clearly defined, control is almost impossible. There is also a greater chance that situations will get out of control when there is no specific definition of what "under control" is. Thus, the system itself becomes the most fundamental control. The more clear-cut and understandable it is, the more effective the other controls are likely to be.

Documentation Documentation is inherent in and implicit to a system. It is considered a separate condition of control because it is essential to creating adequate controls. Without a full, accurate description of the details in a transaction, it is not possible to control that transaction. Documentation enhances communication between departments and permits transactions to be properly analyzed, accounted for, and controlled.

Documentation may serve several purposes simultaneously. In some cases, it is required solely for the purpose of control. For example, the performance of specific tasks is usually documented by the initials or other identification of the person who did them, such as the underwriter's approval of a new application. This affixes personal responsibility to those tasks and permits their supervision. It also serves as a control to check on who did what if errors are subsequently detected.

Documentation primarily intended for control purposes can contribute to other functions. For example, the sequential numbering of documents is employed to make sure that all authorized transactions are fully processed. That also serves to identify and locate documents when needed for other purposes, such as a claim file charge-out form.

Competence and Integrity Systems and control procedures have no value unless people carry them out consistently and conscientiously. Each employee must have a level of competence adequate to the task and enough personal integrity to take responsibility for doing it as well as possible. The competence and integrity of the individuals found in an organization can be influenced by many factors. The most important of these are the organization's reputation and geographic location (availability of experienced personnel); personnel selection, retention, and training policies; the difficulty of the work; the amount and quality of supervision; and the degree of systemization. After employment, competence is fairly easy to judge; integrity may be harder to assess. The presence of effective disciplinary controls, such as supervision, normally provides the needed assurance that employees are competent, that their integrity meets organizational standards, and that conditions of control are adequate. The system and its supervision must be modified as appropriate to the staff's level of competence while maintaining the established level of controls required to keep the organization functional.

Resources Obviously, a system cannot function properly, nor be adequately controlled, without sufficient resources to ensure its viability.

Internal Accounting Controls

Internal accounting control is the organizational plan, procedures, and methods of keeping records that ensure the reliability of financial data and records. It also encompasses the safeguarding of assets through an awareness of what they are, where they are located, and how they are controlled.

Internal accounting controls are designed to provide reasonable assurance that:

- Transactions are executed in accordance with management's general or specific authorization.
- Transactions are recorded as necessary to:
  - Permit the preparation of financial statements in conformity with generally accepted regulatory or statutory accounting principles.
  - Maintain accountability for assets.
- Access to assets is permitted only as authorized by management.
- Recorded assets are compared with existing assets at reasonable intervals, and appropriate action is taken with respect to any discrepancies (such as bond counts or bank reconciliations for cash).

Internal accounting controls consist of basic controls and disciplines over basic controls. *Basic controls* are necessary to maintain the accuracy of the accounting records. *Disciplines over basic controls* ensure the continued and proper operation of basic controls in safeguarding the assets.

The accounting or financial department usually is responsible for installing and maintaining internal accounting controls. Data processing is responsible for conforming to control requirements, and the internal audit function checks that the controls are being exercised. Coordination among various departments is also necessary for an efficient system.

Factors affecting the internal accounting control system can be classified on three levels:

1. The conditions under which control can take place (discussed earlier).
2. The basic controls performed directly on transactions and assets, either individually or in groups.
3. Disciplinary controls that serve to enforce, supervise, and maintain discipline over the operations and their results.

Under different conditions, one control activity may be more important than another. As a general rule, the conditions permitting control and the disciplines over them are as important as the specific control operations themselves. The latter are unlikely to function well without the former.

Basic Internal Accounting Controls Basic controls are designed to ensure that transactions are recorded completely and accurately and that assets are safeguarded. For purposes of internal accounting control, the control system should include steps to ensure that:

- All transactions are initiated, executed, and recorded once and only once.
- Data for a transaction is recorded and transcribed accurately. (Accurate data is essential to make appropriate management decisions.)
- Transactions and their data are executed and recorded in accordance with management's intentions.
- Recorded information (such as rating tables or reserve factors) remains correct and up-to-date.

To achieve that objective, the system should prevent or detect, on a timely basis, errors in execution or recording. Internal accounting control aims at preventing or discouraging unauthorized transactions and errors, but complete prevention is impossible. Rather, controls attempt to provide a way to detect both types of errors, if and when they occur.

Basic controls are just as important in a computerized environment as in a noncomputerized system. They may be even more important when some of the control steps are programmed to take place within the computer. This programming of controls relating to the operation of the computer is embedded in the system software and its operating system, which tells the computer what to do and when to do it. The system software controls the computer and provides the information needed to process application programs, independent of those programs. The programmed control steps in application programs are referred to as programmed procedures.

When EDP systems are properly controlled, they are consistent, they can process information rapidly, and they can generate new, complex reports not easily available otherwise. Many functions for processing transactions can be programmed into the EDP system in advance of the transactions themselves.

There are several areas of concern to management including the following: A complex EDP system cannot be re-created manually, since most information either is not available to users or is too voluminous to handle well. Many computer records can be read only by the computer (usually leaving no visible trace of changes). Most EDP systems allow multiple access, an advantage to users, but a potential control trouble spot. As the use of telecommunications increases, the need for security over system access increases. There tends to be less manual scrutiny in an EDP system environment than in the manual environment. As a result, unusual items not foreseen in systems design may be treated incorrectly and may even go undetected.

When data records and processing are centralized in one computer, disaster planning and adequate segregation of data and duties are imperative. The effects of disasters may be very great (although the chances of disaster may be no greater than they are for manual systems).

Disciplines over Basic Controls   Disciplines over basic controls monitor and enforce basic control tasks. A system without disciplinary controls is conceivable, but it would be error-prone at best. The presence of disciplines gives an organization reasonable assurance that the basic data processing and accounting control operations are functioning as designed. They allow procedures to continue to operate efficiently on a day-to-day basis and help ensure that any errors that do occur are detected on a timely basis.

The value of disciplinary controls has been implicitly recognized for many years. However, they deserve much more explicit consideration than they have received. As with basic controls, disciplinary controls are necessary in order for control objectives to be met.

Three disciplines are essential features of an adequate system of control: (1) segregation of duties, (2) custodial arrangements, and (3) supervision. Segregation of duties allows the work of one person to check the work of another, and prevents access to data and programs not specifically required to do a particular job. Custodial controls are necessary to prevent unauthorized activity of all sorts—from loss or misuse of assets to theft or destruction of computer-generated data or media on which it is stored. Supervising access to the system and those who operate it helps ensure its accuracy and reliability of financial and other data. Supervisory controls may be considered the most important group of controls since they permit the detection and correction of errors caused by weaknesses in other controls. Supervisory controls are often part of a system's programmed procedures.

Segregation of Duties. The separation of one activity from another serves several purposes. If two parts of a single transaction are handled by different people, each serves as a check on the other. For example, one bookkeeper can process a day's cash receipts for premiums received through the mail while another posts those receipts to the computerized accounts receivable records. Checking the total of the postings to the total receipts gives assurance that each operation was accurately performed. Aside from other control objectives, it is usually more efficient to specialize tasks and people, whenever the volume of activity is sufficient. For example, it is usually better to train one person to handle cash (for example, premiums collected) exclusively, and another to keep the related records. When evaluating the costs and benefits of segregating duties, management should recognize that the benefits often include operating efficiencies.

On the other hand, the control features of segregation of duties may be so important that this disciplinary control should be adopted when it actually creates administrative inefficiencies. In fact, it is often worthwhile even if it results in inefficiencies; an analysis of the potential risk of mistakes and even possible theft may justify the segregation of duties even when it is inefficient. For example, the volume of transactions and the dollar amounts passing through a premium processing system justify having one person obtain the totals for accounting purposes and another post the transactions.

Segregation of duties can also serve as a deterrent to fraud or concealment of gross incompetence since one person would need another's cooperation. Separation of responsibility for the physical security of assets and related record keeping is in itself a significant custodial control. An official who signs checks cannot hide unauthorized claims by making false entries in the loss records without access to the computer that holds them. (Only the authorized bookkeeper should have access to the records.) Custodial control is further enhanced if someone else is responsible for periodically comparing the cash on hand and in the bank with the cash records. After making this comparison, appropriate action should be taken if there are any differences.

Since many of these tasks can be performed by the computer, the system should be designed to ensure that a meaningful and proper segregation of duties is possible.

Custodial Arrangements. An internal accounting control system should deal with (1) the separation of responsibilities for the physical security of assets and data, and the related record keeping, and (2) physical arrangements that prevent unauthorized access to assets, data, and accounting records.

Not all physical safeguards are related to accounting controls. If the absence of a custodial control cannot cause accounting errors, the control is administrative rather than accounting in nature. For example, management may consciously risk some degree of pilferage of computer supplies in preference to installing supply room procedures. As long as any losses are accounted for accurately, the books and financial statements can accurately reflect what has taken place.

To prevent all types of unauthorized transactions, ranging from theft to unsanctioned activity that is inconsistent with the system, it is necessary to restrict access to all items that can be used to initiate or process transactions. Such arrangements are most commonly thought of in connection with the physical security of negotiable assets, such as cash, securities, inventory, and other items that are easily convertible to cash or personal use. The need for protective measures applies equally to access to data, computer files, books and records, and the means of altering them—unused forms, unissued checks, check signature plates, files, computer tapes, computer programs, ledgers—in short, everything important to the process.

In its most basic form, physical security consists of such things as a safe, a vault, or a locked door. Such physical safeguards are useless without a discipline that prevents unauthorized people from coming and going at will. For example, computer room sign-in procedures may not be enforced because the person entering is known to the operations staff, but that person may not be authorized to enter. This discipline can be automated to some degree. Computers can be programmed to reject commands or transaction data unless the correct password is used or other specific test for authorization is met. Physical security measures also protect assets and records from physical harm such as accidental destruction, deterioriation, or the results of carelessness.

A variety of physical access control systems are used to regulate an individual's movement within a complex or structure, including mechanical, electronic, electro-mechanical, digital, and computerized methods. In some instances, security requirements demand concurrent use of several methods for restricting access.

Supervision. The third essential discipline—supervision—can be seen as the glue that holds the entire system together. Effective supervision of personnel has numerous benefits. It will lead to modifications of the system when required, corrective action when the errors are detected, and follow-up action on weaknesses. A control cannot be regarded as effective in the absence of adequate supervision.

As well as systemization, supervision is essential to control operations and provides the means for correcting other weaknesses. Without adequate supervision, the best of systems and control operations may become erratic or undependable. Systems and disciplines may be bypassed, reconciliations may be omitted, errors and exceptions may be left unattended, and documents may be lost, mislaid, or not journalized or posted to the appropriate ledgers. Supervisory and administrative personnel may be drawn into the day-to-day work of processing data and correcting errors, and thus not be able to perform their supervisory control duties effectively.

Even in a system that was well-designed to begin with, problems in the accounts may signal a lack of supervisory controls. An inordinate number of errors and exceptions, backlogs and bottlenecks, and instances of prescribed procedures that are not followed should serve as a warning. When problems proliferate, or supervisors are bogged down with detail, or have inadequate knowledge of their responsibilities, management should be made aware that it cannot rely on other control procedures.

Many supervisory controls consist of specific, observable routines. They are designed to ensure supervisors that the specified conditions of control and the required basic control operations are maintained. To be effective, the performance of these administrative routines must be documented by such means as checklists, exception reports, initials evidencing review of controls, reconciliation procedures, vouchers and other authorizations for spending, log books for review routines, and written reports.

APPLICATION CONTROLS

To meet the control objectives of management, several kinds of control techniques are commonly found in computer-based systems, including basic controls exercised by users and the programmed procedures carried out by the computer. These controls relate to applications or programs that accomplish specific tasks such as an inforce/unearned calculation; for example, inforce and unearned premium calculations are usually run monthly, the inputs being the current month's premiums written file. Controls over each such application should take into account the entire sequence of manual and computer processing. Examples of questions that relate to application controls are given under the headings discussed in Chapter 8:

- Completeness of input—have all the claims been processed?
- Accuracy of input—are the effective and expiration dates correct?
- Completeness of update—was the last endorsement included in the inforce calculation?
- Accuracy of update—what is the new inforce amount?
- Validity of data processed—who authorized the additional coverage?
- Maintenance of data on files—are these files the most current, updated files?
- Calculating, summarizing, and categorizing procedures—are these generated totals calculated accurately?
- Computer-generated data—does the system use turnaround documents for renewals?
- File creation and conversion—are they adequately controlled?

Application controls are usually defined by the task they accomplish. They consist of procedures applied by EDP users both before and after data is processed and procedures performed by computer application programs. In this context, users are defined as those who use the computer but are not in systems development, systems maintenance, or computer operations.

Some application controls in computer systems are unrelated to computer processing itself. Examples include checking the mail for applications, endorsements, cancellations, or payments, and ensuring that all transactions are initially recorded. Other application controls consist of clerical procedures that check the results of computerized procedures. An example is checking the extensions and additions of invoices produced by the computer. The objectives of these manual procedures can be met only if the related computer processing is appropriate. For example, investigation of items reported by the computer as missing or exceptional will be effective only if all missing or exceptional items are reported. Still other application controls involve examining and acting on computer-produced reports and thus rely on programmed procedures.

GENERAL CONTROLS

General, or integrity, controls are procedures within the data processing department that ensure the effective operation of programmed procedures. They include controls over the design, implementation, security, and use of computer programs and files, and authorized amendments to those programs and files.

General controls normally pertain to all applications. As with application controls, they consist of basic controls and disciplines over basic controls. Their effective operation may, in some cases, depend on computer programmed procedures, such as software generation of a system log that can be used to review access to data by individuals.

General controls can be divided into the following five major areas:

1. *Implementation controls*—designed to ensure that programmed procedures are suitable and that they are effectively implemented in the computer programs. They apply both to new systems and to subsequent changes in existing systems.
2. *Program security controls*—designed to ensure that unauthorized changes cannot be made to programmed procedures.
3. *Computer operations controls*—designed to ensure that programmed procedures are consistently applied during all processing of data.
4. *Data file security controls*—designed to ensure that unauthorized changes cannot be made to data files.
5. *System software controls*—designed to ensure that suitable system software is effectively implemented and protected against unauthorized changes.

The first three areas relate to controls over the programmed procedures; the fourth area, data file security, relates to the maintenance of data; and the fifth area, system software controls, can relate to either programmed procedures or data files. Since the system software controls the computer, many general control procedures rely on information that is supplied by the system software. The relationship between general controls and system software is similar to the relationship between user controls and programmed procedures.

One important factor influencing the nature of general controls is the structure of the EDP department. Department organization depends largely on the extent of computer processing, the number of people in the department, and the control techniques used. The larger the department, the greater the opportunity to establish a satisfactory system of general controls. The software features available in a large facility can be employed and provide adequate disciplines over the basic controls. These disciplines are easier to establish and enforce when there is a larger staff, since an appropriate division of duties can be maintained.

Implementation Controls

Implementation controls are designed to ensure that the proposed programmed procedures are both suitable and effectively implemented. These controls apply to both new systems and subsequent changes to existing systems.

Implementation Controls in System Development The timetable for new system implementation should be monitored to ensure that the implementation is proceeding as planned. An implementation project team or steering committee is often established to accomplish this. Including relevant user personnel on the committee ensures user involvement at appropriate stages of development.

The procedures concerned with the development of new systems are discussed under the following headings:

- System Design and Program Preparation
- Program and System Testing
- Cataloging

System Design and Program Preparation. System design and program preparation should ensure that programmed procedures are appropriately designed and written into the programs. Effective design requires thorough preparation of systems specifications. The detailed systems descriptions should be reviewed and approved by both the user and computer departments; detailed programming should follow.

If a new claims processing system is to be developed, the accounting supervisor, claims manager, and EDP official should all participate and have input in the design of the system. One of the biggest problems in systems development is the lack of user involvement at the early stages. Making required modifications to an existing system is more complex and much more expensive than during the early stages of systems development.

Also of major importance is the quality of system description if it subsequently becomes necessary to make program changes. It is difficult to make effective changes without a reliable, detailed record of the original system.

Program and System Testing. Program and system testing is normally carried out in three distinct stages: (1) program testing, (2) systems testing, and (3) parallel running.

Program testing consists of checking the logic of individual programs; desk checking and test data are the principal methods used. *Desk checking* is analyzing the logical paths in the program to confirm that the program code meets the program specifications. Whenever practical, desk checking should be carried out by a programmer other than the one who designed and wrote the coding.

Desk checking is often used in conjunction with test data. Test data is fictitious data prepared according to the system specifications for entry into the system. It should be designed to cover all possible processing and/or error conditions, with formal procedures designed to identify and correct errors discovered during testing. The results of running test data should be documented and retained as evidence that the tests were performed; in addition, the same data can be used to test future system changes.

System testing is checking that the logic of various individual programs is consistent and links together to form a complete system that meets the detailed systems specifications. Test data is the principal technique used. The test results should be carefully scrutinized, and test data rerun and redesigned if necessary, until all logical failures in the program are corrected. In addition to common situations that the system is designed to handle, the effect of unusual conditions on the system should be tested. Whenever possible, system testing should be performed and checked by people other than those responsible for detailed programming. Tests should also be made to ascertain the impact of changes to programs or new programs on the system as a whole.

Parallel running consists of operating the complete new system at the same time (or in parallel) with the existing system. The results obtained from the dual processing can be checked to identify and investigate any differences. Parallel, or pilot, running tests the complete system in operation, including all user procedures. Pilot running is done using a particular unit or department's data. Unlike system testing, the purpose of parallel or pilot running is to test the system's ability to cope with real (not test) data and with actual volumes, rather than individual transactions. The new system should be accepted by the relevant user departments, and the existing system be replaced, only after the full processing cycle has been successfully run, as far as practical, on the new system. In addition, recovery procedures should be tested and documented prior to cataloging. The results of testing should be reviewed by people other than those responsible for the detailed programming, whenever possible.

Cataloging. Cataloging is the set of procedures necessary to move tested, authorized programs into operation. It includes both manual and programmed procedures. Important manual procedures ensure that testing and documentation have been satisfactorily completed before the programs go into production, and that the manual procedures for the new or changed system are in place in the user and the computer departments, including written operating and user instructions, which should be reviewed and approved by responsible officials as a part of the final acceptance procedures. There should be a formal manual procedure to transfer new or changed programs, at an appropriate cut-off point, from a test to a production status. This generally includes instructing staff in new procedures.

Software procedures related to cataloging include converting the source programs into executable form. When programs are held on-line, transferring the accepted programs from a test status on the program library file to a production or operational status is often a procedure performed by software.

Reports produced by the software during cataloging will include listings of programs transferred from the test to the production library. These listings should be checked by a responsible official to ensure that the correct versions have moved into production. Listings of the source versions of the new production programs—or programs as written in high-level computer language by programmers—should also be checked by a responsible official to ensure that no unauthorized changes have been made after the catalog was approved, and that the source program was properly converted into executable form. The conversion is performed in the computer by a compiler (or, less often, an interpreter) that first checks the program language to determine that its syntax is correct, and then translates it into machine code. The resulting object modules are linked by a linkeditor to produce executable programs.

Program Changes Making a change to a program usually requires a significant amount of work. (A common change is going from a monthly pro-rata calculation to a daily calculation for unearned premiums.) The controls required for the development of authorized program changes are similar to those for new systems. The change request must be defined properly to form an adequate basis for decisions about its acceptance and design. The changed program must then be tested and properly approved before implementation.

An important practical consideration when making program changes is to ensure that all valid requests for changes are accounted for and promptly acted on. This is necessary since other controls may not identify an ongoing deficiency that the change was designed to eliminate. All such system and program changes should be supported by appropriate written authorization.

Occasionally, production programs may be amended without adhering to standard procedures. This might happen, for example, in an emergency when a processing deadline has to be met or at night or on weekends when the staff is minimal. To control such cases, these amendments must be subjected to the normal authorization, testing, and implementation procedures on an after-the-fact basis.

Program Security Controls

Program security controls ensure that unauthorized changes cannot be made to the production programs that process data. Program security is of special concern when an unauthorized change in a progam could benefit the person making the change (for example, a change made in program processing payments for claims or policy loans that could result in unauthorized payments being made).

Program security controls are necessary for programs both while they are in use and while they are held off-line. Programs in use can be accessed through the system, either by operators processing jobs or through terminals. Off-line programs are held away from the computer, in a library, and must be retrieved for use. A library is a self-contained area that holds programs and data files when not in use. In addition to the basic controls over program security, disciplinary controls should be installed to further reduce the possibility of unauthorized changes to production programs.

Programs in Use The principal methods of controlling programs in use are the following:

- Comparing a comprehensive computer report of jobs processed with the authorized job schedules, to identify any unauthorized accesses of production programs. This report should be reviewed and approved by a responsible official, and any such access properly investigated.
- Authorizing jobs when they are set up, and prior to passing them to operators for processing. It is necessary to ensure that unauthorized changes cannot be made after jobs are set-up, and that unauthorized jobs are not added.
- Periodically comparing production programs with independently controlled copies. These copies, and the software executing the comparison, are normally held either in a permanent, supervised physical library or off-site at a remote location.
- Periodic running of test data by responsible officials.

Production programs that are online to terminals should be protected by security software so that only authorized personnel can access them.

Off-line Programs   When programs are held off-line on tape or disk they should be subject to physical library controls and securely held, preferably in a physical library, issued only on appropriate authority, and promptly returned. Aside from physical removal, programs are relatively safe since they must be mounted on a system to be changed. Back-up copies and program documentation should be protected to prevent unauthorized personnel from obtaining a detailed knowledge of the contents of the programs.

Disciplines over Program Security Controls   With sufficient technical skill and knowledge of their contents, operators may be able to make changes to production programs. Protection is normally provided by an appropriate segregation of duties. When duties are separated, operators cannot obtain a detailed knowledge of the programs and, on the other hand, people responsible for the development and maintenance of the programs cannot gain unsupervised access to production programs. It is important to maintain this segregation of duties at all times, even outside of normal working hours.

Computer Operations Controls

Computer operations controls ensure that the programmed procedures are consistently applied to both storage of data and processing of data. They include controls over physical assembly of the necessary material in the computer department and its subsequent processing. These controls are described under the following headings:

- Job Set-Up
- Operations Software and Computer Operating
- Disciplines Over Computer Operations Controls
- Back-Up and Recovery Procedures

Job Set-Up   The physical assembly of the material necessary for processing is referred to as job set-up. This may include any devices holding relevant programs and data, job control statements, run instructions, and the parameters. In advanced systems there is less need to do physical assembly since the programs are held online in the program library, data files are online, and software controls their use.

The normal way to ensure that valid job control statements and parameters are being used is to maintain approved written set-up instructions. In online systems, software can control much of this process. There is also a need to check that the statements and parameters actually used correspond with those instructions, reviewed and approved by a responsible official. The set-up instructions should cover all applications and system software, including processing flowcharts, information regarding peripherals and files, job control language requirements, and run parameters.

In many cases, the normal updating and maintenance controls (application controls) ensure that the correct data files are being used. However, specific controls over the use of the correct files are still necessary, particularly for files that contain tables referred to in processing (for example, lists of numbers when sequence checks are used).

There may be manual controls over the data files from the time they are issued from the physical library until job set-up, or system software may ensure that the correct files are loaded. When system software is used as a control technique, files held on disk or tape include information (such as the file name or the version number) needed for processing. When a file is loaded for processing, these details are checked by the system. Any operator override of these controls should be reviewed and approved.

Operations Software and Computer Operations Computer processing is organized and controlled by both manual and pro-grammed procedures. In advanced systems, many procedures are carried out by software, and manual functions are restricted to actions required or requested by the software. The principal control consider-ations are that the system software is reliable and that manual procedures do not (due to error or for other reasons) interfere with or affect normal processing.

Controls over manual procedures depend largely on the nature of the system software and the size of the installation. Normally they comprise a combination of procedures designed to both prevent and detect errors. The preventive procedures usually include providing operating instructions for system software, application procedures, restart and recovery procedures, procedures for labeling, disposition of input and output tapes, and—where practical—a suitable segregation of duties.

Disciplines over Computer Operations Controls Reviews of operator actions are usually based on computer-produced reports or, less frequently, manual reports. The system software usually records, on a file, details of all activity during processing. This file is called the system log and its details can be printed for review. Unusual activity such as hardware malfunction, reruns, abnormal endings, and the resulting operator actions can thus be investigated. However, the information recorded on these logs is voluminous and technical in nature, so that a full review is often impractical. Packaged audit software is available, or audit software can be created, that will analyze the entries, and report only the desired information to facilitate their investigation.

Back-up and Recovery Procedures Documented back-up procedures and arrangements should exist so that in the event of a computer failure, the recovery process for production programs, system software and data files does not introduce erroneous changes into the system. Principal techniques that may be used are:

- A security system to copy or store master files (such as loss masters, premium statistical files, year-end inforce-unearned files) and associated transactions so that it is possible to restore any files lost or damaged during a disruption.
- Similar procedures to ensure that copies of operating instructions, run instructions, and other essential documentation are available if the originals are lost.
- A facility for restarting at an intermediate stage of processing, applicable to programs terminated before their normal ending, to avoid the need to reprocess the whole run.
- Written instructions for the restoration of processing or transfer to other locations.

Data File Security Controls

Data file security controls ensure that unauthorized changes cannot be made to data files. These controls are often more important for master file data than for transaction data, because not all master file data elements of accounting significance are subject to regular reconciliation procedures. Any cyclical checking of data on files may not be performed often enough to allow unauthorized changes to be identified on a timely basis.

Data file security controls are also important from an operational standpoint. Operational considerations include protecting files from destruction or erasure, both accidental and intentional, and from theft.

Controls are required for data files both while they are in use—online—and while they are held off-line. Data files in use are files that can be accessed through the system by operators processing jobs, users at terminals, or other access methods. Files in use include tapes and disks that are loaded for a specific processing run but are otherwise stored off-line, as in batch systems, and tapes and disks that are permanently loaded and available for inquiry or updating, as in online and realtime systems. When off-line, data files should be held in a physical library, and their use controlled.

Preventing Unauthorized Access to Data   Traditionally, access to data was restricted by retaining confidential data and records in user departments under suitable physical security arrangements. Similar procedures developed as a result of the proliferation of computerized systems, when data became concentrated in the EDP department. There are growing concerns over security arrangements for computer operations, data files, programs, and updates now that data can be accessed online from outside of the EDP department, or even outside of the organization. Controls are needed to ensure that system use is restricted to authorized users and that access to data is restricted to authorized functions. This access is defined by the system software and security software in use in online systems.

Other controls to accomplish those objectives include physical security; software checks, such as passwords; terminals dedicated only to certain processing functions; automatic disconnect of dial-up terminals unused for a given time or after a specified number of unsuccessful password entries for attempted access; dial-back features, which redial the terminal after it calls in; and controls over the master terminal that controls other terminals and passwords.

Difficulties inherent in controlling data access have been complicated by the phenomenal growth of microcomputer use. Frequently connected to other computers in a network or with a modem, these can create new concerns. Controls and standards for these new users may not exist, since organizations are just becoming aware of the need to control and monitor microcomputer use. Other concerns are what data is gathered and how it is used, how the related recordkeeping may affect compliance with legislation, and controlling and protecting messaging systems.

Preventing Unauthorized Update   A particular threat is unauthorized updates to data on file. In batch systems, files are loaded for a specific processing run, so that the control may be limited to controlling the action of operators during a particular run. Files in online and realtime systems require permanent protection against access since they are available to users. Controls that help guard against unauthorized updating of files are discussed in the paragraphs that follow.

Access by Operators.   The control procedures designed to protect data files from unauthorized access by operators during processing are similar to those described for programs. These procedures, which can usually be carried out at the same time as those for programs, include review of data files accessed during processing, controls over computer operations, and the use of the correct data files.

Access Through Terminals. Data entered through terminals, as in online and realtime systems, must be protected. The entry of unauthorized information that will subsequently be updated on the data files may be possible when access controls are weak. Often attempts made to enter this unauthorized data come from people outside of the organization.

The entry of invalid data may be made to transaction data, often a complete transaction that adds to a balance on file, such as an agent's account, or alters the effect of a transaction already on file. For example, a credit note to match a policy on file would alter the status of the premium amount due. Invalid master file data might consist of a complete record, such as a fictitious policyholder, or a data element, such as a commission rate. The opportunity to alter data elements, or fields, is usually increased when files are online.

When data files are online to terminals, there should be an appropriate implementation of system software, such as properly using the system of password control, and security over terminal access.

Access by Production Programs. In addition to operator and terminal access controls, procedures should be established to restrict access to production data files by programs that do not require those files for normal processing. Accesses to data files can be monitored by security software, as well as the system logs, which can generate reports of all accesses of the programs. Reports on system activity should be reviewed and investigated, as appropriate.

Security of Off-line Files. Off-line files are protected from change because they are not mounted on a system. However, the potential danger to files held off-line is that they can be removed, possibly for unauthorized purposes. They should be physically protected, properly monitored, and their release controlled. The control features that protect against the unauthorized removal of files are discussed below.

To secure off-line files, they should be kept in a locked storage area separate from the computer room. If possible it should be supervised by a full-time librarian responsible for the issue, receipt, and security of all files. Another employee should be assigned similar duties in installations not large enough to warrant a full-time librarian. Access to the library should be restricted to authorized staff.

Procedures are also needed to ensure that files are issued only for authorized processing. This means that processing schedules for all applications should be prepared that specify in detail the files that are required for processing. The schedules should be approved by a responsible official.

Library Records. Each removable storage device, tape or disk, should be given a unique identity number permanently recorded on the device. Then a record of devices can be maintained, either manually or by system software, to account for (and control) both the files issued from the library and those created during processing.

System Software Controls

System software is the set of computer programs that control the functions of the computer and make it possible to use application programs. System software consists of programs that are not specific to any particular application but may be used in the design, processing, and control of all applications. It includes security software, operating systems, compilers, librarian packages, telecommunications packages, and utility programs. System software is important because it assists in controlling both the programs that process data and the data files. Although controls over system software do not affect the programs and data directly, they affect the extent to which one can rely on other general controls.

The system software that may be relevant to control includes programs relating to:

- cataloging,
- reports on jobs processed,
- file handling,
- data communications,
- reports on operations,
- file set-up,
- password protection, and
- library records.

Implementation of System Software Controls required for successful implementation of system software are similar to those required for implementation of application programs. Specific considerations relating to system software are discussed here.

All vendor-supplied system software should be subject to review and approval by a person with sufficient knowledge to determine its impact on existing systems and operating procedures. That person should also be able to determine whether the software will meet the company's needs and objectives. Such a review should encompass both basic software packages and available options.

When new system software interfaces directly with existing application programs, it is imperative to test the software using proven application programs. When any discrepancies occur, they can be identified as resulting from the system software in this case.

Technically competent personnel should review instructions and other documentation for system software and options supplied by an outside vendor. The documentation should properly describe the procedures necessary to operate the software correctly.

Security Controls similar to the program security controls described earlier should ensure that unauthorized changes are not made to system software, either while in use or when being held off-line.

COMPLIANCE TESTS OF CONTROLS OVER CONVERSION TO NEW SYSTEMS

For each component of general controls, compliance tests may be performed to ensure that general controls are functioning as planned. The areas to be tested in each case are addressed below.

Implementation Controls

Implementation controls are exercised over the development of new systems and the maintenance of present systems. They ensure that appropriate programmed procedures are properly implemented and adequately maintained.

Compliance tests of implementation controls may include:

- Examination of evidence to determine that system specifications and documentation are adequately prepared, reviewed, and approved.
- Examination of evidence and reperformance of systems and program testing to establish that testing procedures are adequate to ensure the appropriateness of the programmed procedures.
- Examination of evidence to determine that tested programs or changes are brought into use without subsequent unauthorized alteration.

If implementation controls vary from system to system, then each different type of control usually should be tested.

Computer Operations Controls

Controls over the consistency of computer operations ensure that jobs are properly set up and run in accordance with authorized instructions and procedures.

The tests of controls over the consistency of operations may include:

- Examination of processing schedules, operating instructions, and the job control language used to determine if jobs were properly scheduled and set up in accordance with written instructions.
- Examination of job processing sheets, console log reports, problem log reports, and the like, and reperformance of control procedures to verify that jobs were properly run in accordance with established procedures and that any problems that arose did not adversely affect the results.
- Observation of controls over the restriction of access and exercise of supervision.

Program Security and Data File Security Controls

Program security and data file security controls are designed to prevent unauthorized changes to programmed procedures and data files. Usually, separate tests should be carried out for:

- Off-line programs protected by physical custody controls (such as supervised storage areas).
- On-line program libraries protected by software controls (such as passwords).
- Off-line data files protected by physical custody controls.
- On-line data files and other files protected by software controls.

Tests of file security may include:

- Examination and reperformance of the log of physical movements to determine whether they are recorded and whether files are promptly returned to the library.
- Observation to determine whether overdue files remain in the computer room (they should not) and that access to data files is restricted.
- Examination of the console log or other reports of password-related files to find evidence of the company's investigation of unauthorized attempts to access password-protected files.
- Examination of evidence of password changes to verify that they take place regularly, and that people who leave the organization are promptly removed from the list.

System Software

System software assists in the control of both the programs that process data and of the data files themselves. Therefore, although controls over system software do not directly affect the programs and data, they affect the degree to which general controls can be relied on. The controls over the implementation and security of the system software also will have to be tested.

THE EFFECT OF GENERAL CONTROL WEAKNESSES

Different areas of general controls have different effects on programmed procedures and data, as follows.

Weaknesses in implementation controls generally cause new or modified systems to function incorrectly. Often, such errors are embedded in the system. Accordingly, the erroneous processing continues until the error is identified and corrected.

Weaknesses in program security controls generally mean that unauthorized changes not subject to the normal implementation controls can be made to the system. The organization may not be sure which systems have been changed and which have not; opportunities for the misappropriation of assets are also increased.

Weaknesses in computer operations controls generally allow random errors to occur in the system. Some errors, such as those in master file data, have lasting consequences. The main effect of such weaknesses is similar to the effect of weaknesses in a noncomputerized system—that is, most processing will be correct, but occasional errors will occur. This contrasts with the repeated errors arising from implementation control weaknesses.

Weaknesses in data file security controls generally make it possible for unauthorized changes to be made to stored data. How long it will take to discover these unauthorized changes depends largely on the structure of the application controls. Some errors in transaction data may be discovered fairly quickly through control accounts, mailing statements, and so forth. In a payment system, the error may never be noticed. Errors in master file data usually take longer to detect. Weaknesses in data file security controls, combined with weaknesses in program security controls, provide particular opportunities for almost undetectable misappropriation of assets. Weaknesses in data file security controls, coupled with weaknesses in the application controls over the continuity of the data, increase the likelihood that undetected errors will occur.

Weaknesses in system software controls usually do not have a direct effect on the applications. Such weaknesses may, however, mean that system software relied on for the proper functioning of the other general controls is not appropriate. As a result, one or more of the control areas described previously may be weak.

COMPUTER ABUSE

Although computer systems offer many advantages in terms of efficiency, they also involve unique vulnerabilities. Systems control should include a review of the potential forms of computer abuse and measures to prevent those abuses or reduce their impact.

Forms of Computer Abuse

Generally, the exposures of data processing systems are physical disaster, fraud, vandalism, mischief, and human error. To ascertain exposures, a security review evaluates each area of EDP to determine the security measures used to prevent, detect, and control the potential for abuse and to identify areas where additional control techniques should be employed.

Physical Disaster Many different disaster-causing events occur, which could cause the discontinuance of business. Recovery time varies depending on the cause of the disturbance; in some cases, the damage is irreparable. These events can be intentional (such as bombings and fires), acts of God (such as hurricanes, tornadoes, floods, and earthquakes), or negligence (such as dropping a disk pack).

The primary concern is to determine what and how data and assets should be protected or duplicated to ensure that the business can recover. The type of protection required depends on the nature of the business and, because even similar businesses do not operate identically, the unique protection methods available for that environment.

Probable occurrences can be analyzed by examining disaster vulnerabilities. Cost-effectiveness is then determined after considering the cost of alternative protection techniques. For example, there may be situations where the cost of offsite backup for all tape and disk files would be inordinate compared to the cost of recreating the information. In other circumstances, the cost of offsite backup is a small price to pay for the assurance of continued operations.

Fraud When automated systems were initially developed, few system designers realized the potential for criminal abuse by embezzlement, fraud, or theft of assets. As a result, protection or detection techniques generally were not included in early systems. The complexity of today's systems has made defalcation even more difficult to detect. Data previously maintained in different departments had been compressed and centralized for faster and easier use. In many instances, organizations were restructured and manual processing procedures were replaced by automated processing without accompanying security measures.

Those automated processing systems were designed to require fewer people, with more authority to handle transactions at a faster rate. In fact, fewer people were familiar with the new processes and not many questioned their use. Even fewer understood that data could be fraudulently entered or processed. As a result, individuals who wished to do so had a vehicle for perpetrating crime through unauthorized computer use. In addition, there were fewer methods of detecting fraud by individuals who had access to vast amounts of information.

Elaborate schemes can be developed to defraud an organization for personal gain, as substantiated by computer-related crimes over the past decade. Such crimes may occur because security controls are either missing or lax, and thus can be circumvented. Some personnel have enough knowledge of the system to use it for their own advantage. Very few systems have sufficient controls to detect fraud as it is occurring. Typically, a crime is detected after it has been committed, and it is often detected by accident because the perpetrator makes a mistake or an inconsistency is discovered inadvertently.

Many systems do not have adequate audit or information trails to indicate how a transaction has been processed and the personnel who were involved. Methods commonly used in manual systems, such as journals, ledgers, receipts, and other documents, are automated in an EDP environment. Reports are printed, although source documents used to create these reports are often destroyed. Those with access authority can manipulate data for fraudulent purposes by falsifying transactions and records.

To reduce the opportunities for fraud, adequate controls with prescribed audit checkpoints should exist, to trace complete processing of a transaction from creation to disposition. Cross-checking involving more than one individual should take place, but serves as only a deterrent rather than an absolute means of fraud prevention.

Vandalism Vandalism takes many forms; planned or spontaneous vandalism can arise from external or internal sources. For example, telecommunications lines can be cut, unauthorized changes can be made to programs or data, or computer hardware or programs and essential data can be destroyed.

Disgruntled employees seeking revenge against an employer they believe to be unjust may resort to vandalism. Such destruction is usually camouflaged and is not detected until much later; often it is untraceable. Unprotected storage media such as disks are prime targets. If back-up copies do not exist at a secure location, it may be virtually impossible to recreate the contents of disks. Program modification is another method of revenge perpetrated by introducing destruct instructions or illogical processing instructions that cause a system to fail or to create invalid data.

Mischief   Mischievous acts, unlike vandalism, are usually nondestructive; however, the disruption caused is often serious. Generally the acts are pranks—for example, hiding or purposely misplacing media.

Human Error   Human error is the greatest ongoing cause of disruption within a data processing installation. For example, computer operators may accidentally damage equipment and storage media, the wrong tape may be mounted for a production job, incorrectly coded programs may be entered into production without adequate testing or quality control, or sensitive information may be publicly disclosed through inappropriate procedures. Such error can never be completely eliminated, but security and control techniques that reduce the risk of other exposures can also reduce the frequency of errors.

Preventing Computer Abuse

Without definitive laws, established organizational procedures, and detection/reporting systems, the problem of detecting and prosecuting computer crime and abuse will continue. Growing management concerns have led many to realize how important it is for an organization to protect its systems so that the opportunities for abuse are reduced. The following questions about computer abuse prevention may help develop such procedures for protecting systems:

- Does the organization have a contingency plan that can be activated if computer abuse is suspected?
- If abuse is confirmed, would notification of the proper officials be timely?
- Does the organization have insurance coverage commensurate with the increased risks associated with modern computer technology?
- If computer abuse is suspected, does the organization know its responsibilities to its insurance carrier, and vice versa?
- Is the organization aware of responsibilities to investors, stockholders, and reporting agencies in the event that computer abuse is uncovered?
- Has the organization had a comprehensive diagnostic security study?
- Has the organization had a review of general or integrity controls within the last year? Were all recommendations and directives implemented?

- Is there assurance that the organization's internal audit program is comprehensive?
- Do relevant personnel know the legal limitations regarding questioning individuals, discharging employees, and discussing suspected events with third parties?
- Does the organization have an overall corporate security plan or philosophy?

IMPLEMENTATION OF CONTROLS

This chapter has presented an overview of the relationship between procedures and controls in a computer accounting system in terms of the categories of controls in such a system. The conversion of a manual casualty claim system to a computerized system illustrates the implementation of controls in an EDP system.

The hypothetical manual claim system consists of a series of procedures, some of which are designed to ensure the correctness of the accounting information and to protect the assets of the organization. The first step in the system is the physical delivery of the claims received on a given day, which are taken to the claims servicing department. Next, the completeness of the claim detail is checked by the claims handler. If any critical items are found to be missing, the third step is to track down the missing information. Once these three steps have been compiled, the clerk signs or initials the claims to show that they have been checked. Taken together these three steps form a basic control that ensures both the receipt and the completeness of all claims that arrive each day.

A basic control can consist of a combination of steps or procedures, as it does in this case; it can also be one procedure by itself. This example also illustrates that some procedures in a system are not accounting controls, such as the delivery of claims to the claims servicing department.

The next level in controls in the hypothetical system is the discipline over the basic controls. The claims adjuster supervisor provides that discipline by approving each claim and documenting the approval by the initialing of the claim.

Disciplinary controls are designed to ensure that the related basic controls continue to operate and that assets are safeguarded. In this case, the adjuster's approval procedure serves both purposes. It guarantees that the clerk is following the procedures for ensuring the completeness of claims and will continue to do so; it also safeguards the company's assets since it also serves as authorization for the payment of claims.

If the manual claims system were fully computerized, the same concepts of basic controls and disciplines over them would continue to operate, and the same processing tasks would be performed.

In the computerized system, the second step—checking for completeness of information—is done by the computer and is referred to as a programmed procedure. As part of the program, the critical data fields for each claim are checked and the computer produces a listing of claims with missing information. This list is the exception report, used in the third procedure to investigate errors and to ensure that they have been properly corrected and cleared. Essentially, this step—correcting errors and the fourth step—evidencing error follow-up, remain unchanged from the manual system.

The basic control to ensure the completeness of the claims still consists of the group of three procedures. The major change that has occurred in computerizing the application is that the checking in step two is now handled by the computer. This programmed procedure is only one part of the basic control; the manual procedures in steps three and four are still parts of the control. The basic control will be inadequate if the manual procedures are lacking, even if the computer functions properly.

In this computerized claims processing application, the fourth procedure still constitutes a discipline over the basic controls. Since the procedures that constitute the basic control include a programmed procedure, some questions arise: How do the people who review the report of exceptions know that all exceptions are on the report? In other words, how do they know that the programmed procedures operate correctly?

In the illustration described, two procedures involve checks based on the computer-produced exception report. Therefore, they both rely on the correct operation of programmed procedures for their effectiveness. Two accepted methods can be used to ensure that progammed procedures operate correctly and thus can be relied on. The first is to manually reperform the programmed procedure, which requires that the computer print all the information needed to reperform the procedures and then compare to the results.

The second way to ensure that the programmed procedures operate correctly is to rely on the procedures and controls exercised in the EDP department—the general controls—consisting of both basic controls and disciplines over basic controls.

Essentially, general controls must operate over all applications, such as premiums, claims, investments, or the general ledger, to ensure that the accounting applications are processed correctly. Since the same general controls operate (for the most part) over all applications, a single weakness in those controls may affect every system that uses the computer. This makes the evaluation and testing of general controls a particularly important part of an audit, especially when reliance is placed on these controls.

CONTROL REVIEWS

When proper controls are not built into a system, significant costs and additional losses can be incurred. Since data and system security are essentials in effective control, system resources must be protected from unauthorized modification and destruction. Monitoring system control can ensure their adequacy and evaluate the system's potential processing results. Thus control reviews can be appropriate at any time in the life of a system.

Pre-implementation Reviews

A pre-implementation review is the examination of a proposed computer system or set of programs. Performed during the system development phase, the review determines the extent of planned controls and the auditability of the proposed system. As organizations recognize the need to provide adequate controls over computer environments, management requests for pre-implementation reviews are increasing. Potential inefficiencies in a data processing operation or physical security risks are often uncovered during the pre-implementation review.

The primary purpose of a pre-implementation review is to provide an independent evaluation of the controls designed into the system. The computer system stores data that represents management information and financial records; therefore, it is critical to ensure adequate controls are in place when the system goes "live." The review is not a critique of the basic system design or computer equipment, nor of the methodologies employed for its implementation. Rather it is concerned with the system's ability to function properly with adequate controls.

A pre-implementation review includes evaluating the adequacy of planned testing, the appropriateness of defined user responsibility, and the planned conversion procedures. Also evaluated are the adequacy of audit or information trails and the recovery and contingency capability in the event that the new system fails. The system development phase is the best time to ensure proper controls will be in place so that system data will be entered and processed completely and accurately, in accordance with management's intentions.

The advantage to management in reviewing a new or modified system prior to use in daily production is that corrective action of significant weaknesses can be made based on report recommendations before the system is implemented. Uncovering weaknesses during the annual review might adversely affect the degree of reliance that can be placed on controls. Another benefit is that the user gets an objective review of certain aspects of the planned system. Additionally, an EDP auditor can suggest conversion procedures resulting in a well-controlled implementation.

Pre-implementation reviews should involve a close working relationship between all members of the internal audit staff including EDP audit professionals.

Systems Development Life Cycle Reviews

Following systems development life cycle methodology, whether a systems development project involves one person or a team, an adequate evaluation of the system and its documentation and controls is made at critical stages. Internal auditors, as members of the steering committee or acting as independent reviewers, can perform this important function, which is quite similar to a pre-implementation review.

Some organizations have a function of "manager of internal control" to educate users on controls and their use. Others have the auditor sign off the system during various phases of development to be sure controls have been included. By evaluating these critical stages of systems development, an auditor can include programs or computerized audit routines that will help in future testing and evaluation of applications programs.

An important contribution an internal auditor can make is to ensure that the systems development life cycle is based on procedures and standards.

An implementation review or audit of a systems development project can include a report comparing the cost of developing and implementing a controlled system with the benefits derived, based on an analysis made when the specifications are approved by the user. Management plans and allocated resources for each phase of the system life cycle should be used according to plan. A full definition of system development phases, organization, and resources available is required. The internal auditor can ensure that phases are carried out as defined and properly signed-off before proceeding to the next step.

Post-implementation Review

A post-implementation review is done when the system is already in use. It employs an EDP auditor's expertise and automated testing techniques to identify, review, and evaluate the internal controls in an operational computer-based system. This type of review is done at management's request, for an in-depth review of one or more of their applications, outside of the normal audit review.

Third-Party Reviews

Although the computer service bureau is often an efficient and economical alternative to an in-house computer, the user may suffer a loss of control. While it is obviously impractical to have numerous users or their representatives observe the service bureau on site, the user needs assurance that the service burreau has adequate internal controls. The service bureau must be shown to be processing data correctly with controls over application systems and programs development, implementation, and maintenance, in accordance with management's intentions; completeness and accuracy of processing; confidentiality of data; and adequate contingency planning.

As systems become more complex, management may not be able to maintain control over data processed at the service bureau by using extensive manual control procedures. To address this concern, a third-party review or appraisal of service bureau control policies and procedures is performed by independent qualified EDP audit professionals, in accordance with the auditing standards set forth in the Statement on Auditing Standards No. 44, *Special Reports on Internal Accounting Control at Service Organizations* and the AICPA guide, *Audits of Service-Center-Produced Records*. The review may incorporate both application and general data processing control concerns.

Findings and recommendations are presented in a detailed report to be used by management to make decisions about the reliability of the service bureau's internal control system. It can be used by other auditors avoiding duplication of examinations.

Reports can take various forms, depending on the review's objective. Reports on the general controls or computer environment cover the service bureau's general controls, including organization, procedures, application program and operating system maintenance, access to data files and program libraries, computer operations, physical security, and contingency planning. Reports on the system development life cycle methodology for design of a system or its segments analyze the adequacy of the new application through its development life cycle, focusing on the definition of the system, a feasibility study, general design and detailed specifications, program development and testing, system testing, and conversion and documentation.

Reports on application controls or systems describe the system's input, processing, and output, with emphasis on existence of controls that provide for completeness and accuracy of input and update, validity and authorization of data, and timeliness, accuracy, and maintenance of data on the computer files.

Detail or supplemental reports may cover procedures and controls in greater detail to meet review objectives. Recommendations for control improvements may be made.

Better knowledge of the extent and effectiveness of the service bureau's internal and operational controls is the main use that both service bureaus and users derive from a third-party review. Service bureau management can also benefit from the ongoing discussions concerning the bureau's data processing systems and operations, the identification of operational problems and opportunities, and suggestions for enhanced marketability of the bureau's services.

Transaction Reviews

The transaction review may start at any stage in the flow where the transaction type is readily identifiable. Normally, the auditor traces a transaction all the way from its inception to its termination as an entry in the general ledger. However, one may begin the transaction review in the middle of the flow or at the end, providing all steps in the process are covered at some point.

Transaction reviews are carried out in computer systems for the same reasons as in noncomputer systems, but the computer system may change the methods used. Transaction reviews in computer systems apply to the accounting procedures carried out manually before or after the computer processes the data; to the programmed procedures the computer carries out that relate to the completeness, accuracy, validity, authorization, or maintenance of data; and the calculation, summarization, categorization, updating, or generation of that data (application controls). They also apply to the general controls or procedures within the EDP department to ensure the effective operation of programmed procedures. These include controls over the design, implementation, security, and use of computer programs and files and subsequent amendments.

In a transaction review of manual accounting procedures within computerized systems, one may not be able to trace the same transaction through both input and output procedures because the computer system may hold items (such as orders awaiting shipment) on suspense or on master files before the data is used. Sufficient visible evidence to trace input to output, or vice versa, may not exist. When input transactions are batched or posted to a computer file, one can trace the batch, file, or total rather than the individual transaction, which has become part of the batch, file, or total and cannot be readily traced. The output reviewed may consist primarily of exception reports, since this information is commonly generated by the system.

One may not be able to confirm program logic adequately by tracing transactions through the system, since transactions are often grouped into batches or files for computer processing. A summary report of the procedures applied to the group is usually generated, but evidence on the effect of processing on each individual transaction rarely is. Another consideration is that a particular programmed procedure may include one or more complex programs and several computer files. Each program can include a hundred different logical paths, not all of which have significance for the purpose of the review. An overall review can first identify which paths are significant.

Programmed procedures are usually described in the systems and program documentation. If the documentation of programmed procedures is incomplete, out-of-date, or badly prepared, it cannot be used to confirm an understanding of the programmed procedures. Interviews with data processing personnel can help to determine the accuracy of the recorded programmed procedures.

Working papers should record any transaction review performed. When possible, a worksheet should accommodate several years' evaluations. It can be set up in columnar form, with the numbers of the operations from the flowchart and supporting narratives listed on the left. The operation numbers listed on the worksheet indicate the procedures performed, as shown on the flowchart or narrative. The specific transactions reviewed should be identified in a column of the worksheet. If the work performed is evident from the flowchart, and the document reference is indicated on the transaction review working papers, no further documentation should be required.

When transaction reviews are used to confirm the understanding of the system shown in the flowcharts or narratives, no further work is necessary. If they indicate that the initial understanding of the system was incorrect, one should find out what procedures are actually in effect, revise the system documentation accordingly, and note this on the working papers.

SUMMARY

No information system is complete without the incorporation of adequate controls into the system. Control weaknesses can be devastating in computerized systems, but the computer also offers great potential for control purposes. Internal controls include both administrative controls over efficiency, timeliness, and informed decision-making as well as accounting controls to assure that transactions are executed and recorded accurately, completely, and in accordance with management authorization. Control in any system requires systemization, documentation, competence and integrity, and sufficient resources.

In addition to the application controls discussed in Chapter 8, an insurance information system should incorporate general controls. For example, implementation controls ensure that proposed programmed procedures are suitable and effectively implemented. Program security controls prevent unauthorized changes to the production programs that process data. Computer operations controls ensure consistent application of programmed procedures to both storage data and processing of data. Data file security controls prevent unauthorized changes in data files. Finally, controls over system software are needed to prevent any unauthorized changes in the other general controls.

Weaknesses in any of these general control areas undermine the reliability of the system. Weak implementation controls may allow errors to become imbedded in the system. Opportunities for misappropriation of corporate assets exist when program security controls are weak. Weak computer operations controls allow random errors to occur. Weaknesses in data file security controls may allow unauthorized changes in data files to occur and, when coupled with application controls, to go undetected. Weaknesses in system software controls may prevent other controls from functioning properly.

Information systems are vulnerable to many forms of computer abuse. Physical disasters, either accidental or intentional, can destroy data as well as systems components, disrupting operations. Fraud is always a possibility, and it may be more difficult to detect and trace in a computerized system. Vandalism, mischief, and even human error can also disrupt operations. Procedures should be developed to reduce the organization's vulnerability to these forms of computer abuse.

The conversion of a manual system to a computerized system shows that the same controls must operate even though the audit trail is no longer visible. Thus an evaluation of internal controls requires testing the programmed procedures for assurance that the controls operate properly.

Control reviews are appropriate at any point in the life of a system. Pre-implementation reviews can ensure that adequate controls exist before the system begins operating. System development life cycle reviews ensure that a systems development project adheres to standards and includes adequate controls. A post-implementation review may identify areas for future improvement even though the system is already operating. When a computer service bureau or similar outside organization performs some of the processing, a third-party review can provide assurance that adequate controls exist. Transaction reviews facilitate an understanding of the entire system and its controls. While control reviews of these various types can be useful in many different situations, they are especially useful in the audit process discussed in the final chapter.

CHAPTER 10

Auditing

INTRODUCTION

Organizations cannot rely on computer-based information systems without appropriate controls over those systems. To rely on EDP systems, an audit approach to review and test the effectiveness of controls is needed. Whenever weaknesses or control deficiencies are discovered during such an evaluation, the auditor then must determine if there are controls that compensate for those weaknesses. Without compensating controls, the auditor must judge whether that weakness can have a significant impact on the reliability of the information system. This is a primary concern of an audit of a system.

One successful approach is to divide the audit into manageable component phases that employ standardized techniques and documents. This type of systems approach can be applied to audits of both manual systems and automated systems of varying degrees of technological complexity, regardless of the way data is processed. This approach can be applied to existing systems, new systems development, and administrative or operational audits.

In manual systems, audit concerns include decisions about what data is needed, how the data is gathered or developed, and how those procedures were followed throughout the period. Basic controls over data include disposition of data developed, and whether anyone checks it appropriately. Disciplines over the basic controls are concerned with whether control has been appropriately exercised throughout the period and whether improvements in control are needed.

In computer-based systems, the same concerns take on new form. The same basic controls and disciplines that work in a manual system can usually apply to a computerized system, but some are performed by the computer's programmed procedures. Since the computer performs many procedures, questions arise about what data the programs call for and whether the programs have continued to operate in the same way throughout the period. General controls are relied on to assure continued and proper operation of programmed procedures. Application controls, including programmed procedures, are often designated and evaluated separately from the general controls over EDP as a whole.

THE AUDIT PROCESS

One audit process to assess computer-based systems consists of the following sequence of activities:

- planning, based on audit objectives;
- obtaining, recording, and confirming an understanding of the system;
- evaluating the internal controls by performing compliance tests;
- performing substantive tests; and
- determining and reporting findings and recommendations.

The results of each different phase need to be assessed throughout the audit. Because audit procedures may be modified as part of the evaluation of the control system, the approach should be flexible enough to make adjustments in the audit program if it becomes necessary to amend the planned strategy.

Auditors may refer to guides, reference manuals, control questionnaires, checklists, and forms. Standardized documents have been developed and are useful in maintaining the consistency, thoroughness, and quality of audits. The AICPA Audit Guides, *Audits of Fire and Casualty Insurance Companies* and *Audits of Stock Life Insurance Companies*, which relate to the industry, and the AICPA Audit and Accounting Guides, *The Auditor's Study and Evaluation of Control in EDP Systems*, and *Computer-Assisted Audit Techniques*, and the AICPA Computer Services Guideline, *Audit and Control Considerations in an Online Environment*, which all relate to EDP auditing, may be particularly helpful.

When EDP auditors perform other functions, such as security reviews, operational audits, pre-implementation reviews, reviews of standards, and system development life cycle reviews, a similar audit approach can be applied.

Planning

Adequate planning of an overall audit strategy is an important, integral part of a systems audit approach. The auditor should perform the following steps in planning:

- Develop an overall plan or strategy.
- Obtain and document a preliminary current understanding of each system to be audited.
- Set audit objectives and determine resources.
- Determine the audit strategy that yields the best mix of effectiveness and efficiency.
- Document and communicate the planned audit strategy.
- Monitor, plan, and react to changing circumstances and findings.

Developing an effective audit strategy requires that the audit department understand management objectives. Planning is an essential aspect of an efficient audit. To devise a workable audit plan, the audit department should perform the following tasks:

- Develop audit objectives from management objectives.
- Translate audit objectives into specific long- and short-term goals and develop a plan for implementation.
- Ensure adequate resources, especially time and personnel, and allocate them.
- Assign responsibility for implementing the plan's various facets.
- Schedule EDP audit training to ensure proficiency in technical areas.
- Monitor the plan; make needed changes on an ongoing basis.

The planning process for work done by an internal audit department can be managed within two basic components:

1. Prepare an annual audit program, perhaps within a longer term plan, such as five years.
2. Develop detailed audit strategies or a program for each audit contained in the annual program.

Preparation of the Annual Audit Program Most internal audit groups work with limited resources, which must be allocated effectively and efficiently. An evaluation procedure should be employed to assess use of resources. To establish the priority of the areas included in the annual audit program initially, the auditors can develop a complete list of all possible audit areas. After evaluation of these audit areas, priorities can be established. Factors auditors can consider when evaluating the areas to be audited are:

- Financial statement impact—areas that would have a significant impact on the financial statements should almost always have high priority.
- Previous audit history—areas where previous audits showed deficiencies may require follow-up.
- Length of time since the last audit was conducted—all areas should be audited on a cyclical basis within a reasonable period of time.
- Changes in the industry.
- Changes in policies or procedures—when these have occurred, assurance that there was proper implementation of any substantial changes in company policies or procedures since the last audit should be a high-priority item.
- Changes in governmental regulations, legal requirements, or federal or state tax laws affecting the industry should be audited.
- Implementation of new systems—this includes computerization of a formerly all-manual system or modifications to a computerized system. The level of involvement is based on:
  - Operational exposure
  - Accounting significance of the system
  - Need to determine compliance with established methodologies for implementing the new systems or maintaining current systems.
- Establishment of new contracts or proposals for computer hardware or software.
- Requests from external auditors or state examiners for assistance in their annual audit of the financial statements.
- Specific requests from the audit committee.
- Requests from management—operational managers may be aware of particular concerns in their departments that should be addressed; the internal audit staff should solicit these requests through suitable procedures, such as distributing form letters.
- Use of a service bureau for data processing.
- The resources available versus requirements for special projects, based on past experience.

Once the auditors have evaluated these factors, they can prepare the annual audit program based on that evaluation and the amount of audit time available. Individual auditors should be assigned specific responsibilities for each audit within the annual program. Upon completion, the annual audit program should be reviewed and approved by the audit committee.

Developing Individual Audit Strategies The second step in planning an audit is developing an audit strategy for each of the individual audits within the annual program. When the audit will be of a system currently in place, this planning process can be divided into the following five major steps:

1. Review industry analyses and statistics.
2. Review the latest management reports and identify factors and related risks that may significantly affect the audit strategy.
3. Obtain and document a current preliminary understanding of the systems to be audited.
4. Determine the most effective and efficient audit strategy.
5. Document the planned audit strategy.

When the audit relates to the implementation of a new system, the planning process should include:

- establishing ongoing communication with the data processing and user departments, and the details of those communications, i.e., who should receive them;
- establishing control standards that require internal audit sign-off at the completion of each step of the implementation process; and
- scheduling training for EDP auditors to bring them up to date on the new system, when appropriate, to enable them to evaluate the new, possibly more complex systems and to participate in the system development process.

Obtaining, Recording, and Confirming the Understanding

To evaluate controls or make decisions about the audit strategy or procedures to be applied, auditors must develop an understanding of the system under review. They can obtain this understanding by interviewing personnel, reviewing previous audits, and reading systems descriptions, such as flowcharts and system narratives. Auditors can review such items as correspondence files, business statistics, organizational charts, internal audit reports, consultants' reports, procedural manuals, and external audit reports, including previous comments to management, and can interview on-site personnel, or tour the site.

Reviewing working papers from prior years will indicate what type of work was done in the past and the problems that were encountered. If possible, an interview with the previous auditor can provide valuable insight into problem areas.

Once the research needed to understand system operations is obtained, the auditor prepares a record of the system's audit control procedures. A prerequisite of the audit, this record permits effective supervisory review and saves time on subsequent audits. It also gives the auditor a more comprehensive and accurate understanding of the system as the control procedures are recorded.

Flowcharting As a first step in recording an understanding of a system, the auditor can prepare a computer overview flowchart or a system narrative for each important computer application. Overview flowcharts should summarize all significant input such as files, and output, such as reports.

The flowchart should integrate all procedures, to show the flow of transactions through the whole system. Identification of the transaction types is in itself an important aspect of an audit. When the auditor plans to rely on controls, detailed flowcharting documents the internal control procedures established for processing each transaction type. This recorded understanding becomes the basis for the auditor's evaluation of the system.

An auditor interested in controls requires flowcharts that define the point at which a control begins to operate and the range of procedures covered by the control. (In system-oriented flowcharts, controls are rarely depicted.)

By showing procedures in graphic form, flowcharts improve comprehension and provide superior communication of information. The auditor can identify particular control features in the system, so that their significance can be evaluated to see whether they are meeting the objectives of the overall internal control system. When prepared logically, concisely, and clearly, flowcharting also promotes efficiency and uniformity in the preparation of working papers.

Preparing or updating flowcharts is an integral part of the internal control evaluation process. The auditor who obtains or updates the understanding of the system and its controls should also record the understanding, although the help of EDP audit specialists may be required in flowcharting computer systems.

The auditor usually obtains the needed information to prepare or update flowcharts by interviewing site personnel about procedures followed and by reviewing procedure manuals and other systems documentation. The auditor can do these interviews at the same time as the transaction reviews, especially when updating flowcharts.

Copies of the audit flowcharts can be given to site personnel, who may find the flowcharts useful. The auditor may ask site personnel to provide comments that confirm the accuracy of the flowcharts. System users often provide useful critiques.

Confirming the Understanding Depicted in Flowcharts Where the flowcharts or narrative notes have been prepared or updated, the auditor confirms that the system has been understood and recorded properly. This confirmation can be obtained through a transaction review, or tracing a transaction of each type (a premium or a claim, for example) through the system.

In computer-based systems, the auditor confirms the understanding of the application controls, manual procedures, programmed procedures, and general controls. The objectives of transaction reviews in computer-based systems are the same as those in noncomputer systems, but the nature of computer-based systems frequently changes the methods the auditor uses. For example, a claim transaction is usually batched for processing, and the review follows the batch rather than an individual transaction. The loss of visible weaknesses records all control evidence in computer systems, and growing use of paperless systems where there are no source documents has an effect on the methods the auditor uses. In many such cases, computer-assisted audit techniques are required to perform an effective audit.

Evaluating Internal Accounting and Operational Controls

Flowcharts are usually appropriate for documenting procedures that have significant accounting implications. They should include all operations having accounting control significance: not only to the accounting control objectives and procedures, but also to any compensating controls. Audit flowcharting can also integrate administrative controls. For example, the part of the premium cycle flowchart describing control procedures in the underwriting function may describe such administrative control procedures as maintaining the premium rate files. When efficient, such controls can be discussed in the narratives which supplement the flowcharts. The extent of review of administrative controls and documentation for such a review must be planned before the system review starts.

Preliminary Review Sometimes an auditor starts with a preliminary review and evaluation of controls. Such a review simply provides basic information. It is useful, for example, when it is not possible for the audit department to evaluate all the systems in depth, or to identify systems with major problems that require a detailed review as soon as possible.

Size and Volume of Transactions and Balances Auditors often record information about the size and volume of account balances and transaction flow to evaluate the potential existence of identified accounting control weaknesses or administrative control exceptions.

This information can also be useful to assess the costs and benefits of making changes in the system.

Information about account balances includes the number of accounts or balances in the files and ledgers, and the total net dollar amount split between positive and negative balances.

Transaction flow information includes the number of transactions flowing through a transaction processing system in a certain time period, the total dollar amount, the range of amounts, and the average amount of transactions flowing through a transaction processing system in a certain time period. Also useful, if available, are the error rates in transaction processing. The auditor should give prior notification to site personnel to develop this data, which may not be readily available, or interview on site to obtain the data.

Evaluation of Systems   Computerized processing methods for accounting and management decision support can create changes in the methods of processing and controlling transactions and may result in changes in both applying and evaluating controls. The extent of change depends on the scope of computer processing in each system.

The large volume of transactions in computerized systems and user reliance on programmed procedures usually results in lessened examination of processing output. This increases the need for controls over the continued correctness of data held on computer files. These controls are applied to prevent unauthorized changes to that data, to assure the continued and proper operation of computer software, and so forth.

Evaluation of Application Controls   As part of the audit approach, the auditor can use methods that employ audit documents to evaluate internal controls in computer applications. These documents include a control matrix, a computer internal control questionnaire, and a record of control weaknesses.

The Control Matrix.   The auditor uses the computer application control matrix to evaluate existing computer applications and as the principal recording document for application control identification. A matrix includes a one-page summary of identified controls.

The auditor records the following information on the control matrix for each transaction of audit significance: input or transaction types processed (as documents or records on a computer file) and control techniques for each transaction type.

To use the matrix to perform administrative or operational reviews, the auditor also enters the additional techniques, if they are needed, to ensure timely detection of errors and the timeliness of management reports. The auditor can enter on the matrix an assessment of the efficiency of the controls, and when required, of the other aspects of the system.

Internal Control Questionnaire. The auditor can use a set of questionnaires called the internal control questionnaire for a detailed evaluation of internal controls in computer-based systems. Usually internal control questionnaires contain questions, organized by control objectives, that relate to manual systems and to those manual controls that do not change in computer-based systems. When a control objective requires different procedures to suit a computer-based system, the auditor can use a computer internal control questionnaire designed for the purpose. It covers application controls that are organized by control objectives including controls over master file data, the general or integrity controls over stored data and programs, and so forth. A well-designed computer internal control questionnaire ensures that these controls are covered, although the format can vary.

Record of Control Weaknesses. This is a record of control weaknesses identified in the questionnaire or control matrix. The reason for a separate record is to have one document that includes control weaknesses identified during the evaluation; evaluation of possible effects, including potential errors of a significant nature; audit program amendments, including tests, due to the existence of weaknesses; a record of discussion of weaknesses with local management; and senior management reports or corrective action taken.

A record of control weaknesses also provides an overview, making possible a review of potential effects of weaknesses on the organization's management information systems. This record can be used throughout the later phases of the audit cycle.

Evaluating Management Procedures Audits also include review of management's organizational procedures to ensure that they are being followed and that they meet their intended objectives. Specific actions to be taken and definition of areas of responsibility are defined by good procedures, and become the basis for review, testing, and evaluation. When needed, the auditor can suggest changes in procedures.

Compliance Tests Compliance testing is the process of testing controls identified on a matrix or questionnaire to determine if they are operating as planned. Testing usually consists of examining evidence or reperforming control procedures, and observing whether the planned controls are in fact being performed. These tests are usually documented or recorded within the audit program.

Performing Substantive Tests

Substantive tests and procedures evaluate the accuracy and completeness of data, such as balances on a file. Some substantive testing is usually done as part of the audit. More may be required when there are weak, unreliable, or nonexistent general controls over EDP processing.

There is often a direct correlation between the level of internal control and the amount of substantive testing required. The potential exists in computer systems for improved internal controls over the updating and maintenance of details of account balances and master file data held on computer files. If the results of compliance testing indicate that internal controls are adequate, the auditor may minimize the substantive procedures. When compliance testing reveals control weaknesses that raise doubts about supporting evidence, substantive testing can help alleviate those doubts.

In computer systems where the auditor chooses not to rely on internal controls, substantive procedures can include additional tests or data evaluation to confirm that programmed procedures are operating properly. Additional data work may include the supplemental testing of procedures already planned (such as testing a greater number of the items that make up an account balance), greater depth in the procedures already planned (such as seeking more complete documentary evidence in support of an agent's balance) or auxiliary procedures not previously considered (such as confirming agent's account balances where this has not already been done).

Determining and Reporting Audit Findings and Recommendations

The purpose of control reviews, evaluation, and testing is to make it possible for the auditor to make an informed audit judgment. The audit objectives themselves require that the auditor decide on the extent to which those objectives were satisfied. The external auditor's audit objectives, standards, and regulations are followed according to generally accepted auditing standards (GAAS) and form the basis of an audit opinion. For an internal auditor, the audit approach leads to the audit conclusions and indicates the findings of the audit. When recommendations are possible, they are included.

When the audit is complete, the auditor reports any internal control deficiencies to senior management, in a form and content according to the particular organization's requirement. When weaknesses or deficiencies exist, the auditor may make a recommendation of possible corrective actions to be taken so that adequate controls are implemented. Internal auditors usually prepare formal reports of assessments of the system or area reviewed and comments on internal controls.

The audit report is the auditor's formal written communication with management that provides a concise statement of what was found as a result of the audit. Designed to help management meet its responsibility to establish and maintain an adequate system of internal control, a well-written report identifies deficiencies in control found during the course of an audit and provides a formal record of recommendations regarding those deficiencies. The auditor can often make constructive suggestions on the operations of the organization. In developing the report the auditor should take care to direct management's attention to the more significant weaknesses and make sure that the information can be readily understood.

The degree of detail supplied is largely a matter of judgment, according to management preference. Some managements prefer to have all audit findings reported, no matter how minor they are; others prefer to receive a general description of significant findings. Auditors' ultimate accountability requires that they bring findings of major significance to the attention of executive management and the board of directors.

Audit reports should inform management of the current state of the operations in the area reviewed and whether the area's day-to-day operations are in accordance with management-prescribed standards. Reports should comply with current internal audit professional standards and provide communication of technical audit findings in understandable summary comments. The details can be given in an addendum.

A statement of scope indicates whether the findings pertain to a limited period or remain applicable over an extended period of time and should include the limits of the review. A mechanism for the auditors to state their position on the findings can help management understand the situation from both viewpoints. Then management can respond with the appropriate corrective actions necessary to eliminate control deficiencies. Management response should outline corrective actions chosen or the reasons for not acting.

Scope of Audit Work   Part of the report is a statement of the scope of audit work performed. The data of the audit, as well as the time span subject to review, are essential to inform readers of the period that was the audit focal point. To evaluate elements in the scope of audit work separately, the auditor can consider the following areas.

Adequacy.   A system is adequate if it contains key accounting control procedures designed to prevent or detect material or significant errors or irregularities. The auditor determines adequacy by obtaining an understanding of the system through discussions with the appropriate personnel; by referring to documentation, such as procedure manuals, job descriptions, and flowcharts; and by observing key activities and documenting those observations.

Efficiency. Efficiency here is concerned with the cost of internal controls not exceeding the value of expected benefits. The auditor uses general experience and expertise to judge the practicality of controls in terms of their cost in relation to their benefits.

Effectiveness. The auditor determines the effectiveness of the degree of compliance with the system by performing compliance tests. These compliance tests are designed to provide reasonable assurance that the organization is applying key control procedures. Tests of compliance, for example, with internal accounting control procedures, might require inspection of internal documents to obtain evidence in the form of signatures, initials, and so forth, or observation of certain principles of control, such as segregation of duties, to permit an evaluation of the performance of such duties.

Quality of Ongoing Operations. Operations are the procedures or processes that are designed to satisfy predetermined organizational and control objectives. Management is responsible for ongoing operations and must be confident that the system is meeting operative needs. The auditor should review the system and should evaluate and report on the quality of ongoing operations.

Audit Findings Audit findings are based on a process of comparing what is with what should be. The findings include a statement of the condition and a statement of how it could be. When these differ greatly, if the effect is meaningful, it may be worth reporting. If the deviation is of not practical consequence, the auditor should consider discussing it orally. The auditor must determine the cause of the deviation—an audit finding is not really complete unless it includes the causes of the problem. The next step is the action that is necessary to eliminate or minimize recurrence of the situation, presented as a recommendation. Audit findings should explain reasons behind what is stated, including: statement of condition, effect, cause, and recommendation.

A well-developed audit finding includes all those points and distinguishes each from the others. The reader of the report should have no difficulty understanding what was found, what is thought about what was found, what the effect is, why it happened, and how the auditor thinks it should be corrected.

The auditor should refer to the record of control weaknesses identified through the audit. The auditor can use this record to review the possible effects of the weaknesses upon the organization's financial statements and to weigh the effect the weakness might have on the nature and timing of subsequent audit procedures. The record should also document any discussions with management regarding the finding, as well as any corrective actions management has taken.

Oral Reports. Although written reports are the most common way of presenting findings, at times oral presentation may be more appropriate. Oral presentations are very effective for minor findings that do not require senior. management's attention and provide immediate feedback necessary for findings that require immediate attention.

Oral reports also can promote better relations between the auditors and the auditees, because during those discussions auditees have an opportunity to present their views of the findings. In fact, those discussions may disclose areas requiring additional audit effort.

Technical Findings. The manner of presentation of technical EDP findings depends on who is going to receive the report, since senior management may not be familiar with the control requirements in computer-based systems or the details of systems themselves. To begin the report, many auditors prepare an executive summary that addresses the effect of the control weakness in nontechnical terms. The technical finding is then placed in an appendix to the main report, or is issued as a separate report.

The criteria and recommendation elements of a finding may be affected in an EDP environment by the auditor's inability to obtain sufficient information on each element. For example, management may not have established an adequate system development life cycle. This lack of established criteria may lead the auditor to comment on the desirability of adoping specific standards. The recommendation section, on the other hand, may be complicated by the amount of time the auditor needs to research the most efficient means of correcting the weakness. This is compounded in an EDP environment by the time required to analyze the various options. In situations where it is not practical to recommend a specific or best way to achieve corrective action, a more general recommendation or suggested approach to the problem is appropriate.

Prior to final distribution of the report, the auditor should review a draft copy with management, both as a courtesy and as a form of insurance. In complex systems, the auditor may miss a point or report it incorrectly. Reviewing the report with the department concerned can bring out any inaccuracies of this kind for correction before the final report is issued.

The Foreign Corrupt Practices Act of 1977 made corporate officers accountable for the adequacy of internal controls that affect the organization's financial statements. As a result, identifying and reporting weaknesses and recommending corrective action to management may not be enough. Follow-up procedures should ensure that the organization has taken cost-effective, timely corrective action on control deficiencies and has implemented an adequate system of internal control.

COMPLIANCE TESTS AND REVIEWS IN EDP SYSTEMS

Special testing techniques are available to auditors of computer-based systems. In many instances these tests, performed using audit software, are the only efficient and effective way to evaluate such systems. Audit tests fall into two general categories: tests of controls (compliance tests) and substantive tests. To perform these tests, the auditor chooses a strategy and suitable specific testing methods.

Factors in the Selection of Controls for Testing

There are no absolute rules for selecting controls and determining levels of tests. The objective is to obtain reasonable assurance that a control is functioning properly, while keeping testing to a necessary minimum. To make a judgment about an appropriate level of tests, auditors take into account such factors as the complexity of the transactions, and results of previous evaluations, among others. Some additional factors are discussed below.

Principal Controls The principal controls are those that can be tested effectively and cover the widest range of control. There can be several controls over one application—the principal control is often selected from these for testing.

Frequency of Control Performance In general, the more frequently a control is performed, the more likely it is that it should be tested (even though the percentage of items tested may decline as total volume increases).

Controls over Groups of Transactions In this case, the auditor determines the tests according to the primary evidence of the control, rather than by the underlying individual transactions. For example, in the case of a monthly control over the completeness of sequentially prenumbered documents, compliance testing might be to examine a few monthly reports of missing numbers to confirm that, on the face of it, missing numbers are being identified and investigated. Reperformance based on such reports could involve selecting a number of batches of documents, seeing that any missing numbers had been listed, and reviewing the results of the investigation.

Risk of Undetected Errors In an effective system of internal control, a breakdown in one control will often be detected by the operation of another (normally later) control. The auditor should consider various relevant factors in determining the extent of risk that an error may not be detected.

Disciplines over Basic Controls Effective supervisory controls should identify breakdowns in the operation of the underlying basic controls. In the absence of a supervisory control, and assuming adequate segregation of duties, the auditor may increase levels of tests of evidence that the basic controls continue to operate. Conversely, where weaknesses relating to the segregation of duties exist, and assuming adequate supervisory controls, the auditor may increase tests of the basic controls to obtain assurance of the effectiveness of the supervisory controls.

Interrelated Basic Controls Many basic controls are interrelated. For example, if the controls over the completeness of premium notices break down, this should be detected as a result of the investigation of lapsed policies. (If no notice was received, probably no payment was made, and the policy would lapse as a result.)

Overall Reconciliations When, as part of the regular control procedures, carrying out overall reconciliations (such as insurance in-force, total investments, or outstanding losses) is possible, the auditor may feel justified in testing the operation of such reconciliations and in reducing the level of compliance tests of the related basic controls. When overall reconciliations are done less frequently (such as annually), the auditor may still decide to reduce the levels of tests of some of the related basic controls. (Whenever reliance is placed on overall reconciliations, the auditor should take particular care to examine the controls that ensure the completeness of items in the reconciliations.)

The Justification for Reducing Tests Reducing testing as just described may not be applicable when testing general controls, since they relate to all systems. For example, the auditor should not reduce the levels of general control testing because of the existence of overall reconciliation and reasonableness reviews relating to a particular system. An example is computing on an overall basis interest earned based on an average interest rate. Overall reconciliations rarely cover all the programmed procedures and data files at risk; adequate tests of general controls are still necessary for systems not covered.

The Significance of Potential Errors The significance of potential errors is affected by the stage in the processing system at which the potential error could occur. Errors that occur at the early stages frequently have less significant impact than those that occur at a later stage.

The effects of breakdowns in general controls are often more far-reaching than the effects of breakdowns in other types of controls. Inadequate or incorrect programmed procedures (such as summarizations, overdue premium calculations, or unearned premium calculations) may continue to have an adverse effect long after the program containing them was implemented. Computer system processing involves greater use of summary reports and reports of exceptional items requiring action, with less manual review of the detailed results of processing. Hence, errors in a program or data file are less likely to be detected by application controls, which should be taken into account to test general controls. The same consideration applies to controls over master file data, since incorrect master file data can also have a continuing impact on large numbers of transactions.

Breakdowns that affect controls over completeness can be more important than breakdowns in controls over accuracy or validity of individual transactions. As a result, they require a higher level of testing, because items that should be present but have been omitted during processing are often difficult to locate or to identify.

Spreading of Tests Spreading tests over different time periods is relevant to the levels of tests because the number of items selected must provide an adequate representation of the population during the periods under review.

It may not be necessary to spread compliance tests when the effective performance of the control reveals accumulated errors, including those arising because of a previous breakdown in the control. For example, if bank reconciliations are to be tested as of the year-end date, in most cases compliance tests need not be carried out during the year. However, the auditor should find out how often regular preparation of such reconciliations is done to ascertain any major deficiencies that might be (or have been) corrected prior to year-end.

Tests also do not need to be spread when the particular controls are not significant because of the compensating effect of other controls or procedures. For example, certain controls over the calculation of unearned premiums in a property and liability insurance company during the period prior to the year-end usually have minimum significance and need not be tested. The same controls, however, are significant for the balance sheet date.

When the auditor proposes to test controls that operate throughout the year and that do not fall within the areas mentioned above (such as validity of claims), compliance tests of the disciplines over the basic controls should be spread. This is necessary to obtain assurance of continued operation of the underlying basic controls. If the disciplines over basic controls appear to be operating properly, the auditor can sometimes restrict the reperformance of the basic controls to one period. Often, the auditor will select the latest period available at the time of the test, but the latest period is not required.

Levels of Review As with tests of internal accounting controls, there are no hard-and-fast rules for determining the level of review. The level chosen is a matter for judgment by management, considering all relevant factors. The objective is to review to the minimum extent necessary while determining the apparent existence and proper functioning of the controls.

The levels of review of administrative controls are often based on the effort involved in a particular review procedure, considering the potential financial impact if the control is inoperative. When the additional time to review a control is small, and the potential impact of a control breakdown is large, the level of review of the administrative control should be relatively high. This is normally the case when an administrative control is reviewed in conjunction with the testing of a related internal accounting control.

Noncomputer Control Techniques

Many of the manual tests for computer-based systems are the same as the ones used to test manual systems, although the documents that are examined may be different. Customary manual audit testing techniques can be used whenever:

- adequate evidence is readily available,
- information is presented in normal accounting terms, and
- volumes of data are not too large to carry out the test.

Accordingly, many transaction review techniques, compliance tests, and substantive procedures will not change significantly in a computer-based system.

Some manual audit tests do require special EDP skills. For instance, general controls and program coding are usually described in data processing terminology. Review may require the assistance of a specialist, both to understand the evidence examined and to test the relevant processing functions. In such cases, some type of audit software can often be used.

Manual Checking To perform compliance tests, the auditor can use manual checks that generally include examination, reperformance, and observation.

Examination includes examining reports. For example, a report may indicate that the numerical sequence of prenumbered documents is periodically checked and missing numbers are investigated by someone who does not normally work with those documents. Another example is examining program amendment forms to see that they have been approved by the appropriate people.

Reperformance is selecting items from the report of missing numbers and verifying that the correct follow-up action has been taken, or selecting approved program amendment forms and confirming that the forms and amendments have been adequately designed, tested, and documented, for the examples above.

Observation includes activities like observing the physical restrictions on access to the computer room.

The auditor can test user controls and many of the general controls in the usual way, and thus experience no major change in procedures. Similarly, substantive procedures, even when carried out on computer printouts instead of on traditional lists of balances, can sometimes be performed by conventional manual tests.

Limitations on Manual Checking The auditor will also test certain programmed procedures, which are checked as part of compliance tests on implementation controls or as substantive procedures to provide assurance that a particular programmed procedure is operating. Some evidence that the programmed procedure is functioning is usually available. However, steps taken to produce those results by computer processing are rarely printed out in detail, and the auditor cannot test the operation of programmed procedures in the conventional way. For example, since totals and analyses are usually printed out without supporting details, the auditor cannot check the method used to reach the total or analysis. When exception reports and rejection listings are produced, it is often impossible to manually establish that all items that should have been reported or rejected have been. In examining those reports or listings, the auditor sees only the items that were reported. In both cases, there is a lack of visible evidence showing how the programmed procedure operates within the computer, since only the results of its operations are seen.

Manual Simulation Techniques The auditor can also carry out manual tests when the system does not readily provide full visible evidence. Methods that can achieve re-creation of evidence are known collectively as "manual simulation."

One method of manual simulation is reassembling processed data so that it is in the same condition as it was when the programmed procedure was first applied. For example, reassembling batches of premium payments can be done to test the batch totals that were posted to the premium revenue ledger control account.

Another technique is working on current data before it is sent for processing by the computer. For example, checking the additions of batches before they are sent for conversion can test how a total that was used to control subsequent processing was reached.

An additional method is selecting a small number of items from those submitted for processing and processing them in a separate run. For example, splitting a batch into two batches, one large and one small, and then processing the small batch separately will test whether the computer-produced totals agree with precalculated results.

Simulating a condition that will produce a report if the programmed procedure is working properly can also be used. For example, altering a batch total to an incorrect figure so that the batch is rejected, or withholding a document so that it is reported as missing tests whether these reports are produced. This approach requires careful planning, execution, and the agreement of a responsible user department official.

Another method of manual simulation is requesting a special report of items processed. For example, some systems can produce a listing of invoices included in a total produced by the computer.

Even though visible evidence of the operation of a programmed procedure neither exists nor can be created, and the appropriate condition cannot be simulated, the manual tests just described can still be carried out.

Selection of Items to Be Tested or Reviewed

The respective purposes of compliance tests and administrative reviews are to determine whether specific internal accounting controls are operating and whether specific administrative controls are apparently in existence. The items selected should be representative of the transactions processed. That otherwise similar transactions are processed by different people, or in different locations, is not relevant, provided the basic control procedures are uniform with respect to internal accounting controls. The auditor should be satisfied that such transactions are subject to the same supervisory controls as are all transactions.

Compliance tests and administrative reviews are concerned primarily with the flow of transactions through individual control points, rather than the flow of transactions through the entire system. Different documents within the same transaction processing system may be selected for examination to verify different control points. It may sometimes be more efficient to test or review related controls using the same documents.

When carrying out reperformance tests of general controls, the auditor should select control procedures carried out on programs and files that have accounting control significance, if that is what is being tested. For example, the auditor would normally select procedures relating to changes in programs in the premium revenue system rather than changes in programs in the personnel scheduling system. The auditor can identify appropriate programs and data when obtaining and confirming an understanding of the accounting system and completing or updating an evaluation of internal controls.

When an auditor is reviewing a system, or administrative controls, controls that apply to all significant programs and files are covered. If implementation controls vary from system to system, the auditor should test the different sets of controls separately. Although there are two separate types of general controls that deal with program security and data file security, the same controls may apply to both programs and data files. For example, both may be protected by the same software while on-line. When this is so, only one set of compliance tests is required.

The auditor need not test internal controls in the same order in which they appear in the control questionnaires used. Often the auditor can test supervisory controls before testing the related basic controls, and test controls over groups of transactions before testing controls over the related individual transactions. The results of tests of supervisory or group controls can help the auditor determine the levels of tests needed for underlying controls. It is equally acceptable to test the basic controls first, or the basic controls and the supervisory controls at the same time, if this is more efficient.

Administrative controls should be reviewed in the most efficient order. Review of an administrative control should be carried out in conjunction with the compliance test of a related internal control procedure whenever efficiency will be enhanced. For example, in testing controls over the matching of purchase orders with receiving reports and purchase invoices, the auditor will normally determine both whether routing and other instructions are on the purchase order and whether a cash discount was taken. Since those tests can be done simultaneously, it would be less efficient to do them separately.

When compliance testing finds an exception, it is necessary to establish whether it is an isolated incident or whether it indicates a departure from, or a breakdown in, the system, if a control is not being applied or is not evidenced.

To find out whether the exception is an isolated incident, the auditor determines, through inquiry and examination of the exception, why the exception arose. The auditors also may find it necessary to extend the number of items tested, but should take care to ensure that extending the testing will actually help determine the nature and extent of the exception. When a departure or breakdown in the prescribed systems exists that has not been corrected, the auditor should record it on a document designed for the purpose, such as the record of control weaknesses, and should amend or annotate the audit flowcharts and the control questionnaires or control matrix in use.

If a departure or a breakdown has been corrected, the auditor should note it in the working papers or on the form used to describe the test. If no exceptions are found as a result of the compliance tests, this should also be noted.

Tests of Accounting Controls Compliance testing of basic accounting controls generally should include both examination of evidence and reperformance. In some cases observation alone may be more appropriate. The auditor would do this when complete reperformance would be impractical, for example, in the case of a periodic agreement of open collections balances with the control account. Reperformance might consist of testing the additions of the individual balances to arrive at the total and tracing a sample of individual balances from the ledgers to the listing and vice versa. It would not mean tracing all of the individual balances, since the sample can sometimes indicate the whole performance picture.

Testing of custodial controls and segregation of duties usually involves observation, inquiry, and examination of such items as signatures and initials on documents and records. The auditor normally carries out these tests as part of tests of related basic controls, rather than as a separate operation.

Compliance testing of the supervisory controls, on the other hand, is based largely on the examination of evidence. The primary evidence the auditor examines is the signature or initials of the person exercising the control on the relevant document or record. Particular attention should be given to other evidence (such as exception reports or internal memoranda that indicate the disposition of unsatisfactory documents) or records that have been queried as a result of the supervisory control. In addition, the auditor can observe the application of the supervisory control to current transactions.

Complete reperformance of a supervisory control is usually not possible. The auditor rarely has knowledge and experience of the supervisor concerned; the nature and extent of the checks carried out at the supervisor's discretion may not be clearly evidenced. Reperformance is limited to the tasks that are expected to be undertaken in the exercise of the supervisory control. It normally includes inspection of the supporting documentation that should have been seen by the person exercising the supervisory control, together with evidence of prior checks as required. Using the same documentation for examination of evidence of basic controls can provide increased efficiency. The existence of errors in the application of the basic controls that were not detected by the supervisor may indicate that the related supervisory control is not being effectively applied.

Reviews of Administrative Controls Administrative or operational controls deal with the efficient use of resources. Reviews of operational controls are based largely on the examination of evidence. Such evidence may consist of the items that form the basis for the control, such as an organizational chart or policy manual; a report or worksheet, such as technical performance specifications for computer equipment to be purchased; or exception reports or internal memoranda indicating that the control is being applied. Reviews of some administrative controls may involve observation.

Reperformance of an administrative control may not be practical, primarily because of the large amount of time that may be required. Sometimes, however, the auditor will be able to reperform an administrative control procedure with a limited expenditure of time. For example, using a portion of all premiums, the auditor can reperform a calculation to determine whether an open premium amount is overdue (the balance is open for more than 90 days). Reperforming this procedure for a portion of open balances may be done efficiently.

It is often best to test the general controls before testing the related application controls. Even when application controls are adequate, the auditor may not be able to rely on them if they are related to undependable general controls. For example, there is little point in testing the action taken on computer reports if the programs creating those reports cannot be relied on.

Sometimes the auditor feels that the results of testing application controls and general controls do not provide sufficient assurance about the consistent and proper operation of programmed procedures. At that point, the auditor should consider the use of other testing techniques, such as using audit software, to ensure that the programs are appropriate and operating consistently. Such techniques are often considered substantive tests, not compliance tests, because the auditor is attempting to gain satisfaction with the programmed procedures by direct tests, rather than by evaluating and testing the controls.

Tests of Management-Defined Procedures Consideration and review of each organizational procedure often provides the auditor with a parallel test of the important controls. It also can yield extensive insight into how management expectations are being fulfilled. Tests of compliance applied to organizational procedures may overlap the compliance tests of internal controls.

Recording Compliance Tests and Reviews

Documentation of the program and record of tests performed should be designed to be used for more than one period. When the program of proposed tests and reviews has been recorded, reviewed, and approved by management, the test program can be used in subsequent periods. The auditor should then evaluate the program in the light of experience in carrying out the tests or reviews in previous periods. Any changes in control procedures for the current period, as identified during the preparation or updating of the questionnaire or matrix, can also require test changes.

When a proposed compliance test or adminstrative review is no longer appropriate, or when different or additional tests are necessary, the program is amended accordingly. If the proposed compliance test or administrative review will be performed on a cyclical basis (such as twice a year), that should be indicated. When substantial changes are required, a new program of tests should be developed.

To permit the auditor to conduct the reviews most easily, tests and reviews can be sequenced in accordance with control objectives, and be efficiently presented. For example, tests and reviews of controls relating to premium payment activity might be listed together. Tests and reviews can also be grouped by transaction type or by activity, as shown on the procedural flowcharts. The broad classifications of compliance tests and administrative reviews included in this manner should be entered on a summary sheet.

Preparation of Program Generally, each control objective, with proposed compliance testing or administrative review, is listed with the internal control questionnaire references cross-referenced. Complete details of tests or reviews to be performed should contain details of the work, providing a satisfactory description of the compliance test performed.

If any internal control questions in the questionnaire will not be compliance tested, reasons for not performing the test should be recorded. Management may also want reasons for the omission of reviews of administrative controls listed. In this way, no control for which questions were answered in the questionnaire is overlooked. Tests or reviews may be omitted because there is a "No" answer to a question; the control cannot be relied on because of other "No" answers for the same control objective, or management has decided for its own reasons, which can include efficiency, that testing or review is unnecessary. Proposed levels of test or review are also listed. Then the questionnaire should be reviewed to be sure that all control procedures that should be considered for compliance testing or administrative review are included in the program.

The program is reviewed and approved by responsible supervisory management, usually before the compliance tests or reviews are performed. The program of test development should be carried out at the same time as, or soon after, completion of the internal control questionnaire or control matrix, preferably by the same person who recorded and confirmed the understanding and who evaluated the related controls.

Updating of Program For subsequent periods, the test program should be marked to indicate the continued appropriateness of the proposed compliance tests or administrative reviews.

Summary Sheet A test program summary sheet can be used in each period for each cycle of the internal control questionnaire. This provides evidence of approval by responsible supervisory management of the preparation or updating of the program of compliance tests and administrative reviews, completion by the auditor of the compliance tests and administrative reviews, and review by a responsible supervisor of the work performed.

The summary sheet can also serve as an index to the individual control objectives in each period. If some other activity or grouping is used, the entry should agree with the identification used elsewhere in the working papers.

Management Approval The proposed tests and reviews (or in subsequent periods, proposed changes) should be reviewed and approved by management. Approval should be evidenced by signing and dating the appropriate page. If there were any changes in the system, management should ensure that the program has also been suitably amended.

Completion of Program On completion of the compliance tests and administrative reviews relevant to each individual set of tests, the auditor should sign and date the working papers and, if used, the summary sheet. Any exceptions in the course of compliance tests and administrative reviews should be noted as isolated instances (or temporary breakdowns that have been corrected) or properly recorded on the record of control weakness.

Supervisory Review The audit supervisor should review the completed test program and supporting working papers. Signed and dated, the papers indicate that the program of tests and reviews appears to have been properly completed; exceptions noted have been correctly disposed of; any departures or breakdowns have been recorded on the appropriate documents; and senior management is immediately advised of any significant weaknesses in internal control.

Evidence of Work Performed The auditor should record sufficient detail in the working papers to identify the particular record, document, or other evidence that was examined. When complete reperformance of an internal accounting control is not appropriate, normally it is necessary to prepare a working paper recording the extent of reperformance carried out. For example, when the auditor reperforms the reconciliation of a control account, it is desirable to summarize the reconciliation on a working paper. The auditor can indicate on the working paper the specific balances checked from the ledgers, the extent to which additions were reperformed, and any other tests performed.

For the disciplines over basic controls and administrative controls, the auditor should prepare supporting working papers to record the specific evidence examined, the procedures reperformed, or the nature and circumstances of the observations.

SUBSTANTIVE TESTS OR PROCEDURES

Substantive procedures are performed in computer systems when general controls either do not exist or will not be relied on. The main objective of substantive procedures is to substantiate account balances. The auditor uses these procedures to determine whether the computerized and manual accounting treatment of the related transactions was proper and valid. The processing and resulting account balances should not contain errors or irregularities. Substantive procedures, and related application controls, check that assets and liabilities exist, that they are recorded in the correct accounts at the proper amounts, and that transactions are properly authorized, among other requirements.

Substantive procedures also include identifying and evaluating the accounting principles used and evaluating judgments used by management that affect valuation estimates. Substantive procedures also complement compliance tests, providing additional evidence as to whether the internal accounting controls have continued to operate.

Internal auditors may perform substantive procedures when no reliance can be placed on the relevant internal controls and when assisting the external auditor during the annual examination of the financial statements.

A systems audit approach should be flexible enough to allow the auditor to rely on controls, perform compliance tests, and limit substantive testing. It also should permit the auditor to rely on substantive techniques when reliance on controls appears impractical or less efficient.

The auditor can use judgment to choose the methodology that provides the most effective and efficient approach. However, when the auditor relies principally on substantive procedures, assurance that internal controls are adequate will not be achieved, although it may identify some control weaknesses.

Extent of Substantive Procedures

The extent of substantive procedures depends in part on the following:

- the significance or materiality of account items,
- the composition of particular account balances,
- the correlation of an account balance with other accounts and information,
- the number of exceptions identified through application of substantive procedures, and
- audit judgment.

Materiality of Account Balances   Materiality means the importance in relation to audit objectives. Insignificant differences do not affect the extent, timing, or nature of audit tests. When performing substantive procedures, the audit effort is usually proportional to the significance or materiality of the items being tested.

The materiality principle includes consideration of audit risk. In this context, this risk is the chance that the auditor will state that an account is not significantly misstated when it is in fact misstated. Audit efforts are also affected by the risk of error or misstatement that exists in a particular environment. For example, outstanding and paid losses are likely to present more of a problem than investments in terms of control, valuation, and application of accounting principles, although both accounts may be material. The greater the audit risk and materiality of the particular account balance, the greater the need for extensive substantive testing.

Account Balance Composition   The composition of the account balances also affects the substantive procedures performed. The quantity and value of items, and the amount of judgment required to arrive at the balance, are important. Usually more items are examined in an account balance where judgment is an important consideration, such as reserve factors in a highly inflationary economy. Using audit software to examine all items and to provide useful account analyses can be a great help.

In noncomputer environments, the auditor often relies on the results of compliance testing and some substantive testing when an account balance consists of a large number of items with relatively low individual balances. Using audit software sometimes makes it possible to perform substantive testing of 100 percent of the items. When an account balance consists of a small number of items with relatively high values, auditors usually subject all of the individual items to direct substantive tests. Using audit software in this situation is less beneficial unless the high-value items are an accumulation of a large number of relatively small individual entries.

Correlation with Other Accounts and Information Tests performed on related accounts (for example, correlating the interest charge with the related debt, after allowing for any variations in the amount outstanding during the period) may produce information that reduces the need for substantive procedures. Information the auditor obtained during the course of the audit may also indicate the need to extend substantive tests. For example, a review of performance indicators may reveal unexplained changes in the ratio of premiums to total losses in a given period. This may indicate an error in cutoff procedures and the auditor may wish to expand cutoff tests to see if this is the case.

Information relevant to the audit may already exist as reports generated by the system for management, which may be useful to the auditor. Audit software can also be used to generate reports of desired information.

Exceptions When errors and deviations from established procedures are found with substantive procedures, the auditor should determine the reason for each type of exception. The auditor should also determine the implications of exceptions on the system, both for the proper functioning of the internal control system and for the account balance under examination. The effect on related account balances should also be investigated. A single, seemingly isolated exception may indicate a serious weakness in control. If the breakdown is in a programmed procedure, or if there is a possibly significant misstatement of an account balance, there can be widespread ramifications. The auditor should not change planned tests because of an exception until its significance is ascertained. All significant exceptions should be investigated, and management should be informed immediately of those significant exceptions.

Audit Judgment The auditor's professional judgment affects the use of substantive procedures. Analytical review procedures, such as comparison of current financial information with information from comparable prior periods, anticipated results, or similar industry averages, may indicate to the auditor the need to limit or expand substantive testing. The auditor's experience and professional knowledge make such decisions possible.

The auditor may need to rely on certain programmed procedures that either are part of the system of internal control or produce additional information at the test date, such as account analyses or exception reports. The auditor must be satisfied that these programmed procedures are functioning properly and that the information produced is complete and accurate.

The auditor may choose not to do compliance tests on the general controls when they are weak or when it is more efficient to perform extended substantive tests on the programmed procedures. This usually involves reperformance of the programmed procedure using audit software or test data. Examining the program instructions may also confirm that the program functions properly. The auditor should then follow the procedures when running the program to ensure that:

- the correct version of the program is used,
- it is run against the correct data file, and
- there is no unauthorized intervention.

The auditor should obtain assurance from the tests that the programmed procedures operated properly throughout the period. Tests of programmed procedures may not be simple, since there is often a lack of visible evidence of how the program functions. However, the auditor may be able to create this visible evidence, so that simple manual tests can be carried out. Because specialized computer-assisted testing techniques may possibly be required, a range of testing techniques is available for programmed procedures.

To rely on information produced by audit software, an auditor must first establish by other audit tests that the data on the file examined is complete and accurate. Computer programs examine only data actually on a file; if that data is inaccurate or incomplete, the results will be inaccurate also.

Methods of Substantive Procedures

Substantive procedures fall into two categories: substantive tests of the account balances and their components; and other auditing procedures, such as analytical reviews. The nature of the substantive procedures will vary, depending on the account balance examined. These procedures, which can be performed manually or using audit software, include confirmation, inspection, reperformance, cutoff testing, vouching, analysis of fluctuations, analysis of financial trends and ratios, reconciliations, and account analysis.

Confirmation Confirmation is verification of a fact or condition, such as an account balance, by a third party. Such independent verification so strongly supports the existence of the account balance that bank confirmation often serves as the principal substantive test for cash accounts. The auditor may use audit software to select items for confirmation using statistical, systematic, or random selection techniques. Some audit software can print confirmation letters, subsequently identify missing returns, and print out a second request.

Inspection Inspection is the physical counting or examination of items represented by the dollar balance in an account. Normally staff people perform the count at management's request while the auditor observes and tests the procedures used, but the auditor may actually perform the physical count. This procedure is typically applied to investment (such as bond counts) and, less often, to fixed asset account balances. The auditor may use EDP audit assistance or audit software to save time in the selection of items for physical inspection.

Reperformance Many account balances are the results of a computation or an accumulation of computations, such as unearned premiums and IBNR reserves. Reperformance of the computation is the principal substantive procedure applied to such account balances. When judgment enters into the basis of a computation, reperformance of the computation should include an auditor's evaluation of the soundness of reasoning behind the judgment.

Cutoff Testing Cutoff testing consists of examining transactions—such as applications, endorsements, or cancellations which represent actual policies—to determine that the transactions were recorded in the proper period. The auditor can usually do effective cutoff tests in computer systems, particularly in batch systems. In all cases, testing that the documentation reflects actual transactions that occurred on the dates recorded is necessary.

Vouching Vouching is examining evidence that supports a transaction or item to determine its validity. Vouching includes review of company procedures for supporting documentation, examining that supporting documentation, and a review for unusual items. Vouching is typically used to check claims—such as to check coverage on original application, check adjustees report for proof of loss, and so forth. The auditor can use audit software to speed the process of selecting claims to be vouched or isolating unusual claims for review.

Fluctuation Analysis Analysis of fluctuations in account balances includes identifying unusual changes, or the lack of them, in recorded amounts (such as premiums written by line of business). The auditor compares them with budgeted amounts or amounts for prior periods, obtains explanations, and evaluates their reasonableness in relation to other financial information and his or her knowledge of the organization's affairs. A necessary supplement to the substantive tests, this procedure may reveal audit areas that require particular attention, such as inappropriate entries in the accounts, or items that should receive little or no audit emphasis. The auditor can use audit software that will calculate absolute dollar and percentage changes and indicate account balances with significant fluctuations, which allows the auditor to concentrate on evaluating the differences.

Analysis of Financial Trends and Ratios   Analysis of financial trends and ratios is the review of an organization's financial position and performance. Significant performance indicators, including loss ratios, premiums earned, and net premiums written to policyholders' surplus are all used to express these trends.

The auditor looks for relationships among the trends, obtains reasonable explanations for unusual relationships, and considers whether changes should be made in the nature, extent, or timing of substantive tests. For example, increases in losses in relation to premiums, or reductions in deferred acquisition costs, might cause the auditor to extend tests of the loss reserve. The auditor usually performs analysis of financial trends and ratios in conjunction with analysis of balance sheet and profit-and-loss account fluctuations.

Reconciliation   Reconciliation is accounting for any differences between two amounts that ought to agree (one of the amounts is usually an account balance). For example, the auditor will compare the general ledger balance for agent's balances with the total of the detailed open collections file by agent, or the book balance for a bank account with the balance shown by the related bank statement. If differences are found, the auditor usually performs substantive tests to determine whether adjustments are required to the account balance.

Reconciliations often occur more frequently in computer systems than in manual systems. The individual balances on computer files (for example, policy master files) are reconciled either to an independent control account or to a control record on the file each time the file is updated or if it is reorganized. These regular reconciliations may mean that the auditor is more likely to carry out compliance tests because it is usually easier to investigate items in the reconciliation, and it reduces the audit effort required for reconciliations during the substantive procedures.

Account Analysis   Account analysis includes categorizing and summarizing account details to provide better understanding of the items in the balance. An account analysis can be a summary of activity during the period under examination or an analysis of the composition of the closing balance to determine major items or categories of items.

Exception reports normally produced in a computerized system often include a greater number of account analyses. Computer systems can also produce more complex analyses using data that is not part of the account balance (such as an analysis of accounts receivable in relation to credit limits). Properly used, this type of information can provide the auditor with a better understanding of the nature of items that constitute an account balance than is normally possible in manual systems.

EDP TESTING TECHNIQUES

Audit software makes it possible to audit data that is stored on computer media to access the information in computer-based systems. The auditor can use audit software programs to perform various functions, including creation of reports used for audit examination. Both compliance tests and substantive tests can be assisted by using audit software, depending on the criteria used to generate the reports. Data files and production programs are not affected by use of audit software.

The benefits of using audit software include the ability to examine all relevant items on the data files, providing better audit coverage than manual tests that usually examine only part of the data. Additional information of audit significance, such as claims over a certain dollar amount or claims where the amount paid exceeded the reserve, can also be produced. This combination means that the auditor can usually carry out more effective tests on computer-based systems than are practical with manual tests. In some cases, the proper use of audit software tools for complex, integrated computer systems may be the only way to perform an effective audit.

Using audit software to meet audit objectives is an important technique, but it is not the only one an auditor needs to audit complex systems. It is one part of the repertory of required procedures.

Audit software functions include automated reading of data files, analysis of that information, selecting and summarizing data, totaling, comparative calculations, formatting output, comparing program code, and flowcharting the logic of program code. These functions are similar to the query facilities, report writers, and utilities of data processing software. When these relatively standard data processing methods are known, the auditor can employ them to assist in the audit.

Management information systems usually contain far more data than traditional accounting systems. Relevant data may be stored on computer media that maintain organizational data in a form that can satisfy management requirements. Data stored can include accounting data, historic results, statistical information, computer programs, and operational data (such as computer operating logs).

Even when data is automatically stored, once its usefulness has expired, it is regularly overwritten because of high storage costs on computer media. A special request may be required so that the relevant data is retained for audit examination.

Audit Objectives and Audit Software

Audit software can be used effectively only when it will meet audit objectives, translating them into computer processing functions. This can be accomplished when the auditor knows basic EDP concepts. With a more comprehensive knowledge of EDP, an auditor can prepare and execute the software as well. Computer functions can also be discussed with an EDP auditor or a data processing technician to develop the automated application specifications and prepare the computer programs. The technical ability required depends on the software; when it is very flexible, the auditor needs to know more to use it.

For example, a typical audit objective might be to determine that the general ledger control account balance agrees with the total of the individual account balances included in the subsidiary records. The corresponding computer function would be to foot the amount in the dollar balance field of each record included in the file or data base and to print the total. To prepare for the computer specialist to do this, the auditor would:

- indicate the location of the relevant fields on the records in the files,
- direct that the amounts in those fields are to be added, and
- specify the format of the report on which the totals are to be printed.

Although the previous example is simple, it demonstrates the basic, step-by-step thought process that is required. By following the same process, even complex audit objectives can be translated into specific computer functions.

Exhibit 10-1 illustrates how some of the compound audit objectives relating to premium processing may be translated to basic computer functions, and thus converted into an audit software program.

For purposes of illustration, assume that EDP maintains a file containing insured balance-forward information. This would typically include insured name, policy number, balance due, and the totals of the aging categories within which the amounts comprising the balance fall.

Exhibit 10-1
Specimen Premium Cycle Audit Objectives

Audit Objective	Computer Function
1. Determine that the total of the balances of individual insured accounts agrees with the general ledger account balance.	1. Add the balance due amount for each record on the balance forward file and print total.
2. (a) Request confirmation of amounts due from insured on a given basis of selection.	2. (a) Compare balance, insured name or other relevant information on each record with established selection criteria and select those records that meet or exceed the criteria; print confirmation requests.
(b) Test the aging calculations by selecting individual accounts on a given basis and check the aging of unpaid amounts by tracing to source documents.	(b) Compare selection criteria with relevant information on each record and select those records that meet or exceed the criteria. For each of the accounts selected, print the policy number and amount for items comprising each aging category for manual comparison to source documents.

In addition, a supporting transaction file is maintained, which shows insured name, the policy number, and amount of all items uncollected at the end of the month. To meet some of the audit objectives, the auditor would follow the procedures shown in Exhibit 10-1.

Generalized Audit Software An auditor who knows standard data processing techniques, such as use of computer languages or utilities, may be able to satisfy some audit requirements by using them. When using software extensively, the auditor should use software aids specifically suited to the environment.

Generalized audit software exists because many different audits require similar audit procedures. This software can be quickly adapted to the goals of an audit and is usually cost-effective, especially when compared to custom software.

The auditor uses generalized audit software to examine the information held on computer files and carry out audit tests, such as verification of calculations, totals, or analyses. An example of such a test would be the valuation and summary of investments. The auditor can also make additional analyses of data, such as the calculation to total investment holdings summarized in Schedule D format, and have the analyses printed out in a report. The data held on computer files can be examined to provide totals of such items as preferred stocks and municipal bonds held. The auditor can also select and print out data from the file for subsequent examination. This would be done to provide a sample of normal data, or data that the auditor defines as unusual, such as those holdings identified as not approved by the NAIC.

Application Audit Software Packaged software popularity has shown that data processing functions can be standardized to meet the needs of different organizations, as can audit software tasks for common applications such as accounts receivable (agents balances), accounts payable or claims, general ledger, payroll, and insurance policy reserve calculations. Applicable audit software is developed to achieve common audit objectives in such applications. Using this type of software can save audit time and effort since the audit functions are predefined. For example, for agents balances or uncollected premiums the software can age-analyze the accounts (for overdues), select items for audit testing, produce confirmation letters, and match subsequent cash received. The particular audit concerns can be met by flexibility that is built into the software. To run the software, the auditor's data files are converted into a format compatible with the software package by the auditor, who also determines the appropriate parameters and then executes the software, either alone or with assistance from EDP personnel.

Audit Software for System Activities Audit software also exists that facilitates the review of system activities. This software includes comparison programs, unexecuted code analysis, flowcharting programs, systems log analysis, and data base analysis.

Comparison Programs. Comparison programs are used to compare the source or executable versions of production programs in use with authorized copies held by the auditor. This software can provide listings of the contents of the programs being compared and any differences between them. This is extremely useful in identifying unauthorized changes, or to confirm a lack of changes, in programs. The software can also compare source programs to see whether they are logically identical to their executable form.

Once a program has been properly implemented on a controlled basis, it should not receive unauthorized changes. To ensure that unauthorized changes have not occurred, the auditor performs comparisons to identify additions, deletions, and changes in a program between two points in time. This information helps evaluate program security. When the focus is on the production program, the auditor reviews the controlled version and any production version changes.

This software can be particularly useful when converting from one system to another, to help ensure that programs used are the same. To ensure that authorized program changes are made in accordance with program change requests, a comparison program can flag any changes. These changes can be followed through the request procedures to ensure that all changes were properly authorized and implemented.

Changes in load modules (in machine language) may be especially hard to detect. Software can help determine whether a load module created from a source program is currently unchanged. The source program is compiled or translated into the machine code of an object module. The object modules are linked together by a process called link editing, creating a load module which is entered (loaded) into the computer for execution. Software programs can compare the object module to the load modules or can compare two load modules to determine if any changes have been made. The software can help to ensure that a controlled program produces the same executable code as the current production version, that the source program corresponds to the current version in production, and that no unauthorized changes have been made to production programs. These programs, however, cannot detect a change when the load module has been changed back to its original status.

Such software can be used, for example, when the auditor has identified significant programmed procedures and wants to determine whether they are operating properly. One way to ensure that programs are executed in accordance with management's intentions is to review the source code of the production program, then determine whether the version checked is identical to the one in production. A comparison program can produce an exception report of differences between the object module and the load module. The auditor should consider any exceptions when deciding whether to rely on general controls. A controlled copy of the authorized program can be retained for use to detect program changes during subsequent audits.

This software can be used to test vendor-supplied software, as well as that developed in-house. Vendor-supplied package modules can be compared with those used in production. If the user has customized the software (with the vendor's permission) or has made maintenance updates as prescribed by the vendor, the auditor should consider those changes.

Unexecuted Code Analysis. Unexecuted code analysis software monitors the execution of a program, tracking the number of times each line of source code was executed during processing. To perform code analysis, the auditor should investigate any line of code that is not executed. The auditor may uncover unauthorized, redundant, or erroneous code through this process.

Flowcharting Programs. Flowcharting programs document the steps in programmed procedures for analysis. Flowcharts produced may be too voluminous to be helpful in an audit, but the verb listings and cross-referenced data-name listings also generated are often helpful in program code analysis.

System Log Analysis. The systems in many installations generate a log of computer activity. Software programs that analyze the systems log are used to report on requested items. Using this software, the auditor defines items for tests to ensure that only approved programs access sensitive data sets, and that utilities that can alter data files and program libraries are used only for authorized purposes. Another concern is that approved programs are run only when scheduled and that there are no unauthorized runs. The software can also help ensure that the correct data file generation is accessed for production purposes, or that data sets reported to be password-protected actually are protected. Software is especially helpful in these tests, since the system logs are often too voluminous to review manually.

Many operating systems have built-in logs that report such activity as system and data file accesses and other job-related activity. These analysis programs can eliminate the necessity of going through extraneous data. For example, the auditor can request a report of executions of utilities that may have modified production data files, and then trace these executions to records of authorizations for use of the utilities. The information can help the auditor test whether modifications to production files are authorized, data sets accessed were those required, changes are authorized and documented, and that jobs on the production schedule were the only ones executed.

Data Base Analysis. Data bases linked by telecommunications are sometimes too readily accessible and vulnerable to security breaches. To evaluate controls over data and programs, the auditor can use software for help in understanding the data base structure. For example, the IBM Information Management System/Virtual Storage (IMS/VS) organizes and maintains a large centralized data base for on-line and batch data processing applications. The data can be integrated and shared by different users. Yet this shared data makes it important for the auditor to assess the adequacy of data base security.

Software analyzers can help auditors ascertain whether the documented control standards are actually in place. Part of assessing these controls is understanding the data base structure, the number of data bases, and who can assess them. The interaction between data bases, which terminals can be used to enter transaction types, as well as which on-line transactions can access certain data bases, are important control considerations to assure that data base security is implemented as planned.

System Software and Service Aid Utilities

Systems utilities and service aids provided by computer manufacturers and software vendors are part of the software that controls the system and its activities. As such, the auditor can use them to examine processing activity, to develop data interrogation audit systems, and to test programs and operational procedures.

Program Code Analysis Program code analysis confirms the existence of significant programmed procedures in a program or series of programs, as identified in a control questionnaire. The auditor can examine the code in object form, which may not be practical since machine code is hard to work with, or confirm that the language the programs use relates to the executable programs. Tests carried out on program security controls and computer operation controls can provide such confirmation.

The auditor is most likely to use program code analysis in advanced systems where system software ensures that the source and executable programs are the same and, therefore, can often rely on tests of those procedures. Testing software can check a newly compiled version of the source program in question against the executable program in use, and provides an audit alternative.

Parallel Simulation Parallel simulation is a way to test the proper functioning of programmed procedures and the accuracy of the financial data processed. It consists of taking real data and processing it through test programs. The test programs must perform some (not necessarily all) of the same functions as the production programs being tested.

Parallel simulation checks input validation procedures, data updating logic, and processing logic and controls. All transactions chosen for the test are confirmed. These test programs can be run whenever computer time is available. The method employed depends on the software selected, such as generalized audit software, industry-oriented audit software, application audit software, or custom audit software.

To perform parallel simulation, all data and files processed by the test programs must be in the same format as is required to run the production programs, and the reports should be generated for the same time period. Documentation of controls, or any reconciliations conducted should be retained for future reference.

Parallel simulation test programs may be less complex than the production prgrams they simulate; therefore, discrepancies may occur. It is not cost-effective to amend the test program to conform to processing requirements of production programs, so these discrepancies are often reconciled manually. The auditor can use a program to compare the test processing results and detect any discrepancies. The auditor should fully document exceptions and unexplained discrepancies; corrective measures can be recommended when necessary.

Whenever production programs have not changed in ways that have audit significance, parallel simulation can be repeated using the same testing programs. The auditor should check the program change log and then test it by comparing the current version of the source program to a controlled version of this program to verify authorization of changes. The auditor can check present production programs to see whether there were unauthorized or unrecorded changes using the program code analysis.

Test Data and Integrated Test Facility   To test processing and controls in application systems, the test data method employs real programs to process test data. Processing output can then be compared to predefined results. This audit use of test data should not be confused with the test data used by data processing to test the operation of new programs. Audit test data tests only the particular programmed procedures on which the auditor wishes to rely and is designed to be representative of the actual data processed by the company. When the auditor uses audit test data, tests on other procedures that would otherwise be done manually are sometimes included for efficiency. The auditor uses test data to check input validation routines, error detection, and transaction data control procedures that are integral to the programs, as well as processing logic and controls over master file data. Standard calculations, such as premium transaction types or premium amounts, can be tested. The auditor also can use test data methods for acceptance testing of a system already in use, including manual procedures.

The test data method is applied to program processing verification and evaluation and is not a way to check application controls, such as completeness and accuracy of input or update of data or master files.

Test data can be processed using the operational programs, apart from the actual data, by setting up copies of master files or specially designed dummy files. With approval from a responsible department official, test data can also be included with the organization's data for regular processing.

The second process utilizes an *integrated test facility*. When specific master file records are created or reserved for this purpose and processed for testing at established checkpoints, the facility may be called Base Case System Evaluation.

Ways to create test data include completion of actual input forms so that each condition in the test plan is tested, including creation of master file records, then running the transactions to test processing and controls. Since this is a somewhat lengthy process, another method used is copying actual master file records to create a test master and then running transactions. (Every condition in the test plan should be covered in the processing of master file records.) Another method is to use a test data generator computer program to prepare test data sets. Test data generators are used at a higher cost, but their advantages include a reduction of effort in preparing test data and increased thoroughness in testing input validation routines, error detection procedures, and calculations.

However they are prepared, test data transactions should be run on the current executable programs in the production library. The auditor can observe the run, or ensure that it is handled so that it cannot be tampered with, and can receive its output. Production files should not be affected by the presence of test data. The auditor can then compare output to the expected results, analyze any differences, and rerun the test to confirm the results. Finally, the auditor should document any differences in procedures.

SUMMARY

An audit is a systematic investigation of documents, procedures, and systems. This investigation includes an evaluation of the controls present in the system and leads to recommendations for maintaining or improving those controls.

Although the specific tasks involved vary considerably from one audit to another, the audit process generally consists of the same sequence of activities. Planning the audit includes preparing an annual audit program and developing individual audit strategies. Obtaining, recording, and confirming an understanding of the system under review may require flowcharts or narrative descriptions of the system, which can be confirmed through transaction reviews and interviews with site personnel. Evaluating internal accounting and operational controls documents those controls using a control matrix, internal control questionnaires, and a record of control weaknesses and employs compliance tests to determine whether the controls function properly. Substantive tests, which assume greater importance when controls are weak, evaluate the accuracy and completeness of data. When the audit is complete, the auditor communicates any control weaknesses to management in a formal report that describes the scope of the audit and presents the findings.

Although this sequence of activities should occur in every audit, the auditor's judgment determines the specific tests appropriate to each audit. In selecting controls for testing, the auditor considers the principal controls, the frequency of control performance, controls over groups of transactions, the risk of undetected errors, the disciplines over basic controls, interrelated basic controls, overall reconciliations, the justification for reducing tests, the significance of potential errors, the spreading of tests, and the level of review. Some techniques used to test manual systems, such as manual checking, can be used to test computerized systems as well, although there are limitations, and simulations of manual techniques may also be possible. Compliance tests of accounting controls and reviews of administrative controls should be selected that are representative, inclusive, and most significant for the control objectives evaluated. All compliance tests and reviews should be recorded in a document that shows the preparation of the program, updating of the program, a summary sheet, management approval, completion of the program, supervisory review, and evidence of the work performed.

Substantive tests serve to substantiate account balances when there is reason not to rely on the organization's internal control. The extent of substantive procedures depends on the significance or materiality of account items, the composition of particular account balances, the correlation of an account balance with other accounts and information, the number of exceptions identified through application of substantive procedures, and audit judgment. Substantive procedures include confirmation, inspection, reperformance, cutoff testing, vouching, fluctuation analysis, analysis of financial trends and ratios, reconciliation, and account analysis.

Using audit software to perform substantive tests offers advantages over traditional manual techniques since computer files usually hold large volumes of accounting data. In addition, transaction files often hold detailed records of transactions that were processed during the year. Audit software can examine all data on a file consistently and accurately and perform extensive substantive tests quickly and easily. Generalized audit software, application audit software, and audit software for system activities are readily available, but it is essential to match the audit software to the audit objectives. System software can also facilitate an audit through various techniques, including program code analysis, parallel simulation, and integrated test facilities. Although the purposes of audit tests remain the same, these capabilities enable the auditor to approach the work differently, often with a more thorough examination of transactions and quantification of results.

Bibliography

AAA Committee to Prepare a Statement of Basic Accounting Theory. *A Statement of Basic Accounting Theory.* Evanston, IL: American Accounting Association, 1966.

Alter, Steven. *Decision Support Systems: Current Practice and Continuing Challenges.* Reading, MA: Addison-Wesley Publishing Company, 1980.

Battaglin, Bernard H. "A Changing Role—Insurance Statistical Agencies." *The Interpreter.* December 1984.

Churchill, Neil C. "Budget Choice: Planning vs. Control." *Harvard Business Review.* July-August 1984, pp. 150-164.

Committee on Auditing Procedure. *Statement on Auditing Standards,* No. 1. New York: American Institute of Certified Public Accountants, 1973.

Duggan, T. Patrick. "Can Strategic Planning Improve Insurance Company Results?" Proceedings of the Insurance Accounting and Systems Association, 1981.

Examiners Handbook. Kansas City, MI: National Association of Insurance Commissioners, 1985.

Gane, Chris and Trish Sarson. *Structured Systems Analysis: Tools and Techniques.* Englewood Cliffs, NJ: Prentice-Hall, 1979.

Gibbons, Robert J., ed. *Dimensions of Corporate Strategy: Selected Readings.* Malvern, PA: Insurance Institute of America, 1983.

Glendenning, G. William and Robert B. Holtom. *Personal Lines Underwriting,* 2nd ed. Malvern, PA: Insurance Institute of America, 1982.

Griffin, Ben L., Jr. "Systems Development." in Robert J. Gibbons, ed. *Dimensions of Corporate Strategy: Selected Readings.* Malvern, PA: Insurance Institute of America, 1983, pp. 534-538.

Grossman, Steven D. and Richard Lindhe. "Important Considerations in the Budgeting Process." *Managerial Planning.* September-October 1982, pp. 24-29.

A Guide for Studying and Evaluating Internal Accounting Controls. Chicago: Arthur Andersen & Co., 1981.

Halper, Stanley D., Glenn C. Davis, P. Jarlath O'Neil Dunne, and Pamela R. Pfau. *Handbook of EDP Auditing.* Boston, MA: Warren, Gorham & Lamont, 1985.

Hussain, Donna, and K.M. Hussain. *Information Resource Management.* Homewood, IL: Richard D. Irwin, Inc., 1984.

430—Bibliography

IASA Accounting Research Committee. "Profitability: Management's Need for Information." *The Interpreter.* June, 1985, pp. 5-32.

Insurance Services Office. *Quality of Data Audit Guide.* 1978.

Life Office Management Association. *Financial Planning and Controlling.* (Financial Planning and Control Report No. 52), May 1981.

Maple Flooring Association v. United States. 268 U.S. 564, 45 S. Ct. 582, 1925.

Masterson, Norton E. "Statistics for Management." In G.F. Michelbacher and Nestor R. Roos, eds. *Multiple-Line Insurers: Their Nature and Operations.* New York: McGraw-Hill, 1970.

Membership Information Fact Sheet. Chicago, IL: National Independent Statistical Service, n.d.

Mondanaro, Phillip J. "Tactical Planning: The Vital Link." *Best's Review* (Property/Casualty). March, 1983, pp. 23-26.

National Association of Insurance Commissioners. *All-Industry Rating Bills.* June 12, 1946.

——————.*NAIC Model Market Conduct Examination Handbook.* 1984.

——————."Uniform Accounting." *Financial Condition Examiners Handbook.* 1976.

National Council on Compensation Insurance. *Workers' Compensation Statistical Plan.* 1983.

New York Superintendent of Insurance. *Regulation 103.* "Implementation of Private Passenger Automobile Insurance Statistical Data Monitoring System (SDMA)." November 18, 1982.

Page, John and Paul Hooper. *Accounting and Information Systems.* Reston, VA: Reston Publishing Company, Inc., 1982.

Prouty, William B. "Business Planning: Linking Strategic and Budget Plans." *The Interpreter.* September, 1984, pp. 13-15.

——————."Developing Strategic Planning." *Proceedings of the Insurance Accounting and Systems Association—1981,* pp. 526-528.

Schissler, Dale R. "Organizing an Insurance Company Research Unit." In Robert J. Gibbons, ed. *Research Philosophy and Techniques: Selected Readings.* Malvern, PA: Insurance Institute of America, 1983.

Securities and Exchange Commission. Securities Release 34-13185. January 19, 1977.

Senn, James A. *Information Systems in Management.* Belmont, CA: Wadsworth Publishing Company, Inc., 1978.

Strain, Robert W., et al. *Insurance Words and Their Meanings.* Indianapolis, IN: Rough Notes Co., Inc., 1981.

Thurston, Philip H. "Should Smaller Companies Make Formal Plans?" *Harvard Business Review.* September-October 1983, pp. 162-188.

Uhrowczik, P.P. "Data Dictionary/Directories." *IBM Systems Journal* 12, No. 4, 1973, pp. 332-350.

Walker, Peter B. "Strategic Management—New Tool for Insurers." *Best's Review,* March and April 1982.

Walsh, Myles E. "Update on Data Dictionaries." *Journal of Systems Management.* August 1978, pp. 28-37.

Wu, Frederick H. *Accounting Information Systems.* New York: McGraw-Hill, Inc., 1983.

Index

E

G

H

I

W

Z